VISIBLY FEMALE

VISIBLY FEMALE

FEMINISM AND ART: AN ANTHOLOGY

EDITED AND INTRODUCED BY HILARY ROBINSON

SERIES EDITOR *WOMEN ON ART* FRANCES BORZELLO

UNIVERSE BOOKS • NEW YORK

Published in the
United States of America in 1988
by Universe Books
381 Park Avenue South
New York, NY 10016

Published under license from Camden Press Ltd.
43 Camden Passage, London N1, England

Introduction © Hilary Robinson 1987
The copyright in each of the articles remains with the original copyright holder
as detailed in the Permissions and Acknowledgements pages

Designed by Anne Braybon

88 89 90 91 92 / 10 9 8 7 6 5 4 3 2 1
Printed in the United States of America

Library of Congress Cataloging-in-Publication Data

Visibly female.

Bibliography: p. 312
1. Feminism and the arts.   2.   Arts, Modern — 20th
century. I. Robinson, Hilary.
NX180.F4V57 1988   700'.1'03   88-1150
ISBN 0-87663-540-0 (pbk.)

PERMISSIONS
AND ACKNOWLEDGEMENTS

We are grateful to the following publications for allowing us to reprint the articles in this book. Copyright resides with the authors.

Artforum
Carrie Rickey, 'Judy Chicago: The Dinner Party', *Artforum*, January 1981
Carolee Schneemann, 'Letter to the Editor', *Artforum*, October 1983

Artists Newsletter
Anna Bonshek, 'Feminist Romantic Painting – A Re-Constellation', *Artists Newsletter*, May 1985

Artrage
Karin Woodley, 'The Inner Sanctum', *Artrage* no. 9/10, 1985

Artscribe
'Rose Garrard Interviewed by Fiona Byrne-Sutton and Julia James', *Artscribe* 49, November/December 1984
Rose Garrard, 'Something Omitted?', *Artscribe* 50, January/February 1985
'Mary Kelly Interviewed by Terence Maloon', *Artscribe* 1978

Camerawork
Ros Coward, Yve Lomax, Kathy Myers, 'Behind the Fragments', *Camerawork* 25, 1982
Kathy Myers, 'Towards a Feminist Erotica', *Camerawork* 24, 1982

Centre for Contemporary Cultural Studies
Angela Partington, 'Feminist Art and Avant-gardism', Centre for Contemporary Cultural Studies, Birmingham. Copyright held jointly by the author and the Centre

Feminist Art News
'Judy Chicago Interviewed by Dinah Dossor', *Feminist Art News* 8, 1983

Feminist Review
'Karen Alexander: Video Worker. Interviewed by Mica Nava', *Feminist Review* 18, November 1984

Rosemary Betterton, 'How Do Women Look? The Female Nude in the Work of Suzanne Valadon', *Feminist Review* 19, March 1985

'Alexis Hunter Interviewed by Caroline Osborne', *Feminist Review* 18, November 1984

Heresies

Michelle Cliff, 'Object Into Subject: Some Thoughts on the Work of Black Women Artists', *Heresies*, vol. 4, no. 3 (issue 15), 1984

Lucy Lippard, 'Some Propaganda for Propaganda', *Heresies* 9, 1980

Gloria Feman Orenstein, 'The Re-emergence of the Archetype of the Great Goddess in Art by Contemporary Women', *Heresies*, vol. 2, no. 1 (issue 5), 1982

May Stevens, 'Taking Art to the Revolution', *Heresies* 9, 1980

Link

'Monica Sjoo Interviewed by Moira Vincentelli', *Link* 39

Lip

Judith Barry and Sandy Flitterman-Lewis, 'Textual Strategies: The Politics of Art-Making', *LIP*, Australia, 1981/2

Pandora's Box

Penny Woolcock, catalogue entry, *Pandora's Box*, Trefoil Books 1984

Sense and Sensibility in Feminist Art Practice

Marie Yates, catalogue entry, *Sense and Sensibility in Feminist Art Practice*, Midland Group, Nottingham, 1982

Spare Rib

Parveen Adams, Rosalind Delmar, Sue Lipshitz, 'Using Psychoanalytic Theory', *Spare Rib* 56, 1977

'Reworking Myths: Sutapa Biswas Interviewed by Yasmin Kureishi', *Spare Rib* 173, December 1986

Zena Herbert, '*The Dancer* and *Heat*', *Spare Rib* 166, May 1986

Laura Mulvey, 'Post Partum Document: Mary Kelly', *Spare Rib* 53, 1976

Margot Waddell, Michelene Wandor, 'Mystifying Theory', *Spare Rib* 55, 1977

Square Peg

Kate, Angie, Martine, Sandra, Caroline, 'Sex on Film – Lesbians', *Square Peg* 7, 1984

Ten:8

Beatrix Campbell and Gloria Chalmers, 'Striking Women', *Ten:8* 20, 1985

Undercut

Sandra Lahire, 'Lesbians in Media Education', *Undercut* 14/15, summer 1985

Woman's Art Journal

Lawrence Alloway, 'Old Mistresses: Women, Art and Ideology', *Women's Art Journal*, vol. 3, no. 2, fall 1982/winter 1983

Ann Sutherland Harris, 'Letter to the Editor', *Woman's Art Journal*, vol. 4, no. 2, fall 1983/winter 1984

Griselda Pollock, 'Women Art and Ideology: Questions for Feminist Art Historians', *Woman's Art Journal*, vol. 4, no. 1, spring/summer 1983

Griselda Pollock, 'Reply to Ann Sutherland Harris', *Woman's Art Journal*, vol. 4, no.2, fall 1983/winter 1984

Women Artists Slide Library Journal

Chila Burman, 'There Have Always Been Great Blackwomen Artists', *Women Artists Slide Library Journal*, no. 15, February 1987

To the students at Hull, 1986-87, for whom the personal is becoming political, with thanks for the last year;
and
to Patrick Vidaud, for whom the political has damn well had to become personal, with thanks for the last six years.

Every peak is a crater.
This is the law of volcanoes, making them eternally and
     invisibly female.
No height without depth, without a burning core,
though our straw soles shred on the hardened lava.

Adrienne Rich, poem no. XI from *Twenty-One Love Poems*

CONTENTS

v Permissions and Acknowledgements

1 Introduction

Personal statements

8 Introduction: Raising Issues

10 *The Dancer* and *Heat*
Zena Herbert

13 Sex on Film – Lesbians
Kate, Angie, Martine, Sandra, Caroline

19 Statement from *Pandora's Box* Catalogue
Penny Woolcock

22 Statement from *Sense and Sensibility* Catalogue
Marie Yates

Interviews

28 Introduction: The Shaped Voice

30 Karen Alexander: Video Worker
Interviewed by Mica Nava

37 Reworking Myths: Sutapa Biswas
Interviewed by Yasmin Kureishi

43 Judy Chicago
Interviewed by Dinah Dossor

50 Rose Garrard
Interviewed by Fiona Byrne-Sutton and Julia James

59 Something Omitted?
Rose Garrard

xiii

62 **Alexis Hunter**
Interviewed by Caroline Osborne

72 **Mary Kelly**
Interviewed by Terence Maloon

80 **Monica Sjoo**
Interviewed by Moira Vincentelli

Reviews and Overviews

92 Introduction: Discussion and Re-evaluation

94 Judy Chicago, *The Dinner Party*
Carrie Rickey

97 The Inner Sanctum: *The Dinner Party*
Karin Woodley

100 *Post Partum Document* by Mary Kelly
Laura Mulvey

102 Mystifying Theory
Margot Waddell and Michelene Wandor

104 Using Psychoanalytic Theory
Parveen Adams, Rosalind Delmar and Sue Lipshitz

106 Textual Strategies: The Politics of Art-Making
Judith Barry and Sandy Flitterman-Lewis

118 Feminist Romantic Painting – A Re-Constellation
Anna Bonshek

130 Striking Women
Beatrix Campbell and Gloria Chalmers

140 Object into Subject: Some Thoughts on the Work of Black Women
Artists
Michelle Cliff

158 The Reemergence of the Archetype of the Great Goddess in Art by
Contemporary Women
Gloria Feman Orenstein

Theory

172 Introduction: Tools For The Job

175 Taking Art to the Revolution
May Stevens

184 Some Propaganda for Propaganda
     Lucy Lippard

195 There Have Always Been Great Blackwomen Artists
     Chila Burman

200 Old Mistresses: Women Art and Ideology by Rozsika Parker and
     Griselda Pollock
     Lawrence Alloway

203 Women Art and Ideology: Questions for Feminist Art Historians
     Griselda Pollock

222 Letter to the Editor
     Ann Sutherland Harris

226 Reply to Ann Sutherland Harris
     Griselda Pollock

228 Feminist Art and Avant-Gardism
     Angela Partington

250 How do Women Look? The Female Nude in the Work of
     Suzanne Valadon
     Rosemary Betterton

272 Letter to the Editor
     Carolee Schneemann

274 Lesbians in Media Education
     Sandra Lahire

283 Towards a Feminist Erotica
     Kathy Myers

297 Behind the Fragments
     Ros Coward, Yve Lomax and Kathy Myers

307 About the contributors

312 Bibliography

INTRODUCTION

The aims of this anthology are threefold: to make accessible articles which are for the main part dispersed in various feminist or art magazines; to show the state of feminist art and art criticism in the eighties; and to show the wide range of political and artistic approaches which can be categorised as 'feminist art', thereby extending and strengthening debate in the area.

I have often had women (and men, once or twice) approach me saying 'I was told to come and see you because I want to do some research on women artists – have you got any references?' This book is compiled with the students among them in mind – and their tutors; but it's also compiled thinking of those who do not have ready access to either academic or feminist libraries, whether they are artists themselves or have a more general interest in aspects of feminist cultural production. Its aim is emphatically *not* to follow one particular approach to feminist art and art criticism, but rather to show the diversity of politics and practice in the feminist art world in the UK in the 1980s. Indeed, although all the women included would share one common base in their approach to politics and culture – a recognition of the oppression of women – many would argue with each other about the nature and causes of that oppression, and the best strategies for dealing with it in their work and in their lives. It is a situation which feminists not involved with art will recognise. Over the past two decades, feminism has grown, diversified, strengthened, rather like a rope made of fibres which, looked at close up, seem to twist against each other, yet when seen overall give strength to each other.

So it is too among feminist artists – there is no such thing as a single 'feminist art'; it would be impossible to describe to someone what it looks like. Unlike most other 'isms' of the art world, the term 'feminist art' does not automatically imply a certain approach to the formal aspects of art-making, or the use of certain media; nor does it even imply what the foremost concern of the artist is in making the piece of work. This is different from, say, the concern for the effect of light on local colour which identifies Impressionist painting. Attempts have been made, largely though not exclusively by the art world establishment, to 'contain' feminist art through the implication that it uses one or another particular mode of

1

production. This however is doomed to failure as can be shown by an examination of an exhibition such as *Pandora's Box*, where a large number of the artists were feminists. Here an extraordinarily wide range of media was used by the different artists, and their major concerns ranged from the formal (such as Lois Williams) to the overtly political (Catherine McWilliams, Alison Allnut) to the highly personal (Kathleen Michael, Pascale Petit).

So how is it that 'feminist art' frustrates attempts at containment and definition as one particular type of production? For the simple reason that, as Lisa Tickner said at the 1986 Art Historians Conference in Brighton, feminism is a politics, not a methodology. To say that you are a feminist artist, or that you produce feminist art, is to say that your approach to art making is informed by your feminist politics. The methods and concerns of a feminist artist will alter as her political aims and strategies respond to changing circumstances. Many of the decisions she makes about her work will relate to her politics. These will include such major decisions as whether to attempt intervention in various art world establishments or to work outside them, and in each case, how; and whether to utilise and subvert established visual languages and modes of production (examples: Lubaina Himid, Jacqueline Morreau), or to attempt to create completely new ones (examples: Mary Kelly, Marie Yates).

For many women strategies of intervention, whether in institutions (colleges, galleries etc) or in areas of production such as painting, are the most practical and effective way forward. Yet here the picture is further complicated by the machinations of the art establishment, by which I mean the mainstream private art galleries and Arts Council funded art centres, which feed into and out of the international market (and collectors like Charles and Doris Saatchi); national and international critics, historians and magazines; and last but far from least, the art college system.

Within the colleges, tokenism is rife. The proportion of female students (about 50% in England, 70% in Scotland) is by no means reflected in the proportion of female staff. This has grave consequences for the kind of tutoring that students receive, for their knowledge of women artists past and contemporary, for their understanding of their own position as women and as artists today, for their ability to find role models, mentors or heroines in the way that male students can and do find heroes. For most of the students I referred to at the beginning of this introduction, the intricacies of the development of feminist art theory over the past fifteen years might as well never have happened. A handful of well-thumbed books in the library, someone brought in to 'cover' women and art in a couple of seminars, a feminist artist given a day's teaching, and all too often that is it. The regular, full-time, male members of staff consider 'the matter' is 'dealt with', and so feel no need to alter their own approaches to the material they teach and the students they teach it to. Often the terms 'woman' and 'feminist' are conflated (as in: 'the feminist bunch are making a lot of noise – we'd better get a woman in to teach for a couple of days'). This is an insult to the political sensibilities of all women. It can lead to severe embarrassment for any non-feminist woman brought in to teach as a result of feminist students demanding more appropriate tutoring, and also to feelings of added disappointment and betrayal amongst all students interested in feminist approaches. Tokenism can also lead to ghettoising and containment. Maybe a women's group is set up; but when certain students leave college it folds. Then, a couple of years later, another group is set up; the same ground is painfully rediscovered from scratch because women do not know their history, in the college or outside of it. There is no continuum in the form of women tutors or feminist course input, or the systematic recording of work by or on women. The situation in colleges also has grave consequences for the financial and professional stability of women artists, trying to support themselves, their dependants, and their studios; and also trying to retain credibility in the eyes of the full student body and professional respect from male colleagues.

The 'ism' to have hit the art establishment in the biggest way this decade has been post-modernism (although no-one can decide exactly what it is), and its off-shoot, 'new figuration'. This has been a mixed blessing for feminists, and women in general. On the one hand, it is now OK in the eyes of the art establishment to refer to people, to the personal (whether autobiography or fantasy), to use an assortment of materials, to produce work that doesn't quite fit into any pigeonhole. On the other hand, it's not OK to produce work that is (in the establishment's terms) 'political' – which means that which refers overtly, questioningly, to race, class, sexual politics or issues such as nuclear energy and arms. Where mainstream galleries do show such work (like the *State of the Art* show at the ICA in London – the exhibition of the book of the TV series – where all the work shown has some sort of oppositional impulse) very strange things happen, mainly to do with audience. The politics of what things mean when seen by different people in different contexts become very complex. For instance, what does it mean when Black artists show very angry work in that exclusive gallery context? Or when the white feminist Barbara Kruger is given 100 prime site billboards throughout the country for her piece of work? All the Black artist such as Donald Rodney achieves is the pricking of a few white liberal consciousnesses about South Africa in a trendy gallery; and while Kruger's work deals with sexual politics, it does so in such a way that it will probably cause a similar reaction in passers by as the latest cigarette advertisement. I am not arguing here about the political and artistic validity of Rodney's work, nor with the fact that it is good that a feminist gets such exposure for her work. Rather, I am pointing to the subtle containment of contentious ideas which is something in which the liberal art establishment excels.

In the same way, in the post-modern art establishment sex is in; or rather, the depiction by men of the male hero and the male body is in; but any serious consideration of sexuality by men or women, gay or straight, is conspicuous by its almost total absence. There are very few male artists dealing with sexual politics or male sexuality, and the work of the few that do can't always stand up to feminist scrutiny. An often cited example of a male artist in this country who is dealing in a 'radical' way with sexual politics and who is accepted by the art establishment is Victor Burgin, who still manages to follow a well worn tradition of projecting his ideas of male sexuality onto the female body.

Although post-modernism offers a way out of the more stultifying aspects of modernism and formalism, and into a more personal approach to art that might at one level seem to suit feminists, it has become clear that it also offers a way to continue conventions and traditions that certainly are of no benefit to women. The exhibition considered by critics to mark the return to figuration at the beginning of the decade was not *Women's Images of Men*, but *A New Spirit in Painting*, which although not billed as an exhibition of men's work, included no work by women. The kind of painting now favoured by the establishment embodies what could be seen as macho qualities – the bigger the canvas, and the more aggressively painted, the better (examples: Julian Schnabel, Anselm Keifer), and where 'quieter' painters look over their shoulders to past mythologies (examples: Adrian Wiszniewski, Stephen McKenna) it is in a spirit of romantic, nostalgic retrieval, not one of questioning the past in order to move forward. The patterns repeat themselves, in the artists' lives as much as in their work. As has been the case since the renaissance, the wild boy of one year is the star of the next, and the hero and genius of the year following. This 'star' system favoured by dealers and galleries has found space for a few women, a handful of whom will today identify themselves as feminists (such as Alexis Hunter, Rose Garrard, Susan Hiller); but without wishing to belittle their work, the point must be made again that tokenism is a useful way of both calming dissent and soothing the conscience, and therefore of containing feminist politics.

In the winter of 1985/6 I began researching a specific area of feminist art practice; my resources were those well thumbed volumes in the college library, the exhibitions I'd seen, the artists I could contact. I spent three months sitting in libraries wading through back copies of magazines – feminist magazines, art magazines – trying to find information, reviews, articles, anything to build up a history of what had been happening in recent years. The feminist magazines had little on art; the art magazines had little on women. What was printed was often too short to give anything but the most hazy impression of what an exhibition was like, what an artist's intentions were, what a considered reaction might be, or what form a feminist art theory might take. Writings from a specifically lesbian viewpoint were virtually non-existent, as were articles identifying and discussing work by out lesbians; articles on Black culture or individual Black artists were usually by and about men; I only found a couple of articles on Irish artists, no matter which side of the border or what gender, published in British magazines, and precious little on feminist artists published in Ireland. All of these imposed silences are appalling; it is easy to be cynical about the mainstream art press and say 'Well, what do you expect?'; but the fact that the women's movement allows no room for lesbian artists (for one example) to have a voice is unforgivable.

As I worked, a pile of articles built up, and with it the idea for this anthology. What I found striking about the articles as a group was the energy and enthusiasm they contained in comparison to much art criticism by men. This I am sure is because the women writing them have such a strong, committed and developing political perspective, rather than a stand that is a desperate attempt to maintain a position, either to keep modernism alive, or to find a foothold in a new order that doesn't yet know what it is or in which direction it will go. It has at times seemed a dangerous and stupidly difficult task to select one article for reprinting instead of another; this has been countered by including a bibliography naming many other articles. The layout of the book starts with the individual voices of artists' personal statements, and works through to a section clumsily titled (for want of a better word) Theory. This format echoes the much-used feminist slogan that the personal is political. It aims to show how women respond to different situations, and how this is not a simple matter of isolated individualism, but relates back to the wider political/cultural context. The word 'theory' here means 'how best, as feminists and as artists, to deal with the context you find yourself in'. It is not a monolithic body of knowledge and opinion, static and impossible to engage or argue with.

Each section attempts to show the variety of strategies, activities, and voices which come under the broad umbrella of feminist art in the 1980s. The strategies vary from attacks on racism to explorations of matriarchal religion, the activities vary from documentary photography to performance art, the voices vary from the challenging and academic to the chatty and friendly. I see no contradiction in this: as women, as feminists, as artists, we have a lot to learn from each other and a lot to give each other. I hope this anthology goes some way towards helping that process, both for us today and for those who follow and are looking for traces of their history.

I would like to thank very much all those women asked for permission to reprint their pieces, all but one of whom were both supportive of the general idea and also agreed. Thanks as well to those I have talked to and who have been eager to see such a book published, both those who have supported and those who have challenged my ideas; thanks to those, especially Pat Phippard, who have given friendship and encouragement through a full and difficult year. Last but not least: thanks and amazement to Frances Borzello at Camden Press for saying yes, and then making it happen so quickly and efficiently.

Hilary Robinson
March 1987

All articles use the original style, punctuation and spelling.

PERSONAL STATEMENTS

1   Penny Woolcock, *Living In The City*, 1987, 7'7" by 10'6", acrylic and silver paper.

RAISING ISSUES

The articles in this section show the dialogues that feminist artists have, both internal and external, with themselves and between themselves. The women are not writing as spokeswomen for any particular group or movement, but have written these pieces to complement their work or to make their position explicit.

The opening piece, Zena Herbert's *'The Dancer* and *Heat'*, sets a context for the rest of the book. She highlights in a very direct way many areas that the Women's Movement has taken on board as being political priorities; and she does this by telling us, through her own experiences, how the Movement is failing to deal with them. The whole article raises all the question that feminists involved with art here and now should be asking themselves. Some of them are discussed in later articles; here, I would like to outline the issues that are raised by *'The Dancer* and *Heat'*:

Issues of racism. How do white women, in a country that has colonised so many others, react to work that arises out of a different cultural heritage to their own? And how can the women producing that work make it insist on the readings or interpretations they want, when much of the audience may be white British? What strategies or actions should either of them take if they think that the other has simply got it wrong politically?

Issues of art education. Are colleges able to provide appropriate tutoring for women, for mature students, for Black students and students of colour? And where there are appropriate tutors, what is their position within the college hierarchy? Are they able to cross 'demarcation zones' when necessary – from historical studies to studio work, from painting to film, etc.? What is it about the college structure that meant that Zena Herbert only heard from women tutors who had things to say about the politics, meanings and readings of her work when that work was already on public exhibition?

Issues of imagery. In a culture where women's bodies are the repository for the pornographic fantasies of a large proportion of the male population, is it possible for women to reconstruct images of their own bodies – or have we so internalised sexist visual traditions that we can't help but reproduce them? Where are the languages of joy and celebration for women today? Do we have to work on new visual languages (which may be incomprehensible) or should we subvert the old ones (and run the risk of being misunderstood)? Is the work done by feminists on the meanings of images of women simply leading to new puritanical orthodoxies, or is it an aid to creating visual languages with feminist meanings?

Issues of context. Where do we want to show our work, and why? Would work such as Zena Herbert's have 'meant' something different if exhibited in a show of women – or of feminists – or of artists from non-British cultures? And: who is work made for? If we have the luxury of choice about where to show work, what is the best strategy – to pinpoint an audience, or to intervene in the mainstream? If we show with women are we ghettoising ourselves and having no effect on the mainstream, or are we reaching the audience of women we want and providing a supportive context for each other? And if no choices are available (as, for instance, in a college show) what are the consequences?

The theoretical politics of feminism arise out of personal experience, and are tested by activism on every scale. The theoretical articles in the last section of the book will be worthless if we don't also listen to the direct experiences of the women in this first section and all the others like them.

THE DANCER AND HEAT

Last year I was totally involved yet rendered totally non-existent in the smashed sculptures affair that culminated in the Leeds trial of five women. The gory, inaccurate descriptions in newspapers mentioned that other sculptures were also damaged.

Nobody said those other pieces were made by a woman – me. Damaged means chipped or cracked. The truth was, 'smashed'.

In 1983, aged thirty nine, I began the BA(Hons) Fine Art course at Leeds Polytechnic, working in clay and using African imagery, for chunks of my childhood were spent in my father's village in Algeria. I became tormented by the idea of lifesize, ceramic women, powerful and strong. I believed women, who would instantly identify with such figures, would recognise my motivation; men would be confronted with a statement they could not ignore.

The Women's Movement in the 1960s had really impressed me. My mother is Jewish, my father Algerian Rif-Kabyle. Both Berber and Jewish women have a history of self-determination and despite a rigorous Muslim upbringing, I saw in my female relatives self-assertion based on self-belief. That, and photographs of myself, was the start.

The Dancer began mid-thigh because in the Atlas foothills, where the tents are low, women dance on their knees. I remembered women I had danced with, body jewellery shimmering, lamplit, free together. No arms: I saw no need. No legs: they would not show. Did I make a 'mutilated torso'? I made a velvet headdress with brass bezels and stranded bugle beads from the ears to the breasts. (Nipple and labia rings – and testicle rings for men – are traditional with Rif-Kabyle. I wear them from choice.) The brass half-skirt fastened with beads and a single ring linked the labia. *The Dancer* was not in a sexual situation and had chosen to close her body.

It is a shameful paradox that the vulva is seen, even by many women, as something to be simultaneously pursued and reviled. I find wearing labia rings voluntarily helps change that. One adorns a beautiful, worthy part of oneself.

A second figure began with more photographs. Slithering, scowling defiantly, ferocious: *Heat* (Fig. 2). The two figures represented a year's work. Women in college who discussed my work with me suggested the

2   Zena Herbert, *Heat*, 1984, ceramic sculpture.

sculptures had a powerful presence infrequently associated with women. Men felt uncomfortable and overawed.

On the Friday night the exhibition opened, I was still making *Heat*'s jewellery, based on my own: a copper necklace looped to breastrings and a matching belt carrying little discs from labia rings down the legs. Public reaction that night was positive. There were ceramic horses, vessels and portraits, besides the other figures.

The following Monday some women tutors complained that my work was sexist and racist. They had never spoken to me and I was stunned by such kneejerk reactions by academics. The exhibition was closed for investigations. The next day my women were in smithereens.

The horror of seeing another woman hammer faces and breasts, even clay ones, is indescribable. I felt sentenced, unheard, by a self-appointed executioner-judge. In the brouhaha perhaps someone saw the copper glint and thought it chains, but the shackles described so luridly in court were in the minds of those who saw something that did not exist. There were no manacles, no chains. I made my women free, not slaves. If clay women made from my photographs are obscene then I, by merely being female, must be obscene; and that is ludicrous.

But how does this affect women artists? May we not depict woman other than dressed (nakedness, I was told, is undignified) standing (other postures are degrading) and alone (to be near another woman implies a sexual relationship)? Must we submit our sketchbooks to be told what is proper? May we hold differing views but not express them on pain of violent censorship? The hammer pre-empts dialogue. Is it blasphemy for a woman to depict a naked woman?

We must have the courage to depict ourselves honestly in our art. If this is forbidden, we tread a dangerous and ever-narrowing path. The field will be left to pornography, with the abused image of woman the only one made or shown. If it is thought right that some women have dictatorial jurisdiction over other women, I have misunderstood the whole aim of the Women's Movement.

Over the past twenty years I have been spat at in the street for holding hands with my girl-friend. I have been ostracised at work for saying woman is entitled to her own sexuality. I have been derided as unnatural because I refuse to accept what society says is my proper place. Thousands of us have rejected men's authority: we do not need a 'master'. We have no need of a 'mistress' either.

SEX ON FILM – LESBIANS

On Lesbian and bisexual women film makers producing images of sex between women on film...

Why? As lesbians we don't *need* to film our sexuality...

Counterbalance? The politics of desire? Shock tactics?

Is 'shock tactics' conforming to a heterosexual viewpoint – perversion?

As lesbians, our lifestyle is different to hets and gay men. Many film makers – even those dealing with experimental film and 'abstract' imagery – are concerned with autobiography: so are we.

Therefore: lesbian sex in lesbian-made films.

All mainstream and porn films showing lesbian sex have ever done (including the liberal *Lianna*) is contribute to anti-lesbianism or the lezzies-as-perverts view.

Therefore: lesbian sex in lesbian films.

Feminist arguments like 'men might see it and wank off on it,' have produced images of a de-sexualised sexuality, or alternatively non-erotic images – produced out of fear and repression.

How to be 'explicit' and not exploit? Is non explicit sex on film taken seriously? How to be romantic – to show desire without being het?

We need a new language of subversive imagery.

Where is it?

What five film-makers (four lesbian and one bi) think about it...

Kate

Why explicit sex?

Lesbian films in this country tend to euphemise desire on one hand or turn it into S/M images on the other. Rather than covering up our sexuality 'in case men get off on it' we should be telling it like it is. *For some time Kate has been using images of extroversion and sensuality –women performers, taking the power of expression into their own hands, using this combination to portray the reality of desire.* I have tried to be direct about my sexuality, it is very important... I don't want to be de-sexualised by current right-on ideas about whether you should or shouldn't represent sex. I see sex as connected to politics, to love, to romance. I think my attitude is Jewish rather than gentile, for us, as Jews, sex is part of life, it is a source of life... as a lesbian I don't see that I should have to justify that. I don't want to limit myself, and I want to look at what we do together, if we don't do that we're back in the intellectual middle class rut and making boring films – to me there's no question of what a lesbian film should be, the principle is the same for everyone... to show the reality and not to simply react to who might be watching. There is very little erotic imagery of women together, and very little analysis of sex on a political level, like the much-hated *Salo* by Pasolini which shows fascism in its sexual form.

I am sick of the catholic idea of sex becoming the lesbian one, just because the Christian is dominant, even if they think they are atheist or something... the repression and the fuck ups are still set up as the lesbian form... and I don't see Nazi reflections as solving anything... they are not my concern, I am a Jew.

Angie

I've dealt with different kinds of sexuality in my film work: het, gay male and lesbian and probably will continue to do so.

In one film I'm trying to make about how sexual relationships are manipulated under apartheid in S. Africa, I'll be including a racially mixed lesbian relationship because as a bisexual and with that kind of political awareness I *can't* just show hetero sex. I'm a bit worried that people will look at it and be so obsessed with the gay parts of it that they'll say 'this is a gay rights film, not a film about apartheid' as if dealing with the two issues was mutually exclusive. But that's their problem and they'll have to deal with it. After making a film about my mother's disability, two lesbians asked me to make a film about them – including all the hassles they go through having sex – in the context of their day-to-day lives. They wanted to confront people with their sexuality. Disabled women are denied *any* sexuality, never mind lesbian. They predicted that people would cringe at the sight of two disabled women having sex and wanted people to think about why they would cringe – i.e. because it's not a classically romanticised beautiful set up. I felt that it would be exploitative for me as an able-bodied woman to make this film so I didn't, because I wouldn't be exposing *myself* but I would be using very powerful images without fully understanding the feelings involved. I felt that I'd like to help but that the women should make the film by themselves and use the differences in the technical process such as camera shape, etc. I would treat filming sex between women differently to other sex.

There are set established methods for portraying sex images –simplistically, porn/fetishisation, soft focus/colour/lighting of sex and women's bodies belong to the consumer world – whichever way they're depicted they're used to sell products. Sometimes it's difficult to separate bodies from products. Films from Eastern Bloc countries use a different visual language. Maybe it's something to do with the fact that in those countries fragmented women's bodies aren't used in the same way in advertising, so maybe people see women's bodies without the same exploitative connotations.

Most men want to watch lesbians, so most film-makers have chosen to film lesbian sex so as to pander to men. In filming a sex scene I'd use as natural lighting as possible, not picking out (fetishising) anything in particular. You never get incidental scenes in films or on TV with gays together – in bed etc. – only if the film's about gays (usually as 'freaks').

I'd like to be able to show some sort of alternative. As long as people draw the line at what goes on in bed, it will remain 'dirty', and the logical conclusion of the arguments about portrayals of sex being exploitative would be to get rid of all sex including het sex. It's up to people to change, not to get rid of sex being shown in films.

Martine

I dealt with sexuality in my films before I was a lesbian, usually as part of other ideas, and not as *obvious* representations of sex. I was using medieval imagery – male sexuality represented by knights in armour – like using fairy tales.

That was all more about watching someone else. Since then my work's been more about representing my own sexuality without men. In the film *Faster Princess* I arrive at a party, 'pay homage' to 'Miss Worlds' (who *don't* represent anything real about women's sexuality) dance with another woman, and the film ends with two dolls in bed. It's like a fairy story, without the prince.

I'm working on a film at the moment which is two women's journeys: one on land in a beautiful seaside landscape with sand dunes, and ironically the sort of imagery usually meant to be representative of women; and the other the journey of a siren through the sea. Again it's using elements from a fairy story. Each woman dreams of the other's environment (land and sea) and both are dreams in which they are searching for their sexuality. In the end the women meet.

Using personal experience in films is important, for instance with my work on Catholic Guilt. Maybe there are parallels here – guilt about 'being caught'. Also I've used hard imagery around guilt; this could apply to guilt about relationships with women. People will always say 'this is a sex film', 'this is a lesbian film' – if it *is* a lesbian film they'll have to deal with it. It's quite easy to forget the threat that alternative sexuality poses to established ideas. In terms of film-making and sexuality I was affected by Jean Genet's *Un Chant d'Amour*. It's about romanticism and fantasy, without directly showing fucking. You can't avoid objectifying sexuality in some ways. I'm not thinking of men as an audience – I don't want to feel guilty, I'm not an angel, not perfect. I wouldn't *want* to show a film about lesbian sex to men, but I wouldn't mind. Also, I want to try anyway – I might feel secretive and leave 'bed' to what they think, but eventually what's important is to get the best from yourself – maybe *being* a lesbian is enough. *The* film on lesbians and sex hasn't been made; there are parts in different films I identify with. It's important for women to see lesbians in films. Sometimes the hardest thing for women is the denial of their own sexuality because of isolation.

Partly I'm making films for isolated lesbians, or women who're not quite so heterosexual!

I want to be able to show desire, not just a little interlude in someone's life.

Sandra

For years I've felt left out – seeing straight sex in films and films made by straights. The best attempt at showing lesbian sex I've seen is by Chantal Akerman, and she's not a lesbian – she doesn't know what it really feels like. If I deal with lesbian sex in my films, it's about sexuality being cut up, about pain. Straight people who've seen my work haven't been able to handle this pain.

In *Edge* there's a shot with me kissing another woman's stomach and she folds up – that's about healing.

So far I've only shown pain, but if I do what I want to – showing women being good to each other (for women – I don't want to be compulsive about it) trying to show all aspects of sexuality until I can do something that's a celebration. Heterosexual sex is one of the building blocks of the economy. In this sense lesbians are not 'productive'; in the power relations of this society women have no space of their own. My work on anorexia *(Arrows)* is partly about this. I don't know if I can show anything about lesbian sex on film unless it's showing positive joy and not just wishful. I'm sick of people intellectualising about lesbianism in terms of language, lack of signifier in sex, etc. I'm very aware of the privilege of being at art school and the time spent on abstraction.

I wouldn't ever show heterosexual sex on film – even in the work I'm doing on Sylvia Plath – no matter how hung up she was on the idea of having a male hero/guru.

As lesbian film-makers we need to start a discussion out of silence. There's nothing yet between the bad and the idealised. Soft-focus, male-identified images of women make me squirm – no hairs on their legs, privileged, middle class, 'Chanel No 5' women who've got a head start anyway because of class – I can't relate to that.

From a lesbian perspective, I'm not on the outside, therefore I can't be an automatic consumer. So anything I do is more like the raw end of a nerve. Sex is the most important thing in most people's lives. It's like screaming all the time. I don't just want to show gloom – but joy often turns into power. It's hard to separate real life from my film work.

As far as portraying 'real' sex is concerned I think it's a problem. It could just end up 'aping' sex in heterosexual films. I don't want to use all the 'clouds in front of the moon' or 'pans across the beautiful countryside' devices. I would want to show emotional desire, not two women in bed, and the 'press tab A' type of reactions. If there's some way of showing that desire, I'll do it.

Caroline

Because of my history – coming from revolutionary feminism – I have a really strong awareness of the way images of women are used to exploit, and sexual images of women are *used* by men as a turn on. On the other hand we need to see representations of ourselves, not just heterosexuals. If all we're ever fed in terms of sexual imagery is heterosexual, then this pushes us on to the defensive and keeps us out of sight.

After being involved in feminist film-making for a while, I got a really strong feeling that we needed strong images of lesbian sex that turn women on but threatened men. Because of my anger about the way men exploit women's sexuality it's a difficult combination but not impossible. I don't think as lesbians making films we should be scared of trying – after all we haven't got that much to lose.

I suppose I mean 'threatening' in the way that *A Question of Silence* is threatening in terms of exclusion.

I'd like to be able to show 'explicit' lesbian sex in a film. It's something that could be represented visually in very exciting ways. Film for me is about pleasure, as well as about thought and communication. Technically and given my politics, if I knew how to do it, I'd do it. It could be in any number of contexts, for me it's not a question of form but context *and* form. For instance, in *At First Sight* there's no explicit sex, but it is very clearly erotic and shows desire. In that context sex scenes could have been a 'rip off'.

I think sexual imagery in my own work would be harder, and also that the film would be about sex rather than incidental – I don't make narrative films. Also if it was exclusively about sex, I'd want it to be for women only. I don't think as lesbian film-makers there should be an onus on us to produce *the* perfect lesbian film.

Film covers a very wide area of cultural experience, from experimental films and other low budget films to the multi-million pound industry. At one end of the scale, obvious factors like sales and marketing come into it. Apart from eroticism, lesbian sex is always political.

One way of using sexual imagery in film could be using powerful contrasting images to create not just a sexual image but also a strong political threat. Or using sound as a contrast to the image, or using lesbian 'in' humour which can be both powerful and funny. I'm not thinking about campaign politics as such, but about reality – the everyday politics of life – consumerism, housework, etc. and the actual substance of everyday reality which is not normally considered political in the way that demos are. So I want to produce images of the reality which have political significance – including lesbian sex.

PENNY WOOLCOCK

STATEMENT FROM
PANDORA'S BOX CATALOGUE

...But he feeds on us,
like all of them. His whole life, his art
is protected by women. Which of us could say that?
Which of us, Clara, hasn't had to take that leap
out beyond our being women
to save our work? or is it to save ourselves?

From *Paula Becker to Clara Westhoff* by Adrienne Rich

Part 1 At fourteen, my future appeared to me in frozen stills, sepia tinted daydreams. In one I sit before an oval dressing table, ruched frills to the floor, gazing into its hinged mirrors. On its polished glass surface rests an ivory-backed brush set and a huge powder puff. My adult self, in a 1950s strapless ball gown, head tilted slightly to the right, brushes the iced ripples of her elegant coiffure. She is reflected indistinctly in the mirror along with an enticing double bed and the handsome figure of a husband wearing a suit and tie.

In the other I stand laughing in a loose circle of friends, face clear and hair tumbling over my shoulders. I have on a large brown coat and a striped scarf, poised to return to paint in my London studio.

In retrospect, although naive, the choice seems remarkably perceptive and more than a question of lifestyle. The hours I spent painting in my room in a Buenos Aires suburb felt like taking swims in a different kind of water that made me feel more alive. Instead of curling my eyelashes and despite failing art O-level twice, I set out to make paintings.

It was ten years before I could work without looking over my shoulder. A son, lovers and what I can only describe as an unrecognised desire to be the subject of a great painting drove me to turn my back on it for about four years. I returned like a lost and homesick traveller to liberated lands, camped out in the biggest room in the house and learnt to work with fragmented images, using scrap materials which reflected how I lived rather than some romantic notion. I no longer waited for time, money or permission.

19

Part II It is not incidental to how I breathe, paint, talk, earn money or anything else that I am a woman who has become a mother, a feminist, a revolutionary socialist but neither is the way I do these things prescribed by my politics. Art is not above gender or class and can serve reactionary or progressive ends but it is also specific to itself and not a substitute for other forms of action. There are more effective ways of sharing a vision than spending months painting an image to hang in a gallery patronised by obnoxious Tory connoisseurs who would buy canvases stained with the blood of peasant women if the proportions were right. The thought of succeeding on their terms makes me want to start lying, behaving myself, smiling too much, combing my hair and throwing up.

The crucial factor in the relationship between art and politics lies in what sector of society appropriates it, with or without the artist's consent. Frida Kahlo and Diego Rivera worked figuratively in revolutionary Mexico but at the time of the Russian revolution traditional painters admired by Lenin were Tsarists, while the avant-garde supported the Bolsheviks and formed a movement which expanded into popular culture with unparallelled vigour. The mandarins of the New York art establishement condemned abstract work as a Communist plot until Stalin denounced it as bourgeois and institutionalized social realism as the 'art of the people', upon which abstract painters became the epitome of the capitalist dream. Pieces by members of the Proletkult now change hands at exorbitant prices on the East Side.

The social context, politics and gender of the artist, the composition of the audience and the content of the work, are all variables in a complex picture. A constant factor has been a deliberate blindness to the work of women and a patriarchal bias in the images produced of us, the old fascist favourites, the mother and the whore overshadowing the silent presence of daughters, sisters and wives. Despite the problems of defining a women's, let alone a feminist art, we all carry our common history into the studio on our backs and I think this gives a curiously intimate quality to the work; the sense of an old friend who can still surprise you.

Part III When I came back to painting in 1975 I worked very badly every day but it was a question of survival and I didn't care. I dived into my own space to make huge sails dipped in coloured wax, cloth etchings stitched together and dreaming map drawings. I worked on a collective project with two other women (Kassandra Pardee and Sarah Ainslie) and used all the information at my disposal.

I was a shop steward, looked after my son and stayed up all night scribbling, tacking, staining, sweeping dust and old bus tickets into little bags. Figurative work seemed very restrictive to me and I was inspired by other women, listened to music and sometimes fell in love with inappropriate men. I won a Southern Arts bursary and had a joint exhibition at the Arnolfini both of which deeply depressed me. Unhappy, I painted heavy bitumen black spirals. When I felt better I made drawings of skies and kites and hung rows of broken glass and strips of cloth to cast shadows over them.

In the spring of 1982 I read Monique Wittig's dazzling *Les Guerrilliers* and painted some impressions of it. That painting, although only half successful, pulled me into increasingly more figurative work and I painted a bloody version of Gentileschi's *Judith* and multi-coloured images of Bolivia after a journey there. I had already developed a way of making working surfaces by nailing an old blanket to the wall, covering it with hemmed cotton scraps from jumble sales, cutting around three of the sewn edges and sticking the flap to the blanket with paste or emulsion before priming the whole area. I draw on these stiff skins and use oils and also powdered stage pigments mixed with a gel medium. Sometimes paintings work straight away but a piece may give me trouble and make me jump up and down and attack it with different ideas and materials. If the attack goes too far I destroy it altogether and put it in the bin but interesting things can happen in this way. I am now working on a large piece about life models.

Part IV I worked on the 'Pandora' paintings for about four months and it was a fine time of waking up to breathe and paint what I had dreamed about the night before.

Under the Breast the Bone was painted from photographs of women who have inspired me, friends and strangers, my Pandoras. This painting challenged the negative assumptions of the male myth and substituted a rib cage, a pelvis and individual faces for the bruised tits and bums of the first.

For *Dressed in Glittering Raiment, They Drank Heavily Laughing Loudly* I asked three friends to spend an evening together dressed for each other's pleasure in the sort of clothes women generally wear for men while I recorded the event with slides and photographs. I had originally intended to poke fun at the myth but a more complicated picture emerged. What happened is in the painting along with some of what I was thinking about at the time.

Part V Writing all this has been like pulling out a bad tooth and then having to wear it around my neck. I can't possibly write any more.

MARIE YATES

STATEMENT FROM
SENSE AND SENSIBILITY CATALOGUE

Old Hat, February 1987

On the telephone, you said, 'We'd like to publish that piece you wrote for the *Sense and Sensibility* show catalogue in 1982' and she thought, 'Oh, no. Things have changed so much, we have all changed. The map references have all moved and I can't believe a word of it anymore, and I wouldn't support its sentiments at all now.' She said, 'It would have to be rewritten,' and as she spoke she could see that it needed to be another piece entirely now.

That piece is an old frame, a historical map and as she wrote in the catalogue in 1982, 'The answer can only be *Now*. We can't use an old frame.' We can't fix our desires. It's a viewing of the same landscape but with a different set of references, redefining the limits, reframing the identifications. Desire becomes relocated and new objects are freshly constructed out of the old ones.

But you said, 'We like it as it is,' and she sighed and thought of all the beautiful writing and analysis since then, constructed by women who were changing the maps and moving everything around. In 1987, alternative readings cannot be seen to be 'outside' of anything. For us now, in 1987, pornography is another object entirely, there is a different *Now*, now. Different forms of politicisation, not political positioning. These new forms of politicisation begin with the recognition that meaning is perpetually displaced from the image to the discursive formations which cross and contain it, there can be no question of 'progressive' or 'alternative' contents or forms in themselves. The problem is not to answer the old questions, it is to identify the new ones.

She sighed to herself again, and thought how firmly she now held that women and men are not constituted as uniform and monolithic blocks, locked forever by their respective biological destinies in inevitable, immutable opposition. 'Such a view,' she thought, 'of course rules out the possibility of any sexual politics at all, if politics means change.'

'In 1982,' she murmured to herself, 'it might have been O.K., but now, in 1987, anyone using the word pornography is viewed with suspicion, and

3   Marie Yates, *The Only Woman*, 1985, one of 21 panels, Section 1, *The Gaze*, poster.

rightly so. For to do so is to run the risk of supporting and perpetuating the old legal moralisms and homophobia.'

But for the sake of history, she thought, maybe it would be valuable for us to view the distance covered in five long years, and so with some misgivings and a firm insistence that you the reader view what follows historically, she decided to allow it to appear again, saying to herself, 'This is where we've been, we don't need to go back there'.

With thanks for their views to: Betty Friedan, Angela Carter, Elizabeth Cowie, Victor Burgin, Simon Watney

Sense and Sensibility, 1982

She said, 'I can't imagine an alternative image from inside this one,' but you said, 'meaning is not already there in the image, but is produced in the process of viewing,' and she said, 'but porn puts into circulation images of sexuality that have definite meanings connected with them, sexual pleasure for men is initiation and dominance and for women submission to men's depersonalised needs. The problem is that these meanings feed general definitions of sexual identity and sexual activity.'

But you said 'alternative readings are not just a question of new content but of different strategies of production of the image in relation to the discursive space of all other similar images, remembering that discourses redefine images in their circulation as part of the production of those images.'

'Yes,' she said, 'meaning is given to a representation by its context, use, and the arrangement of its elements, but sexuality itself is framed, bounded for us in mythic dream-time where we become voyeurs upon our own caresses in a charade of maleness and femaleness.'

'Maybe,' you said, 'but it is not possible to preserve one's identity by adjusting for any length of time to a frame of reference that is in itself destructive to it. It is very hard indeed for a human being to sustain such an inner split – conforming outwardly to one reality, while trying to maintain inwardly the values it denies.'

'Yes,' she said, 'and by adjusting to it, a woman stunts her intelligence to become childlike, turns away from individual identity to become an anonymous robot in a docile mass.'

You said, 'Men must learn to enact restraint on their indiscriminate sexual autonomy, while women have to learn the right to autonomous sexuality and not be determined or controlled by sexuality itself. It is an imbalance of incompatible strategies and the weight of responsibility is heavy for all of us involved.'

'Yes,' she said, 'and we need to be able to specify what it is we object to in all these representations. We need to understand how degrading meanings are constructed and reinforced generally. Unless we do this, we run the risk of failing to understand male and female sexual behaviour and the working of power in it.'

'Of course,' you said, 'and within these representations we seek woman-ness and man-ness; we locate what we identify as a clue, and decide on the basis of it that we have discovered a "real" sexual difference located in the person captured in the "reality" of the image. This "location of difference" then becomes the full presence required by the question of the image, and narrative takes hold and places the subject of the image within a framework of events and details. Further, because so much personal reference is required in this production of meaning through involvement with the image, we entail ourselves within the recognition.'

She then said, 'These images may be seen to embody or represent the "feminine", and draw the reader in, constituting the female subject by means of the invocation of certain fixed meanings constructed according to definite and familiar conventions and means of presentation.

'These fixed meanings intrude into a space where they were previously absent. These narratives of presence/absence/image/woman/action/prac-tice/detail constitute a whole baggage of history, identity and effects to be taken on it would seem, by merely being recognised by the reader, who is also, it must be remembered, the woman who is speaking or making the image.'

'And have you ever thought,' you said, 'how the caption operates so that the image of the woman brings into presence a whole body of detail absent in the image alone. It shows us the enormous lack which inhabits the photographic image; the image presents us with no real knowledge, no real presence; for what *is* present in the moment of the shutter clicking, is not ever present in the production of the pattern on paper collected by means of light, not ever present to the reader; but what is present is the construction of the reader's presence in the relationship to the authority of presentation of photo and text, where the tyranny of fixed meanings articulates the reader as subject to it.'

'Alternative strategies of image-making?' she said, thinking that perhaps this also refers to other constructions and readings and entities, yes, not new content but a different position of relatedness to that content, a viewing of the same landscape with a different set of references, redefining the limits, reframing the identifications. Desire then becomes relocated and objects are freshly constructed out of the old ones.

'Perhaps,' you murmured, 'one asks "When did the photograph happen?" at what point did the framing occur? The answer can only be "now". We can't use an old frame except as a historical map reference and yet we do attempt to piece together a collection of old frames, and the more currency that the image has in terms of the unconscious, say with pornography, the more diligently do we assemble our map references, find them in conflict with each other and so despair.'

She sighed, and said, 'If only men could take responsibility for being men, as women are doing for being women.'

'Yes, I know,' you said, 'and then they might see their maleness as a problem, and see the effects of masculinity, to which at present they are blind – it's like you said at the beginning about imagining an alternative image from inside this one.'

The original 1982 catalogue statement is preceded by a new introduction.

INTERVIEWS

4 Monica Sjoo sitting beneath her painting *God Giving Birth*, 1968, oil on hardboard.

THE SHAPED VOICE

Here again is the voice of the artist, but in quite a different form. The tasks the interviewers here have set themselves are varied – to put the kind of questions to the artist that the reader would want to ask; to draw out the artist's explanation of her aims, her overview of art and/or feminism; and to challenge or to support. The overall result is to give the reader more information with which to interpret the artist's work, with the voice of the interviewer shaping the nature of that information.

This shaping is implicit in any interview. The interview with Rose Garrard by Fiona Byrne-Sutton and Julia James, and Rose Garrard's letter in response to the published form of that interview, are printed here primarily because of the discussion of issues arising from Garrard's work; but they do have the added interest of making explicit the editorial process. Any long taped interview will need some editing in order to be published on two or three pages of a magazine. In this case, the interviewers did that editing in good faith; Garrard found her views misinterpreted due to the editing process and wrote the letter; and the interviewers added a rider to the effect that they had tried to contact her about the editing but were unable to do so. Another layer of control is still left concealed: the editorial staff's final say about the form taken by the interview in their magazine, including matters of wording, length, illustrations and so on. In this case, it is not stated to what extent they used this authority, or whether indeed they allowed the interviewers a comparatively free hand in all of these matters. Without wishing to enter the realm of conspiracy theory, it is clear how the containment of an artist's ideas could occur at any point of this process, and I think it important to add a postscript to this particular story – that both interviewers and interviewee are happy to have the interview and letter reprinted as they stand, because of the issues discussed within them.

The interview format can be particularly useful because it can frame an artist's work in a way that cannot be done in a straight-forward review. All of the women interviewed have shown their work outside the mainstream gallery context, which means that they have, on those occasions, 'missed' the chance of getting it reviewed, and, therefore, recorded for the benefit of a larger audience. Two of the interviews in particular are important because of the access they provide to work which might otherwise be little-recorded. Karen Alexander has chosen to work in a community-based project; whilst the importance of this work and the energy it generates can be hugely appreciated on a local basis, it often doesn't get much wider recognition. Monica Sjoo says that she is 'not the least bit interested in modern bourgeois European art'; the art press has responded by ignoring her work. The socialist-feminist press too, with its unease about matters spiritual, and its equation of matriarchalism with essentialism,[1] have also to a large extent ignored her work. The interview format is also particularly useful when a woman has shifted her method of working (as in the case of Alexis Hunter) as this can be examined in a way that would probably not happen in an exhibition.

NOTES

1 Matriarchalism: belief in female deities.
  Essentialism: the belief that 'femininity' and 'masculinity' are innate and biologically determined – ie, if you are born female you will 'naturally' be caring, passive, nurturing; if you are born male you are 'naturally' more agressive, assertive etc., and there is no possibility of changing the essences of the genders through political action. Most feminists argue that 'femininity' is a cultural construct, and therefore open to alteration; some would say that 'femininity' is 'natural' to all women, not to be found at all in men, and should be treated as superior to masculinity.

KAREN ALEXANDER: VIDEO WORKER

Karen Alexander is part of a growing group of black women involved in film and video production. After completing the Visual Communications and Sociology degree course at Goldsmiths' College she joined Albany Video, a community-based video project in south-east London, where her job includes working with local black groups, women's groups and youth groups. She was also involved in setting up the Pictures of Women collective (POW) and worked with them on a series of programmes which were screened by Channel 4 in January and February of 1984.

Here she talks to Mica Nava, a member of the *Feminist Review* editorial collective, about her cultural work and her political commitment as a black woman.

Mica Nava: When did you start working with video?

Karen Alexander: I made my first tape when I was a second year student at Goldsmiths. It was a documentary called *Contradictions in Housing*, about the gentrification of the Lots Road area of Chelsea; it tried to look at housing history and different perspectives in housing policy. During my research I had a lot of help from the local tenants' association. In my final year I decided to make a tape about the Asian Community Action Group. Instead of just saying, 'these people are really suffering, that's why they set up this group', I focused on one woman who worked there and showed her in different settings and taking on different roles, such as Asian expert in a TV interview or militant picket outside the Home Office. I tried to show her as a person who was brought up in this country, who negotiated both Western and Asian cultures and who was using knowledge gained from the former to benefit the latter. I wanted to avoid the cliché of showing an Asian woman trapped between two cultures and unable to cope. But it wasn't a radical tape really; it was just a college project. It didn't change the situation or the politics of the group, though it got them interested in using video.

Mica Nava: Tell me about the work which is done at the Albany Video unit.

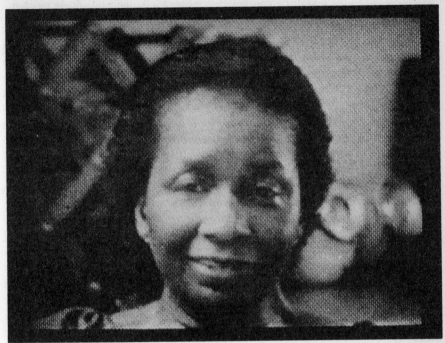

5   Karen Alexander, *Photo Of My Mother*, video. (Photo: Jessica Evans.)

Karen Alexander: The video work at the Albany tends to fall into four main areas: distribution, production, education and training. The unit runs a distribution library with about twenty different tapes made either by us or by similar community groups. They range from *The Irish in Britain* to *Us*, a tape made by and about physically and mentally handicapped people. In production we work with groups and either produce tapes for them or enable them to produce their own tapes. By 'education' I mean sensitizing youth and community workers and groups to the possibilities of video technology as a resource, especially as a discussion initiator about different or difficult issues such as racism, sexism and sexual prejudice. As far as training goes, this may consist of running courses for groups or for youth and community workers who are interested in using video in a constructive and imaginative way. Most recently, my work there has been concerned with fund raising and preparing for another woman worker to join the project. I have also been involved – though not as much as I would have liked – with a group of black women youth and community workers who are producing a mixed media package for use with black girls in youth clubs.

Mica Nava: Have you done much video work with girls and young women?

Karen Alexander: Yes, but it's always quite complicated. You can't just barge into a room and say, 'OK, I'm a video worker and the best thing in your life you can do is produce a video tape'. For example I worked with a group of young mothers – they were all black – in a youth club in Lewisham, and I went there and talked to them for weeks before they felt they had enough confidence to make a tape. In the end they decided to make one about the attitudes they found really annoying when they told people they were pregnant. They made the situation quite comic: they took on the roles of their parents, their boyfriends and the doctors, and really exaggerated them. At the same time they were learning how to use the equipment, and then they edited the tape. The whole process took a long time and some of them got bored after a while, but they didn't have much time – only two hours a week – because of the problem of finding someone to look after the children. I think the experience was useful because before that they wouldn't ever have imagined themselves learning to use video equipment and producing a tape. They probably thought, 'Black women don't use video, it's not for me'. When I work with women's groups, especially black women's groups, they always ask me how I got involved and say it's good to see a black woman doing such things. On the other hand they are really suspicious of people who come from places like the Albany because they think that they are all do-gooders or lefties, or worse still, communists. I think that being a black person gave me one less hurdle to get over when working with groups like that.

Mica Nava: So do you think that the process of making the tape actually changed the way those young women thought about things?

Karen Alexander: I think it may have changed the way they view the media. When you go into a group with a video cassette recorder, camera, microphone and lights, they go, 'Do we need all this for just a little video tape?' Then you can start talking about the way TV programmes are put together and you get them to think about when and where on television they see such things as lights, mikes and cameras. This sort of low-key questioning can happen while they are constructing shots; for example, you can suggest that they use a head-on shot rather than the one they are mimicking from TV; you can point to the types of people who have full mid-shots facing the camera and to the authority that is invested in what those people have to say. It's not thrusting theory down their throats, but trying to make them question the things they look at. Another example of this kind of approach occurs when people I am working with don't like the colour of their skin on the video that we produce. Our equipment isn't very sophisticated of course, but then we start talking about how even on television black people don't appear as black as they should, their colour just doesn't look right. All this leads to a discussion about television technology and how the cameras are set up to give a perfect picture against a test card which consists of a white woman with brown hair; and so you start to talk about the construction of a technology which is often portrayed as neutral, as offering a window on the world.

Another interesting example of this kind happened when I was working with a group of sixth form girls. They had decided that they wanted to make a tape about what they didn't like at school, but then at one point they suddenly stopped and said, 'Look, we can't do this, it's not fair because there aren't any white girls here to say what they think, it wouldn't be balanced if they didn't put their view'. So I just asked when the last time was that they had seen a black woman on television saying what she thought about anything. Then they thought for a bit and said, 'I suppose you're right', and carried on. Those are the kinds of points that come up all the time when you're working with groups, and if you think about how to answer them you can put over quite a lot of information. It's important to my work to point out the whole constructive nature of the medium I'm working with and to relate it to representations of black women; in this way I think I can help to create a consciousness about power and control. But it's also important that the women in the groups I work with gain confidence, learn some skills and feel they are capable of producing something. The thing about video is that it's so immediate, and it's relatively simple.

Mica Nava: Apart from your work at Albany Video, you are also involved in the Pictures of Women collective. How did that project get off the ground?

Karen Alexander: Late in 1981, four women, three of whom had been at Goldsmiths' College, started to meet to talk about setting up a multi-media production group. Our project was to produce visual material by and for women. In order to do this we needed money. At the time that we were meeting, Channel 4 was just setting up and putting out feelers for innovative programmes. During the same period certain issues around female sexuality were being pinpointed for study, and we thought it was essential to look at common-sense assumptions in this area and offer a feminist analysis. We also wanted to use the medium of television in an exciting way. All this constituted enough difference in Channel 4's eyes to get a commission; it was also a time when they were actively looking for applications from ethnic minorities and women. So a lot of our success in getting finance had to do with being in the right place at the right time. I think that if we wanted to do the same thing today, we wouldn't be able to; there is no longer the money or the goodwill around for groups such as ours. Channel 4 took a risk when they commissioned the *Sexuality* series from us because we hadn't done anything for broadcast television before. I learned a lot by working on the series, it's been invaluable in that respect. Perhaps that knowledge and those skills can be passed on to other women to help them produce things as well.

Mica Nava: What are you doing with POW at the moment?

Karen Alexander: We all do one day a week in the POW office. At present I am doing a lot of liaison work, which entails going out with the tapes to do presentations to women's groups or trade unions about the issues dealt with in the programmes. It's important that the tapes have a life after broadcast and are used by interested groups. We want to get some money now so that we can compile short tapes, consisting of chunks from each of the programmes, which can be used to initiate discussion.

Mica Nava: What kinds of responses have you had to the POW programmes?

Karen Alexander: We have recently had a very interesting invitation. We have been asked to go to a women's prison by the education officer there, in order to run a weekend course for prisoners around the themes brought up in the POW series. I am really looking forward to that. Overall it's fascinating to see the diversity of response to the programmes. For example some of my male relatives and their friends asked me about the sexual harassment one. It was at a party shortly after the programme had gone out, and somebody said, 'I hear you have been involved in this women's lib series, I watched the one on sexual harassment at work'. Then they all discussed whether they agreed with it or didn't agree and commented on the things they did or didn't like about particular programmes. I've been amazed at the number of black men that I've spoken to who watched at least one and were interested enough to talk about the issues which were raised. At a friend's house, a guy recognized me from the programmes and started to talk to me about the one on pornography; I thought he was going to say he didn't know what all the fuss was about, or something like that. Instead he told me that it had really made him think about the issues. He said that he and the man he worked with had looked at pornography and he was now asking himself, 'Why are we like that?'. It was quite interesting getting feedback like that from men.

Mica Nava: Independent film and video work is enormously constrained by the funding that is available. What, ideally, would you like your next project to be?

Karen Alexander: One of the things I would like to do is to make a film. I've put in an application for finance to the Greater London Arts Association

(GLAA) with a friend of mine, another black woman. We want to do something about black women and the reflections we experience of ourselves. We want to examine how we view ourselves and what sort of cultural representations of black women are offered up to us to consume. To accompany the visuals we hope to get verbal reflections from black women about the experience of being in a society which continually negates or assimilates our existence. We want to do a film rather than a video because of the quality of the image and because we would like to make something which could go out as a short with a longer independent film.

Mica Nava: Have you got any other plans?

Karen Alexander: In about a year's time I'd like to do a video about my mother and my aunt. I am always interviewing people about their lives, and yet I don't know very much about their history – and to a certain extent their history is my history. I keep telling my mother that I'm going to do a tape with her and she says, 'Any time you're ready'. I'm really looking forward to that. A while ago I did a short interview with her for a seminar I was giving for a Black Women and Representation course organized by the women in Sankofa (a recently-formed black film and video group) and some other black women. What was interesting was the answer I got when I asked my mother about the films she liked. She said her favourite was perhaps *Gone With The Wind*; I told her that many people objected to the way in which black people were portrayed in it, and she said that she would agree with that. I also asked her which bit had the most impact for her and she said, 'The bit I'll always remember is when Scarlett O'Hara holds up the red dust and says "I'll never be hungry again, as God is my witness I'll never be hungry again"'. The way she said it conveyed a whole experience of poverty which I'd never known because I was born here and not in Guyana. It was an indication of the wealth of experience that she hadn't let come to the surface about things which are very important to her. It's also interesting talking to my mother about the types of women she identified with when she was young. They were all white women, but they were all women like Joan Crawford – very strong women. She's seen *Mildred Pierce* again and again. When my mother lived in Guyana, she would go to the cinema once or twice a week.

Mica Nava: I wonder if you would like to say anything about your political commitment as a black person and as a woman. Has this double commitment ever been contradictory or difficult to reconcile?

Karen Alexander: At the time that I left Goldsmiths I didn't know of any black women producing things on video, so I joined Albany Video, a white group which had a history of working with women's groups and black groups. While I was at Goldsmiths I tended to work with women, so in a way it was a natural progression to involve myself with women and women's groups when I left – groups of white women. POW was an example of this. Members of the black community, or rather certain black men, sometimes asked me why I worked on those programmes with all those white women; in effect they were saying that I should be putting my skills to work for black people. During my first year as a video worker at the Albany I felt very confused. I'd get black groups phoning up and women's groups phoning up and I just couldn't do everything; I was being pulled in two directions and I felt equally committed to working in both areas. I was meant to be just a video worker, but because of my sex and colour I felt I was like an extra resource, which was sometimes uncomfortable in spite of the fact that I thought it was important to be visible, to show that black women were getting involved in film and video production.

But more recently the situation has improved. There is a growing participation of black women in the independent sector, and I feel that I am part of that movement. Three black film and video workshops have recently been established, they are Ceddo, Sankofa, and Retake – all mixed groups. The funding they receive comes from a mixture of sources: GLAA, The British Film Institute, Channel 4 and the Greater London Council. So recently there has been a dramatic increase in the number of black women involved in a sector where previously we were conspicuous by our absence. There are also more black women who have done film, media or communications courses at college and who like me are very interested in looking at questions of black women and representation. So overall I now feel that my allegiances lie with the up-and-coming black independent sector in general and towards black women in particular – towards making tapes and films about ourselves and our struggles.

INTERVIEWED by YASMIN KUREISHI

REWORKING MYTHS: SUTAPA BISWAS

Through the ages, women-artists have become closely associated with the use of pastels to paint quiet, delicate images. Sutapa Biswas continues to use pastels, but rejects traditional techniques and notions, by producing huge, strikingly colourful and assertive images. Sutapa told me, when I met her recently, 'I never realised the kind of effect my work would have, because I never made my work to last – it was never precious – I thought, oh well if it gets a hole in it, it gets a hole in it.'

Born in India in 1962, Sutapa came to Britain at the age of four. She studied Fine Art at Leeds University and was the only Black woman in her department at college. Though several of her lecturers were supportive, Sutapa experienced a great deal of racism. 'It was not the kind of racism you can pinpoint, it's insidious.[1] At the time I didn't know of any other Black artists who existed and I felt very isolated.'[2] Since then her work has seen the light of day at the ICA, Brixton Art Gallery, Rochdale Art Gallery and the Tara Arts Centre, to name but a few.

Sutapa's work addresses important issues for Black women and women everywhere, and by using myths and iconography from ancient Hindu mythologies, Sutapa reworks her rich, cultural history to question Western attitudes and assumptions. Sutapa's parents are very proud of her work. They were also surprised to see the powerful way in which she was using images, derived from stories of their heritage which they'd passed on to their children.

It doesn't bother Sutapa if the kind of symbolism she uses isn't immediately apparent to her audience: 'I want people to research into my culture, as I've been doing into European and Western culture'. She sees part of her role as an Asian woman artist to challenge the ignorant and arrogant assumption, that is often made about Western culture, as being somehow 'superior' to Eastern culture. 'All those assumptions are very serious in how they affect our lives, because they become part of that institutional framework that binds all of us. I think there are different ways of challenging them – films, television, photography, for me producing artwork is what I enjoy'.

6   Sutapa Biswas, *The Last Mango In Paris*, 1986, acrylic and pastel on paper. (Photo: Patsy Mullan.) The full title of the work is *The Last Mango In Paris* – an important message for the prospective anthropologist.
   As the hour passed, the distance from the immediate chore fluctuated.
M: If you were to be reborn and had a choice, what would you come back as?
   Bowdi thought for a while.
B: If I were to be reborn, I would be born as an English dog, because in England they look after their dogs really well.

Sutapa explained to me the idea within Hindu culture, that every woman is seen as a goddess, because the idea of gods and goddesses exists in such a strong human form.[3] The goddess Kali for instance, is always represented with a garland of men's heads round her neck and the head of a man in one hand. The garland is symbolic of evil and Kali was created to destroy evil. In Sutapa's painting, *Housewives with Steak Knives*, she depicts a strong, multi-armed woman, wearing a necklace of men's heads, with one arm holding a steak knife, and in the other a decapitated male head. Sutapa's aim is to bring in icons and myths and continue them into her work, past becomes present, Kali becomes *Housewives with Steak Knives*. Hindu culture was originally matriarchal, and yet Sutapa points out, 'The only way in which we now assess Asian culture is to say, Oh aren't they oppressed, what d'you think about arranged marriages? And we have to ask, why is it that women have arranged marriages? Arranged marriages were reinforced as an idea, with the invasion of the British in the Indian sub-continent, because it was a fashionable concept which came from Victorian England. So I'm trying to bring forward these images to make people ask, where is the link?' (Cover picture.)

The Last Mango in Paris shows two women, sitting together, laughing and talking, while they each peel a mango. The caption underneath the painting relays to us their conversation:

M: 'If you were to be re-born, and had a choice what would you come back as?'
B: 'If I were to be re-born again, I would be born an English dog, because in England they look after their dogs really well.'

Any inclination the viewer might feel to use racial stereotypes to label Asian women, are instantly swept away, by the humourous conversation they are having. 'Humour and the use of satire is intrinsic to much of my work.' Sutapa emphasised, and she was keen to stress, that contrary to how Asians are usually portrayed by the media, as having no idea of the real world – we are in fact very much aware of our economic and political situation – why we're here, and what our relation is to the dominant social and ideological thinking i.e. British and European culture. And something which Sutapa sees as lacking, when Asian people are portrayed, is their sense of humour. By taking humour and satire to the extreme in her work, Sutapa wants a platform from which people can begin to address their own racism.

Sutapa was trying to say a lot about domesticity and the domestic life of Asian women in *The Last Mango in Paris*. Sutapa explained, 'Why my work is often about domestic scenes, is that although my mother has never been politically active, she's been active and not passive in the ways she's educated and brought up her own children – influenced their thinking and ideas – it's a very positive influence'. Sutapa does to a certain extent agree with feminists who attack the basic ideas behind the family network. But she went on to make the point that, 'What isn't taken into consideration is the fact that coming from a totally different cultural and historical background, the place of the family and the ties of the family, are very different within Asian cultures and also within Black communities in general, throughout Britain. And because of the social pressures, families have always existed within quite tight structures. I suppose because you need that, it's your only way of getting support.'

Focusing on the positive aspects of Asian family life in her work, I wondered why Sutapa hadn't touched on the problems. Regarding her own experience she told me, 'I've never really felt that oppressed within my family, the only place I've felt oppressed is outside the home. Of course there are many problems within any sort of home life, and I think there are problems within the Asian community, but those problems exist within every culture in society – I think these things have to be dealt with within those societies themselves. I don't see it as important to highlight those issues, because on TV that's all you hear about. The only artwork I've produced that comes close to looking at those issues is *As I Stood Listened and Watched, My Feelings Were, This Women Is Not For Burning*, which is

39

7   Sutapa Biswas, *As I Stood, Listened and Watched, My Feelings Were, This Woman Is Not For Burning*, 1986, acrylic and pastel on paper. (Photo: Patsy Mullan.)

about the physical and mental abuse that women have to undergo. It was making a reference to the dowry system – but not just that – for me the two paintings cross over seas – like Britain and India – the relation between the two countries – the tensions and ties that exist between them'.

So how did Sutapa deal with being a part of two distinct cultures? 'One needs to be positive and say there are things we need to deal with – I don't see it as a problem. I find it difficult in terms of wanting to know about my roots and not having access to that information and knowledge, because of the distance and also because Eurocentric culture is such that it doesn't teach you anything about the Asian continent, nor the African or Australian continents for example – that's what I find a problem, but they are not problems which are intrinsic, they're created.'[4]

What advice then, had she, for aspiring Black women artists? 'It's really important that Black artists are able to make their links very strong, so that they can act as a kind of support mechanism. We don't necessarily need white institutions and spaces to make our work visible, we don't have to operate in those areas – I think it's useful if we do though, because as many different areas we're seen in the better. But from my own experience I've needed other women who are Black and who are artists, and the more we come to realise as Black women, that there are other people who go through exactly the same kind of experiences, the less we feel isolated.'[5]

NOTES

The following notes have been added by the artist for the republication of the interview.

1 Sentence should read: Though some of her lecturers were supportive, (Fred Orton, Lorraine Leeson, Griselda Pollock) and many other students (Jane Brake, Symruth Patti, Pat Forbes, Isabelle Tracy, Emma Ayling, Jane Glasby, Liz Colebrook, Andrew Rodgers, Andrew Edwards – to name but a few), the overall structure of the fine art course was Eurocentric. Its basic structure was reflective of the cultural imperialism predominantly taught on most art history and practice courses in Britain. Therefore, it is not surprising that she experienced a great deal of racism.

2 I have some friends who were at the time studying fine art at the Polytechnic, Leeds, who are Black (Smyruth Patti, Pat Forbes, Raj Batra). They experienced more overt racist attitudes than myself, from tutors on their course, who showed little or no support. (An inquiry was set up by the governors of the Polytechnic, to hear submissions from any person wanting to make a contribution about the course, and a written report was made to the governors.) Other than Symruth, Pat, and Raj, at that time I didn't know of any other Black artists who existed. Certainly, not any Black artists who were 'successful' and exhibiting their work in the mainstream spaces one normally hears about. Consequently, it meant that it was difficult to feel as if one had a voice, and therefore very easy to feel isolated.

Of course, this all changed when I started to do research work for my dissertation, 'Contemporary Black Women Artists in Britain – One Hell of A Big Subject'. I met up with an amazing artist called Lubaina Himid, who has been, and continues to be, a major influence and point of inspiration in my life, and in the lives of a large number of Black women artists.

3 It is important to note here that Hinduism is not a religion. Hinduism is a sanatana dharma. Sanatana means perennial. Religion and dharma are not synonymous.

4 Sutapa Biswas has recently returned from a long trip in India. Whilst there she travelled 8,000 miles across country.

5 The artist demands that her work should be read within a broader art historical context in both its form and content and that its reading should not fall into the current ghettoized misinterpretations of artwork produced by Black artists.

JUDY CHICAGO

Judy Chicago was in Liverpool, England, in October 1982 lecturing and teaching at the Great Georges Community Cultural Project. This recorded conversation was taken partly from group discussions with students from Dartington College of Art who came to Liverpool to work with Judy and the Community Cultural Project, and partly from an interview which I held with her after the discussion.

Dinah Dossor: Do you think that art can be a tool for social change?

Judy Chicago: I don't know how you come up with the idea of art and social change at all because I don't believe in art simply as a tool of social change I believe in art as art. One can use art as a tool for social change or one can make art which has as one constituent the changing of social and political circumstances, but after all that is over art will continue to exist as beautiful images.

Dinah Dossor: But surely anything which is objectified, reified and put into a public gallery will become a commodity and be out of your control.

Judy Chicago: I'm going to tell you something – I wouldn't mind if my art became a little more of a commodity. Actually it's the opposite problem for those of us who come from disenfranchised groups – it does not even represent a threat because not being able to enter the cultural commodity pool as a market is one of the things which makes us disenfranchised. Art is inherently or potentially powerful – images are powerful and have the potential to speak out of the human spirit and express things that are uncontrollable – nobody can control an artist making a mark on paper. The object itself can be controlled, the artist can be made to feel terrible, but that act can only be controlled psychologically, or the product controlled by the market-place. Therefore that is an act that is inherently anti-social – that's one of the good things about it. Unless the artist submits to the values of the culture, the artist can say something that has never been said before, and therefore alter cultures. And all societies attempt to control and suppress their activities. I don't think there is any country in the world that has a good model for the position of the artist in the culture. Dissent is essential to the development of a civilisation. Now, to what extent can society tolerate dissent? That seems to be where the problem is.

There can be many different models for social change art but I think one of the criteria for that art is whether or not, in my estimation, it's good art and two, whether it's effective, and that means in actual real ways, in seeing actual change take place in values, in ideas or change in personal lives. Art is action, and I think that's one of the things that people get really mixed up about. It's not just the art activity that's the action: art itself is action. The act of making a work of art is action: the act of looking at a work of art is action.

Dinah Dossor: Do you think that everyone can be artists?

Judy Chicago: No. And it doesn't have to be to do with skills, it's to do with vision. Not everybody has the same vision. People have all different skills and abilities, but it's only when we come to art that people think that everybody can do it. Nobody would say everybody can be a scientist. But when it comes to art, our commonsense fails us. Artists are special people just like people who have mathematic skills are special people. It has to do with how your brain is formed, what your genetic disposition is. I know it's not a popular idea, but I believe it. All people can make art but that doesn't make them artists.

Dinah Dossor: Do you think that a distinction exists between art and craft in contemporary art practice? Not necessarily the historic distinctions but perhaps something which is more appropriate to contemporary culture?

Judy Chicago: Yes. I do think there's a distinction between art and craft, and I think it's a distinction that needs to be maintained. However I do not think it's the historical distinction. I think the historical distinction is – if men do it it's art and if women do it it's craft. I think there's a tremendous amount of sexism and racism and classism in the traditional distinctions between art and craft, and what I use myself as a working distinction is that in art, the technique or the material is in the service of meaning, and in craft, the technique or the material or the process is an end in itself.

Dinah Dossor: If we take the case of a Navajo blanket this presents us with a few problems because though it may be exhibited in the Museum of Modern Art, it would have been made for a particular function.

Judy Chicago: Yes, but that's use, and I didn't say anything about use; I think that Navajo blankets are in the service of meaning. That's why they speak to us, because apart from their use as blankets, they have symbolic meaning.

Dinah Dossor: Would you say then that an object acquires the service of meaning, for example the furniture made by the Shakers?

Judy Chicago: No. I think that it had the meaning and we just learned how to appreciate it. They transmitted their whole value system through these objects, and we get it when we look at them. That's what makes the difference, for example, between their chairs and Mies Van de Rohe's chairs which are beautiful wonderful craft objects but they do not have any spiritual dimensions.

One of the tasks of having a vision is not only to translate that vision into form but also to discover whether the forms have meaning to anyone outside yourself. And that brings us to audience. For whom do you make the art? Art is inherently communication because otherwise why do you spend all that time making a form that doesn't communicate?

Dinah Dossor: Is there such a thing as a definition of an artist?

Judy Chicago: Yes. Someone who makes art.

Dinah Dossor: In that person's own terms?

Judy Chicago: Well – because we live in culture, in community, it seems to me that one of the tasks of having a vision, is not only to translate that vision into form but also to discover whether the forms have meaning to anyone outside yourself, and that brings us to audience – for whom do you make the art, do you make the art only for yourself? Well, if you make the art only for yourself then your own definition that you're an artist may not have any resonance in the world. I myself would not be happy with that, for I think that the function of art is communication.

Dinah Dossor: Does the audience decide whether or not the art is successfully communicating?

Judy Chicago: No. Why give all the power to the audience? For me the discovery of an audience meant that I found out that there were more people who could respond to my work than I had been traditionally told in art school. I went to china painting shows and I went to quilting shows and I saw all these thousands of people there, and I thought, they're going there for the art, and that's the only kind of art they can respond to, so I thought, well – there's something here I want to take a look at. How come they all come to see this art which I consider bad, or irrelevant, or imitative when there's so few people in the galleries?

Dinah Dossor: Was it mainly women at those shows?

Judy Chicago: Tell me something. When you go to a gallery in the day-time who's mainly there? It's women. Women are the major culture consumers. Who else can go to the museum at two o'clock on a Tuesday afternoon? So I thought, if I want to broaden the audience for my work what can I do without compromising my commitment to beauty – I always thought art was about truth and beauty and I've never really swerved from that idea. One thing I thought about all the people in these non elitist art shows was that they could understand it. Whereas they couldn't understand all the work in the museums, particularly contemporary work. So I set about, in the seventies, trying to make my forms more accessible, so you didn't have to read *Art Forum* to appreciate it. It's not an easy problem to make form more accessible without compromising quality, particularly for me because I was an abstract artist.

Dinah Dossor: Why can't men set up a work situation like the one you have?

Judy Chicago: Well, it has nothing to do with sex, that is, gender. It has to do with power relationships between men, and my working situation is based on co-operation and my forms come out of the way women communicate. Women don't communicate well in a competitive situation; they communicate best in an open, sharing, taking turns situation where silence is allowed, and that is a situation that men do not feel comfortable with, so I just don't think it's possible for a long time till men's personalities change.

Dinah Dossor: Why do you think that people continue to think of you as somehow exploiting the women that you work with, particularly when you've always made it clear that you work co-operatively, not collectively?

Judy Chicago: That's always the avenue of trying to invalidate me.

Dinah Dossor: You write very fully in *Through The Flower* about the particular kinds of support that you get from working with other women. Is there anything you could add to that account, looking back on that period?

Judy Chicago: I don't think I'd be able to work if I didn't have that kind of support, since I don't have the traditional support. If I had not built a network of support I couldn't work, and even if I did work, my work wouldn't go anywhere or do anything, and there would be no resonance, and I would go mad I'm sure. I think it's very hard to imagine the isolation of a woman with vision and how as one moves along that vision and an achievement out of it is not rewarded, it's punished, and the farther you get the more punishment you receive, including from ignorant women. That's just another form of punishing me because I've done good and I get punished all the time because I did good. I got punished for *The Dinner Party* and I did something wonderful. It's like it's not okay to say 'you've done something wonderful'.

Dinah Dossor: In terms of the working process of working with women, is there any difference between, say, *The Womanhouse Project* and *The Dinner Party*?

Judy Chicago: In *The Womanhouse Project* I facilitated my students in producing the rooms and the work, and *The Dinner Party* and *The Birth Project* are all my images. I think I was looking for a way to put together that kind of working situation with my own art-making impulse in it and for some years I didn't know how to do it. They were separated, I would work in my own studio as an artist while, at the same time facilitating the growth and production of those people who worked with me, and I think that that's also more acceptable because I was being the mother, and I think it's really hard for women to let other women not be mothers. It was when I brought it together that actually I began to operate full tilt as an artist and that meant that I needed a support system, but that is what every artist who gets to a certain point in their development needs to realise themselves. What we as women need to do is to provide our visionaries with that kind of support. I think a lot of this has to do with education in teamwork. Men have that sort of education, they know how to work together – that there's one quarterback and one lineman and one person doesn't feel diminished because another person makes the goal, they feel like they all did it together. And that actually is the spirit of people who work with me, they feel they're doing it together. My images are the vehicle.

Dinah Dossor: One thing I found odd about *The Womanhouse Project* was that the women who were all working in the same building said that they felt isolated.

Judy Chicago: Yes. Isn't that peculiar? I'll tell you something. I've learned not to listen too carefully to all those things because sometimes they're just expressions of anxiety, and I think one of the things we as women need to do is not take every expression of anxiety quite so seriously.

Dinah Dossor: Do you think the women who choose to work with you are to some extent a self selecting group of people?

Judy Chicago: Yes. You see a lot of these people aren't artists – they don't see themselves as artists.

Dinah Dossor: Have you worked with an artist of your stature?

Judy Chicago: I've tried.

Dinah Dossor: Was it qualitatively different from working with women who didn't have that self-image?

Judy Chicago: It's a different kind of relationship. A collaborative relationship is different from a co-operative relationship. I love to work with people who are my peers.

Dinah Dossor: You've been very successful at facilitating other women

47

without over-mothering them and you've developed a tremendous range of skills to help people grow and restructure their own personalities without taking them over. Can you say something about this?

Judy Chicago: I appreciate that. Do you know what's basic to it? First of all I think it has to do with my attitude towards power which is there's only one kind of power I'm interested in and that's creative work in the studio. It's also very humbling because no matter how famous I get and 'powerful', those are always other people's terms, that's not how I see myself. I don't think of myself even as successful because in my goals for art I'm just at a very early stage and I just hope I can make a contribution to a new sense of what art can be in the culture. I don't think I can achieve my goals in my lifetime, and therefore my idea of success is a future thing. I think that's one of the keys of how I work with people because fame and money are not interesting to me. I tend to treat people like people and one of the things about fame which is actually a pain in the ass is that then people treat me differently, they tend not to treat me as a person. The evolution of people working with me goes from seeing me not as a person to the point where they actually treat me as a person and that's when our relationship moves to a place when I feel comfortable. The other thing I feel very strongly about is that the one right that women are deprived of is the right to struggle. I feel that every human being has to struggle for what they want. So I provide support for struggle, and I would never invade someone else's right to struggle and to find their own way to their own form of personal power. I don't have role expectations and I don't judge people. I think that's presumptuous.

Dinah Dossor: Can you say something more about the concern which you expressed earlier that there have not been more spin off projects from *The Dinner Party* and your other co-operative work, because it is surprising that some of the women didn't go on to establish further programmes.

Judy Chicago: I think that what it's told me, although people get upset when I say this, is that everybody's not me. You see I think there's such pressure against the idea of a woman ever being unique and individual. I think that's a lot of the root of our oppression and we women perpetuate it too – it's taken me the longest time to think that I might actually be unusual, even though my family tells me I was unusual from the day I was born! Also, all the people that work with me get put down. They have to defend themselves and their decisions. I think another thing that women have a lot of trouble with is building on each other's achievements and acknowledging them – it's as though you lose points if you acknowledge that it was other women who nurtured you and supported you. I feel proud of the fact that I turn to other women for support but I think that it is real hard for us to acknowledge ourselves in each other, and that's one of the problems of living in a society that denigrates women.

Dinah Dossor: What do you think of women's art movement work which may be invisible because of the belief that what's important is the art-making process, not the product?

Judy Chicago: I think that's being ladylike. As long as what you're doing isn't noticed you're not violating any of the canons of what a woman's supposed to do. You come out into the public and you force a confrontation with the society and you say 'look at me – what I'm doing is important'. There are some feminist artists in America who really are trying to move into visibility and I think that's a very important step.

Dinah Dossor: Do you find there are general patterns in the development of the women you have worked with?

Judy Chicago: Yes there are general patterns in the development of the ego. The first thing is you need to have a private space to do it in. When I was working at Cal Arts my students had tremendous problems as soon as they walked outside the door of our space because they were confronted directly with the preponderance of the values of that institution which were all traditional male art values, so they felt invalidated as soon as they walked outside the door. That is a very difficult thing to combat if you're working in a traditional institution where girls are denied and diminished.

Dinah Dossor: Do you think it would be good for consciousness raising to be part of the course in an art school?

Judy Chicago: Oh, probably ... absolutely! I use a completely different kind of structure which is non-authoritarian and I think that's something people get really mixed up with – there's a leadership, but that's not inherently authoritarian, and one of the things we've been doing in the last ten years is building non-authoritarian forms of leadership. Leadership is necessary, it just needs to be a new kind of leadership and we need to trust women so that we can develop forms of leadership that are positive and growth enhancing and not be so suspicious of each other –it's unbelievable how we can't even trust the forms that we've developed.

ROSE GARRARD

Fiona Byrne-Sutton: Tell me about the title of your touring exhibition *Between Ourselves*.

Rose Garrard: 'Our' is a non-gender word, so the title is all inclusive... it's also about confidences; what most artists' work is about, a form of trust between the artist and the audience.

Fiona Byrne-Sutton: In the video accompanying the show you say the work is about the relationship between men and women. But while you particularise women 'types' like the Virgin Mary, Eve, Pandora, you don't do the same for men.

Rose Garrard: I think women are in a Catch-22 situation in this respect. Men have both positive and negative role-models – hero or villain – while the point of focusing on women role models is that for the most part they are a combination of positive and negative. The dilemma for women is: they are encouraged to go so far in emulating these models but if they really do the consequences are bound to be disastrous.

Fiona Byrne-Sutton: Perhaps you could use male and female models strategically, almost as protagonists of particular positions?

Rose Garrard: My work has never been oppositional – your suggestion sounds like a very male statement! Male motivation tends to be competitive and oppositional and I'm very aware of my own male side and of enjoying that side of myself if I want to, without losing the beneficial aspects of my female conditioning.

Julia James: To excavate women artists from history in an attempt to answer the question 'why have there been no great women artists?' is one of the biggest traps we can fall into. There is a current argument that we have to acknowledge a patriarchal hegemony in which women aren't left out completely but are given a specific place. It's from that premise that we have to find a way forward.

Rose Garrard: My starting point is myself: the difficulties of a woman trying to make a professional action and finding herself in a situation where apparently there are no historical models and then discovering models, finding out why one hasn't learned about them. So the point about 'reconciliation' of male and female in the show, is not that women have to adjust themselves to fit back into a male world, but that women are, I feel, opening out an enormous psychological territory for themselves, whereas it seems men's roles are becoming less fulfilling.

Fiona Byrne-Sutton: In your *Models* series the shift in scale between your own blank silhouette and the portraits of women from art history is formally very effective, but your relationship to these women remains ambiguous. It would be possible to imagine you are overwhelmed by them (Fig. 8).

Rose Garrard: I think that would be to completely miss the point – that would be a very subjective interpretation. You have to look at the whole structure of the work. There is a cleaning, or a retaining of the ground of the image; what is left within the skin of the painted portrait is my own silhouette. There is a determination of a role through the process of copying, or replicating a pre-existing image – the woman from history – but at the same time there is a retaining of the white ground which is myself, still undetermined.

Fiona Byrne-Sutton: It seemed almost as if you'd gone through ten years work to come back to this position – Rose as a white 'absence'.

Rose Garrard: Well, those works are deliberately ambiguous in some other aspects. I made the silhouette image of myself – holding a book, pointing a gun, and so on – in my studio clothes and the assumption of many viewers has been that these are male figures. There is no contemporary image for a female artist. We only recognise a female if she's wearing a petticoat. Also, I wanted a womb-like sensation, of being enclosed within a figure from history. There was comfort in that, a sort of conspiracy – even though some of these images were actually originally painted by men.

Fiona Byrne-Sutton: Do you think the point of *Models* might have been made more effectively if they were shown in a more enclosed space – literally creating a site for a woman's 'coming to speech'?

Rose Garrard: Well, the work was conceived to be flexible. At the ICA I was able to see the pieces as they were originally visualised, working in pairs from the outside moving in. There is a movement from the floor up into the frames of the first pair, which continues upwards and sideways in the middle pair in an optimistic flow.

Fiona Byrne-Sutton: On your current 'visibility'...you are in a privileged position which at the same time is double-edged: you are being promoted as an individual as well as the token 'woman artist'. In the latter role you can be used to appease the conscience of 'liberal' men in the art system through the process of positive discrimination – teaching, exhibitions, interviews and so on.

Rose Garrard: Isn't it extraordinary that in attempting to do something which is actually 'universal', one is somehow honed-down into some kind of figure-head. Again, in this situation a woman stands for the particular and a man for 'mankind'. At my ICA talk recently, ninety percent of the audience were women. So one isn't really reaching this point of adjustment where one can have this kind of conversation with people who aren't already sympathetic.

Julia James: There is a great desire within the contemporary women's art movement for new role models. Female students in particular want to be reassured that there is a place for them, so they will look to you as someone who appears to be confident and dealing with the issues which they know to be relevant to their own situation.

Rose Garrard: I remember last year Stuart Brisley talked about his *Peterlee Project* as a 'blueprint' for how artists should operate in the future. It wasn't what he did but this way of seeing the work that intrigued me; this idea that an artist can be free enough and unegotistical enough to feel that others should take up the same position that he was beginning to operate. In the same way I feel I might be gradually stumbling upon and opening out a system which it would be possible for others to adapt and make their own; that seems at the moment to be critical of a system and yet not totally outside of it. That's a dangerous position to be in but at present it seems to be the only one I can operate. With my middle class background it's inevitable that I should be something of a fence sitter, balanced between the art school system with its male tutors and male values, and my work as an artist. It's this which becomes the focused-upon issue. On the point of 'reconciliation' it isn't a question of wiping one thing out in favour of another – I do think some male values are essential.

Fiona Byrne-Sutton: Another aspect of the *Models* is the 'quality' of workmanship and how you manipulate ideas of 'good' and 'bad' drawing. You don't seem to paint so skilfully here – as you did in *Incidents in a Garden*, for example.

Rose Garrard: My priorities are the meanings of the images, not the meaning of the marks. It would be a luxury to get into the meaning of the marks – which is where most male artists' work begins. The point of rightness for me isn't to do with stylistic considerations.

Fiona Byrne-Sutton: When I saw the nude in your show at the Venice Biennale, for example, the first thing I looked at was the way it was done.

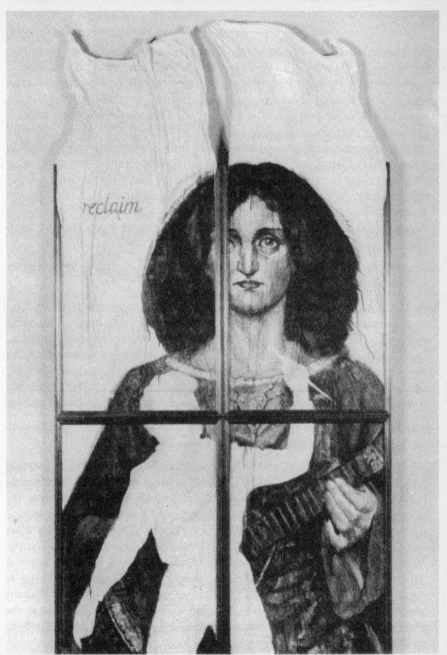

8   Rose Garrard, *Window. Reclaim: Model by Woman Artist*, 1983, acrylic on plaster panel on wood (fresco).

Somehow you had drawn attention to this aspect which you wouldn't have done if it had been painted very neatly, or minutely.

Rose Garrard: I did paint it minutely! But after I'd painted it I then swamped it with paint, I 'threw it away' as it were. I can't technically *not* 'do it well' but I question my *need* to do it well. So often there's a chopping-up of the image, or staining – like the stained bedspread at the ICA. The Venice piece is the 'post-piece' to the bedspread. This autumn I want to start some work that addresses this problem of the 'well-made work'. There's something interesting about the whole issue of copying a pre-existing image. For instance, the Mary Cassatt self-portrait is so amazingly painted, there's so much energy in it; but it's the distance of the reproduction in the book that I'm trying to replicate, not the original gesture. I suppose there's a watery look to a lot of my pictures – a dripping, crying surface, which is as far as I've gone because it takes a lot of physical painting to develop that personalised mark.

Fiona Byrne-Sutton: To incorporate that as part of the subject matter would be to engage with 'the cultural'.

Rose Garrard: This seems to be a recurring point in my conversations. I get to this brick wall all the time which is my increasing need to think of expression being integral to the way in which the work is created. I've kept them slightly apart until now because I'm always so aware of the ways in which these gestures are read. In the last year or so it would have been very easy to make expressionistic work because it's current; but that style is about a particular value system that I'm not at all convinced by.

Fiona Byrne-Sutton: How do you perceive expressionist painting by contemporary women, Thérèse Oulton for example?

Rose Garrard: I'm jealous! Entirely jealous that a woman artist can feel that free. I feel hedged round with misunderstandings. It's the reverse for me – I feel totally inhibited by questions of style: how the paint would go on, the texture or colour of a sculpture. I can't afford to think about formal questions beyond a certain point, at least not at the moment. The work has to be read – that's my priority. If I think the 'signs' are uncertain in how they read, then I can't work with them. So my point of entry is 'cleaning' the signs, cleaning the language. The advantage of being to some extent in the limelight, is that I know people are contextualising my work. I can move to that freer ground without inhibition because the audience will come to the work with a framework which I had something to do with creating.

Julia James: Why do you return to the Virgin Mary, Pandora, and Eve so often?

Rose Garrard: Something I read in the conceptual/minimal days said that one is solo, two is oppositional, three is infinite – so it's not necessary to go beyond three. The Virgin symbolises the whole of what Christianity stands for in terms of 'the woman'. Pandora is the pre-Christian Eve and she returns us to a period before stories were written down. Eve emerged out of Pandora, so there are Old and New Testament references.

Fiona Byrne-Sutton: The problem with presenting these figures in the way you do is that you are putting forth female models – the mother, the temptress – without any disruption or intervention. In fact it's almost as if you are reinforcing these stereotypes.

Rose Garrard: That's where others will start. I really feel like a focusing device, not a propaganda machine. I want people to look at the work and then come up with these questions – 'Is it a reinforcement or a criticism?'.

Fiona Byrne-Sutton: The focus in contemporary theory has shifted now, from 'production' to 'social reality' ...

Rose Garrard: There have been very real changes. I'm absolutely sure the work I do now could not have been received five years ago. I'm always aware I'm arriving on the heels of other women whose work *hasn't* been received. The press have brought the women's movement into public consciousness, no matter how stereotyped or limited the view. In my 1983 *Frameworks* exhibition when I was talking about the cut fabric pieces, I didn't have to explain that this was a valuable women's skill and that it was of equal value to painting.

Julia James: There is a quote from Pierre Bordieu's article, 'The Aristocracy of Culture'. He says 'There is a notion of the popular, that it requires a wholehearted and unselfconscious involvement in cultural events and that the audience will tend to accept formal experiments and specifically artistic effects only to the extent that they can be forgotten and do not get in the way of the substance of the work.' How do you use 'the popular'?

Rose Garrard: I've chosen to work with images which are the least exclusive, which will let my audience enter into the work. There would be no point in my involving myself with abstract painting, say, because I'd be lost before I'd even started. The sort of people I want to include in my audience aren't the sort of people who would feel comfortable coming into an elite art language. So there has always been in my work a hook of reassurance from which a popular audience might be able to go deeper.

Fiona Byrne-Sutton: What sort of feedback do you get from the general public on the feminism in the work? How do they perceive 'feminism'?

Rose Garrard: Well, there's usually surprise: 'Gosh, aren't you nice – I didn't think feminists were nice.' Surprise that the work is relaxing to be with, that it's visually comfortable, it doesn't assault you; surprise in that you come to the gallery knowing what art is and then find out you're not wrong, which gives you the confidence to come and talk to me directly. I think it's unfortunate that we're forced to talk about feminism as if it were a style that one adapts from somewhere outside oneself, something that might fall in and out of fashion rather than something which is ethical. This is the greatest misunderstanding. At the end of the interview in *Harpers & Queen* they wrote 'The risk that Rose Garrard runs by adopting feminism is that she steps outside one rigid frame to another.' Which to me is an example of absolute non-communication because feminism is an open explanation, it is a means of understanding and changing one's possible future. And on the subject of the media I was very intrigued last night by a few seconds of TV news on the Territorial Army manoeuvres in Germany. Some ten thousand of them had been shipped over there on full pay. How did they present it? They showed footage of a woman commanding male troops. I just had to sit there and think 'This is goddamned clever'. Here is a woman in a new role, commanding a powerful force – they've put women in a position of criticising women.

Fiona Byrne-Sutton: Where is the pleasure in making the work?

Rose Garrard: It's in not letting go of the problems. For instance with the bedspread in *Adam and Eve* – I didn't know quite how to contextualise it, it couldn't be shown as it was because it would have been an absolute negation, just a traditional canvas except that it would be horizontal, flat on the floor. I impose a harsh questioning onto an initially intuitive approach, which is where the crossing over between media occurs. With the horizontal canvas I had the idea of a plinth to be covered in canvas, which would stand for a bed. The pleasure of the work is this wonderful galloping process which is half logic, half intuition.

Fiona Byrne-Sutton: In the video you refer to the photograph of Henry Bate's sculpture of Pandora, describing the dark space surrounding the statue as the 'darkness beyond the frame'. This seems to employ an essentialist notion of femininity, what Montrelay calls 'the uncolonised continent' – a pre-patriarchal femininity which falls into the trap of 'romantic feminism' since it is ahistorical.

Rose Garrard: I think there's a subjective judgement in your perception of darkness as negative. Darkness is as infinite as lightness.

Julia James: In *Feminism & Psychoanalysis – The Daughter's Seduction* Jane Gallop mines Lacan's discussion of female sexuality. Since female identity passes through what Lacan calls 'the name of the father' which is patriarchal myth and patriarchal language, there *is* no authentic identity for women. They do not exist in themselves because they are nameless.

9 Rose Garrard, *Tumbled Frames*, 1984, installation with video. (Photo: Analogue Productions.)

Rose Garrard: But saying one is nameless, is a naming. What you've said sounds very depressing. I don't feel that sense of loss and I don't think other women do. There's a marvellous dilemma going on trying to discover 'who am I?' which seems to be an extremely rich, optimistic situation.

Julia James: To start from oneself as the only possible place is a very lonely position.

Rose Garrard: Absolutely. Maybe that's where every woman starts in trying to move 'beyond the fragments'.

Fiona Byrne-Sutton: You rarely insert yourself in your work as a fragment but rather as an 'I'-centred subject.

Rose Garrard: There isn't another choice quite honestly. I struggled unconsciously for years asking myself – how on earth do I put a face on a female figure? It seemed immoral to me to use any face other than my own. How could I pass the buck? Which is not to say that by using a mask of myself I have arrived at a solution that is without questions, without errors.

Julia James: The figurine used in *Tumbled Frames* reminds me of a brightly painted Sunday School Madonna (Fig. 9). Where did you get that from?

Rose Garrard: I had both a Protestant and a Catholic parent and this was the original Madonna from my bedside which I had there from a very early age. She was a very comforting presence standing for kindness, humanity, and compassion. Within my limited understanding at that age she was someone to emulate.

Fiona Byrne-Sutton: What about the place of self-love for women within Christianity?

Rose Garrard: I had an excellent teacher for religious instruction who taught it as metaphor not dogma, which was very interesting. As I had both a Catholic and a Protestant Bible we discussed what happened in translation. The word 'Yahweh' can be a verb meaning 'I am', so if you say 'I am love' love is also 'in you'. The choice is both the answer and the question. A 'cursing' was often a naming of the choice so when Cain killed Abel the mark on his forehead meant that he would always know the choice; that's what Eve also brought, the ability to choose.

Julia James: In *Tumbled Frames* I couldn't perceive the reason for your transition from the 'unknown model' to the Madonna.

Rose Garrard: My idea of the room was that it was womb-like, an infinitely comfortable black space that softened the hard black walls. It's a dilemma piece about the price one pays for becoming a mother. Mike Archer said 'What Garrard's work insists upon is that to offer someone the choice is insufficient' since these choices are imposed ones. In the new Channel 4 piece I actually become the Madonna for a brief period – not looking very happy about it. You see the mother and child was one of my starting points. Something that's not really understood is that the choice of having or not having a child is with a woman every day. With *Tumbled Frames* the hopefulness was that the sheer number of frames, and the number of Madonnas would allow a union, an image of woman within a frame of her own determination.

Julia James: I would perhaps see these as two untenable positions. They both march together but they're not going to get anywhere, however much you multiply them they still lack meaning.

Rose Garrard: This is a central question at the moment. The lovely thing in postgraduate colleges I visit is the increasing number of women who've had a family, and whose children have now reached school age. The children of the male staff are with their wives who trained as art students and gave up. These women are talented enough to come back and do postgraduate work, and the feeling is that they are held back by children, whereas having children is an enrichment of their lives – a centering of their work. So we've now got the beginnings of a new role model, the woman artist with child. Hopefully we'll have a new role model of male artist with child – 'Oh it's another father and child painting'. I do see a shift now in male art students' perception of woman's value, which I find extremely optimistic. Their inquiry is genuine, not paternalistic, which I suspect is the real case with my generation.

ROSE GARRARD

SOMETHING OMITTED?

Dear Artscribe

A sensation of absence...invisibility...a feeling familiar to many women in this culture which vastly over-rewards male values, and under-rewards female values to the point where the latter are often seen as 'worthless' if recognised at all...but a sense of absence while reading an interview between two feminist colleagues and myself, that is a shock! *Rose Garrard interviewed by Fiona Byrne Sutton and Julia James* (*Artscribe* No. 49); an apparently straightforward title but it omits to mention the term *edited without consultation with the artist.*

The replies to at least eleven of the twenty-eight published questions, though composed of phrases, sentences and sometimes even whole paragraphs that I recognise, have had the emphasis of their meaning so shifted (or in two cases actually edited to suggest the opposite meaning) that they no longer represent my views.

My work is frequently concerned with exploring and uncovering where power resides; in television, radio, newspapers and magazines power resides in the act of editing. The subject, filtered through the conscious or unconscious bias of the presenter/s, has little chance of being 'visible' unless this bias coincides with the subjects. My assumption that some basic views were held in common by myself and my questioners may have led me to understate the obvious, but that the precise signification of my primary values has been subsumed by the dominant values of the 'filter' is destructive not only to me and my work, but to the efforts of many other women artists informed by Feminism who have been working with similar concerns.

I *do not* believe (apparent answer to question 2) that the consequences of emulating 'types' such as Mary, Eve, Pandora (Joan seems to be forgotten here) are 'bound to be disastrous' for women! Histories and myths created by dominant male values and fears have sought to make us believe this. And *this* is the 'Catch 22' syndrome of the propagandised female role-models, where the positive and useful attributes of these visible women have been undermined by creating disastrous consequences which conjure up women's conditioning to fear male disapproval, to fear her independence from man, because while such fear exists male status, power and control over women is maintained. Until recently the absence of female role models from the 'history' of art has reinforced women's fears that we are intruders in a male domain. Who knows how many trained and talented women artists have not survived this undermining of the very foundation of our presence this century, let alone how many were working in ways that were not recognised as valuable by those filtering and recording a history based on the primacy of male values in the last 500 years? I refuse to stand outside the history of art. I refuse to believe that the values I hold as a woman artist are of less worth than those held by male colleagues. I refuse to allow the conditioning that encourages women to be as afraid of 'success' as we are of failure, to go unchallenged. I refuse to let male images of women prevent me from attempting to create images of women (and men) that question the primacy of their view, and one day hope to create images that inherently express the values of women as valuable to 'man' (meaning female and male equally). I refuse to let male values convince me that I am an outsider to art, life, or any other activity that I'm engaged in. I refuse to allow fear of disapproval to dominate my life, disapproval by male or female, feminist or non-feminist.

In common with many other women artists I take on an active responsibility for re-claiming and re-contextualising roles and images of women which have been so negatively coloured by male fears and values. Fiona Byrne-Sutton's accusation that I am 'putting forth female role models – the mother, the temptress – without any disruption or intervention. In fact it's almost as if you are reinforcing these stereotypes,' is replied to by 'me' in an irresponsible and uncharacteristically unchallenging way. That this issue of the subversion of meanings of images from male to female values is one of the most important concerns of informed women artists today, and that the serious discussion of when, where, how, why, and *if* it is being achieved by artists is vitally important to art in the 80s, makes my apparently dismissive reply a destructive act which does nothing to help create a dialogue with others. I do not 'disrupt or intervene' through using the 'mainstream' stylistic conventions of innovatory mark-making which seem to me to be far too highly rewarded. I see instead my replication and repetition of 'the unique image' and its *re*-presentation in formal contexts which undermine the hierarchy of categorisational judgements, as means by which I do 'disrupt' its original message and which at very least question the supremacy of the value system which had coloured its meaning. My work attempts to make the viewer aware that other equally important value systems exist, and to encourage her or him to question the basis of the unconscious value systems we all bring to bear when judging an experience. This 'heightening of awareness' talked of by artists is fused for me with the 'consciousness raising' which the women's movement has informed and encouraged. Art for me has always been engaged in this active process of questioning meaning and value, art history however has persistently recorded only those works whose physical durability and interpretable message are most valuable to a competitive, aggressive, sexist, commodity-based culture. In such a culture many works which I value by both male and female artists are seen as marginal to the 'mainstream'. I refuse to devalue, make invisible, or omit the presence of those creative artists whose work encourages such a culture to change, from my concept of the true history of art.

I don't recall the question 'What about the place of self-love for women within Christianity?'. However I did discuss at some length how histories and myths are arrived at, and the central role that translators' 'errors' have played in determining our concept of the first woman and a male god. My comments have been hacked about to create an 'answer' until they have lost all sense. The word 'Yaweh' is the Hebrew word for 'God'. It isn't a noun but comes closer to a verb in English. We have no equivalent word. The nearest we can come to understanding its meaning is in the present tense of the verb to be, 'I am'. This autonomous statement of self-responsibility means that each of us *is*, ('Yaweh'), when in an active, aware state of being. To qualify the verb with a noun destroys this meaning, and to suggest that I would have made the romantically Christian statement 'I am love, love is also "in you"' is a gross distortion.

My 'reply' to the question 'Why do you return to the Virgin Mary, Pandora and Eve so often?' seems to be a fabrication of sentences taken from other contexts. I do not believe the simplistic statement 'The Virgin symbolises the whole of what Christianity stands for in terms of "the woman"', but use Mary and Eve to examine the damaging polarisation of women's sexual roles into 'Virgin or Whore'.

Ridiculous mis-translations of my views are so numerous that I can only indicate them by pointing out that though for some 'Feminism is an open *explanation*' for me it is an open *exploration* through which women are discovering and naming both our female and 'male' qualities. 'I do think some male values are essential'...yes...but not those which inhibit, restrict, threaten or destroy the ability and confidence of women to determine for ourselves who we might become, or which seek to misrepresent and make invisible that process of becoming because it doesn't conform to the views of those in power.

In haste! Rose Garrard

These professional differences were resolved, and both sides are now amicably reconciled (Ed.).

ALEXIS HUNTER

Alexis Hunter was one of several artists during the 1970s who addressed themselves to current debates within the Women's Movement, and worked from an intentionally feminist perspective to reach a specifically feminist audience. At the same time she both challenged, and intervened within, mainstream art practice. Alexis Hunter came to London in 1972 from New Zealand, where she had been received as a promising young painter. Soon afterwards, she became actively involved in the Women's Workshop of the newly-formed Artists' Union. The Workshop attempted to provide a sympathetic environment as well as to organize campaigns around the discriminatory conditions affecting working women artists with children.

From 1976 she was involved in running the exhibition space at the Women's Free Arts Alliance. While supporting herself by working in film and animation, she began to produce work which integrated the reality of women's lives, from a socialist feminist perspective, with a personal examination of women's psycho-social identity.

For Alexis Hunter, visual representation is a feminist issue: her work, from the 'alternative' media and conceptualism of the mid-1970s to her recent return to painting, provides an insight into general questions concerning women artists today.

We have used the interview format not to endorse the idea that artists hold 'the meaning' of their work, but in order to highlight how general issues debated within the Women's Movement percolate through the personal experience of one particular artist to affect, if not actually to produce, her work. In this way we hope to open up the relationships between the formation of an artist, her work, its reception, and its meaning(s). It is also intended to touch upon current discussions around feminism and cultural production in order to underline their importance for a wider feminist audience.

Caroline Osborne: Our readers will probably be most familiar with your photographic narrative sequences from the mid-1970s, some of which were exhibited at the 1978 Hayward Annual Exhibition in London (Pollock, 1979). The critics' reviews of that show singled you out (along

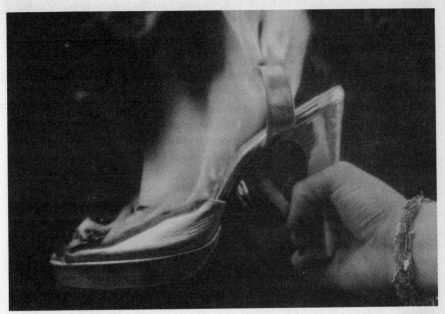

10   Alexis Hunter, *Approach To Fear XIII: Pain – Destruction Of Cause* (detail), 1977–8, colour photographs.

with Mary Kelly) as being a 'feminist artist' and often accused your work of not being 'art' at all. Earlier you had been a painter. Why did you decide to change your medium at that time?

Alexis Hunter: Painting has been overloaded with the same meaning for hundreds of years and I wanted to explore different meanings. I wanted to deal with the reality of the change in women's lives which was happening in that decade, to confront the fear of independence.

Sometimes I think that paintings paint themselves and that you're just a cipher standing over them with a paintbrush. With photography you have to have a good idea of what you are going to do: even though I tried to take photographs intuitively, the narrative is clear. If I was going to burn a shoe – as in *Approach to Fear XIII: Pain – Destruction of Cause* (Fig. 10) - - I literally had to burn one and it would not turn into anything else. If I painted a burning shoe it might turn into something else, the fire might look like a bat, the shoe might turn into a tree. In a painting I've just been doing called *The Struggle Between Instinct and Logic* I don't know why a mermaid/merman started appearing, but it must unconsciously mean something about change or need, as water or drowning is interpreted in dreams as change, rebirth, a new life.

Caroline Osborne: Does this relate to changes that are taking place in your own life, or to women in general?

Alexis Hunter: Both. In the 70s I did work about the burden of change on women who had been socialized into being dependent, but my new work is about being totally independent and struggling with decisions without fear.

Now I have the freedom to work emotionally and passionately. Of course it helps to have a certain amount of success, the support of the Edward Totah Gallery, to know that the work does not always have to go through a committee of women and men who don't want women to define their own cultural identity.

From 1972, when I first came to England, women artists who tackled feminism as a subject were treated as lepers. This exposed the most abusive misogyny within the art scene – in colleges, among reviewers and in the Arts Council especially. Back in the 1970s, women artists tried to be objective about their emotions. It was as if to be too emotional was in some way anti-art, unprofessional. Through making personal issues political and public, I think feminists have changed the demands people make from art, and the viewer expects to see content now instead of just form.

Caroline Osborne: Reviews of women's art during the 1970s suggest that critics lacked the necessary conceptual tools with which to approach the work. They saw it only from a gender-conscious and dismissive viewpoint or at best in terms of contemporary art movements such as conceptualism, instead of relating it to debates that had been generated within the Women's Movement and the Left. I'm thinking in particular of developments in film theory and around Freudian and Lacanian psychoanalysis. They also neglected the collective organizations and discussion groups that formed a basis for so much of the work.

Alexis Hunter: There was such a prejudice against what we were trying to do. It is in their own interests for critics to support a star system. They get a reflected glory when the artist becomes successful. A lot of art comes out of an aggressive individualism but without a society to work in, and against, the artist cannot produce anything of real worth. I have the sort of obsessive personality when I am creating which makes it difficult to work truly collectively in an art context, but I have done projects with writers and poets.

Caroline Osborne: On a more personal level, do you have a conflict between emotional needs and the ambition to express yourself as a woman, to other women, through your work?

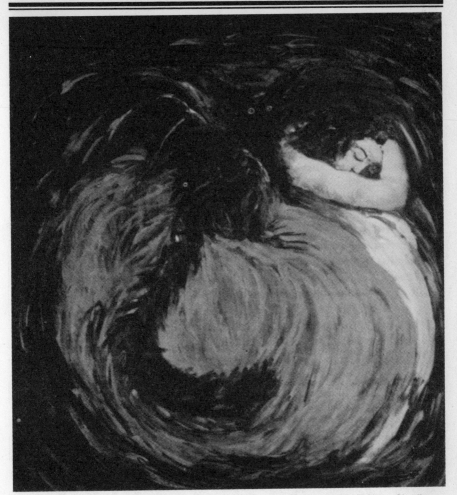

11 Alexis Hunter, *The Struggle Between Ambition And Desire*, 1983, 5′6″ by 6′, oil on canvas.

Alexis Hunter: Yes. The painting entitled *The Struggle Between Ambition and Desire I*, which shows a woman sleeping with a chimaera on top of her bed, is concerned with this. The contradiction in the title is to do with having to cut yourself off from people if you are to achieve something. Ambition to express oneself is a desire, and desire can also be something separate, a desire to be protected or sexual desire. (Fig. 11.)

Caroline Osborne: Ambition is one desire at the expense of others.

Alexis Hunter: And sexual desire can be a contradiction to other desires as well. The woman (the artist or whatever) is asleep and the chimaera sitting on top of her represents her Jungian animus – the projection of her creativity. It is influenced by Fuseli's paintings of the *Nightmare* which I saw when very young. In that painting the woman's back is arched back over the bed and the incubus, which has a dog's face and wings, is sitting on her stomach. In my painting she has turned away from the incubus, refusing to be possessed by it. The night circles around like black fingers. Whether the chimaera represents ambition or sexual desire I don't know – the elements are all part of the same thing. In the end you can't separate them and that is why they haunt you, that is the struggle. These paintings are not feminist in the sense of being educative, but they do relate to issues which surround sexuality and individuality versus the collective, issues which have been raised in *Feminist Review* itself.

In the beginning of this wave of feminism, talking about pornography and eroticism would have been confused with 'sexual liberation'. When the media was out to destroy the movement with hostile ridicule, some questions were avoided as too complex and divisive because we had to appear united. In 1977 I was giving lectures at art schools explaining the difference between sexism and eroticism, and it was really hard going. People are beginning to see through art history and understand that some artists were just projecting male masturbatory fantasies and their paintings are just soft porn illustrations after all.

Caroline Osborne: Does your recent work refer specifically to Judy Chicago's notion of 'female forms' such as circular, organic forms and a central aperture (1982)?

Alexis Hunter: Yes, I'm trying to break down phallic perspective in the paintings. But I would not do a painting around centralism alone, and as I mentioned earlier there are other aesthetic reasons as in how we see with our unconscious, dreaming. Also I want the viewer to be dragged into the content. Maybe that's why some people find these paintings frightening.

Caroline Osborne: I wonder why that is? I don't.

Alexis Hunter: Feminists that have visited the studio haven't found them frightening. Maybe it's because we analyse our conflicts all the time, write about them, discuss them. I don't want to work unless there is some meaning – so that by painting I can communicate something personal and political. By political I mean that the subject of the work comes out of reality – out of life, out of society – and I'm not talking about party politics.

As painting is ambiguous, sensuous and has to come from your core, you relocate that core and work from there. I might, say, refer to the female nude now but she is always active, symbolic of female action: and although painted in a sensual style she is not up for sale, not offered to the viewer. Now I am influenced by John Berger's (1980) essay on animals looking at us which seems very true – the more we make animals like us, castrate them or make them into breeding machines, the more we want to be natural and savage like them. It has parallels with Valerie Solanas's *S.C.U.M. Manifesto* (1971) where she says men want to oppress women because they want to be like women.

Caroline Osborne: Do you see your recent work as being as historically specific as the work you did in the 1970s?

Alexis Hunter: In regard to feminism, I hope that it concerns itself with a positive, strong expression of the female ego which one can identify with. But the idealistic battles we fought in the feminist art groups, herstory, and within film theory in the 1970s are more important historically because we broke so much new ground.

Caroline Osborne: Can you tell me something about your background as an artist?

Alexis Hunter: As a child I worked in a natural, undisciplined emotional style which shifted around as it became influenced by other painters. In the last year at Art School my style had settled into a romantic academic vein, very influenced by art history, which I had had to take on as an extra subject. I reacted to the preponderance of women as models in art by making my subject man-as-model. I came up against opposition when I wrote my thesis on my own work after the painter Rita Angus declined to let me write it on hers. I had no interest at all in writing for a whole year on a male artist, not that I didn't appreciate their work, but I couldn't relate to their *life*. What had angered me about art history was that it was written as if 'masterpieces' just popped out of time like magic, and that these productions hadn't come from real lives which were lived in real societies and are just as much in the end about paying the rent as about glorious spiritual passion.

In 1971 I started making small sculptures about the division of understanding between the sexes. I came to London in 1972 and joined the Artists' Union soon after. Like many women then I started questioning the difficulty of painting to carry an unambiguous message, and using an establishment form to carry a revolutionary message. Not that painting carried an inherently reactionary force (though it has been used as a reactionary tool in the past), but that the way people perceived paintings in the 1970s was too formalistic and conventional. Now, because of the experimental nature of conceptual art, video, film, performance, sound tapes and political contextual work, we can insert ideas in painting in a fresh way. People now automatically ask me what I mean by using a combination of images in a painting, instead of *why* I did the painting.

I struggled through a lot of different media during this period of rediscovery in the early 1970s. It was very frustrating because I had to keep learning new skills all the time, as well as juggling with this new content of feminism. I tried film-making (too expensive), photo-realist painting (too 'provincial', skill overtaking reason), expressionist painting (too ambiguous, not detached enough) and montage (good for working out ideas but unsatisfactory as finished work).

I felt that film making was the most politically effective medium, even though I was not in a financial position to make films and knew that it would be impossible to get any grant aid because my ideas didn't fit into either the avant-garde art house film-making genre or into agit-prop. The films I made tried to explore the sensibility of women and their relationship with each other across class boundaries: how women care for each other under the gaze of men. The narrative photographic sequences are actually storyboards of the films I couldn't afford to make. I didn't make videos because I knew the problems my friends had with borrowing monitors and with equipment breakdown, apart from the fact that 'third area' art tends to be shunted off into a corner. The sequences became influenced by, and aimed to compete with, television advertising, so I felt there might have been inadequate separation if I used the same form.

Caroline Osborne: The form of the photo sequences is derived from film storyboards but from where did their content develop?

Alexis Hunter: I used to have to live in my studio and I'd climb up on the roof to be able to see the horizon. One day I was particularly depressed and started thinking about suicidal impulses. I went over to the edge of the roof and began to wonder at what stage one would actually die. I took experimental shots with a camera to try and capture the visualization of panic, fear and hopelessness when a person carries through such an act. The sequences of photography were extended into other types of violent death and their visualization. They led into the *Approaches to Fear* series.

These crushingly depressive moments in my life have led to my best work. It is through them that I reject a whole lot of garbage stored up about what art should be like, and concentrate on total expression and communication. I'm a modernist in that sense only – trying to push out the boundaries of my own provincialism and conventionality. I was surprised when the sequences were taken up as avant-garde.

Caroline Osborne: Do you think the Women's Movement in England is supportive of artists?

Alexis Hunter: No, not really. Individual women involved in the movement have been, but the movement generally doesn't seem to be interested. Here it is more socialist than in the States, but because of that, anti-art.

Anyway, I don't think an ideology can really be supportive in the way of a genuine friend. I've written before (Hunter, 1981) about the difficulties of political artists – having to withdraw from one's friends in order to communicate to people one may never meet. An ideology can work as a base for ideas, a mission, a cause, a reason for working, an expression of conscience: but to rely on feminists totally for support is unrealistic and wouldn't be fair to them. One's life as a political artist is too hard, and they have their own lives to lead. I suppose if friends were all feminists there wouldn't be this division. I don't expect feminists to share the same kind of ideology. I think that all the different kinds of feminism make a broad base from which to operate. Theory has its place alongside radical action – they both need each other. Each member of the movement should work according to her temperament and ability.

Caroline Osborne: Do you regard your feminism as the result of your past in any particular way?

Alexis Hunter: When I was very young, as hard as I tried to please everyone, I felt as if I had been picked out to pay some kind of price for society's evils, especially after being attacked by a complete stranger when I was eight. Not that it was a sexual attack; I thought he was going to kill me. That incident changed my attitudes, I became more introverted and depressive. I had been exceedingly compliant, but after the attack I started carrying a knife and infuriated the teachers in school by refusing to learn the most simple spelling or sums. I didn't have any respect for anybody in authority.

Caroline Osborne: What effect did being a twin have on you?

Alexis Hunter: If you are a twin you have to go through everything three times. Firstly, you experience what is actually happening, then you share in the humiliation of your sister who has to watch, and then the feeling of guilt at causing such humiliation. I was expected to compete with Alyson who was top of the class, but instead just faded out to be with my friends – the misfits in the bottom grade. I had to wake up, of course, when I was sixteen, and pass exams to get into art school. Working in factories in the holidays brought home the awful future I was sentencing myself to.

Germaine Greer, writing about Artemesia Gentileschi in *The Obstacle Race* (1979), said that after she was raped (by her tutor), then tortured by the authorities (to see whether she was telling the truth), then made out to be a whore (to save the tutor's reputation) she had nothing to lose by being an artist. She had already lost her social respectability and reputation. Something else also happens when you are put off the rails when you are a child – you can't lose your trust in anybody because you never had it anyway. Even though I fantasize about the kind of dreams

12   Alexis Hunter, *Considering Theory*, 1982, 24″ by 30″, acrylic on paper.

that trap a lot of women, I know that whatever I want I have to strive for by myself, and that the only gilded carriage that carries me off at midnight is the 29 bus from Soho to Camden Town!

I suppose it was my background that made me a feminist, but it was in my *nature* to be sensitive to oppression. But it did make me need to develop my powers of expression, and my impressions of the world through art. It made it important for me to be successful, to exist as an individual, and patriarchy got in the way.

Caroline Osborne: Why did you move back to painting in 1981?

Alexis Hunter: I felt the *Approaches to Fear* series had worked itself out, and to keep its essential integrity intact I had to finish it. Art can take over life too, and it started to become too emotionally dangerous to use myself as a cipher. The sequential work was an insertion into the artworld, to start people thinking about the demands of a female audience, and to let them know they couldn't push us under the carpet. It was just part of this revolution called the Women's Movement – a quiet, painfully slow, divisive, but magnificent revolution. It is really the only thing that can stop total carnage – making people think a bit more.

In 1982 I started a series of large acrylic paintings about woman's cycles and the premenstrual syndrome. I experimented with style, trying to reject all my training and go back to when I was fifteen and working in a converted chicken coop. Then I started the *Male Myths* Series, to try and expose Greek and Christian myth as patriarchal propaganda by using visual parody, as in *Considering Theory* (Fig. 12).

Caroline Osborne: What do you think is the most important factor facing women artists at the moment?

Alexis Hunter: In England the most important factor facing artists now is their poverty, which dramatically affects the production of art. Cora Kaplan made a very pertinent comment on the Channel 4 programme 'Voices'. She said that if we want to build a cultural bridge between men and women it becomes impossible when women don't have the financial resources to build their half of the bridge. We have the cultural engineers, the workers and the desire, but we can't buy the steel or pay the wages. In England women artists were treated as failures from the start, and they began to comprehend themselves after a while as failures (look at the life of Gwen John, for example). I feel my confidence draining out of me if I stay in England for more than a year without going abroad. I am trying to think what is going to change, what I can force to change and what I cannot, and be realistic about it.

MARY KELLY

Terence Maloon: You've said that your *Post Partum Document* comes out of consciousness-raising experiences within the Women's Movement.

Mary Kelly: Yes. I've always maintained that the *Document* should be located within the theoretical and political practice of the Women's Movement. It was the conjuncture of this practice and the personal experience of having a child which resulted in my work on the mother-child relationship. Previously I'd been involved in the Berwick Street Film Collective in the making of *Night Cleaners* and after that in the exhibition *Women and Work* which documented the division of labour in a particular South London industry. Both projects showed me the extent to which all the women we'd interviewed were intensely involved with their life at home, with their family relationships. This seemed a lot more 'real' to them than their circumstances at work. The significance of this involvement was underlined by the debate within the Movement at that time about domestic labour and by the notion that the family had a dual function – ideological and economic, and that it wasn't reducible to one or the other.

Terence Maloon: So the *Document*'s your contribution to a feminist analysis of the family?

Mary Kelly: Yes, but my initial conception differed from the way the project turned out. Initially I'd tried to bring in some socio-economic issues. In the first section of the *Document* I'd included material on, say, the number of fathers who participate in child-care, and I'd related the post-partum experience to other economic factors, like the number of children and the living conditions ... It became obvious that it wasn't possible to integrate all this material, and that the strength of the document, if it had one, was precisely that it was concerned with giving a place to the mother's fantasies and not with giving an account of child development, nor with providing more material for a sociological analysis of housework. Ultimately it had nothing to do with those matters and it had everything to do with how femininity is formed in a psychological sense.

72

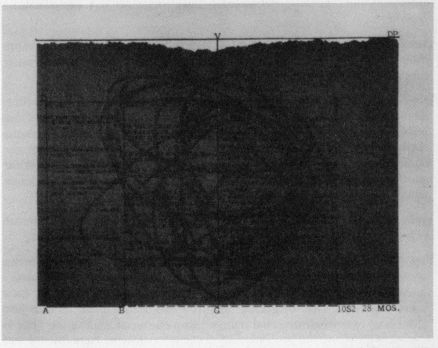

**13   Mary Kelly, *Post-Partum Document*, (detail), Documentation III, 1975, 10 units, 14"
by 11", crayon and pencil on paper. Tate Gallery, London.**

Terence Maloon: Maternity's the crucible as well as the culmination of
female conditioning?

Mary Kelly: I always saw femininity very much as something constituted
within a social process, not simply as conditioning. It's crucial to locate the
founding moment of 'difference' in the child's entry into language,
although most feminists tend to emphasize the period of adolescence,
because that's the moment when women realise that their sexuality, their
pleasure, is appropriated in patriarchy and subordinated to their capacity
for reproduction. This moment is very repressive, very conspicuously so. I
think I originally felt that the moment of childbirth culminated, over-
determined this process. I looked at it as the moment in which femininity
was somehow sealed. Then I came to see more clearly the specific ways in
which maternal femininity is constructed at a very deep level, that is, at
the level of the unconscious. There is a profound desire to have a child,
and having one gives real satisfaction and pleasure. Unless you
understand that, you can never understand why women would subscribe
to the idea of 'biology-is-destiny' at all. The pleasure of having a child

makes it possible to see the capacity for maternity as 'natural' and inevitable, and then to see the sexual division of labour as being somehow expedient.

Terence Maloon: This is the point at which women artists often give up their pursuits. There's a counter argument that men make art because they can't have children.

Mary Kelly: I think that the main reason women don't make art when they have children is because they're actually looking after them. One of the implicit statements in the *Document* is that there had been a dramatic change in the division of labour in my own situation. This came directly out of consciousness-raising on the part of Ray and myself. We lived for quite a long period in a communal household with other men and women who were trying to change their personal lives.

Terence Maloon: What was the relationship between your maternal responsibilities and your commitment to art? Was there a conflict?

Mary Kelly: It was quite frightening in the early stages of the work. Some writers (Sollers and Kristeva) have suggested that the first few months after childbirth are very close to the condition of psychosis, at least metaphorically. The imaginary identification between the mother and child is so overwhelming that it's not just a matter of finding the time to work, it's finding the psychological space to breathe in. Actually, the way the material was worked on, the events that took place (like weaning from the breast, learning to speak, starting school) were lived through in a very spontaneous way. It's not as though I thought about it 'scientifically', but the Women's Movement had made me self-conscious about the importance of these events. It occurred to me that I could actually try to record my feelings about them at the time. It took years after each event to analyse the material, so there are two levels to the work, my lived experience as a mother and my analysis as a feminist of that experience. But I wouldn't want to give the impression that the experience and the analysis were separate.

Terence Maloon: Isn't an acceptance of the child as a whole, indivisible being at odds with an analytical breaking-down of the mother's experience? Is the work about split-consciousness, moments of divided feeling?

Mary Kelly: No, not exactly moments of divided feeling, but moments of realisation or recognition of the loss of the child, because accepting the child as you say, 'as a whole', and more importantly, independent being means accepting that he will inevitably grow up and away from you. The loss of the child is really the loss of plenitude one can associate with having the phallus. The child's a means whereby the woman perhaps disguises her lack, her negative place. It actually provides her with a positive identification which she only relinquishes with difficulty. Almost everyone sees some evidence of this in their relationship with their mother, the way she continues offering you food, for example, or looking after the way you dress. These are all different expressions of the way in which women fetishize the child, which is in fact a compensation for their sense of lack. In a way the art displaces that fetishizing of the child. That's why all the objects in the work are fetish objects, very explicitly, to displace the fetishizing of the child and also to make an implicit statement about the fetishistic nature of representation. It's almost comical in that the value of the objects is minimal in any commercial sense, yet their affective value – in terms of what Freud called 'libidinal economy' – is maximum for me.

The objects in the work – the stained nappy-liners, the scribblings, the hand-imprints, the insect specimens, and in the recent work the inscriptions of Kelly's pre-writing – all these constitute a strand of extra-linguistic discourse within the *Document*. They're recognition points, particularly for mothers, but at some level for everyone in their relationship with the mother. The juxtaposition of the objects and the diaries, the diagrams and the footnotes, locates the work in such a way that the full impact of the theoretical language can be felt, though there's an antagonistic relation between various levels of discourse. The footnotes don't talk about art at all. They provide you with my reading of the events, and of course that's not the only reading possible – it's more a matter of what Freud called 'secondary revision'. All this is a way of working through those experiences and locating them temporally, in an historical process. The diagrams introducing the documents do so in a rather schematic or mechanistic way (for example, a chart on metabolism, one on patterned speech, two by Leonardo, one on perspective and another on perceiving objects). So as a whole the work doesn't propose a homogeneous notion of science. It doesn't represent a 'true' interpretation of the topic, but it sets up all those ways of seeing and reading in a discursive relationship.

Terence Maloon: The formats reinforce the notion of fetishes in various ways.

Mary Kelly: It's the kind of fetishizing you get in museums, where fragments of significant historical events are set out, labelled, explained. That's why it's presented clinically, with the various markings that give it authenticity. It's only a mock-authenticity though. It's an archaeology of the female subject constructed from a specific case history. I think the most interesting reading of this history will be the one that follows it, rather than my own – that is, the reading the Women's Movement will be able to make of it in the future, in the sense of its representation of a particular historical moment within the Women's Movement, and also within the discourse of pop art. (Fig. 13.)

Terence Maloon: How do you see your work relating to past art?

Mary Kelly: I haven't talked about this in the past, precisely because there's a tendency to ghettoise women's practice, a refusal to locate it historically. When I first showed the work at the ICA it was important for me that the men who'd shown there, like Venet, Burgin, Robbins, Art Language, were artists whose work I was very interested in. Those very important years of so-called conceptual work following Kosuth's article refuting synthetic propositions in art was a way of purging art of its level of connotation, of shifting from the metaphorical axis to a metonymic one, emphasising visual syntax. It was implicit in Systems work, Minimalism. Conceptual work restated it explicitly in words – or rather, meta-linguistic paradigms. It provided a polarisation in the history of art practice which subsequently artists could debate openly. It was important that this point should be made in a rigorous theoretical form rather than in some garble about the 'art of the real'.

These events in art coincided with a general development which had brought all the humanities within the sphere of scientific investigation through the developments in linguistics and semiology. It had an effect on anthropology, on psycho-analysis . . . It was very important in terms of my own work – the reading that Althusser gives of Marx, which Lacan gives of Freud. These were only made possible by developments in Linguistics. For the first time it provided a way of analysing the production of meaning based on the premise that the symbolic dimension includes sign-systems other than language, of which art practice is one. These don't mimic language, but they're understood in relation to it.

Terence Maloon: So-called synthetic propositions have made a come-back though, even among post-conceptual artists.

Mary Kelly: When synthetic propositions re-emerged they did so with an altogether different self-consciousness than before. This is true of what I suppose you'd call 'post-conceptual' art, though I think you can't understand the post-conceptual outside of the perspective we've just discussed. I mean, you can't be post-conceptual by simply going on as if conceptual art hadn't happened, like making a jump from pop to neo-dada, or punk if you like.

Terence Maloon: Another contributing factor was the crisis in the avant-garde's self-definition. Since about 1955 virtually any avant-garde manifestation was almost instantly recovered by the establishment (museums, the market, etc). They could swallow up any dissension, any aberration from the prevailing norms – however eccentric, outrageous and 'impossible' they seemed. The only stance left to the avant-garde was philosophical, and when that proved recuperable, radical politics.

Mary Kelly: Perhaps we're in the moment of discovering that that's recuperable as well – precisely because art practice in itself isn't an agent of social change. On the other hand it isn't insignificant that the 'death-wish', which seems to be the ultimate characterisation of the art of the recent past, was an expression of the 'sons' against the 'fathers', which is what the avant-garde is always about. Women were kept largely outside of that, not being part of the discourse with the 'fathers'. It allowed someone involved in feminist practice not to be intimidated by the crisis, but rather to use it constructively. Everything was open to women because it had been closed. So I think this period has been liberating for women, as well as for men. The levels of language in my work depend to a large extent on reworking or subverting various forms of signification developed in particular avant-garde practice.

Terence Maloon: How essential is the format you've chosen for your work? Would it make much difference if the text wasn't, say, typed on cotton swatches, or if it were compiled in book form?

Mary Kelly: It's absolutely crucial. One of the things generally under-estimated in the use of texts in art is that it's as important as any painted sign or mark. The formal qualities of a typed script are very important, as well as the internal construction of the *Document*. The diary text is worked over in the same way that, say, poetry would be. The theoretical text is coherent within its own terms . . . They're all integral to the totality of the work. I always find the suggestion of a book form rather irritating. There's a confrontation betweeen the affective levels of the objects, the texts, and the separateness of the footnotes. It may be necessary at some point to present the material in the form of a book, maybe because it's cumbersome, to make it available to more people. It was crucial in the conception of the work that it would operate within an exhibition context.

Terence Maloon: How does your work differ from the Radical Feminists' tendency in art?

Mary Kelly: Perhaps shall I confine the answer to talking about art practice, or try to give an overview of the movement, which is quite complex? Well, I subscribe to the universality of language. I assume in my work that both men and women enter into the same symbolic order. Then I try to work out a woman's problematic relationship to that culture. Given that it's patriarchy we're talking about, the privileged signifier is the phallus.

The work is trying to make sense of the lack. Radical Feminists would maintain that there is no lack, that there is some alternative symbolic system in which we should be represented in fullness. It leads to a practice which is very diverse, but which could be characterised as being concerned with excavating a kind of essential femininity, either cultural or biological. Do you want some examples? Well, say, Judy Chicago's *Reincarnation Triptych*, which tries to rescue 'great ladies' of the past, to appropriate the myths of amazons and matriarchs who are really representations of the phallic mother, the uncastrated pre-Oedipal mother who contains all good things. Or you have the valorisation of the woman's body. Quite a lot of recent feminist art uses the body, particularly the female genitals – as in Suzanne Santoro's *Towards a new Expression* which indulges a kind of primordial auto-eroticism. Then there's a category of art which foregrounds what you could call feminine 'experience'. Most European performance artists are involved in that. Usually the artist uses herself as signifier, as object, and of course necessarily as fetish.

Terence Maloon: The danger is that woman-as-sign is ultimately so recuperable, particularly with the theatrical lighting, the mirrors, the video, and what have you.

Mary Kelly: Right. The artist needs some very powerful means of distancing. This usually takes the form of the text, or of the word as an intervention. But I don't want to seem wholly disapproving of these tendencies. It's been an extremely progressive step for women to have consciously attempted to articulate the feminine. Although they've subscribed to an essential femininity, although they've equated the feminine with the unconscious, with the marginal and the extra-linguistic, these representations have still got to be seen as part of the productive processes of meaning. They do produce new definitions of women, but it's not as though we're going to discover the 'true' representation of 'real' women. What we're dealing with is the production of the category 'woman' within a particular signifying system.

Terence Maloon: Are you bothered by the possibility that the theoretical ramifications of your work won't be generally understood, that sections will be opaque to a lot of people?

Mary Kelly: I hope that there's an immediate sense in which the work is graspable, but there are simply other levels of discourse included. I've always been very clear about who my audience is: the Women's Movement, other women artists and people generally interested in the issue of patriarchy. Perhaps that's a wider audience than the following for projects which endeavour to generalise.

Terence Maloon: It was interesting to note at the *Art for Society* exhibition how almost all the politicised men's art abjured qualities of sensitivity, tentativeness and 'inwardness'. The women's work was more absorbing, and more effective for that reason.

Mary Kelly: It was only in the work by women artists that the personal statement could be political, because the Women's Movement has argued from the beginning that the personal *is* political. I also think that it's a token of the lack of recognition of that position, which is implied in the work by men when they don't deal with it. When they don't deal with the personal, it means that women are still ghettoised. The critique of patriarchy is still one made by women. I think that one of the most exciting prospects for the future is a critique of patriarchy by men.

Terence Maloon: Do you see an exhibition devoted largely to women's art at the Hayward as a significant breakthrough?

Mary Kelly: Of course I do. It will be the first Annual to have more than merely token representation for women. The organisers made an impressive effort to see, and include, a wide spectrum of work by women artists. Its limitation is that a general women's exhibition doesn't make much point beyond that. Perhaps that was true for the *Art for Society* exhibition too. It was very inspiring that so many artists were willing to show together in support of a common commitment to social content or purpose in art, but it needs to be followed by shows dealing with more specific issues, like, say, patriarchy or racism. One very important point which applies to all so-called politically engaged art is that there's no such thing as a homogeneous mass-audience. You can't make art for everyone. And if you're engaged within a particular movement or organisation, then the work is going to participate in its debates. This is the kind of intervention which is needed now.

MONICA SJOO

Moira Vincentelli: Can I ask you how it was as a Swedish person you first came to Britain? Was it by chance you chose to settle here?

Monica Sjoo: Completely by chance. I left Sweden and went bumming around Europe with another girl. I worked as an artist's model in art schools in Paris and Rome and also worked in vineyards. This was during the Suez crisis in 1957. I just happened to get together with someone in Paris who was from Bristol, got accidentally pregnant, got married in Sweden and then settled in Bristol for many years.

Moira Vincentelli: When you settled here were you happy in the new country?

Monica Sjoo: Not at first. I complained about everything all the time from the draughts and cold to the extreme bad taste I saw around me. Coming from Sweden with its long tradition of functional aesthetics I was used to good design, beauty and simplicity of form. Coming to this country was like coming from the supreme to the grotesque, everything seemed incredibly ugly, but now it has turned the other way round and when I go to Sweden everything is so efficient and so perfect, so clean that I can't stand it and I am relieved to come back here and see a bit of ugly railway station or quaint Victorian design. The attitude that goes with British people is akin to anarchism with its individualism and friendliness.

Moira Vincentelli: And you feel more comfortable?

Monica Sjoo: Yes. In Sweden everything is streamlined, everything has to conform to certain patterns. That is one of the reasons why I left Sweden in the first place.

Moira Vincentelli: Having left school at sixteen do you feel you have suffered educational disadvantages? You see yourself as an artist and writer, quite intellectual things in many ways.

Monica Sjoo: Well, you can call me a working class intellectual, an autodidact. I left school at sixteen. Everything I learned was through my own reading and lived experience. I used to devour a massive amount of

80

books but not through academic schooling. Where could you go to university to study matriarchal history?

Moira Vincentelli: At what point did you become interested in such a thing as matriarchal history?

Monica Sjoo: About twenty years ago. The first book I came across was Robert Graves' *The White Goddess*. Like everyone else I was looking through different religious thinking, and people were involved in Buddhism and Yoga and Hinduism and the whole Existentialist thing. Everywhere I found that women were totally put down or left out or defined as the negative and passive principle.

Moira Vincentelli: Do you think you also came to this interest through your experience of motherhood and marriage?

Monica Sjoo: Perhaps, but my education was travelling in Europe and having to survive, learning about people and places and reading on my own. To a young girl of sixteen travelling on her own around Europe men are carnivorous. It's like running a gauntlet. Whereas women who carried on studying in art schools, universities and so on had a very cushioned existence. I feel that hard experience taught me a hell of a lot about women's position. I could never develop a liberal view and believe that things are not that bad because I have seen a lot of the worst side of things. I waited fifteen years for the Women's Movement to start. I spent four months in Italy when I was seventeen and I was also in Spain and saw the way women were treated. I came out hating the Catholic church and reactionary politics with undying passion.

Moira Vincentelli: How did you first begin to paint?

Monica Sjoo: Both my parents were artists and that makes a lot of difference. All my childhood I was my mother's favourite subject and I spent summers with my father on the coast in Sweden where he painted. I spent all this time watching and they were both good artists. My father became successful, my mother did not.

Moira Vincentelli: Your first husband wasn't an artist?

Monica Sjoo: No, but he became a silversmith under my influence I should say. Working practically, and having to survive is a good schooling. My mother gave me two pieces of advice: one, never become an artist, it only leads to poverty and misery, and two, never marry an artist. I didn't follow the first advice but always followed the second. From my own mother's experience as an artist such a marriage was disastrous. It got to the point when visitors came to see their work, my artist father would turn my mother's paintings to the wall. When offered a big joint exhibition she stood back and said it would be more important for him, being a man, to take it and that was the exhibition that made his name and he broke through. He went from success to success, she into obscurity. I had this background. My mother always told stories of failed women artists. My mother was very kind, a beautiful lovely woman. I am much tougher seeing what happened to her. My whole life I feel has in a way been dedicated to taking revenge for her and what happened to her which I can never forget or forgive. I feel she was killed by patriarchy. She was destroyed by the male dominated art world. Somehow what she was not able to do I was going to do because she lives in and through me. During my early teens I was totally disinterested but when I was sixteen I suddenly started to feel that I wanted to be an artist – that I had to do this. I knew how she suffered because she was not able to carry on painting because of poverty and because of having another unplanned child when she was forty three. She had had all that training, seven years, I just knew her suffering and frustration and knew how she felt humiliated. I tried to get into an art school but had no money to pay for it. I started working as an artist's model. It's an awful job in which you are treated as a part-time prostitute but you get paid cash in hand. I had no idea how I was going to start painting. I began making jewellery with my first husband. That was a good training because you had to think in terms of forms and shapes all the time. Although I have not gone through art school I have had training of sorts even though unorthodox. I spent a year studying theatre design at Bristol Old Vic Theatre School in 1964. There I got interested in Brechtian theatre: total honesty, being absolutely straightforward, and Socialist message. He has in some ways inspired my painting much more than other art. Films like Eisenstein's films, about Mexico and Russia and certain black and white photographs have also meant a lot to me in the past.

Moira Vincentelli: In other words, you are interested in powerful images. Would you say that your work is dedicated to conveying a political message and very specific meaning?

Monica Sjoo: Well, not really. I never see myself as a 'propagandist'. I have been accused of being everything from a 'Bolshevik' to a ' mystic'! I was doing my painting long before the Women's Movement. But what should I be talking about in my work if not about myself and my own experience and I am a feminist woman? All art is indeed political and so is abstract art even when this is denied!

Moira Vincentelli: Don't you think your work has specific meaning – indeed like Brecht?

Monica Sjoo: He is also a great artist, not just a 'propagandist'.

Moira Vincentelli: Are you implying by that that someone who is too dedicated to conveying political meaning cannot be a great artist?

Monica Sjoo: Yes, I think if your attention is solely to make propaganda I don't think that is good art. What I was seeking was a form which expressed what I wanted to say about my experience and women's experience generally. Without that excitement and tension, an image does not convey the message you want to get across. Painting is holistic, it reaches different layers of consciousness. Painting is a Shamanistic act and I consider myself a Shaman.

Moira Vincentelli: Would you then compare yourself to some painters in India who work in a Yogic state, seeing the act of painting as a spiritual activity in itself?

Monica Sjoo: I see it as a spiritual activity although some of the paintings have a highly political content. I never saw a division between what I am saying and the means I am using to say it or between spirituality and grass roots political action. Unless I experience that kind of 'tripping' feeling of going into another reality I would never sit down and just do a political image.

Moira Vincentelli: Other people, however, might read your work as being propaganda because there are such strong images in your painting. Your pictures are made up of lots of images, almost like dream images. It means there is a strong tendency to 'read' the pictures and try to understand what the images convey. Modernist painters and the conventional 'art college' attitude would be very suspicious of this literariness.

Monica Sjoo: Precisely. I didn't have an art school training. If I had gone through that I would not have been able to do it. I never had a guilt trip in my head telling me you can't possibly do this. I couldn't care less. Quite honestly I feel much more in tune with artists' work from the Third World. I am not the least bit interested in modern bourgeois European art. I think it is a little flutter on the surface of reality, good for a few hundred years but it will disappear just like that.

Moira Vincentelli: Do you think there is a danger that feminist art could become absorbed into the culture? Could your art become 'women's art of the 1980s' and be absorbed as a fashionable modern category as for example in Edward Lucie-Smith's book *Art of the Seventies* where his categories include homo-erotic art, erotic feminist, ecological along with abstract, figurative, expressionism etc.? Do you think there is a danger that you could be categorised and therefore de-politicised?

Monica Sjoo: I doubt it. I seem to be very unabsorbable, indigestible. In fifteen years I would have thought there would have been an attempt at that by now and I haven't noticed anything. Sure there is a whole feminist art world and gallery scene. I think it is a class thing also. That whole scene is run by people with whom I have nothing in common. Some women who come from that background would not feel alienated. I wouldn't condemn women who want to be part of it and 'successful' within it. I want to support women wherever they are. We have to be seen. We have to become visible. There is a saying in the women's liberation movement 'anonymous was a woman'... we have got to change this.

Moira Vincentelli: Can you tell me about your experience when you exhibited with other women at Swiss Cottage Library in 1973? Was this when you got a certain amount of publicity?

Monica Sjoo: The first unpleasant publicity was already in St. Ives in 1970. My paintings were hounded there.

Moira Vincentelli: *God Giving Birth* particularly caused people to take offence, did it not? (Fig. 4.)

Monica Sjoo: Yes and I could never understand that. The painting was very much grounded in my own experience of childbirth. My second child was born naturally at home and it was a very powerful and spiritual experience. I believe in the Cosmic Mother, the creator of all life in the earth, as a living body, a Mother that we are all part of. That we all come from and will return to. So it was based on my experience both as a physical mother and my belief in the Cosmic Mother. To me it was a sacred image. I was absolutely astonished by the response to it!

Moira Vincentelli: Is the offence caused because you appeared to represent God as a woman or because it was a scene of birth?

Monica Sjoo: Both, a combination. In patriarchal culture the male is defined as sacred, positive, active and the woman is defined as negative, passive, profane. There is a split. So in patriarchal culture it is a contradiction in terms for a woman to produce sacred images based on our woman's sexuality. Ruling men and the Church spent 300 years persecuting witches, i.e. sexual menstruating women. I am like a present day witch. To them what I am doing is blasphemy. To me the whole Christian thing is blasphemous as it denies the Cosmic Mother.

Moira Vincentelli: You sound a bit like you want to turn the tables. Do you believe in equality?

Monica Sjoo: I do not believe in any form of economic inequality for anyone. I do not believe in any form of hierarchic class, race or gender structure but I do believe that those who create life should also make the decisions about that life and should be responsible for the organisation of communities.

Women are the life creators and women created ancient cultures. There is no way someone else should make decisions about that life. But at present men make all the decisions about life – about war and about death.

Moira Vincentelli: About abortion?

Monica Sjoo: It is the most cruel thing you can do to force a woman to bear a child that is unwanted by her.

Moira Vincentelli: Do you see your art as carrying this message and being able to influence people?

Monica Sjoo: I see my art as empowering women – as reaching into the deep consciousness and I have found many people, men and women, who have had strange visions and experiences from my paintings. A German woman in Denmark told me how she dreamed that she was being reborn within the earth after she had seen the slide showing of my work.

Moira Vincentelli: Do you think your paintings communicate better with women?

Monica Sjoo: I think as long as men are hanging on to their patriarchal lack of consciousness they can feel them as aggressive. They project their own aggressions on to my paintings. That is their hang-up, not mine.

Moira Vincentelli: Have you been accused of making aggressive paintings?

Monica Sjoo: Anyone who is trying to change anything is accused of being aggressive. I have never painted in an aggressive state of mind but I have done paintings with feelings of great pain and sorrow in the past. Men don't want to identify with these images. They are so used to seeing the world and women from a pornographic point of view. Men want to see women as beautiful and sweet and lovely, as seductive and heterosexually alluring, a sort of Pre-Raphaelite image. To see powerful women who are not pleasing and sexually titillating to men is seen as aggressive. Even the way I use colour can be misconstrued. For example, red to me does not represent aggression and warfare or danger. To me it represents life-giving and menstrual blood. Red ochre was used by the ancients in just this way as the colour of rebirth. So we have different emotional reactions to colour and even to form. So often it is a non-recognition in men of the source of the image.

Moira Vincentelli: But this could be so also for women who are imbued with the same values and ideas.

Monica Sjoo: Yes, but an awful lot of women have felt a sense of coming home, a recognition deep somewhere from within.

Moira Vincentelli: Can you say something about the *Woman Magic – Celebrating the Goddess Within Us* exhibition. How has it toured and what response has it had?

Monica Sjoo: In 1978 I went to Ireland with another woman and we visited New Grange, an ancient Neolithic temple of the Goddess which is a mound, a womb and tomb – a place full of maternal forms and images. I felt like 'coming home', here was my Mother's image and that of my ancient sisters and we also came across images of the Sheela-Na-Gig, ancient Celtic images of the Goddess that you find in Ireland. That visit inspired us to take the initiative and organize this exhibition celebrating the Goddess using images that specifically related to women's spirituality. We are living in a time when the assault on the Earth of our living Mother is so enormous. The whole of the patriarchy and the military and industrial complex is setting out to mutilate and utterly destroy Her. I suppose without consciously thinking so at the time, that is the reason that we felt this exhibition to be very urgent.

Moira Vincentelli: You saw it as an antidote to the direction in which the world was moving.

Monica Sjoo: It is absolutely vital to visit the sacred places and to connect with the Earth, but also through imagery we are re-establishing that Earth is sacred and offering a holistic view of life civilized in the image of the Goddess. We have very little time, and I see taking this exhibition round Europe and doing slide shows and talking about the issues as an integral part of the Women's Movement like 'Women for Life on Earth' and women's peace camps. We were first offered a gallery space in Leamington Spa in the winter of 1979. Then it went to Bristol and to London and then the Matriarchal Study Group in Sheffield toured it up North to a number of cities. Nearly always it was shown in alternative spaces such as libraries and theatre foyers and it was always groups of women taking it on. Very often the support has come from lesbian women. In 1982-83 there was a network of interested women who took the exhibition from Denmark to Germany and back up to Sweden. That is the way I like to work. It's presently in Stockholm.

Moira Vincentelli: Are you planning another exhibition of that kind, and how would you like to see your work develop? Would you like to achieve some more official recognition?

Monica Sjoo: I have no plans. I tend to wait and feel when something is right. If it is the right thing to happen it will happen.

Moira Vincentelli: When I look at your work it would work well in poster form or even postcards.

14 Monica Sjoo, *Corn-mother at New Grange*, 1981, oil on hardboard.

Monica Sjoo: I have produced single colour reproductions of the paintings for many years as posters.

Moira Vincentelli: Would you like to do full colour posters?

Monica Sjoo: Yes, but lack of finance makes it difficult.

Moira Vincentelli: Have you ever tried to get financial aid? Would that be bringing you too much into established ways of working?

Monica Sjoo: On several occasions over the years I have tried to get grants from the Arts Council, South West Arts Association and the British Council and I have always been refused. Every time I found hostility. Considering I have been working about fifteen years in this country I think this is hard and I don't think my work is entirely unknown or lacking in importance in the development of women's art. But I do not expect official support.

Moira Vincentelli: What about your writing?

Monica Sjoo: My first book *The Ancient Religion of the Great Cosmic Mother of All* has been sold quite widely, here and in Europe at large. It contains both text and illustrations based on my paintings. In America it has been distributed by *Woman Spirit* journal and I think it has been going fairly well. It is now being translated into German and will be published there soon.

Moira Vincentelli: You are just finishing a second book, are you not? What is the title?

Monica Sjoo: *Spiral Journey – Stages of Initiation into Her Mysteries.* In the last six years now I have made journeys or pilgrimages to many ancient sacred sites, stone circles, standing stones, holy wells and mounds in Wales, elsewhere in Britain (Ireland and Scotland), in Brittany and in Crete. I find that the ancient energies of the Goddess are still alive and vibrant. It is important the way you travel to these places. You cannot just go in a car, arrive and drive away.

Moira Vincentelli: You see it as a pilgrimage?

Monica Sjoo: Yes I do indeed. My first such holistic experience was at Avebury and Silbury. My experience was very powerful. I wouldn't be living in Wales, I am sure, if I had not had that experience. I felt that the Mother, the Earth, communicated with me and what She communicated was Her pain at the destruction of Her living body.

Moira Vincentelli: So you feel you had a mystical experience on that occasion that has redirected your life?

Monica Sjoo: My first mystical experience was the natural birth of my son and that set me on my search. Both times it was related to a birth experience. To me Silbury is the womb of the Earth. It is women who feel these things. I felt the most immense sorrow and pain there. Men can partake in these experiences through women but without that men become like dangerous automatons as we can see.

15 *Goddess At Avebury*, 1978, 8' by 4', oil on hardboard.

Moira Vincentelli: What particularly motivated you to settle in Wales?

Monica Sjoo: It was very much to do with going to the sacred places. I lived the last three years in Bedminster, a dirty polluted part of Bristol. I felt I could not breathe. It was a good and friendly human community but at a physical level it was dreadful. This cottage where I now live came available at a time when I had had enough of living in a city.

Moira Vincentelli: Do you ever feel cut off living in the country without transport?

Monica Sjoo: No, I am in continuous letter contact with women from all over the world. I get lots of people visiting. I am in contact with a whole international women's network, and a whole alternative society. I am a European after all. Many British people are very isolated and insular – isolated from what is happening in Europe. It is an English language imperialism. In that I have much sympathy for Welsh nationalism.

Moira Vincentelli: Do you feel yourself transitory here? Would you learn Welsh?

Monica Sjoo: Evening classes are held too far from where I live so it is not a question of not wanting to learn but there is not the opportunity for me to do so. But I don't feel transitory. I feel it is important that people have roots. People must feel responsibility for the patch of earth they live on.

Moira Vincentelli: When you came here to Wales you began for the first time to include the landscape in a more straightforward way in your painting and even make small sketches and drawings.

Monica Sjoo: Yes, but in general I prefer to work on a large scale and I usually work straight on to the full sized hardboard without any sketches beforehand. These are often as big as six to eight feet across.

Moira Vincentelli: But it is interesting to see how strong they remain in their reduced form when used in your books or posters. But let's return to landscape.

Monica Sjoo: Well, both my parents were landscape artists of the old school and as a teenager I felt very bored with landscape painting as a result. When I first began painting I even experimented with abstracts to start with. Then I concentrated for many years on images of women, sometimes incorporating textural elements onto the surface of the hardboard. I used to experience years ago that I was mystically used as a 'medium', that the images I created came through me from an ancient era and they often had a kind of 'archaic' quality about them. I felt that ancient Neolithic women communicated, dreamed and recreated themselves through me. In the last five years I have turned to landscape. The land round here has inspired many of my paintings such as the one of *St. Non's Well, Cromlech Power* or the one I call *Neolithic Landscape*. For me the whole Earth is Her living body and the landscape around the ancient sites is imbued with meaning and significance. We must again experience the Earth as sacred and live with Her in learning co-operation and peace. It is that mystical spirit that I hope to convey in my paintings.

REVIEWS AND OVERVIEWS

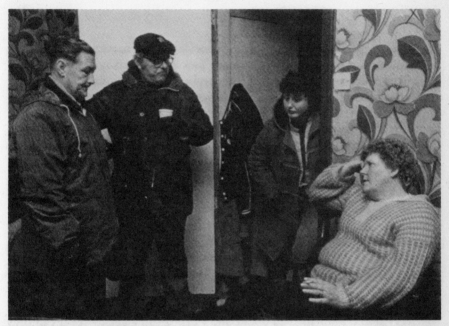

16 'The Buggers'. Pickets share a sense of betrayal with their wives: NACODS executive decides to override 82% ballot in favour of striking. October 17, 1984. Photo: Raissa Page/Format.

DISCUSSION AND RE-EVALUATION

There is an appalling lack of substantial reviewing of feminist work. One of the reasons for this is (obviously) the lack of exhibiting space open for feminist work; but even so, given the number of exhibitions that women do have, the amount of reviewing space devoted to women is small. We have to contend with the fear and the prejudices of mainstream critics and editors. Feminist writers can tell more than their fair share of stories of work being returned by editors as 'too emotional', or 'just not appropriate for our publication'. In addition to this, the feminist press seems to have inherited the Left's distrust of visual art. Films will be reviewed, and literature; but visual arts are still seen as elitist, incomprehensible and inaccessible. This is despite the fact that exhibitions by women can attract huge audiences, of whom a large proportion are women. Shows that spring to mind include *Women's Images of Men* and *Pandora's Box*, both of which toured the country; *Gwen John* at the Barbican and *Frida Kahlo* at the Whitechapel (both in London). Some of these broke attendance records where they were shown.

Women want to see work by other women, so there's no reason to think that they don't want to read about shows they can't get to see. I can only suggest to women that if they are confused or moved by seeing feminist work they should write about it. It can be heartbreaking if a magazine then says no, but if it says yes, then another woman has had her work recorded.

Many of the reviews I read were only a couple of hundred words long. Very few were long enough to explore the complexities of a woman's work and the complexities of the writer's response, or to examine the artist's aims and discuss how far she had achieved them, or to research and discuss issues arising from the work. The articles reprinted here were allowed the space necessary to achieve some of this.

The Dinner Party and *Post Partum Document* have in many ways become icons of achievement to younger feminist artists. They have some similarities: both took years of sustained work; both are full exhibitions in their own right; both have had to be recognised as major works by the mainstream art establishment, and at the same time have had repercussions outside the art world; both have had fully descriptive books published that complement the exhibition; and experiencing both can be like a voyage of discovery. In addition, both artists have been accused by feminists of elitism - - Kelly because of the complexity of the psychoanalytical theory she uses, and Chicago because of her attitude to her co-workers on *The Dinner Party*. There, however, the similarities end. As can be gleaned from these reviews and from the earlier interviews, the intent and strategies of the artists are radically different.

All of the articles in this section have been chosen for their discussion of the 'meanings' generated by the images – those interpretations that give the images their place within history, within politics, within culture; but at the same time are never fixed and static but always shifting, elusive, up for discussion and re-evaluation.

CARRIE RICKEY

JUDY CHICAGO: *THE DINNER PARTY*

An interior dialogue occasioned by *The Dinner Party*:

It is not a hoax, it is not hokum: *The Dinner Party* is a Pop phenomenon on the order of bra-burning and *The Women's Room*. That is to say, an artwork that's larger-than-life, perhaps larger even than the 1,038 lives it honors. It addresses all aspects of social, esthetic, and religious practice. From the moment of its installation at the San Francisco MoMA last year, it became, indisputably, a landmark – a monument to art and the women's movement. I envision historians and critics of feminism, feminist art, and goddess-spiritualism adopting the chronological abbreviations, BDP and ADP – 'Before Dinner Party' and 'After Dinner Party'.

Monuments are built to be defaced. DP indeed! A Displaced Person in every sphere! It's pooh-poohed by feminists and non-feminists alike for its female imagery which reduces the history of women to 39 labia, and continues to depict Women-as-Vessel in its 39 patens and chalices. Disowned in the art world for being sociological, The Dinner Party *additionally suffers from the reverse stigma of bringing the Consciousness Raising group into the museum. Believers and agnostics alike reject* The Dinner Party *for its pop-sacramental attributes, the believers reacting against the deification of mortals along with goddesses, the non-believers chary of mixing religion with art.*

The sensitivity of the secular! Art has *always* been responsible for inspiring awe – religious or emotional. And art has often been conceived and made in a communitarian way, mixing social and spiritual needs, as in the great Gothic cathedrals, whose function was to educate their populace in belief systems, legends, and history.

But the architecture and function of the cathedral grew out of religious practice. Judy Chicago and the community that produced The Dinner Party, *on the other hand, aren't dealing with symbols that have evolved from a belief system; rather, they're self-consciously constructing a pseudo-iconography in criticism of patriarchal Christianity's icons. It's as though they expect a theology to develop out of their jane-built symbols! This is reactionary art of the worst sort. In place of patriarchal Christianity,* The Dinner Party *substitutes a matriarchal Supreme Court – a Sanhedrin*

94

comprising both ecclesiastical and civil figures, freely associating Church with State. In place of the crucifix (a symbol of suffering and injustice), The Dinner Party *substitutes the delta, a reference (equilateral, non-hierarchical, to be sure) to female fertility and pleasure.* The Dinner Party *replaces* The Last Supper *with* The First Supper, *39 representations of legendary and real women, their blood (in the chalices), their flesh (on the patens).* The Dinner Party *is less spiritual paradigm than religious parody. Does Chicago expect that by changing the 'hymns' to 'hers', several thousand years of malign neglect can be corrected?*

It is crucial for women to be aware of their history in order to determine their future. The biographical material related in *The Dinner Party* is staggering. Were all aware of such figures as St. Bridget, patron saint of Ireland, who headed a flourishing monastery where Celtic as well as Christian beliefs were fostered? Or of Trotula, the eleventh-century Italian physican who compiled *Diseases of Women?*

So why not a history, à la Plutarch, of the lives of these women? Honor Thy Mother, yes, but why the insistence on veneration? Isn't substituting patriarchal authoritarianism with matriarchal authoritarianism just old whine, new chalice?

You keep harping on the spiritual appurtenances of *The Dinner Party,* the embroidered vestments and decorated porcelain relics, without seeing the possibility of using a ritualistic framework on which to build a secular piece, a ritual that is not a religious experience, but an esthetic one.

And you keep skirting the contradiction of exploiting religious icons for their esthetic frisson. Isn't this a safe, best-of-both-worlds strategy? Those who wish to read religion into The Dinner Party *can, and those who don't can read it as art. What of the DP's art attributes? Doesn't it capitalize on the rediscovery of forgotten crafts techniques to gain its esthetic pungency in much the same manner it capitalizes on the rediscovery of forgotten women to validate its content?*

Certainly the research into various ceramic, weaving, and embroidery techniques – not to speak of the painfully long trial-and-error experiments in relief ceramics and jiggering on the plates – contributes to *The Dinner Party's* aura. It's a glossary of the so-called 'lesser arts' – tatting, lace, weaving, making ceramic household vessels, embroidering – that women have been consigned to for thousands of years. But that all these crafts are brought together, synthesized for a ritual (and it's men who usually make the ritual art in preliterate cultures), is just one of the canny reversals *The Dinner Party* undertakes. It proposes that the sum of the lesser arts is great art.

But you're arguing a rearguard, reactionary line. You're saying that The Dinner Party *is important esthetically because it demonstrates the significance of the traditionally woman-made, lesser crafts vis-a-vis the traditionally man-made, ritual art. You're not saying it's important on its own. On the content level, too, you're arguing that rearguard polemic, citing the educational importance of women learning their history so they can take charge of their future. You're particularly slippery about the religious angle, by saying on the one hand that it's important to know about goddess worship, that female deities were once venerated as authoritarian religious figures, and on the other hand that* The Dinner Party *exploits religious ritual only to give coherence to its presentation of 39 heroines. The sum total of your rearguard actions is to say, 'The history of the world is but the biography of great women'. To say, 'You gotta have a gimmick, a framework, for this and the DP's gimmick is heroine-worship'. Judy Chicago wrote in her DP journal, 'Sometimes I feel as if I take five steps backwards for every step forward'. This piece is about looking backwards, it has the naive belief that gods are despotic, goddesses benevolent, that men are authoritarian, women libertarian. This is history using the Great Women theory; what happened to the anonymous women?*

The DP is about education and celebration, not retardataire revisionism. You can't criticize a project this large for not doing everything – at least it does something, namely, making the history of women accessible to an enormous population ignorant of it. You rant about its policies and politics for not being forward-looking, but don't mention anything about the optimism of the piece. The way *The Dinner Party* illustrates the history of women as progressing from the flatness, the primitivism, of the Primordial Goddess, to dimensionality. The way the twentieth-century women emerge from their plates, as the relief ceramic on Georgia O'Keeffe's paten, illustrates that until now, the confines of culture have flattened them. Politically speaking, you're the social cynic and *The Dinner Party* the cultural optimist, suggesting the liberation of women from their one-dimensional image.

But that is The Dinner Party*'s most serious failure – its reliance on metaphor. Normally, a metaphor is a figure of speech that likens one thing to another, thus conveying meaning.* The Dinner Party *employs metaphors awkwardly, mixing them into oblivion. The metaphor of each woman is her symbolic paten, the metaphor of Woman's progress ranges from the flatness on the first plate to the increasing depth of form. Metaphor ceases to be a conveyor of meaning, instead, metaphor becomes conveyor of metaphor. Impossibly,* The Dinner Party *asks its audience to get deeper into progress, a mixed metaphor that perfectly sums up this mixed message of an exhibition. It's prepared to progress along a historical surface, but at the same time wants to probe beneath – a feat of mental acrobatics that falls flat on its keester.*

What you're trying to say is that *The Dinner Party* is dense – in both senses of the word.

KARIN WOODLEY

THE INNER SANCTUM:
THE DINNER PARTY

It is a struggle to see the relevance of a reinterpretation of the Last Supper 'from the point of view of those who have done the cooking throughout history'. However, this is how Judy Chicago conceived her much acclaimed exhibition, *The Dinner Party*, and it is an apparently welcome and accepted reinterpretation, if whispers within the inner sanctum of the exhibition were heard and interpreted correctly by me.

An exhibition which attempts to show the contribution of women to Western civilisation using a triangle banqueting table strewn with altar cloths, 39 place settings representing 999 women grouped together according to common experience, achievement, historic period or place of origin within the context of a sacramental celebration, in my opinion is doomed to failure. The representation of each group of women by a plate beautifully crafted as a vagina conjures up the same old misconception of women's sexuality, that of offering not taking. Judy Chicago may pose the problem 'why are there no images of flying vaginas in art?' but her exhibition fails to provide any answer or analysis and compounds the problem by placing the vagina on an altar cloth and putting it figuratively in the control of the 'church'.

Judy Chicago's use of thousands of unpaid volunteers also begs serious questions, especially in the light of the fact that it is Chicago's name that rests as a figure head on all publicity, and Chicago's analysis that seemingly pervades the work. It serves the purpose of such an exhibition to speak of the 'bringing together of women and skills' for one objective and a 'collective approach' to developing the project further. It also serves Judy Chicago's interests to set herself up as the mentor of unpaid workers, whose skills she needs. But it is Chicago who takes the credit for their work, and refers to their support in the most patronising and unspecific terms. The overall dominance of one woman effectively undermines and negates the purpose of such a work.

The role of black women in the project and the representation of black women in the work itself is another area of real concern. Of the thousands of volunteers in the project apparently only one of them mentioned is black,

17   Judy Chicago, Sojourner Truth ceramic plate from *The Dinner Party*.

and her involvement was for a couple of months within the ten years of work. The first series of place settings at *The Dinner Party* are metaphysical representations of women, portrayed as mythical characters. The rest relate to real women in history. On both planes the relevance of black women is undermined. A huge proportion of the mythical characters who present an analysis of the 'essence' of woman are black. These are the deities whose roles in mythology provide the basis for contemporary religions. However, unlike the latter part of the exhibition where black women are described as such, no reference is made to the fact that these characters are black. If *The Dinner Party* is attempting to address the misrepresentation of women in history it should have taken a clear position on issues relating to the portrayal of black women. Instead it takes an inconsistent approach where black women are described as black women from the eighteenth century to the present day, and no statement is made about women who are part of ancient civilisations and their mythologies. This inconsistency is an example of the West's refusal to accept that those ancient civilisations on which its culture is based were black.

Twenty-four historic black women are represented in the rest of the exhibition, all are American. Twenty of these women are grouped in one place setting, the remaining four are incorporated into three other settings. The ceramic plate that sums up black women's contribution to Western civilisation is the only pictorial plate in the exhibition and the only one portraying a negative image. This artificial grouping of black women under an image of a black woman weeping goes against the grain of an exhibition intending to celebrate women's contributions to Western civilisation. In addition, it is an example of the patronising attitudes of white feminists to black women's achievements, and their inability to see the historic contributions of black people in any other context but slavery. The place setting is a token gesture and offers no challenge to the dominant historians' view of black people and black women.

Judy Chicago's insistence that *The Dinner Party* should be seen as a work of art and not a political statement undermines the reason for its existence. It is this lack of political analysis and political motivation that has created such a superficial and inconsistent exhibition. *The Dinner Party* is a shrine to an unknown woman; a woman whose colour, sexuality, class, struggles and achievements are without political context.

LAURA MULVEY

POST-PARTUM DOCUMENT
BY MARY KELLY

Traditionally, the ability to produce children and the emotional relationship that ensues has been held up as the reason for women's lack of creativity. Now, with the women's movement, it is beginning to be possible to bring motherhood, with all the deeply traumatic emotion and unrecognised elements involved, into the kind of examination it desperately needs. Mary Kelly's exhibition *Post Partum Document* is a crucial contribution to this. As an artist she forces into public view the unacceptable combination of roles mother/artist – a slap in the face for old guard concepts of the artist as freewheeling genius; as a feminist she focuses on the contradictory emotions that necessarily come with motherhood, which have been almost taboo as a subject for art in male dominated culture.

It is quite clear from the attention Mary Kelly's exhibition has received in the establishment press that it was a direct provocation to conventional concepts of 'art'. It is the form of the exhibition, rather than art-object-for-critical-evaluation that causes so much outrage. A painting of a mother changing her baby's nappy would be easily overlooked as kitsch, but not so with dirty nappy liners annotated and placed within a discourse that needs work to be unravelled, and refuses to place the figure of the mother on view.

The exhibition comes within a radical art practice which refuses to see art works as purely objects in themselves but rather takes an exhibition as space to give documentation the force of argument. It deprives the object of any market value and its meaning only truly emerges if the work put in by the artist is complemented by work put in by the spectator in reading the documentation and understanding the theories. But the complexity of the language in *Post Partum Document* and the many different ideas presented simultaneously did place a great burden on the spectator.

Mary Kelly described her previous exhibition *Women and Work* produced collectively with Kay Hunt and Margaret Harrison as 'a document on the division of labour in a specific industry, showing the changes in the labour process and the constitution of the labour force during the implementation of the Equal Pay Act. At the same time we were discovering how the division of labour in industry was underpinned by the division of labour in the home and that the central issue for women was in fact

100

reproduction.' Real objects, records (written, taped, filmed, videod) were collected together as evidence focusing attention on a particular economic situation. Individually they may have been without meaning, but linked and organised by the artists, the whole took on a new level of significance.

In the *Post Partum Document* Mary Kelly uses her relationship with her infant son as her raw material. The exhibition has two distinct parts: objects and records acting as factual evidence of the past, framed and hung on the gallery walls, and written, separate documentation using Freudian psychoanalysis to give a commentary and structure to the actual exhibits.

The first room contained the (now famous) nappy liners and baby's vests dating from the period in which the child's needs and the mother's work meet to produce a complementary relationship (the dyad). At this point the mother's frustrated anxiety and the child's frustrated helplessness can be soothed by pleasure, partly through the eroticism of physical inter-dependence and partly through narcissistic satisfaction at their complete-ness as a couple. The second room contained an infinitely more complex record of the child's gradual acquisition of language and the mother's notes as she tries to cope with the sense of loss that overcomes her as the child takes his first steps to social independence. The completeness of the two is broken as the father as authority and the nursery school introduce the child to another world of 'law and culture'. (Fig. 13.)

In its appearance and presentation Mary Kelly's exhibition reduces the passion involved in this process to the minimum; her aim is to distance the emotion by putting the dilemma into a wider context: the way women's unconscious is shaped by the patriarchy. The exhibits themselves are touchingly reminiscent of women's traditional means of self expression (her diary showing so much self doubt, painfully collected and guarded memorabilia). She organises this material in an attempt to turn the most unspoken and culturally repressed of everyday experiences (mother-child relationship) into an art work inspired by feminism and psychoanalysis.

Mary Kelly's use of psychoanalysis is a direct result of recent work by feminists (Juliet Mitchell's book *Psychoanalysis and Feminism* and the conference on patriarchy held last May in London), and growing interest within the women's movement. This interest stems from the realisation that biological difference becomes overlaid by a cultural concept of sexual difference suited to the needs of a particular social order, which psychoanalytic theory can help us to understand. Thus 'femininity' can be understood not as a natural essence but as a complicated edifice which the patriarchy demands in order to give 'masculinity' meaning and strength. The little girl enters society 'negatively'; her lack of penis gives the phallus significance and allows the male to fear castration.

Mary Kelly evokes the impact that producing a child has on women whose unconscious desires are formed within the confines of the castration complex: 'During the ante-partum period (gestation inside the mother's body) and continuing during the breast-feeding phase of early post-partum, the mother's negative place in the patriarchal order – more precisely the Symbolic – can be "mis-recognised" because in a sense the child *is* the phallus for her.' (Experimentum 1. Weaning from the Breast.) As the child grows through the various stages of increasing independence from his mother, she experiences a sense of loss that Mary Kelly describes as reliving her own previous Oedipal drama, undergoing castration for the second time and re-learning the fact of her negative place in the symbolic order. Within these terms, the mother has two possible roads open; recognition and acceptance of her secondary place or rebellion against it. Her rebellion takes the form of fetishisation of the child (as substitute phallus), clinging to the couple relationship and refusing to allow the child to emerge as an independent entity. Part of the fascination of the *Post Partum Document* lies here: the exhibition in all of its obsessive detail fetishises the child, but in this case, the mother has reconciled her 'natural capacity' with her work as an artist. The art object as fetish replaces the child as potential fetish.

The exhibition throws a spotlight on the need to explore further the labyrinthine unconscious structures that lie behind the natural looking facade 'motherhood', but Mary Kelly is limited by a theory biased – though not invalidated – by patriarchal assumptions. The influence of the French psychoanalyst Jacques Lacan is heavily apparent in the *Post Partum Document*. But one important aspect of the exhibition prevails: it gives a voice to the pain and pleasure women have lived as mothers, understood by each other, despised as domestic by dominant culture. Mary Kelly's work comes in the footsteps of some of the very few women in the past who managed to be 'artists' and constantly returned to the mother-child relationship in their work, women such as Mary Cassatt, Berthe Morisot and Julia Margaret Cameron.

MARGOT WADDELL, MICHELENE WANDOR

MYSTIFYING THEORY

Dear *Spare Rib*,
Mary Kelly's exhibition, *Post Partum Document*, which was at the Institute of Contemporary Arts this autumn, aroused much publicity and some

notoriety. We are concerned about some aspects of the exhibition which were ignored both by the media and by Laura Mulvey in her largely explanatory article.

We recognise the importance of the issues Mary Kelly has chosen to treat as an artist (the mutual mother-child socialisation process in infancy), and the seriousness and ambitiousness of her project. However, we feel that the gap between her intentions and her actual achievements is so great that it has the very opposite effect of its apparent aims.

She draws on a relatively new area of psychoanalytic theory to transform selected moments of her relationship with her own child. Using a variety of framed objects – nappy liners, vests, diagrams, charts – she demands an active participation from the viewer as part of the process of appreciation/comprehension/learning from the exhibition. At a superficial level it is possible to walk round the walls and either be turned on by the 'pictures' or not. But any deeper understanding, presumably meant to help provide a basis for women to theorise their own experience and struggle on the basis of that, cannot be got from the 'pictures' alone. Either the viewer must bring the psychoanalytical/linguistic knowledge with her, or make use of the folder of notes Mary Kelly provides.

However, the notes themselves are highly selective, and quite obscure to anyone unfamiliar with the concepts and terminology. While there's nothing wrong with pitching a work of art at a high intellectual level, surely Mary Kelly must be aware that such brief notes, far from extending understanding and closing the gap between theory and art, serve to mystify theory even further.

The exhibition, free to anyone who wants to walk in, appears to be open and accessible; in fact it is opaque, and not so much participatory as excluding and exclusive. This mystification of the theory and the art rebounds on the impact of the framed objects: they cannot carry the weight of significance attributed to them and become weak visual metaphors for an esoteric intellectualisation. At its worst they come across as disconnected visual clues to some academic discourse which do little more than expose the ignorance of the viewer.

We do not simply demand longer and better notes, but question the whole form of presentation Mary Kelly has chosen; such a heavy dependence on an inadequately presented theory can only distract attention from the 'artistic' nature of the work. And because of the inadequacy, we think the exhibition is in danger of provoking impatient and philistine anti-theory responses such as 'this is a load of crap', or 'look, the Empress isn't wearing any clothes'. Two important related effects of this are firstly, the depoliticising of vital feminist issues, and secondly, a confusion about the nature of psycho-analysis, in particular the relationship between psychoanalysis as a theory and a clinical process.

These criticisms do not, of course, deal comprehensively with the exhibition, and we could expand on each of our points at greater length; we simply want to contribute to an important debate within socialist-feminist culture.

Margot Waddell
Michelene Wandor

PARVEEN ADAMS, ROSALIND DELMAR
SUE LIPSHITZ

USING PSYCHOANALYTIC THEORY

Dear *Spare Rib*,

Michelene Wandor and Margot Waddell's comment on Laura Mulvey's article and Mary Kelly's exhibition would be more of 'a contribution to a debate' had any of their points been argued. Instead, they present us with a series of assertions which we need to question and clarify in order to even begin discussion. In doing so we leave to one side two points that they raise. First, their speculations about Mary Kelly's 'intentions': only Mary Kelly can tell us about those. Secondly, their claims about the exhibition's 'difficulty' and 'obscurity' for the visitor: any exhibition, *Post Partum Document* included, will meet with a mixed response and to construct a single general response seems an unnecessary and unilluminating enterprise. There are however, other more concrete questions.

a One of the strengths of Laura Mulvey's article is that it treats the exhibition as a product of artistic practice. This dimension is entirely missing from Margot and Michelene's comments. What is also missing, therefore, is any indication of how they understand the relationship between the work of an artist and the theoretical position which informs that work. The relationship is by no means a simple one. Mary Kelly's exhibition exposes, rather than suppresses, the difficulties involved.

b Their account of her work consequently reduces it to a question of the 'issues' involved, simply and somewhat blandly described as 'the mutual mother-child socialisation process in infancy': a sociological categorisation which misses an important point. Mary Kelly's work is original in that it deconstructs the assumed unity of the mother-child relation in order to give a place to the mother's phantasies of possession and loss. She links the exploration of the psychic forces involved to the social relation in order to indicate the way in which motherhood is a constructed meaning rather than a biological truism. But in her account this deconstruction is achieved through the work of uncovering the interplay of unconscious desire with the conscious activity and physical and mental labour demanded by childcare. This aspect is not even mentioned by Michelene and Margot.

c This brings us to the question of the 'relatively new area of psychoanalysis' – 'new' for the women's movement or 'new' within psychoanalysis? Two points can be made here. First, Margot and Michelene seem to see such a new position as an already constituted body of knowledge which people already have or do not have: 'the viewer must bring the psychoanalytic/linguistic knowledge with her, or make use of the folder.' They advise the artist against the 'exposure of ignorance' which may arouse anger and the philistine response. But what is wrong with the exposure of ignorance, or indeed the exposure of the need for further work? It may cause discomfort, but might also be productive. And of course, the work *did* provide a philistine response, 'a load of crap', unsurprisingly, since at a certain level that was what part of the exhibition literally was. Margot and Michelene make a connection between philistinism and anti-theoreticism, but then fail to explain why they think that Mary Kelly should have adopted a conciliatory stance. After all, it is not the work which 'depoliticises' the issues, but the response which, political in its own way, attempts to reduce the work to the level of sensational eccentricity. Their position appears to be one which evades the reality and consequences of ideological struggle.

d Perhaps Margot and Michelene could be more explicit about what they mean by 'a confusion about the nature of psychoanalysis'. Psychoanalytic theory is used to structure the exhibition but this contains no overtones of a 'clinical process'. It is not a psychoanalysis of Mary Kelly or her child. Laura Mulvey writing about Allen Jones in *Spare Rib* has shown how fruitful a psychoanalytic approach can be – there again with no question of psychoanalysing Allen Jones. The attempts to use the theory produce problems, but its use is important in that it emphasises the ideological positioning of women and explores the phantasy of the loss of the phallus: in *Post Partum Document* in the centrally important figure of the mother. If there is to be a debate it would be useful to know what specific importance Margot and Michelene attach to the movement towards the use of psycho-analytic theory as a means of exposing the mechanisms through which we are formed as women within patriarchy.

Parveen Adams, Rosalind Delmar, Sue Lipshitz.

JUDITH BARRY and
SANDY FLITTERMAN-LEWIS

TEXTUAL STRATEGIES: THE POLITICS OF ART-MAKING

To say that there is a crisis in contemporary criticism might seem like overstating the case for a situation in which critical definitions and methods merely lack precision and rigor. Yet it cannot be disputed that in terms of the feminist issue of the representation of women and the figuration of female sexuality in art, a crisis does exist. In order to develop a truly effective feminist artistic practice, one that works toward productive social change, it is necessary to understand the question of representation as a political question, to have an analysis of women's subordination within patriarchal forms of representation. This article emerges from the need for a feminist re-examination of the notions of art, politics, and the relations between them, an evaluation which must take into account how 'femininity' itself is a social construct with a particular form of representation under patriarchy. We have come together, a feminist film theorist and a feminist artist, to discuss these issues, and more specifically to determine to what extent current definitions of art as a political activity are limited. It is indeed a crisis of definitions and methods where women are concerned.

Traditional notions of art have emphasized personal expression, from the subjective lyricism of the Romantics to the individual virtuosity of the avant-gardists. Initially in the women's movement feminists emphasized the importance of giving voice to personal experiences; the expression and documentation of both women's oppression as well as aspirations, provided women's art with a liberating force. However, a radical reconceptualization of the personal to include more broadly social and even unconscious forces has necessitated a more analytic approach to these personal experiences. The experiential must be taken beyond the consciously felt and articulated needs of women if a real transformation of the *structures* of women's oppression is to occur.

While we recognise the value of certain forms of radical political art, whose aim it is to highlight feminist issues that are generally submerged by dominant cultural discourse, it seems that this kind of work, if untheorized, can only have limited results. These more militant forms of feminist art such as agit-prop, body-art, and ritualized violence, can produce immediate results by allowing the expression of rage, for example, or by focusing on a particular event or aspect of women's oppression. But these results may be short-lived, as in the case of heightened activism resulting from an issue-oriented art work. A more theoretically informed art can prove capable of producing enduring changes by addressing itself to the structural and deep-seated causes of women's oppression rather than to its effects. A radical feminist art would include an understanding of how women are constituted through social practices in culture; once it is understood how women are consumed in this society it would be possible to create an aesthetics designed to subvert the consumption of women, thus avoiding the pitfalls of a politically progressive art work which depicts women in the same forms as the dominant culture. Consequently, we see a need for theory that goes beyond the personal into the questions of ideology, culture, and the production of meaning.

To better understand the point at which theory and art intersect it might be useful to consider women's cultural production in four categories[1]. Our attempt here is to describe a typology rather than criticise these positions for their shortcomings. In evaluating these types of women's art, our constant reference point will be the recognition of the need for a theory of cultural production as an armature for any politically progressive art form. When we talk about culturally constructed meaning, we are referring to a system of heterogeneous codes that interact. The meaning we derive from any interaction is dependent on our knowledge of a set of conventions ensnaring every aspect of our lives, from the food we eat to the art we like. Every act (eating an orange, building a table, reading a book) is a social act; the fundamentally human is social. Theory enables us to recognise this and permits us to go beyond individual, personally liberating solutions to a *'socially'* liberated situation. Any society will impose a certain selection or priority of meaning upon the multiplicity of meanings inherent in a given situation. Culture as a mechanism that imposes an assumed unity on this diversity of codes, has a naturalising function in that it makes this constructed unity appear as given and enduring. Theory, as a systematic organisation of the range of cultural phenomena, can produce the tools for examining the political effectiveness of feminist art work.

Each of the four categories in our typology of women's art-making implies a specific relation between strategy and action. By examining each of the categories and applying the definition of theory that we have suggested, we can ascertain the assumptions that characterise these relations. From doing this it should be clear that sets of assumptions do not constitute a theory, although they may be sufficient to establish a particular type of artistic practice. When we speak of the political in discussing art work we must ask the question, 'Action, by whom, and for what purpose?'. Each of the four categories will propose different answers to these questions, because they each have different goals and strategies.

One type of women's art can be seen as the glorification of an essential female art power. This power is viewed as an inherent feminine artistic essence which could find expression if allowed to be explored freely. This is an essentialist position because it is based on the belief in a female essence residing somewhere in the body of women. It is an orientation that can be found in the emphasis on 'vaginal' forms in painting and sculpture; it can also be associated with mysticism, ritual and the postulation of a female mythology. It is possible to see this type of art which valorizes the body as reversing the traditional dichotomy of mind over matter. If we accept the premise that Western metaphysical thought hierarchises binary opposition so that one term always predominates, this form of art can be seen as an aesthetics of simple inversion. Within the context of a logic that reduces the multiplicity of difference to the opposition of two positivities, feminist essentialism in art simply reverses the terms of dominance and subordination. Instead of the male supremacy of patriarchal culture, the female (the essential feminine) is elevated to primary status.

Much of the art work in this category has as its aim the encouragement of self-esteem through valorization of female experiences and bodily processes. This art seeks to reinforce satisfaction in being a woman in a culture that does the opposite. The strategy is that by glorifying the bodies of women in art work an identificatory process is set up such that the receivers of the art work (the women for whom the work is intended) will validate their own femaleness. This type of art work can also be seen to redefine motherhood as the seat of female creativity from which spring female deities, witchcraft and matriarchal cultural heritage. Operating on the assumption that our society isolates women and inspires competition, this kind of art seeks to encourage the mutual glorification and bonding of women. One of the main ways some of the art works achieve this is through emotional appeal, ritual form, and synaesthetic effects in performance, with the aim of enveloping spectators in feminine solidarity.

One example of women's art that would fall into this category is the work of Gina Pane, the French body artist whose performances for the last ten years have involved self-mutilation and the ritualised drawing of her own blood. She defines the incision of her face with a razor blade in one performance as a 'transgression of the taboo of the sore through which the body is opened, and of the canons of feminine beauty,' and at least one critic has appropriated current terminology in his praise of her work because it 'privileges the signifier on the side of pain.' Complications arise, however, when the assumptions underlying this type of art are examined. When an aesthetics of pain is counterposed against the assumed pleasurable discourse of dominant artistic practice, a rigid pleasure/pain dichotomy is already accepted as given. By confronting one half of the dichotomy with its opposite, Pane's work is seen to offer an act of artistic contestation. However, this confrontation seems rather to continue the dualistic tradition of Western metaphysics.

The very definition of opposition thus comes into question. By evaluating pain to the status of an oppositional artistic force, it would seem that Pane is simply reinforcing a traditional cliché about women. If women are assumed to be outside the patriarchal discourse, would the first rumble of self-expression take the form of very traditional pain or self-mutilation? Pane's comments about her work seem to indicate that she feels in wounding herself she is wounding society. However, because her wounds exist in an art context, they are already ritualised and easily absorbed into an artworld notion of beautiful pain, distanced suffering, and a whole legacy of exquisite female martyrdom. The solidarity in suffering that this work seems to want to promote is actually a form of solidarity that has been imposed on women for centuries. It is bondage rather than bonding.

Hannah Wilke adopts a related strategy of body art by creating an art work that has as its aim 'that women allow their feelings and fantasies to emerge... (so that) this could lead to a new type of art.' In her *S.O.S. Starification Object Series* (1975) she says, 'I am my art. My art becomes me.' She sets up an equivalency between her body's poses and its alteration after vaginally shaped pieces of chewing gum are attached to the exposed areas, and language where the meaning of a word or series of words is transformed by a slight change or modification in the letter(s) – scarification becomes starification. Wilke explains that 'my art is seduction'. Often her poses take on the characteristics of a centrefold, her eyes directed to the assumed male spectator of nude paintings and *Playboy* magazine. In *Ways of Seeing*, John Berger points out 'Men look at women. Women watch themselves being looked at. The surveyor of the woman in herself is male; the surveyed female. Thus, she turns herself into an object.'[2] In objectifying herself as she does, in assuming the conventions associated with a stripper (as someone who will reveal all), Wilke seems to be teasing us as to her motives. She is the stripper and the stripped bare. She does not make her own position clear; is her art work enticing critique or titillating enticement? It seems her work ends up by reinforcing what it intends to subvert. In using her own body as the content of her art, in calling her art 'seduction', she complicates the issues and fails to challenge conventional notions of female sexuality. The consequences are such that they permit statements like the following to issue forth from male critics: 'By manipulating the image of a sex kitten (female sex object), Wilke manages to avoid being trapped by it without having to deny her own beauty to achieve liberation.'

Wilke and Pane are only two, very divergent, types of women's art that fall into our first category. Yet they both enable us to draw certain conclusions about this type of art-making. Because this kind of art has no theory of the representation of women underlying it, it presents images of women as unproblematic. It does not take into account the social contradictions involved in 'femininity'. In much of this art, women are re-installed in society as the bearers of culture, albeit an alternative culture. In this way what is assumed to be a progressive position is actually retrograde. Although the content of this art is different (19th century women instructed their children in art appreciation and manners, here they embody and illustrate the virtues of womanhood), the function remains unchanged; in both cases they are the custodians of what is deemed true, good and beautiful. Being-a-woman is the essential presupposition underlying this art work: what this notion entails is assumed to be generally accepted, uncontra-dictory, and immutable. Whether the art focuses on pain (immolation) or pleasure (eroticism), it does not challenge a fixed and rigid category of 'femininity'.

The second strategy or type of feminist artistic practice views women's art as a form of sub-cultural resistance. It postulates a kind of artisanal work, often overlooked in dominant systems of representation, as the 'unsung province' of women's art activity.

An example of this type of work is the valorization of crafts, such as patch-work quilts, and the activities of women in the home. It posits the development of a feminist counter-tradition in the arts, by the valorization or reconstruction of a hidden history of female productivity. The strategy here is one of encouragement and nurturance and has the positive effect of stimulating women's creativity in the discovery of new areas of female expression. By redefining art to include crafts and skills heretofore neglected, it obviates the ideological distinction between 'high' and 'low' cultural forms. In so doing, it emphasises that this distinction is a tool of patriarchy that has served to downplay or negate creative avenues for women.

However, this can also be seen as an essentialist position since it views women as having an inherent creativity that simply goes unrecognised by mainstream culture. It therefore cannot be seen as a broadly effective political practice because it emphasises the personal at the expense of the social, and thus is ineffectual in transforming the structural *conditions* that oppress women. This is not to say that this kind of art-making is unimportant, but simply to point out the limitations of an untheorised strategy.

Although Jackie Winsor is not usually considered a feminist artist, she does fit into our second category of women's art, and in fact at least one critic considered her a feminist artist when she first came to attention in 1970-71 (Fig. 18). Her constructions of wood, hemp and other 'natural' materials

18   Jackie Winsor, *30 to 1 Bound Trees*, Halifax, Nova Scotia, 1971.

convey a post-minimal fascination with geometric forms and the imposition of order and regularity. While she lists her concerns as repetition, weightiness, and density, there is in her work-process itself careful attention to craft-like details, particularly in the spinning-like monotony of some of the hemp and wood pieces and even of the actual carpentry itself. In *From the Center*, Lucy Lippard characterises her work in the following way: 'Repetition in Winsor's work refers not to form, but to process, that is, to the repetition of single-unit materials which finally make up a unified, single form after being subjected to the process of repeatedly unraveling, then to the process of repeatedly binding or to the process of repeatedly nailing into wood or to the process of repeatedly sticking bricks in cement or to the process of repeatedly gouging out tracks in plywood.'[3]

Jackie Winsor's work is considered much 'tougher' than the work of other women who might be placed in this category, for example the 'pattern painters' such as Harmony Hammond. Her work has been seen as speaking a rugged female masochism encompassing the outdoors, and including skills usually reserved for men. Yet, in discussing her work Winsor often ties the origin of a particular sculpture to an early emotional childhood experience, as in *Nail Piece*. When she was a child, her father planned a house which her mother built while he was away at work. At one point, says Winsor, 'My father gave me an enormous bag of nails and left, saying to nail them down to keep the wood in place. I did . . . and used the whole bag of nails to do it. The part he told me to nail down needed about a pound of nails. I think I put in about twelve pounds. My father had a fit because I'd used up all his nails. They made such a fuss about it that it left quite an impression on me.' And like much traditional women's work, Winsor's pieces conceal the actual labor involved in their construction.

A parallel might be drawn at this point between this aspect of Winsor's work and a related phenomenon with regard to women's craftwork as in quilts or baskets. The mechanisms of repression have functioned traditionally in patriarchal culture to negate the complexity or degree of work involved in women's traditional handiwork. By foregrounding this 'other' of conventional high art, the art work that falls into our second category emphasises that there *is* another art, which has a history, and which has been repressed due to specific historical needs of the dominant culture. The 'alternative tradition' approach emphasises the social and functional aspects of things such as weaving or pottery-making in communities. We agree that this type of contribution to feminist art-making is an important one; however it is equally important to point out the limitations of a form of self-contained subcultural resistance, one which does not work in a dialectical relation with the dominant male culture. A possible consequence is the 'ghettoization' of women's art in an alternative tradition, thereby limiting its effectiveness for broad social change.

Our third category of women's art derives as well from this aspect of isolationism. This category of women's art views the dominant cultural order as a monolithic construction in which women's cultural activity is either submerged or entirely outside its limits. This position is an antidote to feminist essentialism in that it recognises that what has traditionally been known as the 'form' and the 'content' of culture both carry meaning.

However, ironically, it is also the basis of *both* 'separatist' (artists who do not identify with the art-world) and non-feminist (women artists who maintain that they are people who happen to be women) argumentation. Thus this category includes two groups of women at opposite ideological poles. One group wants to establish a separate social order unaffiliated with the patriarchal culture. The other group, women who disavow their sex, attempts to ignore the issue of 'women in crisis', seeking total identification with the patriarchy.

The strategy of the first group is that by establishing their own society, women will be able to combat the patriarchy. However, by failing to theorise how many women are produced as a category within the social complex, or how femininity is a social construction amidst a whole range of intersecting determinations, these artists lose sight of a solution that is workable in practice. As with many utopian visions, lack of integration within the wider social sphere presents obstacles. It is particularly difficult in the case of feminist separatism in that the postulation of an alternative separate culture can often be founded on simplistic notions.

The example of Terry Wolverton presents both the benefits and the limitations of the separatist strategy. As co-director of the Lesbian Art Project (which provides a programme of Sapphic Education) and producer-codirector of a feminist science fiction theatre exploration, Wolverton informs her art work with the desire to shape an alternative female culture. This takes the form of validating craft projects such as bread-dough sculptures and costumed happenings because they are produced by lesbians in the community. One positive consequence is that this type of art allows women to explore their feelings and attitudes, enabling them to develop self-esteem and pride in the discovery of their love and trust for one another. The productive result is an attack on the destructive dissatisfaction with being a woman that patriarchal culture fosters. However, the separatist position seems to be an example of this self-validation gone awry: the very notion of positive (lesbian) images of women relies on the already constituted meaning of 'woman'. Again, this unproblematic notion of 'femaleness' does not take into account that meaning is a dialectical process which involves an interaction between images and viewers. By failing to theorise how this meaning is produced within the social complex, this art considers the notion of femininity as unproblematic and positions women's culture as separate and different from mainstream culture. This can produce very disturbing results, as in the case of some of the art work validated by Wolverton, in which the prominence given to the exposed breasts of the subjects of the art work is strikingly similar to that in the photography of Les Krims, an artist noted for his particularly virulent expressions of misogyny.

The second group of women within our third category of artistic practice cannot be said to have a strategy because they do not view themselves as artists engaged in the feminist struggle. It is at this stage that women who have been favored through more strident forms of careerism make the assertion that women's art has outgrown its need for feminism. For these women, feminism is no longer useful, primarily because it was seen as a means to an end. But this form of separatism – women who deny their sex – does not necessarily have to exploit feminism. Artists falling into this category, such as Rosalyn Drexler ('I don't object to being called a woman artist as long as the word "woman" isn't used to define the kind of art I create') and Elaine de Kooning ('We're artists who happen to be women or men among other things we happen to be – tall, short, blonde, dark, mesomorph, ectomorph, black, Spanish, German, Irish, hot-tempered, easy-going – that are in no way relevant to our being artists') simply deny that their work is embedded in a social context, or that art-making, like being a woman, is a form of social practice. Yet in the dialogue in which these two artists made the above statements, when each describes how she began her career in art, both mention being 'taken' to an exhibit by a man (husband or teacher) and being thereby 'introduced' to certain aspects of the art world.[4]

The final type of artistic practice situates women at a crucial place within patriarchy which enables them to play on the contradictions that inform patriarchy itself. This position sees artistic activity as a textual practice which exploits the existing social contradiction toward productive ends. Accordingly, this position takes culture as a discourse in which art as a discursive structure and other social practices intersect. This dialectic foregrounds many of the issues involved in the representation of women. In these works the image of women is not accepted as an already produced given, but is constructed in and through the work itself. This has the result of emphasising that meanings are socially constructed and demonstrates the importance and functioning of discourse in the shaping of social reality.

In discussing our fourth category of feminist art-making, we can clarify the issue of theory by underlining the difference between women making art in a male-dominated society and feminist art working against patriarchy. Activism alone in women's art has limited effects because it does not examine the representation of women in culture or the production of women as a social category. We are suggesting that a feminist art evolves from a theoretical reflection on representation: how the representation of women is produced, the way it is understood, and the social conditions in which it is situated. In addition to specific artistic practices that fall into this category we should point out that important critical work is being done in theoretical journals such as *m/f*, *Camera Obscura*, and *Discourse*, all of which contain articles analysing cultural production from a feminist perspective.

In *Post-Partum Document* Mary Kelly deconstructs the assumed unity of the mother/child dyad in order to articulate the mother's fantasies of possession and loss. By mapping the exploration of psychic processes, she indicates the ways in which motherhood is constructed rather than biologically given. One section, displayed as a series of transparent boxes, is a record of 'conversations' between mother and son just as the child is leaving the family to enter school. Each box contains a drawing done by the child, remarks by the child, the mother's reaction, and the mother's diary. This information is supplemented by a Lacanian psychoanalytic text describing the constitution of the mother's subjectivity under 'motherhood' (patriarchy). This method allows the spectator to construct several positions simultaneously.

In a September 1976 press release Mary Kelly described her work in the following way: '... I am using the "art object" explicitly as a fetish object in order to suggest the operations of the unconscious that underly it. The stains, markings and word imprints have a minimum sign value in themselves, but a maximum affective value in relation to my lived experience. In psychoanalytic terms, they are visual representations of cathected memory traces. These traces, in combination with the diaries, time-tables and feeding charts, constitute what I would call a discourse which "represents" my lived experience as a mother, but they are consciously set up in an antagonistic relationship with the diagrams, algorithms and footnotes, thereby constituting another discourse which "represents" my analysis, as a feminist, of this lived experience.'

Martha Rosler's video tapes address the ideology of bourgeois culture. In *Semiotics of the Kitchen* an antipodean Julia Child demonstrates the use of gourmet cooking utensils within a lexicon of rage and frustration alluding to a less civilized time when preparing the meal had more to do with survival than commodity fetishism. In *Losing – A Conversation with the Parents* an at-home TV interview style is adopted as two middle class parents describe the death of their daughter by anorexia nervosa, the self-starvation disease that afflicts (mostly) teenage women from middle class families. In the attempt of the parents to present a 'coherent narrative' of their misfortune, many of the social contradictions contained in their position(s) are indexed, most specifically, 'starvation in the midst of plenty'.

Rosler's bound volume of three post-card novels is entitled *Service: A Trilogy of Colonization*. Each novel, *A Budding Gourmet* (about a middle class housewife who takes a gourmet cooking class because she feels 'it will enhance "her" as a human being'), *McTowers Maid* (about a woman employee who organises the workers in a fastfood chain), and *Tijuana Maid* (about a Mexican woman who comes to San Diego to work as a maid in a middle class household – the novel is in Spanish with the translation appended in the trilogy), deals with women and food in relation to issues of class, sex, and race. Originally Rosler sent these food novels through the mail as postcard series, one card about every five to seven days. As she makes clear in an introductory note to the trilogy, the spectator or reader of an art work is an integral part of the piece itself. 'Mail both is and isn't a personal communication. But whether welcome or unwelcome it thrusts itself upon you, so to speak, and must be dealt with in the context of your own life. Its immediacy may allow its message to penetrate the usual bounds of your attention. A serial communication can hook you, engaging your long-term interest (intermittently, at least). There was a lot of time – and mental space – around each instalment of these novels, time in which the communication could unfold and reverberate. So they are long novels, and slow ones.'

When various representations are placed in a crisis in a work of art, the work has a fissuring effect, exposing the elements that embody its construction. This is important to Judith Barry (our third example of art work in this category) 'in considering how women are represented by art, particularly in performance art where diverse conventions/disciplines intersect making possible a natural dialogue within these cultural conventions.' In *Past Future Tense* woman's position as icon is juxtaposed to a disparate psychological and social narrative detailing the question of woman as subject. The format of this piece calls into question the taken for granted assumption of a unified 'ego' of the woman, making apparent her real heterogeneity in its place. *See How To Be An American Woman* situates feminist social theory clichés informing seven horror stories of women's existence via a pre-recorded multi-track tape (rape, childbirth, abortion, marriage, divorce, old age, etc.) against the naked, immobilised body of a woman in an Italian arcade and museum. Several dualities are telescoped: American feminism's unproblematic relationship to the body of the woman/European body art (including another duality: nudity/pornography), woman as individual subject/popular history, performer/spectator, and the art world/larger social world. These dualities are readily identifiable, yet because they are not resolvable they remain in a contradictory stasis.

Kaleidoscope, a series of eight five-minute scenes employing conventions from TV, cinema, and theatre, explores the relationship of middle class feminism as it shapes the private and public lives of a heterosexual couple. The contradictory positions exhibited by the two protagonists (both played by women) as they attempt to live their beliefs, underscores the unresolvable contradictions contained in even the most progressive views of social organisations. Barry says of this piece, 'It is in trying to come to terms

116

with the world as perceived (a perception which is ideological) that psychoanalysis intervenes. As dreams, jokes and neuroses indicate, the unconscious does not describe a one-to-one relationship with the world. Jacques Lacan has shown that this unconscious is produced in language, hence the identity of the individual as speaking subject is fictional. Consequently, ideology's arbitrary nature within the domain of this fictional subject becomes apparent and yet simultaneously must remain unknown on some levels.'

From our descriptions of the work of these three artists it should be clear that an important aim of the art in this category is the critical awareness (both on the part of the spectator, and informing the work) of the social construction of femininity. For it is only through a critical understanding of 'representation' that a representation of 'women' can occur. We do not want to simply posit a definition of 'good women's art', for at this historical moment such a definition would foreclose the dialectical play of meaning that we are calling for. Our intention is to be suggestive rather than prescriptive. One strategy of this fourth type of art transforms the spectator from a passive consumer into an active producer of meaning by engaging the spectator in a process of discovery rather than offering a rigidly-formulated truth. Moreover, the art work strives to produce a critical perspective that questions absolute or reified categories and definitions of women. Both the social constructions of femininity and the psycholanalytic construction of sexual difference can be foregrounded if the art work attempts to rupture traditionally held and naturalised ideas about women. Finally, a theoretical approach implies a break with the dominant notion of art as personal expression, resituating it along the continuum connecting the social with the political and placing the artist as producer in a new situation of responsibility for her images.

NOTES

This article was published in *Screen*, Summer 1980, in a revised and edited version. The version printed here is the original form printed in *LIP: Feminist Arts Journal*, 1981/2.

1 An initial formulation of these categories has been made by Laura Mulvey in an interview in *Wedge* No. 2, Spring 1978.
2 John Berger, *Ways of Seeing*, Penguin Books 1972, p. 47.
3 Lucy Lippard, *From the Center*, New York 1976, p. 203.
4 *Art and Sexual Politics: Why Have There Been No Great Women Artists?* edited by Thomas Hess & Elizabeth C. Baker, New York 1973, both quotes p. 57.

ANNA BONSHEK

FEMINIST ROMANTIC PAINTING –
A RE-CONSTELLATION

'In fact, it is true to say, that all written history is guilty of playing down, or even negating women's responsible actions – as though to remove action itself, and critical insight, from her sphere.'

Maria Chevska, *Pandora's Box* catalogue

Of all the women painters working today, two seem to be receiving a remarkable amount of criticism/'success' in comparison to many others. These women, Maria Chevska and Therese Oulton are, despite being exceptional in their work, exceptional as women painters *gaining recognition* for their work. Of course both are deserving of this attention and appraisal but it should not be forgotten that there are many women artists working today who might not come to our attention so easily. Apart from this, no-one has as yet seriously discussed the importance of feminism for these women, or indeed for all women, or further for society generally. There has been no effort to 'site' women's creativity and action within the context of feminism. This tells us a great deal about how the most important and interesting work being done today (by women) is continually being 'diluted' by the efforts of critics to absorb this work into male mainstream trends. In the light of this I would like to give an introduction to the discussion of Maria's and Therese's work by looking generally (and briefly) at the concerns of women artists and those in the feminist movement, in order to contextualise the two artists' work. I will mention the American influence; the 'second phase' of feminism; the links with socialism; the rejection of painting; the current diversity within feminism and finally provide a 'background' to Romanticism before addressing the artists' work.

There are numerous texts which we may refer to today in order to understand the history of women's oppression, both generally and in the art world, such as *Conditions of Illusion, Sexual Politics, Women Evolution, Old Mistresses* and *Women's Consciousness, Man's World*. In this last volume Sheila Rowbothom says: 'In the 1960s Margaret Mead was left wondering about the "retreat into fecundity". It was evident that the mere existence of

118

social data was not enough to reveal what a woman was. The political force of the need to keep women within the "role" capitalism has assigned to them was sufficiently strong to turn any discoveries about the position of women in completely different cultures into a justification for the existing structure of sexual relationships.' Each volume seeks to present a critique of the patriarchy and tries to define (for ourselves) 'what is woman'. Along with these there have been films such as *Rosie the Riveter* (USA), which documents how women were called to take 'men's jobs' in support of the war effort during World War II, and just as quickly were expected to relinquish these jobs when the war was over, and *For Love or Money* (Australia) which covers women's oppression throughout the twentieth century to the present decade.

There was a clear sense of what the women's movement was about in the seventies in Great Britain and the States. Women seemed united as they fought together for equal rights – equal pay, legalisation of abortion, maternity benefits for the 'working' woman – amongst many other important issues raised by the new Women's Liberation Movement. In art practice we claimed the 'personal as political' and as Alexis Hunter says 'I . . . know the idealistic battle we fought in feminist art groups, history and within film theory in the 1970s are more important historically because we broke new ground'.[1] The 'pluralist' 70s allowed more scope for varied art practice and attention was given to women's work. A lot of women were concerned to work mainly in film, photography, performance and installation, seeing these as areas within which there was a possibility of starting fresh with examples like Maya Deren (1940s independent film-maker/theorist, USA) for a role model, whilst painters and sculpters (i.e. Judy Chicago, Louise Bourgeois) grappled with the problem of finding a 'female imagery' and created work that was gender specific. Women worked from their bodies and found that 'circles, domes, eggs, spheres, boxes, biomorphic shapes, –maybe a certain striation or layering',[2] constituted this female imagery. However within the entrenched, male-dominated discipline of painting (both historically speaking and up to the present day), women felt they could not define the 'liberated' role of the new woman.

In America, the women's movement seemed particularly strong and welcomed women artists. Much of the work being done there was seen as an example to women working in this country and those such as May Stevens and Judy Chicago worked to expose themes of oppression. The latter chose to employ sexual imagery and address her work to the invisibility of women creators throughout history and thereby retrieve women's cultural heritage. We have, only recently, had the opportunity to view her *Dinner Party* at the Edinburgh Festival 1984 and in London in 1985. In the 70s women also explored ancient mythology to rediscover powerful personifications of womanhood, such as Ishtar, Inana, Mycenean and Minoan goddesses,

Artemis,[3] and were looking for a feminine principle[4] which was autonomous and creative. Although Julia Kristeva presents a critique of this 'second phase' of feminism (see her 'Women's Time' in *Feminist Theory*, Keohane, Rosaldo and Gelpi, Harvester Press) this 'phase' can be seen as a searching for a sense of difference and separateness – in order to reclaim our own experience, to find our own experience, to find our own voice, one which wasn't oppressive, denigratory and confining. We were also examining the ways in which women had been made 'invisible' by the patriarchy.[5]

As the American movement gained momentum much work was produced in the arts.[6] There were also projects such as *Womanhouse* and the periodical *Heresies* which acted as a forum for feminists and feminist artists. These progressions influenced us and we too have our *Feminist Art News* (first published 1980) and the Women Artists Slide Library, Fulham Palace, London, along with a number of women's bookshops and The Feminist Library, Hungerford House, London. However, in the States it was possible for a show like the 1979 *Women Artists 1550–1950* to take place in Los Angeles and provide women with an opportunity to view 'the history' of women's painting from the Renaissance to the present century. Nothing quite on that scale has occurred here. British artists have never had quite so much support and exposure. In part this may be due to a prevailing attitude in this country where the activity of artists and what they produce is not given merit. Whether the women's movement itself has been supportive of women artists is a question which has been answered by Alexis Hunter: 'Individual women in the movement have been (supported)... , but the movement generally doesn't seem to be interested. Here it is more socialist than the States, but almost totally anti-art.'[7] The few women who've gained recognition in Britain this century are exceptions, like Barbara Hepworth, Bridget Riley and Gillian Ayres, and they are not necessarily involved with the efforts of the women's movement.

Jon Thompson provides a sketch of America's cultural dominance over the past few decades in his 'Reversing the Trans-Atlantic Drift', *British Art Show* catalogue, 1984–85. However it seems that there has always been less support and respect for artists in this country as earlier this century we looked to Europe as well as the States for influences, and at the present time we do not even merit support from our own government, as politics are introduced which effectively close art schools and reduce staff, whilst withdrawing vital financial aid. In addition exhibitions of 'new' trends in art (i.e. *New Spirit of Painting*, Royal Academy 1981, *New Art*, Tate Gallery 1984 and *The British Art Show*, Arts Council 1984–5) do little to instil confidence in the British woman artist. In these exhibitions very little (if *any*) of the work exhibited was by women!

Meanwhile shows of women's work throughout the country get much less 'press'/prestige although the eighties sees the diversity of feminism opening even wider definitions for women and the quality and abundance of women's work in this country continues to increase. It has been noted that the eighties have brought 'many different kinds of feminism'.[8] Some women see feminism and socialism as inextricably linked, as does Elizabeth Wilson who states that feminism must have a relationship of some kind with socialism since the changes fought for by the women's movement, within society, are not compatible with capitalism.[9] However as Ann Rosalind Jones points out, 'One of the contributions feminism has made to political discourse is the questioning of male-dominated procedures, through critiques of the male Left as well as the Right, and through counterpractices'.[10]

I would like to suggest that women's art practice in this country, by virtue of its critique of the patriarchy and by bringing a female sensibility to creativity, informs critical practices generally and within the art world, and provides new standards and values with which an art work might be read or assessed. Women now work even more diversely under a wider umbrella of 'feminism' than has been defined in previous decades.

At present we have had shows such as *Pandora's Box* touring the country and women such as Eileen Cooper, Paula Reago, Lubaina Himid, Amanda Faulkner, Laura Ford, June Redfern, Alexis Hunter, Avis Newmann, Maria Chevska and Thérèse Oulton are regularly exhibiting work amongst many, many others of us who may be less well known, but nonetheless active.

Painting has been regarded as a male enclave and as I have stated, women have often steered clear of this mode of activity fearing it may only serve to reinforce the status quo. It is an isolating activity and the myth of the artist as a gifted, individual 'set apart' from the rest of society also conflicts with how many women perceive their own creative process, let alone the way they live their daily lives. Women have need to collaborate and feel they can come together and dismantle any enshrined idealism which supports the ego-centric individual (genius).

Women have worked very successfully together in areas like film, for example *Bred and Born* (collectively created) which was shown on Channel 4 this year, on their *Women Direct* series. (See *Circles*, Women's Film Distribution, Roman Road, London.)

During the late 18th and early 19th century, certain artists were working in what has been defined by writers and historians as the Romantic school. Baudelaire termed this school as 'modern' and of all the painters in France at that time, Delacroix was seen as the figurehead. According to Baudelaire it was a 'singular and persistent melancholy that emanated from all (Delacroix's) works', which defined the artist as a Romantic. The painter also referred to Mediaeval or Renaissance history and contemporary writers (i.e. Shakespeare, Byron, Dante).

Generally speaking, the age of Romanticism signified the polarisation of the sexes and there was 'both a masculine and feminine way of experiencing nature'.[11] At this time there arose the 'cult of motherhood' which is discussed by Carol Duncan in 'Happy Mothers and Other New Ideas in 18th Century French Art'[12] and exemplified by Elizabeth Vigée-Lebrun's paintings (see her mother and child paintings in the Louvre).[13] Although religious groups such as the St. Simonians[14] with their deification of women envisaged the coming of a female Messiah, and Bachofen's re-interpretation of the Greek myths led him to suggest an existence of the matriarchy prior to the patriarchy,[15] whilst Mary Wollstonecraft published her *Vindication of the Rights of Women*,[16] women of the day were still confined to stereotypes and these were polarised out into Mother/Whore and both situated women *in relation* to man.

It was an age when painting was executed by the male artist (with very few exceptions) and the artist sought to depict nature and the landscape, and to represent through these, passion. Nature was symbolic of a spiritual realm free from the influence of the industrial revolution, and 'she' (for Nature was seen as feminine) also represented the realm of violent emotion, mystery, fugitive spiritual states, a watery world, stillness, birth and darkness. Woman was fruit[17] and vessel, both container and concealing that which is contained. She was the site of desire, the desire of the active male. She, the signified, he the signifier. Her creativity was never allowed to come into being.

Today two women tackle a 'landscape of the imagination and desire'. Looking at the work exhibited by Thérèse Oulton and Maria Chevska in the Serpentine show *'Landscape, Memory and Desire'* 1984, I can see how the links with Romantics have seemed so obvious (especially with Thérèse's work) and as Tony Godfrey writes in the catalogue, 'Before anything else a painting is a place; a site of imaginative possibilities'.[18] However, the sensuality and compositional structure (which is anti-phallocentric) of Oulton's canvases, also link them with work mentioned above by women such as Chicago and Hunter and the concerns of women artists from the 1970s. Maria Chevska's canvases evoke a literal reading, allowing personal narrative to surface whilst owing much to artists such as Munch and Nolde in their contrasts with the other paintings (by men) in the exhibition. Her work is provocative in that it supports the 'woman as creator' and locates *women's desire*.

In reference to Walter Benjamin's definition of 'reconstellation', Gyatri Spivak explains how the gesture of wrenching a word, concept, metaphor, emblem out of its appropriate context and citing it might give it 'revolutionary use-value. To cite is to re-constellate'.[19] Therese by being a woman painter and referring to the Romantic tradition inverts the view of women exemplified by the Romantic period. She re-contextualises the activity of painting – citing woman as creator – defining her own 'passion'.

19 Thérèse Oulton, *Untitled*, 1983, 30" by 40", oil on canvas.

By virtue of 're-citing' a particular tonal device or compositional structure (referring to a past genre) she provides a 're-constellation' whilst the surface of the canvas itself, the paint, worked in a gestural flurry, owes much to the twentieth century movement of abstract expressionism. As Catherine Lampert has suggested, 'Special references are made to the penumbra of the chiaroscuro approach, the escapism of the French 18th century... '[20] Oulton's work transforms itself before the eye, the supremacy of the paint manipulation giving primacy to gesture, yet motif and metaphor come into being and freeze, like iconographic signs.

In her early work *Untitled* (Fig. 19) there is a whirlpool effect – a toppling landscape – as if the very substance on the canvas has been caressed into a centrifugal pull to give a kind of drama. This dramatic, this shifting ground, seems to pull us into a vortex, as does John Martin's visionary landscape *The Great Day of His Wrath*, which can be seen at the Tate Gallery. In the latter painting (dated 1851–3) the image has a literal – but theatrical – reading and here we are confronted again with a collapsing/exploding landscape. In this apocalyptic work, Nature is shown as the instrument of 'His Divine Wrath' – Nature is destroyed by God/is God. We read the biblical meaning of the piece despite its expressive composition. Oulton's painting invites us to react directly, not merely 'suspend disbelief', but to bring our personal response, through our eye, through the body. The image relates to our body.

Looking at the work shown at the Serpentine (and later at the Museum of Modern Art, Oxford), the image first 'feels' sensual – inviting one to enjoy the richness of the paint. The source of light in each work (particularly those of a diagonal composition, i.e. *Cardinal*)[21] suggests an opening, yet the 'illumination' therein appears to suggest life beneath. And birth! Blood reds, siennas, ochres and blues (*Cardinal, Moral Coil, Quicksilver*) – are worked with the artist's fingers and become like pared flesh or wounds (reminiscent of Rembrandt's painting *The Slaughtered Ox*, 1640, (Glasgow Art Gallery). Then somehow the forms become decipherable and a stairway might lead us out (or into?) a void. The iconographical clues are at once references and 'memories', they connect our experience to the image and become meaningless again as they resume their status as pure wisps of paint, pushed, pulled and poked layers of pigment. Will stairs, pools of light, columns, fountains lead us anywhere but back to ourselves ... our bodies ... and back to the painting itself? These signs masquerade as points of departure, ways to read the paint, but they are confined by their own position within the composition and their secondary status, as the sensuality of the paint itself and effects of chiaroscuro take hold and spell out the realm of woman's desire.

Our eye is led in, engulfed by the 'landscape of Romanticism' – that space signifying the site of passion/desire. The 'melting' pigment, the 'melting' composition is like liquid metal in a furnace where lies latent the possibility of a new structure. These are fugitive clues, all enmeshed, layered, fragmented so that forms appear and are lost again as in Turner's landscapes.

As with Turner, Maria Chevska's 'landscape' is often 'sea-scape'. Her *Crossing the Water* (Fig. 20) refers to the anthology of that title by Sylvia Plath. Many women, including the film-maker, Sandra Lahire,[22] have been similarly inspired by and incorporated the work of the poet in their art. Maria uses comparable visual metaphors.

> *Cold worlds shake from the oar.*
> *The spirit of blackness is in us, it is in the fishes.*
> *A snag is lifting a valedictory, pale hand:*
> *Stars open among the lilies.*
> *Are you not blinded by such expressionless Sirens?*
> *This is the silence of astounded souls?*[23]

Maria's canvases themselves are layered with washes, glazes of pure colour – like waves across their surface. *Crossing the Water* – passing from one state into another. I see this journey by boat (vessel/woman) like a womb, carrying the spirit (idea/desire) into flesh, into being; in harmony with the artist's own feelings and thoughts which come into being through

20 Maria Chevska, *Crossing The Water*, 1984, oil on canvas.

the poetry of her painting. Is this journey from one of confinement to one of hope? The 'flag' flies – white (a surrender?) – a salute to the hand reaching from the depths. A woman's face illuminated by some inner source dominates the painting. Her *Crossing the Water* seems to speak in the same breath of Plath's words and appear in vision like Delacroix's *Barque de Dante* in the Louvre (Salon 1822 – Dante *Inferno* Canto VIII).

These later paintings contrast with the earlier work (as was shown in the *Pandora's Box* travelling exhibition), where the compositions are more claustrophobic and oppressive and the artist used heavier, more opaque layers of paint. In the recent work Maria seeks economy during the creative process and wants to ensure every mark has meaning – there is no 'filling in'. In the paintings and drawings bodies and objects are absorbed into the ground/space or are submerged or spinning in the air, so that body and environment are interrelated, not separate. Underwater bodies entwine and are fluid themselves – echoing the properties of their outer, surrounding world. Some of the later drawings (as exhibited at the Air Gallery),[24] were made at the swimming baths. Here the artist was working from children as part of an artist in schools programme organised by the Whitechapel Gallery, London. The same watery theme is exploited. Like Laura Ford's drawing *Ophelia*,[25] the figures themselves become water-weed or sea-weed as their limbs float upward in an eddying mass of contours. The outline of the figure is drawn over and again, the boundaries constantly retraced, like the late sketches of Michelangelo.

The new paintings seem to represent survival – a 'crossing', and Maria herself acknowledges that the time is ripe at present for women to become creators. As artists are having to restructure their world position, women have a chance to redefine their own experience through painting. Woman can be signifier, not just signified. Woman no longer has to accept the role of the muse – but will make representations of *herself*. She is active, and 'whole' woman. However Maria still recognises the difficulty of painting the female figure – without it becoming 'just flesh' or an allegorical type. In this it is important that the work has integrity and expresses the 'truth of woman'.

For me, the underwater themes represent freedom of movement, flexibility, mobility, an un-namable world, the underbelly of everything we think we can see/know. We drift, or steer ourselves, in a passage from here to a shore unknown, but which represents the realm of hope.

> *Our lady of the shipwrecked is three times life size,*
> *Her lips sweet with divinity.*
> *She does not hear what the sailor or the peasant is saying –*
> *She is in love with the beautiful formlessness of the sea.*[26]

Romanticism has often been described as a movement which served as an 'escapism' in an ever-repressive industrial age. As I have indicated above, the roles of men and women were distinctly polarised and the human populace seemed to be categorised in order to fulfil the aims of that industrial society as it rapidly developed. Ideas about 'free love' and expression of emotion and passion were transmitted through the medium of the (male) artist and poet. During the eighteenth and nineteenth century, notions of a socialist utopia abounded and theorists such as John Stuart Mill and Rousseau were held in great esteem. Though the notion of childhood (as we understand it today) arose at this time (with beginnings of the importance of education for all), such developments as the cult of motherhood did little to revolutionise the position of women in society. In our age of postmodernism,[27] the activities of feminists, women artists, groups of women such as those at Greenham Common, 'feed into' a critique of our society. The women painters discussed above undoubtedly seem to link their work with that of a past age, but as they do so they bring to bear their own position within this period of time within this society (from their own perspective in terms of gender, race, class) and re-invest in that material which has remained 'unacceptable' to feminist artists, until now.

Women here challenge any restrictive definition of the materials that

21 Maria Chevska, *Untitled*, 1984, 40″ by 28″, charcoal.

they can re-work or use critically, and through their work they give it
'revolutionary use-value'. Women widen the parameter of their own
expressive possibilities, of their own vision and experience and bring to it
their *own meanings*. By bringing their sensibility to this material they create

new meanings not only for themselves but also for others.

Catherine Lampert says of Thérèse, that her 'personal attraction to the bitterness of dichotomy is like her questioning of a masculine standard of successful painting. She seems to respect perseverance and prowess but be repelled by authoritarianism and analytic reductiveness. Preserving the intimacy and candour of female behaviour in its raw emotional state is a method of protecting the artist from painting with another person's values'.[28] Although I would like to reiterate much of what Jacqueline Morreau describes in her introduction piece to the *Pandora's Box* show catalogue, I will be content to quote her: 'Women are still an undersubsidised, undervalued group within the British art world...in spite of the fact that many men have told me...that women are doing the only really interesting work these days.' Which they are! And she says further '...we are the voice of our time...'[29] So why was there not an equal ratio of women to men represented at the Serpentine show *Landscape, Memory and Desire* and *The British Art show* and even *New Art*? There are more than enough brilliant women artists working in this country. Artists such as Jayne Parker, Mary Kelly, Susan Hiller, Paula Reago and Therese Oulton represented women in *The British Art Show* but where was there any serious or detailed discussion of the influence of feminism in the catalogue?

As Maria Chevska said, 'creativity in the human soul does not recognise sexual barriers'.[30] However society still seeks to confine women and disguise their actions. By disregarding the influence of feminism in women's (and men's) work and thinking, the oppression of women is reinforced. Women's work and sensibility in all forms of creativity (as action and *recognition of action*) alters, and potentially repairs, the imbalance within this society.

NOTES

1 Alexis Hunter interviewed by Caroline Osborne, *Feminist Review*, Winter 1984.

2 *From the Centre*, Lucy Lippard, New York, 1976 (page 81) 'What is Female Imagery?'

3 *The Paradise Papers*, Merline Stone, Virago.

4 *The Moon and Virgin*, Nor Hall, Women's Press.

5 See: *Old Mistresses*, Rozsika Parker and Griselda Pollock, Routledge and Kegan Paul, London, 1981. *Man Made Language*, Dale Spender, Routledge and Kegan Paul, 1981. *The Female Spectator, English Women Writers before 1800*, Mary Mahl and Helen Koon, the Feminist Press, 1977.

6 For example – Linda Nochlin, Ann Sutherland Harris, Lucy Lippard, Kate Millet, Susan Griffin.

7 Alexis Hunter interviewed by Caroline Osborne.

8 See: *Notes from Three Women Artists*, Laura Knoblock, Trisha Cox, Anna

Bonshek, in *Feminist Action 1*, Battle Axe Books, 1984 (page 154).

9 'Beyond the Ghetto, Thoughts on Beyond the Fragments – Feminism and the Making of Socialism' by Hilary Wainwright, Sheila Rowbotham and Lynne Segal', Elizabeth Wilson, *Feminist Review* No. 4, 1980.

10 'Julia Kristeva, on Feminity, The Limits of a Semiotic Politics', Ann Rosalind Jones, *Feminist Review* No. 18, 1984.

11 *Art in the 19th Century*, Werner Hofman, Faber, London 1961 (p.319)

12 See: *Feminism and Art History: Questioning the Litany*, edited by Norma Broude and Mary D. Garrard, Harper and Row, New York, 1982.

13 See *Old Mistresses*.

14 Rosa Bonheur – artist whose father was a St. Simonian; see *'Women Artists 1550-1950'* Ann Sutherland Harris and Linda Nochlin, Alfred A. Knopf, New York, 1979, p.223.

15 J.J. Bachofen *Myth, Religion and Mother Right, Princeton*, NY, 1967.

16 *Vindication of the Rights of Women*, Mary Wollstonecraft, first published 1792, Penguin, 1982.

17 See: *The Great Mother*, Erich Neumann (trans. by Ralph Manheim) Bolligan, Priceton 1963, (p. 120) for discussion of this symbolism.

18 *Landscape, Memory and Desire* (catalogue), 'Towards a Painting of Desire' by Tony Godfrey, Arts Council, 1984.

19 Gyatri Spivak, Literary Theory Conference, Hong Kong University, 1983.

20 'Following the Threads' from catalogue *Fools' Gold*, Gimpel Gils, by Catherine Lampert.

21 See: 'Following the Threads' for artist's use of compositional devices.

22 *Arrows* by Sandra Lahire (GB 1984) 16mm., 15 mins.

23 *Crossing the Water*, From *Crossing the Water* by Sylvia Plath, Faber & Faber, London 1971.

24 Exhibition *10 years at AIR*, February 1985, AIR Gallery, London.

25 135 Upper Street, Islington, London, *Sculpture and Drawing* by Andrew Sabin and Laura Ford, February 1985.

26 *Finisterre*, from *Crossing the Water*, Sylvia Plath.

27 See: *Postmodernism, or the Cultural Logic of Late Capitalism*, by Frederic Jameson, *New Left Review*, No 146 (critique of postmodernism).

28 See: *Following the Threads*.

29 'Gaining Ground', in *Pandora's Box* (catalogue) 1984, Jacqueline Morreau.

30 *Pandora's Box* catalogue.

Books referred to by me at the opening of article: *Conditions of Illusion*, Papers From the Women's Movement, Feminist Books Ltd, Leeds 1974; *Sexual Politics*, Kate Millet, Virago; *Women's Evolution*, Evelyn Reed, Pathfinder.

Anna Bonshek thanks Maria Chevska, Thérèse Oulton, Liz Ellis and Michael Harrison for their help in preparing this article.

BEATRIX CAMPBELL and
GLORIA CHALMERS

STRIKING WOMEN

As a result of the 84/85 miners' strike, many women have changed relationships with each other, their families and the communities around them. *Striking Women – Communities and Coal* is an exhibition which looks at the roles and lives of women during the strike. This is a discussion of some of the issues it raises.

Gloria: It is ironic that these photographs, which were available for use by the media during the miners' strike, have only been used to any extent since the strike ended. The Format photographers in particular found that there was no great market for their photography during the strike and that even the Left magazines wanted 'action' shots from picket lines. Only after the strike ended were there requests for photographs showing 'social' conditions.

Bea: It seems the photographs were not news. Fleet Street would consider that women's work, whether in the home or not, would not be of 'news value'. Therefore photographers looking at the role of women in the strike start off with a problem. Most of the occasions on which the soup kitchens were addressed was through broadcasting, because sympathetic TV reporters wanted to do a show on the 'real lives', i.e. everyday life in the strike.

Gloria: The Photographers' Gallery state that one of the objectives of the exhibition was to document the 'changing role of women' during the strike, to use 'positive images' of women and portray them in a non-stereotypical way. The concept of 'positive images' of women has been familiar to women photographers since the 1970s, but I wonder if it is an adequate objective in the 80s. One of the main criticisms of this form of representation is that it merely replaces traditional 'feminine characteristics' (e.g. passivity in front of the camera) for more 'activity', without examining how photography plays an important role in the creation of 'femininity'. An unfortunate consequence of this strategy has been the creation of a new set of stereotypes, which have exactly the same effect as the old ones, in that they short-circuit 'meaning' within photographs and

130

22 'We sat down in the road. Greenham women were there and gave us courage.' The first large-scale picket outside the steel works at Port Talbot organised by the South Wales Women Against Pit Closures group, Port Talbot, July 23, 1984. Photo: Imogen Young.

have a reductive effect. For example, Imogen's photograph of the women sitting in the road shows in the foreground a woman with striped sweater, looking quite calm and serene as she is being dragged off by police (whereas the woman in the foreground is quite frightened by the experience). (Fig. 22.) The caption states that the women from Greenham came and gave them support and courage, but simply because the photograph is reminiscent of Greenham in that it includes a woman who is a recognisable 'type', I think it fails to suggest new links between Greenham and the women of the strike. It does, of course, mobilise whatever feelings the viewer has about Greenham and confirm them one way or another, but it closes off any further meanings which might be generated by use of a different kind of image.

Bea: With writing, in terms representing the labour movement and struggles there's always the risk of being 'spartish', which is like the *Morning Star* or *Socialist Worker*. They create sentimental images of 'heroic' workers, muscular, with banners fluttering in the wind, or alternatively as abject, victimised, and living a terrible life. This is done by Left journalists who don't set the thing within the context of an argument, who reduce politics to completely simplistic oppositions, and don't explain anything. This is important for us, as women, because we want to bring a critical awareness to bear on dominant assumptions on the Left. Therefore there are two functions for the radical journalist – one is to set out the struggle against its enemy, and the other is to clarify to our own side and expand its knowledge. It is especially important in the case of the women in the miners' strike because what was printed was along the lines of 'Isn't it great, the women on the same side as the men ... united communities ... happy families ... and, this is the moment we've all been waiting for when men and women are struggling *together* on the same side'.

What most of the work did not do was to investigate the struggle the women had and how they were changed by it. But also how the men were changed and what it all meant. So you have women supporting the strike, potentially very subversive, but 'coralled' by the men through specific jobs they took up which were still contingent on the men's positions. Men up and down the country, including the national executive, were opposed to the women getting together and being involved. To go back to the point, the 'spartish' tendency showed 'plucky' women and a united class. A lot of what was written was along those lines. Unless you were privy to the arguments, then there was no way you could record it and there was a premium on suppressing the argument because unity was so important. We have to clarify the meaning of the struggle or situation for the culture that we create on our way. What is important about it for political principles? What does it mean for the dominant culture within the labour movement? What is it they are stabilising? What is it affirming?

Gloria: Reading the exhibition, there is an awareness of looking at a historical document. We know that it was a 'failed' strike and so that knowledge affects how we read the photographs and text. Some of the photographers have said that it was unfortunate that the commission from the Photographers' Gallery came so late. That, having spent so much time snatching a few days here and there whenever pressure of other work and finances would allow it, suddenly there was money and therefore time. But by then the strike was almost over. Raissa, for example, felt that an earlier commission would have given her a different kind of 'status' in that she could have explained to the women how the photographs would be used. All four photographers spent time gaining the trust of the women, in contrast to the normal distanced role of the photojournalist. And perhaps the commission would have enabled them to make more demands of the women concerning the kind of photographs they felt were appropriate. It is interesting to think how the exhibition would have happened, say, in June 1984 rather than January 1985. And also in what ways it would have differed if the strike had been

23 'Picketing was waiting a lot of the time. The action was over in a few seconds.' The Neath and District Women's Support Group on the picket line at Treforgan Colliery, South Wales, February 18, 1985. Photo: Imogen Young.

won. But perhaps this exhibition and many of the books recently published would not exist if the strike *had* been won. The books tend to be writing history from specific political points of view, and maybe an exhibition celebrating a *successful* strike would not have the same public appeal.

Bea: But in a sense the books are written as if the strike had actually been won. It is a myth now, which almost represents the strike as if it *had* been won. Indeed, Arthur Scargill refused to call it a 'defeat'. And consequently those myths could be seen to be writing history. There were no defeats, but only betrayals, and the undoubted heroism of the coalfield communities and the way that this heroism gets represented can support those myths.

Picketing was a problem during the strike and there are now terrific debates about picketing tactics. One of the strengths of this exhibition is that it reveals the ordinary, little and trivial details about picketing during the strike. Endless hanging around, a kind of determination just to be there, and brief encounters with the scabs. What this exhibition focuses on is the work of the women which, as it happens, was one of the triumphs of the strike. But from the point of view of the photographers,

24 Glenys Kinnock, one of the speakers at the Abertillery Rally, the first women's rally in South Wales, July 27, 1984. Photo: Imogen Young.

and feminists in particular, it must have presented some real problems. How do you represent collective housework as a triumph? Picketing often gets represented as the heroic moment of the strike. Actually it usually failed in its objectives. It went on and on but rarely stopped goods or people moving. Therefore, you haven't got a failure of picketing because it wasn't enough. What you do have is a record of the most spectacular failure, which is Orgreave, with mounted police routing workers. What you don't have is Polish coal at the dockyards and dockers not allowing it in. That would have been a record of a triumph. What you do have are picketing pictures either of people standing around talking to nobody but themselves (a defeat) because they weren't allowed to. Or people shouting in vain at strike-breakers or militant pickets being routed by police.

Gloria: There are some photographs in the exhibition of women on picket lines, but they are quite different to those used by the media. The one by Imogen of Treforgan Colliery is a dramatic picture, but with no actual 'drama' taking place. No action is being frozen by the camera, but it tells quite a story about the activities of being on a picket line. Knowing the outcome of the strike affects how the picture tends to be read. It has a

25 'Just like the thirties.' Colliery Row, Woolley Edge, Barnsley, South Yorks, 1985.
Photo: Raissa Page/Format.

sadness because you get a feeling of so much time passing, and ultimately the strike was lost. But because *we* know the outcome of the strike, there is a strong sense of being in possession of knowledge which those women didn't have at the time. And that adds to the sadness. (Fig. 23.)

Bea: Its strength also lies in the women just standing around quietly in the dark, not doing anything, not 'being happy', not the 'singing pickets'. It is as though each of those women is somehow responsible for herself.

Gloria: The picture of the meeting in Abertillery with Glenys Kinnock on the platform is striking. To have a political platform, the kind of thing we are used to seeing in a large hall, plonked down in the middle of beautiful countryside, looks so unreal. It de-naturalises the relationship between expert speaker and audience. And Arthur Scargill is no more than a minor character for once, rather than the centre of attention. (Fig. 24.)

The picture of Colliery Row tends to suggest the 1930s, through the landscape, which hasn't changed much since then, and the girl in the foreground, who looks kind of 'timeless' because of her hairstyle and glasses. (Fig. 25).

26   The Bitterness Remains. Striking miner's wife Maureen Page, Armthorpe, near
Doncaster, South Yorks, 1985. Photo: Raissa Page/Format.

Bea: The 1930s remains a kind of benchmark of poverty, class, and so on,
which has partly been created through photographs. We are continually
reminded about it. Images of children in the thirties are important in
terms of the way we think of that period. For example, they didn't have
shoes, so our generation looks at the 1930s in terms of 'not having' and
everything since then is about 'having'. But the girl in the foreground of
the photograph is not 'deprived'. She's got shoes, but there is an
assumption that she *is* deprived because she is in a deprived environment.

   The picture of the woman standing beside the 'scab' graffiti leaves me
not knowing anything about the woman. Perhaps I don't want to be
reminded that this brutality exists. It is one of the worst characteristics of
the strike, although I can understand why people feel it. It is such a part of
our culture, the sanctioning of hatred. I am sure both men and women feel
that there is a division in the mining communities now. (Fig. 26.)

Gloria: So the exhibition spends most of its time creating the feeling that
the community is a 'whole' in terms of men and women who are working
together for the strike, and then finally reminds us that there is a perm-
anent division between strikers and scabs. It is very significant that this

27   Clipstone Women's Support Group outside their soup kitchen, the welfare hut they took over for a year. Photo: Brenda Prince/Format.

has been chosen as the final image in the exhibition, probably to generate an emotional response. But it tends to shift the *blame* for the failure of the strike to the *scabs*, by giving the viewer a visible target for their emotions.

The concept of 'community' is used widely both in this exhibition and elsewhere in books and articles about the strike. It often seems an artificial description imposed by middle-class culture workers, through an Orwellian kind of romanticism of the working-class.

Bea: In this case it is a matter of the *wish* and not the *reality* being alive, but in so far as it is a reality, women are at the centre of it, so that in the strike it was women's work which *created* the community. It didn't exist prior to the work that was carried out which brought people together. So the fact that they did something representing 'community' spoke of the absence of it normally. The fact that you have pictures of women in rooms talking to each other are examples of 'community' – they weren't there before. The fact that they are worth photographing bears witness to the fact that they were absent before. The trouble is that people represented it as *evidence* of the community. That's why what women did was so significant, because they generated the emotional infrastructure that we recognise as 'community'. (Fig. 27.)

Gloria: But the photographers, in drawing together and emphasising specific activities, give a specific 'meaning' to those activities, which we recognise as 'community'. It wouldn't be a matter of recording, but actually constructing a coherent image of the community through their own photographic skills, bringing together pubs, soup kitchens and other activities. Pubs have always symbolised community, partly because of being the centre of leisure activities, but also because they have been the subject of vast amounts of documentary photography produced in the thirties and seventies, in an attempt to search out the 'essence' of the working class. So the pubs refer back directly to previous photographic images.

Bea: It would be an image which the women would also believe in, but it brings us back to the absences. There is no evidence of the arguments, the fact that we have the picture of the women who took over the hut because the welfare wouldn't let them have the cash. So why is there no picture of the man from the welfare who didn't let them have it, and perhaps it would disrupt the myth of the community?

It is as if there is a lacuna in the middle of it, i.e. that everyone said 'It's amazing what these women have done,' but you don't know why. And you don't know why unless you tell the stories of the struggle they have. What they came out of. What was in their heads. What you have is women saying 'My life has changed. Before this strike I was a woman who never went out without my man... I was just a housewife, and now it's all changed, etc'. But we don't have evidence of men changing, so we can't see the momentousness of what the women did.

Gloria: So in the interests of unity, those conflicts between miners and their wives have been suppressed, even by feminist photographers, who have shown only the more 'public' side of 'private' life. The arena of public life may now include the women getting together, the interiors of women's houses, and private moments shared with their men when they faced difficult situations together. But it doesn't include difficulties in their relationships.

In photography there are always ethical decisions to be made about whether to use photographs which are in some ways compromising or embarrassing to the subject. There are limited opportunities for altering photographs and the choice can often be to take a risk or self-censorship. There isn't the opportunity, as in writing, to change characters, merge them, create total fictions, as a way of getting across facts about people without causing embarrassment. As feminist photographers, they would want to support the women and that would mean taking pictures which the women would condone and the strength of that is that it is respectful of the subject.

Bea: It would be difficult to document the private attrition, the secret life of the strike, which is about the women's struggle for their right to be in it. So what you have is only a picture of the women's triumph, rather than their struggle. The relationship between the photographers and the women of the mining communities may be a difficult one, but as feminists there is no way you couldn't feel a criticism of the conduct of the strike being a 'macho' mess. The women were strong, but still subordinated.

Gloria: It is difficult for women in photojournalism to maintain a confidence when they are battling against an ideology which is continually sustained by male photojournalists who tend to give editors what they want, and what they are used to. Not photographing the 'action', and showing divisions, while it is important that the strike be won, is quite a task. And it would have been 'outrageous' and perhaps would have jeopardised feminism to have highlighted those divisions.

Bea: Perhaps the risks are too great when feminism is uncertain of its ground in relation to socialism and in particular a strike that was impregnated within meanings for what became a sectarian struggle within socialism itself. It would have been fascinating to see pictures at Ollerton, when women went to the picket lines to have a look. There were villages which suddenly had rows of police in the streets. Women would be going to the shops and they would come across masses of police. Would there have been a way of looking at the strike which would have highlighted that?

Gloria: One of the most memorable photographs of the exhibition is the one where the two pickets are reporting back to Maureen Page and Jill Fox the result of the NACODS's executive not to strike. A private moment of disappointment.

Bea: Men and women communicating with each other. It is one of the most telling pictures in an exhibition which is mostly about heroism and success. This is one of the few pictures which shows a relationship between men and women that must have been pleasurable for the women involved in the strike. The women were being reported to and consulted. The way it is composed, the woman sitting down is the central person. They are all actually doing nothing, being silent and thinking. You see the activity of thinking.

MICHELLE CLIFF

OBJECT INTO SUBJECT: SOME THOUGHTS ON THE WORK OF BLACK WOMEN ARTISTS

In my room there is a postcard of a sculpture by the Venetian artist Danese Cattaneo, done in the mid-sixteenth century – *Black Venus*. The full-length nude figure is bronze. In one hand she holds a hand-mirror in which she is looking at herself. On her head is a turban, around the edges of which her curls are visible. In her other hand she carries a cloth – or at least what appears to be a cloth. Who was she? A slave? Perhaps in the artist's own household, or maybe that of his patron – one of the many Black women dragged from Africa to enter the service of white Europeans. I have no idea who she actually was: she was an object, then as now.

Around this image are other images of Black women: Bernadette Powell, who killed the man who beat her and is now in Bedford Hills; Fannie Lou Hamer; Billie Holiday; Elizabeth Freeman, who sued for her freedom and won it, in Massachusetts in the nineteenth century; Josephine Baker; Harriet Tubman, portrayed in a linocut by Elizabeth Catlett; women students making basket furniture at the Hampton Institute; Lucy Parsons; Ida B. Wells-Barnett; Audre Lorde; Phillis Wheatley; two women in Botswana seated around a gourd; Sojourner Truth; women in the Black Liberation Movement in England; Betye Saar's Aunt Sally HooDoo; a girlchild balancing a basin on her head in southern Africa.

My moving toward the study of the work – written and visual – of Black women has been a moving toward my own wholeness. My interest in this work is a deeply personal interest, because through these words and images I begin to capture part of who I am.

I should begin with my title – *Object into Subject*. What does it mean? We live in a society whose history is drenched in the philosophy and practice of racism, the oppression of Black and other Third World peoples. This is the point at which my definition begins. If you study racism – if you understand the history of the United States – you will find that under racism the person who is oppressed is turned into an object in the mind of the oppressor.

The white anti-racist southern writer Lillian Smith was among the first to offer a metaphysical and psychological explanation of racism as a personal and political American practice.[2] One essential to the maintenance of things as they are in this society. Smith – whose influences included Kierkegaard, Jung, Freud, and Sartre –traced the origins of racism, and its more apparent manifestation, segregation, to that place in the human mind she called 'mythic': that place where dreams, fantasies, and images begin; where they continue and take form as art, literature, politics, religion. The mythic mind is a source of psychic energy – it contributes the motion necessary for sustained thought. But the mythic mind needs a structure in which to function, so that its products will be understood. This structure is provided by reason. Reason, Smith argued, is merely a technic, an enabler; its sole purpose is to create the form which will support the ideas moving out of the mythic mind. Reason is incapable of moral judgment, and therefore will support any idea or image, regardless of its moral basis.

When the mythic idea of whiteness, the obsession with skin color which is the irrational and immoral basis of racism, is given a construct from which the myth takes its form – i.e., the philosophy of white supremacy – the result is cultural or institutionalised racism, contained in the politics, literature, art, and religion of the dominant culture. An insane idea now exists within a reasonable reality, not an irrational dream.

Whatever we may feel about Smith's analysis, or her sources for that matter, her treatment of American racism as something embedded in the white mind, regenerating itself within a psychological construct, is extremely important. She recognised early on the character of racism as in a sense 'larger than life', something which could not be removed by congressional legislation or Supreme Court decisions, unless these actions were the result of a completely radicalised mind-set within the dominant culture. I think that the resurgence of white racism in this country today bears witness to her understanding.

Within the rationale reason lends to racism, Smith argued, is the practice of objectification, an absolute necessity in the racist effort to oppress. (I use the word 'effort' because it is and has been so; one which has been carried on on every level of this society, against constant, historic opposition.) Through objectification – the process by which people are dehumanised, made ghostlike, given the status of Other – an image created by the oppressor replaces the actual being. The actual being is then denied speech; denied self-definition, self-realisation; and over-arching all this, denied selfhood – which is after all the point of objectification. A group of human beings – a people – are denied their history, their language, their music. Their cultural values are ignored. This history, this language, this music, these values exist in the subculture, but in the dominant culture only certain elements are chosen, recast, co-opted, and made available to the definition of these people. And these elements presented by the dominant culture tend to serve the purpose of objectification and, therefore, oppression.

The practice of objectification stands between all Black people and full human identity under the white supremacist system: racism requires that Black people be thought different from white; and this difference is usually translated as less than. This requirement has been stated in various ways throughout the history of America. Did you know, for example, that Thomas Jefferson held the popular view that the Black race was created when Black women mated with orangutans?[2] (I do not know where the original Black women were supposed to have come from.)

Last October on my local PBS station I watched the film *Birth of a Nation*, introduced by a rather hearty film buff as an American classic, the work of a 'tragic poet'. I had never seen the movie, nor had I read the book *The Clansman*, upon which it is based. I felt I 'had to watch it'. The first thing I noticed was that all the Black characters were portrayed by white actors in 'black-face'. Throughout the film the thing most evident to me was that this was a playing-out of a white American's image of Black people, crude and baroque to be sure, but not that far removed from *Gone with the Wind* (another American classic), or even from such white-inspired television programs as *The Jeffersons*. If anything, the very coarse brutality of *Birth of a Nation* is closer to the history of the slavocracy than perhaps any other American film. I could see as I watched this film how white people were capable of committing both the acts of the slave period and the lynchings which flourished during Reconstruction and thereafter. D.W. Griffith's imaginings of Black women and men attempted to justify this history by replacing a people with the fantasies of his tragically racist mind. The very title gives his intention away.

The playwright and activist Lorraine Hansberry, in her essay *The New Paternalists*, observed:

> America long ago fell in love with an image. It is a sacred image, fashioned over centuries of time: this image of the unharried, unconcerned, glandulatory, simple, rhythmic, amoral, dark creature who was above all else, a *miracle of sensuality*. It was created, and it persists, to provide a personified pressure valve for fanciful longings in (white) American dreams, literature, and life...I think, for example, of that reviewer writing in a Connecticut newspaper about *A Raisin in the Sun*...and marvelling, in the rush of a quite genuine enthusiasm, that the play proved again that there was a quaint loveliness in how our 'dusky brethren' can come up with a song and hum their troubles away. It did not seem to disturb him one whit that there is no single allusion to that particular mythical gift in the entire play. He did not need it there; it was in his head.[3]

Just as this white reviewer could hear Black people humming as he watched Hansberry's play, others could declare it a play about insurance money, one which proved that all Black people really wanted was to live alongside whites. Many white people perceived the ending of *Raisin* as 'happy', unaware perhaps of what it meant for a Black family to move into a white neighbourhood in Chicago in the post-World War II years. Did any of these white people know of Hansberry's own childhood experience when her family moved into a white Chicago neighbourhood? The response to this move was white violence: the eight-year-old Hansberry had a brick thrown through her bedroom window by the white mob. Her father, supported by the NAACP, took the case all the way to the Supreme Court and established a precedent for nondiscriminatory housing – but nothing in Chicago actually changed.

If anything, the ending of *Raisin* is hopeful, not happy. And the hopefulness one feels derives not from any expectation of a white change-of-heart, but from the fact that Hansberry has tested her characters throughout the play and they have emerged as people of integrity, capable of facing reality and white racism. She was, I think, attempting to create Black characters who would disrupt white imagery of Black people. But many in her audience could only see these characters through their own screen of objectification.

It is objectification that gives the impression of sanity to the process of oppression. The centuries-old image of which Hansberry speaks, actually a collection of images, is necessary to maintain racism. To hate with no justification for hatred, to oppress with no reason for oppression, would be recognizably insane. Once an object is provided – an object endowed by the oppressor with characteristics that allow hatred, that allow oppression – then hatred and oppression of the object can be defended as logical. An insane idea has been made rational. Lillian Smith portrayed this basic insanity of segregation in the South she knew:

> As I sit here writing, I can almost touch that little town, so close is the memory of it. There it lies, its main street lined with great oaks, heavy with matted moss that swings softly even now as I remember. A little white town rimmed with Negroes, making a deep shadow on the whiteness. There it lies, broken in two by one strange idea. Minds broken in two. Hearts broken. Conscience torn from acts. A culture split into a thousand pieces. That is segregation. I am remembering: a woman in a mental hospital walking four steps out, four steps in, unable to go any further because she has drawn an invisible line around her small world and is terrified to take one step beyond it...A man in a Disturbed Ward assigning 'places' to the other patients and violently insisting that each stay in his place.[4]

'Segregation', for Smith, described a phenomenon deeper than legal statute or town custom. She saw segregation as a form of dichotomizing within the white Western male tradition. She observed, for example, that white women are segregated from Black women and also objectified within the dominant culture:

> Another split took place...Somehow much in the white woman that (man) could not come to terms with, the schizophrenic split he had made in her nature – the sacred madonna and the bitch he had created of her – could now be projected, in part, onto another female: under slavery, he could keep his pure white 'madonna' and have his dark tempestuous 'prostitute'...Back of southern people's fear of giving up segregation is this fear of giving up the 'dark woman' who has become a symbol which the men no longer wish to attach to their own women.[5]

Smith's observation is important: white and Black women were/are both objectified and split from one another. I feel that Smith oversimplified the split, however. For example, the sacred madonna, in order to maintain her status (and most often she was intent on maintaining her status), had to objectify the Black woman according to the white male imagination. The white woman on the slave plantation knew that white men used rape against Black women. She knew that Black women were for the most part fieldhands, working alongside men – when they were pregnant, when they were nursing. The Black woman was made into a sex object, yes, but Smith's use of the word 'prostitute', even in quotes, suggests more choice than any slave woman ever had. It also denies or glosses over the use of rapism by white men against Black women as an instrument of terror, of oppression.

Black women have been doubly objectified – as Black, as women; under white supremacy, under patriarchy. It has been the task of Black woman artists to transform this objectification: to become the *subject* commenting on the meaning of the object, or to become the subject rejecting the object and revealing the *real* experience of being. In her essay 'In Search of Our Mothers' Gardens', Alice Walker ponders the degree of difficulty faced by a Black woman with artistic ambition: 'What did it mean for a black woman to be an artist in our grandmothers' time? In our great-grandmothers' day? It is a question with an answer cruel enough to stop the blood.'[6]

In her novel *Sula*, Toni Morrison makes the following observation about the seemingly destructive nature of her main character:

> In a way, her strangeness, her naiveté, her craving for the other half of her equation was the consequence of an idle imagination. Had she paints, or clay, or knew the discipline of the dance, or strings; had she anything to engage her tremendous curiosity and her gift for metaphor, she might have exchanged the restlessness and preoccupation with

whim for an activity that provided her with all she yearned for. And like any artist with no art form, she became dangerous.[7]

Sula's tragedy, and the tragedy she represents, is 'cruel enough to stop the blood'. Because of her race, perhaps also because of her sex, she has been shut out from art and denied access to art forms. She is an intelligent, thinking woman, who ultimately has nowhere to go.

The objectification of Black women has taken many forms: The Mammy, Mama – wetnurse, midwife, cook – usually large, usually dark, combining humility and capability. The temptress, sex-object, whore – sometimes mulatto (from the Latin for mule, i.e., a creature unable to reproduce herself) – misbegotten and tragic, the power of the master coursing through her powerless veins. These are but two examples which recur in white Western literature and art. And these have been repeated by white women as well as white men. There is, of course, 'Mammy' in *Gone with the Wind*; and there is Julie, the woe-begone quadroon in Edna Ferber's *Showboat*. Another novel, *Imitation of Life* by Fanny Hurst, attempts to 'deal with' both Mammy and mulatto.

By many accounts, Fanny Hurst was a well-intentioned liberal. Much has been made, for example, of the fact that she employed Zora Neale Hurston as her secretary in 1925. But some of that history suggests Hurst's insensitivity to Hurston's identity as a Black woman, not to mention a brilliant novelist and writer, among whose subjects was the self-definition of Black women. On one occasion Hurst, intent on integrating a restaurant in Vermont, prevailed upon Hurston to accompany her – passing Hurston off as an 'African princess'. Hurston remarked, 'Who would have thought that a good meal could be so bitter?'[8] In this incident Hurst, the would-be liberator, reveals herself as objectifier. This phenomenon occurred over and again during the Civil Rights Movement. It was most commonly expressed in the notion that unless Black people behaved in certain ways, allowing whites to oversee and control their access to liberation, that liberation would not be achieved. What is present is the need for whites to maintain power, and limit the access of Black people to that power, which, finally, is the power of self-definition.

Imitation of Life, published in 1933, concerns the relationship between two dyads: a white woman and her daughter and a Black woman and her daughter. Both pairs are essentially alone in the world. The Black woman, Delilah, is hired to run the house by the white woman, Miss B., who has been recently widowed. Delilah carries with her various recipes, and these prove to be the 'salvation' of Miss B. and family. In a relatively short time, Miss B. is the proprietor of a chain of restaurants in which Delilah's food is the main attraction, and which are recognised by a likeness of Delilah on the sign. When Miss B. hits on the idea of photographing Delilah as the advertising gimmick for the enterprise, she dresses Delilah as a chef. Delilah, faithful servant throughout the book, in this one instance asks her employer not to humiliate her but to allow her to wear her best clothes.

Miss B., however, prevails. Hurst describes the final result: 'Breaking through a white background, as through a paper-covered hoop, there burst the chocolate-and-cream effulgence that was Delilah'.[9] Here is Aunt Jemima; the female server of Sanka; even Mrs. Butterworth, whose color literally pours forth. Here is an instance of the brainchild of a Black woman, her recipe, her art form, passed through generations of Black women, co-opted and sold, with a caricature of the artist used to ensure its success.

In and around the main theme of the novel – the 'success' of Miss B. as an 'independent businesswoman' – is the subplot concerning Delilah's light-skinned daughter, Peola – unable to be white, unwilling to be Black, in the course of her dilemma denying her mother. Peola moves west, works as a librarian, passes for white, and marries a white man. She has herself 'sterilized', eliminating any chance of 'throwback'. Her husband is also mutilated, having lost part of a hand. Perhaps he is all she is entitled to. Delilah has the final say: 'Black women who pass, pass into damnation'.

Taken together, Delilah and Peola represent what George Frederickson has characterised as 'soft' and 'hard' stereotypes.[10] Bell Hooks also juxtaposes two stereotypes of Black women: Mammy and Sapphire.

> It is not too difficult to imagine how whites came to create the black mammy figure...She was first and foremost asexual and consequently had to be fat (preferably obese); she also had to give the impression of not being clean so she was the wearer of a greasy dirty headrag; her too tight shoes from which emerged her large feet were further confirmation of her bestial cowlike quality. Her greatest virtue was of course her love for white folk which she willingly and passively served...In a sense whites created in the mammy figure a black woman who embodied solely those characteristics they as colonizers wished to exploit.[11]
>
> As Sapphires, black women were depicted as evil, treacherous, bitchy, stubborn, and hateful, in short all that the mammy was not. White men could justify their de-humanization and sexual exploitation of black women by arguing that they possessed inherent evil demonic qualities...And white women could use the image of the evil sinful black woman to emphasise their own innocence and purity.[12]

To talk about the history of Black women in America, and of the various images I have mentioned, we must begin with the woman who was a slave. Who was she? How did she survive? How many of her did survive? What did she teach her children? What was her relationship to her husband? What were her options?

She could be lynched, beaten, tortured, mutilated, raped. She could have her children sold away from her. She was forbidden education. She was considered a beast of burden. She was subject to the white man's power and the white woman's powerlessness masking as whim. Her womb was a commodity of the slavemaster, and her childlessness, a liability of the slavemaster. She was not expected to love – but she did. She was not expected to run away – but she did. She was known to commit infanticide and induce abortion rather than have her child be a slave. She was known to commit acts of violence and rebellion – with magic, poison, force, even with spit. And she sometimes learned to read and write and sustain the art forms she had carried with her.

In 1960 Lorraine Hansberry was commissioned to write a play about slavery for national television. She wrote *The Drinking Gourd*, about a Black family and a white family under slavery. In it, as in *Raisin*, Hansberry attempted to contradict the myths about Black people and to recapture and recast history. Her play was never performed; it was judged 'too controversial' by the network. Hansberry had described Lena Younger, her mother-figure in *Raisin*, as an 'affirmation', as

> the black matriarch incarnate, the bulwark of the Negro family since slavery, the embodiment of the Negro will to transcendence. It is she, who in the mind of the black poet scrubs the floors of a nation in order to create black diplomats and university professors. It is she, while seeming to cling to traditional restraints, who drives the young on into the fire hoses. And one day simply refuses to move to the back of the bus in Montgomery. Or goes out and buys a house in an all-white neighbourhood where her children may possibly be killed by bricks thrown through the windows by a shrieking racist mob.[13]

With her mother-figure in *The Drinking Gourd*, Hansberry went further. Rissa, the slavemother, does what the Black mother-figure in white American mythology has never done: she, in effect, kills a white man (the 'good' white man), and gives his guns to her children, after her son has been blinded for learning to read. The play ends as Rissa and her band of revolutionaries escape into the woods.

We know that Black women – mothers and nonmothers – have been intrinsic to the activism of Black history. There is the following story, for example, quoted by Angela Davis:

> She didn't work in the field. She worked at a loom. She worked so long and so often that once she went to sleep at the loom. Her master's boy saw her and told his mother. His mother told him to take a whip and wear her out. He took a stick and went out to beat her awake. He beat my mother till she woke up. When she woke up, she took a pole out of the loom and beat him nearly to death with it. He hollered, 'Don't beat me no more, and I won't let 'em whip you'.

She said, 'I'm going to kill you. These black titties sucked you, and then you come out here to beat me'. And when she left him, he wasn't able to walk.

And that was the last I seen of her until after freedom. She went out and got an old cow that she used to milk – Dolly, she called it. She rode away from the plantation because she knew they would kill her if she stayed.[14]

This story tells of a Black woman in the act of freeing herself. A selfish need for freedom, and a recognition that freedom is their right, is something usually denied to Black women historically, even when they are recognised as liberators of their race. But Fannie Lou Hamer, Ida B. Wells, Mary McLeod Bethune, Sojourner Truth – and the many women whose names we do not know – all felt a personal desire for freedom, which came from a feeling of self-esteem, self-worth, and they translated this into a political commitment that their people also be free. Harriet Tubman said:

I looked at my hands to see if I was de same person now I was free. Dere was such a glory ober eberything, de sun came like gold trou de trees, and ober de fields, and I felt like I was in heaven.

I had crossed de line of which I had so long been dreaming. I was free; but dere was no one to welcome me to de land of freedom. I was a stranger in a strange land, and my home after all was down in de ole cabin quarter, wid de ole folks, and my brudders and sisters. But to dis solemn resolution I came; I was free, and dey should be free also; I would make a home for dem in de North, and de Lord helping me, I would bring dem all dere.[15]

The artist, like the liberator, must begin with herself.

Edmonia Lewis (1843-1900?) is the first woman of color we know whose work as a visual artist was recognised by the dominant culture. During her life as a sculptor she was confronted with the objectification of herself as Black and female. While her work was not ignored, it was given a secondary place of importance by most critics. Lewis was seen as a 'wonder', a work of art in herself – a curiosity. The following excerpt from an abolitionist newspaper describes the artist and her marble group *Forever Free* (1867):

No one...could look upon this piece of sculpture without profound emotion. The noble figure of the man, his very muscles seeming to swell with gratitude; the expression of the right now to protect, with which he throws his arms around his kneeling wife; the 'Praise de Lord' hovering on their lips; the broken chain – all so instinct with life, telling in the very poetry of stone the story of the last ten years. And when it is remembered who created this group, an added interest is given to it...Will anyone believe it was the small hand of a girl that wrought the marble and kindled the light within it? – a girl of dusky hue, mixed Indian and African, who not more than eight years ago sat down on the steps of City Hall to eat the dry crackers with which alone her empty purse allowed her to satisfy her hunger; but as she sat and thought...of her homeless state, something caught her eye, the hunger of the stomach ceased, but the hunger of the soul began. That quiet statue of the good old Franklin...kindled the latent genius which was enshrined within her, as her own group was in marble, till her chisel brought it out. For weeks she haunted that spot and the State House, where she could see Washington and Webster. She asked questions, and found that such things were first made in clay. She got a lump of hard mud, shaped her some sticks, and, her heart divided between art and the terrible need for freedom...she wrought out...an admirable bust of Col. Robert Gould Shaw, white Bostonian commander of a company of Black troops organised due to pressure from Frederick Douglass.[16]

When this article was written Lewis was a well-known sculptor living in Rome, with a degree in liberal arts from Oberlin College. She had studied sculpture with Edward Brackett, a prominent neoclassical artist. She was not particularly interested in creating likenesses of Franklin, Washington, or Webster – her interest in these pieces would have been purely technical, not inspirational. The only 'leader' of white America she ever depicted was Abraham Lincoln. All her other subjects were drawn from her history as the daughter of a Black man and a Chippewa woman, and her consciousness of racism.

Just as the author patronizes the artist, so does he minimise the political statement of her work. For instance, he uses the word 'gratitude' rather than 'pride', or 'triumph', in his comments on the male figure; he focuses on the arm which embraces the woman, rather than on the hand which is raised, the broken chain dangling from the wrist. He cites the struggle of the last 'ten' years with typical white solipsism. In addition, his 'Praise de Lord' does not allow us knowledge of the politics of Black Americans, to which religion has been historically intrinsic. Rather, it can be read in such a way that the triumph is taken from the hands of those who have won it and placed somewhere 'out there'.

It is commonly believed that the slaves were freed by white Northerners. But as W.E.B. Du Bois observed: 'In proportion to population, more Negroes than whites fought in the Civil War. These people, withdrawn from the support of the Confederacy, with the threat of the withdrawal of millions more, made the opposition of the slaveholder useless, unless they themselves freed and armed their own slaves'.[17] The journey out of slavery was one in which Black people played a dominant role. It is this that Lewis is commemorating in her work. She had earlier commemorated the slave-woman in her piece *Freedwoman on First Hearing of Her Liberty* (which has been lost to us).

In an interview with the *Lorain County News*, Lewis spoke of her childhood:

> My mother was a wild Indian and was born in Albany, of copper color and with straight black hair. There she made and sold moccasins. My father, who was a Negro, and a gentleman's servant, saw her and married her...Mother often left home and wandered with her people, whose habits she could not forget, and thus we were brought up in the same wild manner. Until I was twelve years old, I led this wandering life, fishing and swimming...and making moccasins.[18]

Alice Walker speaks about looking 'high – and low' for the artistic antecedents of Black women; she speaks specifically of her own mother's garden – how this was the place of her mother's creative expression, the background against which Walker's own work proceeded: 'Guided by my heritage of a love of beauty and a respect for strength – in search of my mother's garden I found my own'.[19] This statement makes me think of Lewis's mother, her independence and her craft. The fact that she trained her daughter in her art form. That she taught her strength.

Lewis's sculpture, because she chose primarily to depict subjects directly related to her own and her people's experience, has a certain power. Where her pieces lose power is in the style she adopted and the material she used: the neo-classical style, with its emphatic focus on Greek idealization, and the pristine whiteness of the marble, which supports the narrowness of the style – so that a black face must appear white and be carved according to principles of beauty which are white, 'fine' features as perfection. The nineteenth century was the century of jubilee, of a women's movement, and of a revolutionary movement in Europe. But these moral reactions need to be understood against the immorality which dominated that century: the 'white man's burden', the political/religious/economic affirmation of the supremacy of the white race. The neo-classical style arose quite naturally from all this, based as it was on the imitation of fifth-century Athens, a slave-owning, gynephobic society, but one popularly regarded as high-minded and democratic. In Lewis's *Forever Free* the limitations placed on a Black and Indian artist working in this style and with this material are evident: the curly hair of the male figure and the broken chain are the only signs that these are people of color.

Of her sculpture *Hagar* (1875), Lewis said: 'I have a strong sympathy for all women who have struggled and suffered'.[20] Again, we have to look beyond the actual figure to the story Lewis is illustrating to find the political/historical statement in her work. Hagar was an Egyptian, a woman of color, the slave of Abraham's wife, Sarah. Hagar was 'given' to Abraham by Sarah so that he might have an heir; and she was the mother of his first-born son, Ishmael. Then Isaac was born to Abraham and Sarah. The book of Genesis continues the story:

> Sarah saw the son of Hagar the Egyptian, whom she had borne to Abraham, playing with her son Isaac. So she said to Abraham, 'Cast out this slave woman with her son; for the son of this slave woman shall not be heir with my son Isaac'. And the thing was very displeasing to Abraham on account of his son. But God said to Abraham, 'Be not displeased because of the lad and because of your slave woman; whatever Sarah says to you, do as she tells you, for through Isaac shall your descendants be named...' So Abraham rose early in the morning...and sent (Hagar) away. And she departed, and wandered in the wilderness Beer-sheba.[21]

It is quite impossible to read this story and not think of the Black woman under slavery, raped by the white master, serving the white master's wife, bearing a child by the white master, and bearing the responsibility for that child – with no power over her own fate, or that of her child. Lewis's choice of Hagar as a symbol for Black slave-women also fits into the Black tradition in America, one immersed in the stories of the Bible (often the Bible was the only access slaves had to the written word), and characterized by the translation of these stories according to Black history.

In reading this account from Genesis, I am also thrown back to Lillian Smith's description of the split between Black and white women. It is Sarah who is made responsible for the banishment of Hagar. Her husband and his god remain blameless, even noble.

After approximately ten years of recognition, Edmonia Lewis 'disappeared'. This sort of falling out of fame is usually seen as tragic, but I wonder what happened to her? Was her disappearance by choice? Or did she disappear because she was a Black woman artist who was no longer in vogue, because she was no longer seen as 'exotic'?

In contrast to Lewis's white marble sculptures, Elizabeth Catlett's figures are done in brown wood or terra cotta, or another material which suggests the color of her subjects, or at least that her subjects are people of color. No white Western features replace the characteristics of Black and other Third World people. But Catlett is a contemporary artist, one who relatively early in her career left this country and moved to a country of colored people – Mexico.

Yet her piece *Homage to My Young Black Sisters* (1969), when we make allowances over time and across space, is not that far removed in political intent from Lewis's *Hagar*. In form the differences are enormous: Hagar's hands are clasped in front of her, in resignation, in supplication – in the wilderness she has to turn to Abraham's god to save the life of her son. The female figure of *Homage* has one arm raised in a powerful and defiant fist. The similarity between the two pieces is that both, I think, represent part of the history of Black women, particularly Black motherhood, in America. The midsection of the *Homage* figure is an open space, which I take as Catlett's statement of the historical white denial of Black women's right to motherhood in any self-defining way, and of the theft of the children of Black women, and of what these children represent – whether through the laws of the slavocracy or those of postindustrial America.

Catlett uses the theme of Black women and children often in her work, depicting over and again the heroism required of Black women simply to survive. In her lithographs, engravings, and linocuts, Catlett seeks to tell the history of Black women, breaking away from the objectification of the dominant culture. We might, for example, look at her wood engraving of Harriet Tubman (1975), in contrast to Judy Chicago's Sojourner Truth plate in the *Dinner Party*.[22] Catlett's Harriet dominates the foreground; one powerful arm points forward, the other holds a rifle. She is tall and she is strong and she is Black. In the background are the men and women she leads. What is interesting to me is the expression on Tubman's face – she is fiercely determined. This expression is repeated in the group she leads. There is no passivity here, no resignation, no impotent tears, no 'humming'. Rather, this is a portrait of the activity of a people in conflict with their oppression.

Catlett has stated that art should be obviously political, available to the people who are its subject. We have no such clear statement from Lewis, but we must wonder for whom her work was done, finally: and whether she stopped working as she did because of a distance between her art and her subjects.

Harriet Powers (1837-1911) was a quilt-maker (only two of her quilts are known to survive). She worked in appliqué, a method of needlework devised by the Fon of Dahomey, brought to this country on slave ships.[23] Betye Saar is a collector; an artist who constructs images with various objects, mementos, photographs, bits and pieces picked up here and there and saved; things used in another context, by other hands. Both Powers and Saar endow their work with a belief in the spiritual nature of the ordinary. Powers's quilts, constructed from the scraps saved by a poor Black woman, convey a real portrait of one Black woman's religion and politics. Marie Jeane Adams states: 'The more one examines the style and content of Harriet Powers's work, the more one sees that it projects a grand spiritual vision that breaks out of the confines of folk art'.[24]

The employment of once-used objects by these artists is one aspect of their work which needs further thought. In the history of white Western art there is an obsession with the purity of materials. And also with their value. For one example: in the art of fifteenth-century Italy, and even earlier, the color ultramarine was often used to depict the most important figure or feature in a painting or fresco. This choice was made with the knowledge that the color was created by crushing lapis lazuli, the most expensive source of pigment after gold.[25] And this choice extended to the very meaning of the work produced. In the art of Powers and Saar, the sources of the artist's materials are also important, but the choice is more deeply personal. We might ask: how much does the power of a work of art consist in the material which makes up that work? What is the difference between a work of art made with things specifically employed in that work and never before? Is one more useful than the other? More magical than the other?

We know of Harriet Powers's work partly because of a white woman – Jennie Smith, herself an artist – who left an 18-page monograph on the artist. She recorded the following in 1891, when Powers finally agreed to sell her a quilt:

> I found the owner, a negro woman, who lived in the country on a little farm whereon she and her husband made a respectable living...Last year I sent word that I would buy it if she still wanted to dispose of it. She arrived one afternoon in front of my door...with the precious burden...encased in a clean crocus sack.
>
> She offered it for ten dollars, but I told her I only had five to give. After going out consulting with her husband she returned and said, 'Owin' to de hardness of de times, my old man 'lows I'd better teck hit'. Not being a new woman she obeyed.
>
> After giving me a full description of each scene with great earnestness, she departed but has been back several times to visit the darling offspring of her brain.[26]

Powers's second quilt – now in the Boston Museum of Fine Arts – was commissioned in 1898 by the wives of professors at Atlanta University. This quilt, known as the second Bible quilt, consists of five columns, each divided into three frames. All the frames deal with the theme of God's vengeance and redemption, illustrated through Biblical images and representations of cataclysmic events in eighteenth and nineteenth-century America.

> This...much-exhibited quilt portrays fifteen scenes. Ten are drawn from familiar Bible stories which concern the threat of God's judgment inextricably fused with His mercy and man's redemption, among which are the Fall, Moses in the wilderness, Job's trials, Jonah and the whale, the Baptism of Christ and the Crucifixion...Four others depict astronomical or meteorological events, only one of which, an extremely cold spell in 1895 in the eastern United States, occurred in Mrs. Powers' adult life. Given Mrs. Powers' intensely religious outlook, she interpreted these events in the celestial atmosphere as messages from God to mankind about punishment, apocalypse, and salvation.[27]

The one frame which does not fit into this categorization is the one which, as Marie Jeane Adams observes, is the key to the quilt. Powers left a description in her own words of all the scenes in the quilt; of this particular frame she said:

> Rich people who were taught nothing of God. Bob Johnson and Kate Bell of Virginia. They told their parents to stop the clock at one and tomorrow it would strike one and so it did. This was the signal that they had entered everlasting punishment. The independent hog which ran 500 miles from Ga. to Va. Her name was Betts.[28]

The frame has a clock in the center, stars and a moon scattered around, two human figures. At the bottom is the independent hog named Betts, the largest figure of the quilt. Metallic thread outlines the clockface and creates a tiara around the head of the white woman Kate Bell. Betts is made from gray cloth, but she is placed over a swatch of orange so that her figure unmistakably stands out.

This quilt represents a great spiritual vision, but it also represents a great political vision: as well as hope, it represents rage. It is a safe guess that Bob Johnson and Kate Bell of Virginia were a son and daughter of the slavocracy. They stand surrounded by scenes representing the punishment meted out to those who are arrogant and self-serving, and the redemption promised those who are righteous. In this particular frame it is their sin of pride which has damned them; and Powers is clear in her belief that their damnation is well-earned. In contrast is the dominating figure of Betts, who in an act of self-liberation goes free. Her 500-mile flight from Georgia to Virginia is, as Adams points out, a reference to one route traveled by runaway slaves. And Betts is undeniably female – her teats hang down from her gray-cloth body. I think of Dolly – the cow in the anecdote cited above – being ridden away by a Black woman. And I think of the white idea of Black women as beasts of burden, 'mules', farm animals; of the image of Harriet Tubman being forced to draw a wagon for the entertainment of white folks. I take Betts to be a metaphor for this experience. Angela Davis has quoted Frederick Law Olmstead's description of a slave crew in Mississippi returning from the fields:

> (I saw) forty of the largest and strongest women I ever saw together; they were all in a simple uniform dress of a bluish check stuff; their legs and feet were bare; they carried themselves loftily, each having a hoe over the shoulder, and walking with a free, powerful swing like chausseurs on the march.[29]

It would be very simple to romanticize this group of women. But, as Davis says, it is not slavery and the slave system that have made them strong; it is the experience of their labor and their knowledge of themselves as producers and creators. She quotes Marx: 'labor is the living, shaping fire; it represents the impermanence of things, their temporality.' Davis makes a brilliant connection here:

> ...perhaps these women had learned to extract from the oppressive circumstances of their lives the strength they needed to resist the daily dehumanization of slavery. Their awareness of their endless capacity for hard work may have imparted to them a confidence in their ability to struggle for themselves, their families and their people.[30]

Black women were not dehumanized under slavery; they were dehumanized in white minds. I return again and again in my own mind to the adjective 'independent', which Powers uses to describe Betts, a 'chasseur on the march'.

It is not that far a distance from Lewis's *Hagar*, to Catlett's *Homage*, to Powers's Betts, to Betye Saar's *Aunt Jemima*. Saar's construction, entitled *The Liberation of Aunt Jemima*, is perhaps the most obvious illustration of what I mean by the title of this essay: 'Object into Subject'. Here is the most popularized image of the Mammy – in the center of the piece she is a cookie jar, the source of nourishment for others; behind her are faces cut from the pancake mix. In front of the central figure is another image of Mammy, holding a white baby. And there is a broom alongside the central figure. But she also holds a pistol and a rifle; and the skirt of Mammy with the white baby forms an unmistakable Black fist. Saar's message is clear: Aunt Jemima will free herself.

In an interview in *Black Art*, Saar described the components she uses in her work:

> They are all found objects or discarded objects, so they have to be remnants. They are connected with another sensitivity so it has to be a memory of belonging to another object, or at least having another function.[31]

Aunt Jemima has been created by another sensitivity than that of the artist who has made this portrait. Aunt Jemima has a memory of belonging to someone else, of being at the service of someone else. She exists against an image, which exists in another mind. The cookie jar is a remnant of another life: most likely she 'lived' on the kitchen counter of a white family, maybe Saar found her discarded on a white elephant table, or at a garage sale. She has appeared to me in my travels, usually turning up in rural antique stores or church basements, labelled 'collectible'. The picture of Mammy with the white baby reminds me first of old magazine advertisements, usually, as I recall, for soap or cereal or other necessities of the servant role. And I additionally recall the many films of the forties and fifties about white middle-class America, in which a large Black woman who worked in the kitchen was always present but only occasionally given a line to speak. She was played by Louise Beavers, Hattie McDaniel, or Ethel Waters – and she was usually characterized by her loyalty to the white family for whom she worked. She also appeared on television: *Beulah* was a program in which she was featured. She was kind, honest, a good cook, always with a song to hum her troubles away; and as usual, devoted to those white folks.

All but three of the elements in Saar's construction are traditional to Aunt Jemima; the two guns and the fist are not. Saar, by including these unfamiliar aspects, has changed the function of the figure she is representing. She has combined the myth with the reality of Black women's historic opposition to their oppression.

This representation of Aunt Jemima is startling. All of us who have grown up with the mythical figure of Aunt Jemima and her equally mythical attributes – whether or not we recognized they were mythic – have been affected. We may not have known her, but aren't we somehow convinced that somewhere she exists, or at least has existed? The last thing we would expect would be that she would carry a gun, or raise a hand. As a child in Jamaica I was taught that the women who worked for us were to be respected and obeyed, and yet I remember my twelve-year-old light-skinned self exercising what I felt was my authority over these women, and being quite taken aback when one of the women threatened to beat me – and my mother backed her up. Just as I was shocked to find that another houseworker had tied up my cousins and shut them on the verandah because they were interfering with her work.

So while we may know the image is an image, the expectations of Black women behaving according to this image persist. As far as I can tell, Harriet Tubman carried both a carbine and a pistol. And she threatened to shoot any slave who decided to turn back on the journey north. Just as Lorraine Hansberry's slavemother armed her children and set out with them – after leaving a white man to die.

NOTES

1 For Lillian Smith's definition of racism, see 'The Mob and the Ghost' and 'Words That Chain Us and Words That Set Us Free', in *The Winner Names the Age*, ed. Michelle Cliff, New York: Norton, 1978.
2 Erlene Stetson, 'Studying Slavery', in *But Some of Us Are Brave*, eds. Gloria T. Hull, Patricia Bell Scott & Barbara Smith, Old Westbury, N.Y.: Feminist Press, 1981.
3 Lorraine Hansberry, quoted in *Les Blancs: The Collected Last Plays of Lorraine Hansberry*, ed. Robert Nemiroff, New York: Vintage, 1973, p. 206.
4 Lillian Smith, *Killers of the Dream*, New York: Norton, 1949, p. 31.
5 Smith, *Winner*, p. 204.
6 Alice Walker, 'In Search of Our Mothers' Gardens', in *Working It Out*, eds. Sara

Ruddick & Pamela Daniels, New York: Pantheon, 1977, p. 94.

7 Toni Morrison, *Sula*, New York: Bantam, 1975, p. 105.

8 Quoted by Robert Hemenway, *Zora Neale Hurston*, Urbana: University of Illinois Press, 1977, p. 24.

9 Fannie Hurst, *Imitation of Life*, New York: Harper & Bros., 1933, p. 105.

10 Although Frederickson's *The Black Image in the White Mind* deals primarily with stereotypes of Black men, with some alterations his categories apply to stereotypes of Black women.

11 Bell Hooks, *Ain't I a Woman*, Boston: South End, 1981, p. 84.

12 Ibid., p. 85.

13 Hansberry, *Winner*, p. 210.

14 Angela Davis, 'The Black Woman's Role in the Community of Slaves', *Black Scholar*, 1971, p. 13.

15 Quoted by Sarah Bradford, *Harriet Tubman; Moses of Her People*, Secaucus, N.J.: Citadel, 1974, rpt., pp. 30-32.

16 Quoted by Phebe A. Hanaford, *Daughters of America*, Augusta, Me: True, n.d., pp. 296-97.

17 Quoted by Sara Bennett & Joan Gibbs, 'Racism and Classism in the Lesbian Community', in *Top Ranking*, eds. Bennett & Gibbs, Brooklyn: February 3rd Press, 1980, pp. 14-15.

18 Quoted by Eleanor Tufts, *Our Hidden Heritage*, New York: Paddington, 1974, p. 159.

19 Walker, 'Gardens', p. 101.

20 Tufts, *Heritage*, p. 163.

21 Genesis, 21:9-14.

22 For a brilliant analysis of the Sojourner Truth plate in Chicago's *Dinner Party*, see Alice Walker, 'One Child of One's Own', in *But Some of Us Are Brave*.

23 This detail, and most of the information about Powers and her quilt, comes from Marie Jeane Adams, 'The Harriet Powers Pictorial Quilts', *Black Art*, vol. 3, no. 4, pp. 12-28.

24 Ibid., p. 16.

25 Michael Baxandall, *Painting and Experience in Fifteenth-Century Italy*, London: Oxford University Press, 1972, p. 9 ff.

26 Quoted by Mirra Bank, *Anonymous was a Woman*, New York: St. Martin's, 1979, p. 118.

27 Adams, 'Powers', p. 14.

28 Mrs. Powers's description of the quilt appears in both Adams and Bank.

29 Davis, 'Black Woman's Role', p. 11.

30 Ibid.

31 Betye Saar, 'Interview with Houston Conwill', *Black Art*, vol. 3, no. 1, p. 9.

GLORIA FEMAN ORENSTEIN

THE RE-EMERGENCE OF THE ARCHETYPE OF THE GREAT GODDESS IN ART BY CONTEMPORARY WOMEN

As the archetype of the Great Goddess reemerges into consciousness today, women artists, through transpersonal visionary experiences, are bringing to light energic psychic forces, symbols, images, artifacts and rituals whose configurations constitute the basic paradigm of a new feminist myth for our time.

> When a psychological need arises it seems inevitably the deeper layers of the collective unconscious are activated and sooner or later the memory of a myth of an event or an earlier psychic state emerges into consciousness.[1]

Evoking the memory of an earlier psychic state, one in which divinity was seen to reside in matter and the energies of the earth were revered as sacred, the Goddess has become that symbol of transformation which activates those forces within woman identified with holiness and with creative power. If the artist is the avatar of the new age, the alchemist whose great Art is the transformation of consciousness and being, then contemporary women artists such as Mary Beth Edelson, Carolee Schneemann, Mimi Lobell, Buffie Johnson, Judy Chicago, Donna Byars, Donna Henes, Miriam Sharon, Ana Mendieta, Betsy Damon, Betye Saar, Monica Sjoo and Hannah Kay, by summoning up the powers associated with the Goddess archetype, are energising a new form of Goddess consciousness, which, in its most recent manifestation is exorcising the patriarchal creation myth through a repossession of the female visionary faculties.

This new Goddess consciousness might be described most effectively as a holistic mind-body totality. As we move away from the cultural dominance of the masculine archetype, characterised by a mind-body duality, we find that the model of the sorcerer's vision serves as a corrective alternative for a

158

consciousness expansion in which intuitive body-knowledge is reaffirmed as a faculty of intelligence. Transcending the false dualities and dichotomies established by patriarchal systems of thought which split mind from body, spirit from matter and sacred from profane, the Great Goddess as a psychic symbol suggests the rebirth of woman to a holistic psychophysical perception of the sacred, as a new form of her feminist evolution.

Artists who are in touch with the archetype of the Goddess are now using the female form in both image and ritual as an instrument of spirit-knowledge. They are training the body so that it functions as a conscious perceptor and transformer of the powerful energies that reside in matter, both animal and vegetable. Through the psychophysical participation in Edelson's magical ceremonies of evocation, through the transformation of the body into a living totem in Damon's rituals, through the stimulation of the body via meditation upon the power points in the body icons of Kurz's self-portrait as the Durga, or Mailman's mirror image as God, through the fusion of the body with the earth itself in Mendieta's alchemical burials, through the sacrilisation of the body in Lobell's Goddess Temple, and through merging with the spirit of the Goddess in Suzanne Benton's masked ritual theater, women are gradually repossessing the powers long associated with the various manifestations of the archetype of the Goddess.

This new art (in which the archetype of the Goddess plays a catalytic role) is not based upon an original creation myth connected with the fertility and birth mysteries. In its modern transformed meaning, it is about the mysteries of woman's rebirth from the womb of historical darkness, in which her powers were so long enshrouded, into a new era where a culture of her own making will come about as a result of a new Earth Alchemy.

If the alchemy performed by the male magician sought essentially to purify brute matter by transforming it into spirit, taking gold or the philosopher's stone as the symbol of spiritual enlightenment, the supreme goal of alchemy for women artists today is to restore the spirit already inherent in the natural world; to consider matter itself as a storehouse of the potent energies most available for transformations in their natural organic state. Women are attempting nothing less than the magical dealchemising of the philosopher's stone, the reconstitution of the Earth Goddess's original herborium on the planet and the energising of the self through the internalisation of its sacred spirits. It is no mere coincidence that the alchemical symbols of 'witchcraft', the magic of the wise women who worshipped the Goddess, are herbs, grains, plants and seeds. The desire to alter both mental and physical functioning translates an impulse to integrate the Earth Goddess's chemical secrets into the body and to carry the Goddess within the self. In so doing, women now activate a Goddess consciousness within matter by means of which all contemporary culture will be awakened.

Jung said: 'To carry a god around in yourself is a guarantee of happiness, of power, and even of omnipotence in so far as these are attributes of divinity.'[2]

Contemporary woman's need to carry a 'god' around within the self, her desire to transform herself into the image of the Goddess, arises from a deep historical imperative. Research into the history of Goddess worship gives ample evidence of the desecration of Goddess temples, shrines, altars and sanctuaries, and of the systematic erasure of all traces of Goddess worship from the face of the earth. Through the persecution of witches, sacred knowledge of the Old Religion had to be transmitted through visual and oral lore from generation to generation. Where once the Goddess was worshipped at sacred natural sites with the Earth identified as the body of the Great Mother, today women are transforming their own bodies into those sacred repositories of Goddess knowledge and energy.

The repossession by woman of the attributes of the Great Goddess is necessary in order to provide fundamental changes in vision and reality. Under the hegemony of patriarchal religions, notably Christianity, which has conditioned Western consciousness over many centuries through image-making and ritual, a profound mystification has been perpetrated on so large a scale that one of the first functions of this new art is to exorcise the sexist impact and interpretation of all sacred imagery. Christian art, for example, by establishing the paradoxical image of the Virgin Mother, has encouraged women to hallucinate an impossibility as if it were a natural image of reality. In order to re-establish the validity of the natural image of Mother and Child as incorporated in the archetype of the Fertility Goddess, contemporary artists are celebrating sexuality by invoking ancient images of the Great Mother that exalt procreation and superimposing them over the former image of the Virgin and Child.

Another integral part of the process of Goddess-culture art are the expeditions to caves, mounds, sanctuaries, shrines or megalithic sites in search of the energy evoked and the artifacts or symbols of veneration left by ancient cults which worshipped the Goddess. In this kind of search artists are making the heretofore invisible, manifest again. The visionary technique of rendering the invisible and the real visible once more and ultimately abolishing the separation between the spiritual and the material plane reestablishes the human and the natural as the legitimate realm of the divine. The energy formerly required to accept Christian illusion is now released for the accomplishment of the true work of alchemical transformation – that of preparing and retraining the mind-body perceptor so that women may now perform their highest functions.

This exaltation of natural energies releases enormous potential so that women may begin to transform themselves into living repositories of sacred knowledge, storing their total history within their bodies, their psychic memory and their art as a natural form of protection against future persecution or annihilation. As bearers of sacred tradition, contemporary feminist artists use ritual to resacrilise the female body, creating a new sacred space for the enactment of those magical rebirth ceremonies that are first coming into our culture through art.

In *Beyond God the Father*, Mary Daly, redefining God as a verb, as a participation in being, rather than anthropomorphically as a being, suggests that women's participation in history, her new sisterhood, is a means of saying 'us v. nonbeing'.

> What we are about is the human becoming of that half of the human race that has been excluded from humanity by sexual definition...What is at stake is a real leap in human evolution, initiated by women.[3]

The Goddess, then, is that archetype which mediates between image, energy and history, evolving and unfolding destiny through the redirection of energy into a revolutionary manifestation of being. When imaged and celebrated in contemporary art, the Goddess signifies Being as a verb, as a creative energy, as a transformative energy, as sacred earth-energy and as psychic energy. Contemporary women artists are using the documentation that is being gathered on the various manifestations of the Goddess from the Upper Paleolithic and Neolithic communities to the present both as visual and as informational data, as elements of the new art works or events they are creating in accordance with the elaboration of a new myth synonymous with the exigencies of female culture in the 1970s.

Architect Mimi Lobell and two other women, one a Jungian, have designed a Goddess Temple which expresses the theme of initiation and rebirth into a Goddess-centered culture. They consider the temple to be the externalisation of an archetypal structure that exists within the psyche. The temple, whose eventual site will be a mountainous region near Aspen, Colorado, is conceived as analogous to the body of the Goddess through which the initiate will pass in a ceremony of transformation. Its form and materials function as a catalyst for this process. According to Lobell, 'To go through the temple will be to experience an initiation into the mysteries of the feminine and activate a prelogical consciousness'.[4]

As planned, the temple is approached via an uphill walk along a 'sacred way' lined with figures of animals. The entrance is at the lower level, which appears to be buried in rock. Deep in this rock the veiled entry leads to a nine-ring labyrinth. Reversing the process of birth one enters through the vaginal orifice and journeys toward the third eye of enlightenment. The walls of the labyrinth are covered with exotic fabrics and tapestries, weavings, batiks, silks and lace from various ethnic sources. In the center of the labyrinth lies the sunken grail pool, inscribed with a serpentine spiral. A helical ladder, 15 feet high, rises out of the pool and ascends to the upper temple, which at eye level becomes a 360-degree open-windowed panorama of the mountains and valleys. Over the windows are 29 perforations in the shape of the moon, one for each of its monthly day cycle. The altar is a part of the Great Eye of Vision of the Eye Goddess.

> We are one with that all receptive 360 degree panoramic perception in the Oculus of the Eye Goddess, warmed by the fires of Vesta, the libidinous energy that keeps us integrated with our bodies and with all of our sensuous lenses onto the mysteries of the universe. The water of the hydrolunar force has been transmuted into the fire that ignites the feminine wisdom of Sophia and the Muses and the Oracles and Sybils.[5]

Becoming conscious of the presence of Goddess imagery in one's work is a long arduous process of visual reeducation. Carolee Schneemann, who in childhood saw the radiant face of the Great Mother in the moon and believed that the world was permeated by invisible energies, unconsciously made her first Goddess image in 1963 when she was working on her theater piece *Chromolodeon*. In her desire for a companion figure for the piece, she made the head of a horned bull and mounted it on a clothed dressmaker's dummy. Seven years later she was to discover that the bull was the sacred beast of the Great Goddess. In the 1960s Schneemann did not yet understand the real significance of the bull iconography in her work. In her series of body pieces, such as *Meat Joy* of 1964, she began to put the materials from the static works onto herself, and in *Eye Body* (1963) she used two snakes on her body in a set of transformative actions. Later, reviewing her artistic evolution through the 1970s Schneemann came to understand that the serpents in her earlier works were related to the Minoan Snake Goddess through a series of iconographical similarities and personal connections.

The figure of the Minoan Snake Goddess, arms upright, is currently featured in much Goddess-culture art. This merging of the self with that of the Goddess functions as a mirror reflection in which women see themselves as the Goddess and the Goddess in themselves.

The process of the evolution of Goddess consciousness itself became the theme of *Homerunmuse* (performed at the Brooklyn Museum during the Women Artists 1550-1950 show, Fall 1977). In a meditation upon the female and the muse, whose presence is indicated in the word 'museum', but whose usual absence from the institution was made obvious by the fact of the women artists' show, Schneemann rejects 'the abstracted token Muse as fragmentation'. Through a collage of texts Schneemann reiterates the theme of woman remaking herself into the image of the Goddess.

Israeli artist Miriam Sharon performs desert rituals that are rites of exorcism overthrowing the patriarchal model that constructed alienating cityscapes of concrete over the ancient earth shrines and sacred sites. Her pilgrimage to the desert put her in contact with the Bedouins, 'the last survivors of the Earth Living Culture'. Her own *Space Project-Earth People* which grew out of her stay in the desert is a ritual act of identification with the Earth Culture. Through meditation rituals in the wilderness, Sharon expresses the wish to recreate an ancient lost myth of the Earth. Sharon's reclamation of the barren earth as the natural holy shrine and her use of the desert as a temple for meditation exemplify the return to primal matter as holy matter. Her participation with the Bedouins in the life of the desert as Goddess-space parallels the initiatory experience of Lobell's Goddess Temple. However, Sharon defines 'holy' as without shrines or temples, holy in its being only.

> The Bedouins (whom I adopted some years ago as part of my work) are part of this 'meditative' existence of the desert. They meditate daily in front of the wide seas or wide wilderness of the desert. They kiss the earth for their existence. They never thanked their 'god' by building huge temples; but just kissed the sands. When they will disappear they will never leave behind any traces for their existence, except the stones of their burial places. I try through my art, not to build static sculptures or monuments in the spaces but only put human energy through my art (a ritual art) into something that is disappearing.[6]

Sharon's recent *Sand Tent Project* involved the participation of a Bedouin tribe and a Kibbutz settlement (Kerem Shalom). The Bedouin Mother who taught her how to create such a tent is the last survivor of the tent life in that area. Sharon's apprenticeship to the wise women who know the secrets of the earth is an affirmation of woman as Goddess-incarnation. The desert, for Sharon, symbolizes patriarchal spiritual values (the barren emptiness) which must be exorcised and is, at the same time, that pure clear space of the new frontier, representing the new female space of herstory upon which our lost traces will be reinscribed and our new destiny will be written.

Ana Mendieta, who came to the U.S. from Cuba in 1961, thinks of the Earth as the Goddess. She recalls a mountain in Cuba, La Mazapan de Matanza, that is in the shape of a reclining woman. Her transformational rituals explore the boundaries between spirit and matter. In a piece she did in a labyrinth, *Silueta de Laberinto* (1974), she worked with the metamorphosis of the self that occurs in sorcery and trance. In this piece someone traced her silhouette on the ground. When Mendieta left the labyrinth, her image was imprinted upon the earth, suggesting that through a merging with the Goddess spirits are evoked that infuse the body and cause such occurrences as out-of-body journeys or astral travel. In Earth Sorcery, of which all her works are examples, the Earth Goddess is the shaman and the spell is invoked through a magical rite in which unification with the Earth Mother transpires. Mendieta is concerned with rebirth and her grave and burial mound pieces suggest that material death does not imply spiritual death.

In some of her works, Mendieta wraps herself in black cloth, imposing her mummified form upon the ground which is then dug out around her. A series of these imprints is eventually lit with gunpowder, leaving silhouetted after-images embedded in the earth as a testimony to the magical site of transformation, the dwelling of the Goddess, where the human and the divine had come to mingle as preparation for a new destiny. Her art concretizes that process of Earth Alchemy, using prime matter itself as the alchemistic vessel through which spirit will be made to reenter matter and transform woman into the vital incarnation of the Earth Goddess once more.

Buffie Johnson's paintings celebrate the natural symbols of the universe which were recognized as sacred in the worship of the Great Goddess. The plant and animal manifestations of the Goddess are energizers of transformation which function like the star and cross in the Judeo-Christian tradition. They are reminders of the numinous state in which all of nature was held to be sacred. Erich Neumann writes:

> Because originally human life was so strongly affected by its *participation mystique* with the outside world that stone, plant, and man (sic.), animal and star were bound together in a single stream, one could always transform itself into another.[7]

These symbols reinforce in us an awareness that we are all manifestations of the one 'single stream', the spirit of the Mother Goddess.

The general 'theme' of Johnson's work since the late 1940s is drawn from the Jungian concept of the collective unconscious and from her scholarly research on the Great Goddess. The paintings which evolved with specific reference to the Goddess show her aspects as *Mistress of the Beasts* and *Lady of the Plants*. Around the latter, she has created single-image plants in varying aspects of cyclical transformation, which stimulate the unconscious and evoke mythic memories. The paintings serve as sacred icons to resurrect the layers of consciousness in which our most primordial images, those of the Great Goddess and of our true origin, lie buried. In *Ariadne (Barley Mother*, 1971), the Goddess of Vegetation is evoked by the image of the long-grain barley flowing gently down in a skirt of rain. A pomegranate bursting from within (*Pomegranate*, 1972) recalls the myth of Persephone and Demeter and their connection with the life-giving powers of the Feminine. The monolithic opium seed-pod *Lapis* (1970) is a cosmic starglobe exploding with life, a metaphor for the Goddess from whose womb all is born. In *Pasiphae* (1976) the image of the iris, the sacred lily of Crete, merges with that of a bovine head, so that both animal and plant symbols of the Goddess coalesce in a new charged sign. References to the myth of the Minotaur and the labyrinth are suggested; the labyrinth of the Goddess being the place where one loses and finds oneself again – the unconscious. The collective symbols are here employed as forces of awakening, the artist reaching deep into the buried past when the Goddess and all of nature were revealed as One.

Donna Byars' work shows the creative processes at work in the deciphering of the oracle of the Goddess as She speaks to the artist through the labyrinth of dream and visionary experience. *Oracle Stone Grove*, for example, evolved from a dream.

> A stone woman who sat in a grove of trees spoke to me in vapors, not words. She was very poetic and mystical and spoke only in truths. All of a sudden, like in a faint, she slid from her chair into a hole in the underground. I grabbed her before she went underground and when she came up she was no longer able to speak. I woke up with a terrible feeling of sadness.[8]

In the piece itself, 'All the components...sit on the floor and do not occupy any wall space, two stones are arranged perpendicular to each other sitting on an old paint scratched rocker in a grove of four weeping fig trees'. For Byars, the Grove becomes a shrine.

In works such as *Vested Relic* where stone and silver wings are enclosed within a blindfolded cage, creating a secret altar and a reliquary, Byars preserves the magical objects that reveal to her the presence of the Goddess as a guardian spirit in her world. The blindfolding of the cage symbolizes that these sacred objects can only be perceived with the inner eye. Byar's glass collages make visible the apparitions of the Mother Goddess in images of a winged being and a shaman, who appears to us during altered states of consciousness.

For Byars, the world is vibrant and alive with signs and guideposts. Many of her pieces are themselves omens, assembled from objects and materials which spoke to her in oracular modes. One such object is *Swathe*, which combines feathers and a wing on a swathed ironing board that has lilies of the valley wrapped in chamois placed upon it. These totems and talismans conjure up archaic imagery from the distant past. Animal horns, wings, feathers, shells, trees, serpents, brought together in these mythopoetic assemblages, activate intimate relationships between natural materials, objects and living things that illuminate essences which were formerly only visible to seers and shamans. The presence of the Goddess is thus revealed and brought into contemporary consciousness.

Mary Beth Edelson's work has long been intimately involved in the explorations of the Goddess. In 1961 her painting of Madonna and Child entitled *Godhead* introduced concentric circles as sources of energy from the Madonna's head. In these early paintings[9] her women were frequently depicted with their arms uplifted, reminiscent of the posture of many early Goddess figures. The primal image of the outstretched arms of the ancient

Goddess, whose power must be reclaimed by women for themselves today, is seen by Edelson not only as a spiritual signifier, but as a contemporary symbol of our political activism.

In 1969 she began to evolve a more defined and specific area of archetypal imagery, out of which emerged the exhibition *Woman Rising*, revolutionary in the way it brought to consciousness psychic material about the Great Goddess. Her most innovative images for today have been the body images she has created through performing private body rituals where the body itself is the house of wisdom. In these, the artist calls upon Goddess energy, using her own body as a stand-in for the Goddess and as a symbol for Everywoman, whose expanded states of body-consciousness and multiple transformations are evoked through contact with powerful natural energies.

On March 1, 1977, Edelson performed a mourning ritual ceremony for her exhibition, *Your 5,000 Years Are Up*, entitled *Mourning Our Lost Herstory*, at the Mandeville Gallery, University of California at La Jolla. Ten women sat in a circle in the center of a fire ring, the only source of light, chanting and wailing while seven silent eight-foot high black-draped figures, which had previously seemed to be an uninhabited formal sculptural installation on the back wall, came alive and began to move around the cavernous gallery. More recently, she performed a mourning-reclamation ritual at A.I.R. Gallery, New York City, entitled *Proposals For: Memorials to the 9,000,000 Women Burned as Witches in the Christian Era*. This ritual, based on research about witch burning in relation to women who were Goddess worshippers evoked the spirits of individual women who were tortured during the Inquisition. Edelson is not content, however, to exorcise the past; her art is about mythic recreation of holy spaces for women's culture today.

Donna Henes's *Spider Woman*, a series of process environmental sculptures, makes reference to the Mother Goddess of the Navaho Emergence Myth about whom Sheila Moon has written, 'She is the protective feminine objectivity. Spider Woman is the unobtrusive but powerful archetype of fate – not in the sense of determinism, but in the sense of the magical law of one's own "gravity" which leads always beyond itself towards wholeness'.[10] In a state of trance and meditation, Henes spins her web of various kinds of fibers in natural settings and in public places, where they can be altered by the specific environmental conditions of each location. Her manifesto[11] defines the web as a map of the subconscious and as a form of primal meditation.

Henes performs a yearly winter solstice celebration *Reverence to Her: A Chant to Invoke the Female Forces of the Universe Present in All People*. The winter solstice is the time when 'the Great Mother gives birth to the sun, who is Her son, and stands at the center of the matriarchal mysteries. At the winter solstice, the moon occupies the highest point in its cycle, the sun is at its nadir, and the constellation Virgo rises in the east'.[12] Henes's participatory chant invokes the Great Goddess, the archetypal female principle of communal creation and continuity, and gives reverence to the female power 'who exists in all beings in the form of consciousness, reason, sleep, hunger, shadow, energy, thirst, forgiveness, species, bashfulness, peace, faith, loveliness, fortune, vocation, memory, compassion, mother, fulfillment and illusion'.

If the webs are a materialization of a female spirit-presence in the environment, a kind of feminine structure within matter itself, her work makes us visualize this presence, evokes it, and brings it forth out of the void, making manifest the interconnectedness of all space and time through the weaving of the great web of life, which is the work of the Mother Goddess. This is the actualization of a creation myth which posits the female life-force as an energy that is at work in the universe in invisible ways.

Betye Saar's work, through its mystical, visionary imagery, probes the collective unconscious for those images of female power specific to black women. By delving deeply into the religious practices of Africa and Haiti, Saar resurrects images of the Black Goddess, the Voodoo Priestess and the Queen of the Witches, collecting the amulets and artifacts of these cultures and placing them in her boxes in order to create potent talismanic collections of magically charged objects and icons. For Saar, contemporary black women are all incarnations of the Black Goddess, and in reclaiming black power, women are instinctively venerating an ancient female force still worshipped in other cultures today. *Voo Doo Lady W/3 Dice* (1977) is a mixed-media collage on fabric that identifies black woman in her image of oppression with the mystical Black Goddess, implying through its iconography that women should worship the deity within themselves, and that a familiarity with occult and mythological traditions will reveal the true face of the Goddess to all women.

In her piece *7,000 Year Old Woman*,[13] performed publicly May 21, 1977, Betsy Damon covered herself with small bags of colored flour which she punctured in a ritual ceremony. As each small bag of flour emptied, like a miniature sandtimer, it was as if the artist and her assistant, through intense concentration and meditation, had incorporated a bit of lost time into the aura of their consciousnesses. This piece demonstrates how contemporary Goddess-culture art seeks to transform the body and the consciousness of modern woman by infusing it with a sense of herstory, reclaimed and reintegrated into the present sense of the self.

Damon has been performing rituals in nature for several years, working collectively with women, creating rites of anger, rebirth and transformation, such as the *Birth Ritual*, in which each woman gives birth to another, chanting, 'I am a woman. I can give birth to you'. In the *Naming Ritual*, performed in Ithaca, women chanted, 'I am a woman. I give you my hand.

We are women. Our circle is powerful'. After the chanting they intoned the names of all the women in the ritual. It was during her performance of *Changes*, in Ithaca, that she dreamed of the *Maypole Ritual*. This fertility rite was held in that same city and participants brought corn, food, poetry and other offerings to the celebration. They painted their bodies, danced and wove maypoles out of colorfully dyed gauze.

Hannah Kay, an Israeli artist living in New York, paints the ultimate breakthrough of Earth Goddess energy that parallels the advent of female autonomy in the new era of feminist consciousness. She writes that in her art, woman 'became a landscape and then the whole universe. A woman's body is, in itself, the whole universe: birth, life, death, and communication. The human body manifests all the laws of the universe; and for me the woman's body is the sensuality of the universe. The sensuality of mountains, and oceans, and planets in their orbits about the stars.'[14] *Enclosed* invites us to hallucinate the female form as the basic force behind the intertwined branches of the worldscape. In this visionary art we come to see the spirit that resides in matter: our perception is altered so that the invisible being of the Goddess becomes manifest, and we are transformed into seers whose eyes may behold the divine revelation of the existence of a female principle at work in the universe.

Judy Chicago has made a major contribution to this tradition by conceptualizing and creating a traveling multi-media exhibition, *The Dinner Party Project*, an environmental recasting of the history of Western civilization in feminist terms.[15] Accompanying *The Dinner Party Project's* exhibition, is a book in the form of an illuminated manuscript of five sections, some of which include a rewriting of Genesis as an alternate creation myth in which the Goddess is the the supreme Creatrix. It also contains a section of myths, legends and tales of the women, a vision of the Apocalypse which is a vision of the world made whole by the infusion of feminist values, and the Calling of the Disciplines, a list of the women represented in the table relating who they were and what they did.

Chicago's work has long been making links between female iconography and a feminist reinterpretation of the Creation Myth. In her series of porcelain plates entitled *The Butterfly Goddesses: Other Specimens* (1974) which includes *The Butterfly Vagina as the Venus of Willendorf, The Butterfly Vagina as the Great Round*, etc., sexuality is expressly connected to spiritual transformation. For Chicago, the butterfly symbolizes both liberty and metamorphosis. The new specimens in *The Butterfly Goddess* series represent a new breed of women: these are women yet to be born to a world in which the Goddess is recognized as the original deity; women whose sexual energy is accepted as a legitimate form of creative power.

Her *Womantree* series suggests the principle of a female Tree of Life out of which these 'Ancient New Beings' will emerge, possessing all the secrets of the matriarchal past transmitted over time through the sacred matrilineage women now reclaim. Chicago's flower forms, seed shapes and pod forms relate to the principles of feminist alchemy and suggest the final transmutation into 'The Ancient New Being' of which the butterfly is her prime symbol.

Chicago's dream has always been to bring art out of the world and back into the culture so that it will effect the people as it once did in the Middle Ages.

Monica Sjoo's synthesizing of artistic, political and mythological material has served as a catalyst of Goddess-consciousness in England. Her underground pamphlet, *The Ancient Religion of the Great Cosmic Mother of All*, is a poetic attempt to cull all information that can be obtained through a feminist occult reading of history, symbolism, myth, art and literature, and bring it into a powerful reevaluation of many of the philosophical underpinnings of contemporary thought. Her art works create Goddess emblems which narrate the story of the real crucifixion, that of women who have been sacrificed upon the cross of patriarchal culture. They speak of female rebirth into a new ethos through the revolutionary force of women as workers and visionaries.

Contemporary Goddess-culture art, with its many varied manifestations, is creating a whole new constellation of charged signs, aspirational images, icons for contemplation, talismanic artifacts, and symbolic rites of passage that constitute the source of a new reality for women.

Artists of the Surrealist tradition like Leonora Carrington, Leonor Fini, Meret Oppenheim, Frida Kahlo and Remedios Varo, artists participating in the Sister Chapel exhibition (*Woman-art*, Winter 1977) such as Diana Kurz and Cynthia Mailman, Canadian artists Jovette Marchessault (totemic sculptural figures) and Suzanne Guité (stone sculpture), Thérèse Guité (batik) and other contemporary American artists such as Faith Wilding, Suzanne Benton (welded sculpture and mask ritual theater), Julia Barkley etc., are creating a new feminist myth in which woman becomes the vital connecting link between all forms of life in the cosmos; the great catalyser and transformer of life energies. By the repossession of Goddess power and by a full participation in Her Being, women are bringing into existence a vastly expanded state of ecstatic consciousness.

Through the many ceremonies of rebirth and reclamation, the rituals of mourning and self-transformation, the energizing of new psycho-physical centers of being, the activation of a new Earth-Alchemy, the rewriting of sacred texts, myth and history, and a new scanning of the universal system of hieroglyphics, using trance, meditation and dream, women artists are bringing about a planetary goddess-consciousness revolution, a cycle of female rebirth and a new feminist ethos in our time.

NOTES

1 June Singer, *Androgeny: Towards a New Theory of Sexuality* (New York: Anchor, 1976), p.71.

2 Jolande Jacobi, *Complex, Archetype, Symbol in the Psychology of C.G. Jung* (Princeton: Princeton University Press, 1959), p. 101.

3 Mary Daly, *Beyond God the Father: Toward a Philosophy of Women's Liberation* (Boston: Beacon Press, 1973), p. 34.

4 Mimi Lobell, 'The Goddess Temple', *Humanist Ideas in Architecture* (Vol. XXIX, No. 1), p. 20.

5 Lobell, p. 21.

6 Miriam Sharon, personal communication, Dec. 10, 1977.

7 Erich Neumann, *The Great Mother* (Princeton: Princeton University Press, 1955), p. 262.

8 Quote by artist from dream narrative.

9 'Mary Beth Edelson's Great Goddess', *Arts Magazine* (Nov. 1975).

10 Sheila Moon, *A Magic Dwells* (Middletown: Wesleyan University Press, 1970), p. 152.

11 Donna Henes, 'Spider Woman Manifesto', Lady-Unique-Inclination-of-the-night (Cycle III 1978).

12 Neumann.

13 Betsy Damon, 'The 7,000 Year Old Woman', *Heresies* (Fall 1977), pp. 9-13.

14 Quote from unpublished statement by the author.

15 Arlene Raven & Susan Rennie, 'Interview with Judy Chicago', *Chrysalis* (No. 4), pp. 89-101.

THEORY

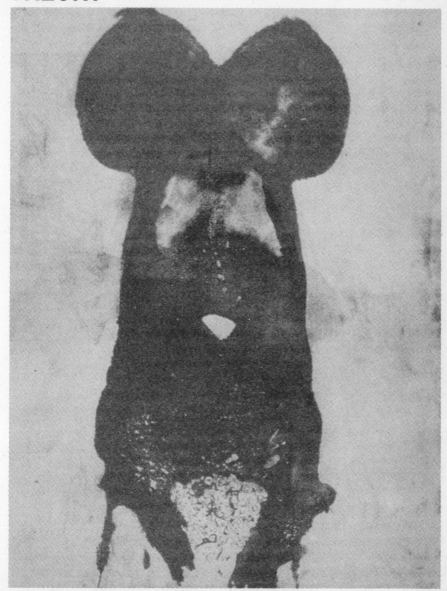

28   Chila K. Burman, *Self-Portrait Body Print*, 1985, sugar-lift and aquatint.

TOOLS FOR THE JOB

This is the only section of the book to have abandoned the alphabetical layout; instead it reflects some of the flow of debate. The word itself, 'theory', is a difficult one as it implies abstract thought rather than 'hands-on' experience. For feminists, theories must be like tools, made to aid and clarify certain activities. Their very existence will affect those activities, and they will be modified or discarded as and when appropriate. The tool and the practice (whether art or politics) feed into and out of each other constantly.

These articles as a whole are an exploration of what the most appropriate tools might be for the practice of feminist art. Taken individually, each one might be recognised as an appropriate tool by the reader – or as one that is seviceable, but needs modification. Some are easy to use, some take a lot of learning; but each, I think, will help in the building of strategies.

An example of this is the debate around art history, and exhanges about art history are central to this section. The division between art history and criticism of the art of today is, I think, a destructive one. Art history is presented to us all too often in a form that has little relevance to our needs and interests and little relation to what happens in studios. It is impossible to understand one without an understanding of the other; yet historians hate being called on to be critics or reviewers, as if looking at today's work were somehow a lesser task.

As in other areas of feminist activity, approaches to art history have been developing over the past fifteen to twenty years. Much of the work that feminists did in the seventies in their writing about women artists was an excavation of the past, researching our foremothers, finding out what they did, and how, and why. Two of the crucial texts in this respect are *Women Artists 1550-1950* by Ann Sutherland Harris and Linda Nochlin, and *Old Mistresses: Women, Art and Ideology* by Roszika Parker and Griselda Pollock. Included here is an exchange of views between Griselda Pollock and Ann Sutherland Harris. Just as there is not a single monolithic entity called 'art history', so too there is no single 'feminist art history' to set in opposition. Here we can see quite clearly how two feminists, trained as art historians, have responded with different strategies to the needs of women today to know their histories and contexts. A rough summary of their

172

differences (as shown here) might be this: that Harris works as an archeologist, painstakingly turning over every stone and examining it; whilst Pollock works as a translator, looking at the overall text (the ideology of the time) and giving each piece a meaning within it.

The function of feminist art theory today is to make sense of the past, and from that foundation to work out the strategies for today and tomorrow. 'The past' includes the immediate past, and the work done by feminists in the seventies – the tools they have handed to us which can be criticised and modified to suit our own purposes. One of the criticisms will surely be that they left much invisible, not recognising the *differences* between women in their need to proclaim a sisterhood. The exploration and demonstration of different identities is in particular being undertaken today by many Black women artists and writers on art, and also by some Lesbian artists – both projects of making visible what has previously been invisible.

Another criticism might be about the division between what is seen as 'history' and what is seen as contemporary work, and how this has been tackled. Harris and Nochlin, for instance, sought to avoid the problem by stopping their account at 1950 (not an unusual habit amongst art historians); Parker and Pollock did not, but through their investigation of how ideologies work, they have developed specific ideas of what strategies feminist artists should employ today.[1] The discussion in the final chapter of *Old Mistresses* of post-1970 feminist work has a sudden narrowing of focus upon one particular way of working[2], in sharp contrast to the wide-ranging, inclusive earlier chapters. The approaches in both of these books obviously have their own inbuilt problems for women involved in producing work now, and for those trying to come to terms with that work. For both groups, the historical context has to include yesterday, and has to show the full range of yesterday's endeavour – which is not to say that it cannot be critical of certain aspects of that endeavour. What is heartening is the way in which many artists have taken on the job of researching and writing about the work of other women. In many cases, as can be seen here, the historian, the strategist and the practitioner are combined in the same person. The wider political framework combines with the attention to detail necessary for the activist/practitioner.

NOTES

1 Griselda Pollock in particular has written many influential and important articles about the problems facing women artists today, about strategies that can be developed, and about the artists and practices that she feels are tackling these problems most successfully. (See bibliography.)
2 The concentration takes the form of a long discussion of the work of Mary Kelly, who works within what would now be described as a photo-text or scripto-

visual' tradition, which develops practices initiated by conceptual and Marxist artists in the US. In common with other artists in this tradition, she makes use of semiotics and psychoanalysis in her work (see articles in the interview and review sections of this anthology). This is examined by Parker and Pollock in some detail through a discussion of Kelly's *Post Partum Document*. There are four lines in the book describing the 'diversity' and 'plurality' of work by feminists, but there is no further discussion at all of (for instance) painting, performance, collective or community work, nor about how feminist political positions vary from the Marxist to the Matriarchist – all of which are reflected in work produced by women since 1970.

I would like to mention as a postscript the essay by Lisa Tickner in the catalogue of Nancy Spero's work published by the ICA in 1987, too late, unfortunately, for inclusion here. It makes use of much of the psychoanalytic and literary theory that is being produced by French feminists, which has by and large been unavailable in translation until recently. Tickner's essay is the first major piece to be published in this country applying this work to a feminist art practice; and it will, I think, be influential on that practice in the next few years.

MAY STEVENS

TAKING ART TO THE REVOLUTION

The questions of the nature of aesthetic experience and the basis of aesthetic judgement are left untheorized in current sociology of art. Which means that the heart of the matter – which is where the artist works every day – is still an unaccountable mystery to scientific analysis. But it seems clear that different forms of logic prevail in different worlds. The aim of art is not clarity and orderliness, each thing in its place, fully explained. The tools of sociology are able to replace phenomena with ever more complex diagrams, finally substituting for each element only a full description of its components. The algebra of reductionism may make an elegant graph which may even replicate a work of art but the quality of art rests upon its surprise, its mystery, its inexplicability. Else why would we want it, why would we care, why would we engage in this discourse?

Art as propaganda. All art can be placed somewhere along a political spectrum, supporting one set of class interests or another, actively or passively, at the very least supporting existing conditions by ignoring other possibilities, silence giving consent.

Art as not propaganda. The meaning of art cannot be reduced to propaganda; it deals with many other things in addition to those revealed by class and sociological analysis.
    Both definitions are true; they are not opposites, but ways of measuring different properties.

Philistinism. Fear of art. Unclarity of meaning, inability to demonstrate immediate social usefulness, difficulties of definition and standards make art seem untrustworthy to the philistine mind (which may be highly trained in other areas of culture). An activity that encourages emotion and individuality, that permits eccentricity and obsession, is necessarily suspect. But art is not subject to social engineering – in this sense: there is no formula for artmaking; art schools do not produce artists (in any positive numerical ratio); high morals do not produce art; effective propaganda does not constitute a definition of art.

That art is amorphous and infinitely variable is one of the properties that defines it and gives it value: here is one area of life where dreams and passions can work out their meanings. That which we feel is worth devoting one's life to and whose value cannot be proven, that is art. Artists create spirit traps, forms to catch our minds and spirits in. These forms may be two- or three-dimensional, of long or short duration, planned or spontaneous. They may engender social action (in delayed time or unforeseen ways) or not. Only a philistine mind could imagine an art accessible to all, accountable to social and political needs, and unconcerned with the hunger for beauty (for color, for tactility, for sensation) and transcendence.

A didactic art, aimed at instructing and organizing the working class, is one possibility for art. It may be that the deepening economic crisis and the crisis of culture in our time demand an art that focuses on just how effective the tools of art can be when applied to specific social needs. This in no way validates either 1) acceptance *as art* of activities and products that are exclusively socially useful, or 2) denigration of art that functions as meditation, catharsis, emotional/aesthetic experience.

To the philistine, the aesthetic experience is either trivial or non-existent. Philistine criticism of art is often a species of puritanism; it is equivalent to criticism of sexuality by the impotent or the non-orgasmic.

But the aesthetic experience is important – regardless of class, age or sex. People unintimidated by class or fashion have a sure sense of style – in their lives, their clothes, their language and what they put on their walls. Social thinkers who see non-intellectuals as a *mass* have little awareness of everyone's sense of and need for art. But people grow and arrange flowers; choose objects, this one over that one; put 'useless' things on walls, shelves, mantelpieces, automobile dashboards and locker doors. These are aesthetic objects, reminders of what one cares about, dreams of, needs to stir one's feelings – through visual codes. Whether it is movie star or sports hero, pin-up or sad-eyed cocker spaniel, the sacred heart of Jesus, sunset or sunflower, the Pieta in the Italian barbershop or the ruffled doily in the back of the Hispanic automobile – people need and love 'useless objects', art of their own choosing, culturally defined, educationally conditioned. The problem is not with people's taste (often called 'kitsch' by superior minds) but with defining art as one thing only. Art is that which functions as aesthetic experience, for you. If a certain art works that way for enough people, there is consensus; that becomes art. For a while.

The clipping on my wall (a news event that has aesthetic meaning for me; a face, a body that moves me) is as much art as the O'Keeffe iris and the Cunningham magnolia or the Ellsworth Kelly black and white shaped canvas that I see in the museums/galleries and whose replicas in media reproductions I also pin to my wall. I must assume I share with 'ordinary', 'unsophisticated', 'less educated' people the same need for a quality of life that includes beauty as *I, for myself, define it,* as *they, for themselves, define it.* To make any other assumption, for example, that 'art' as it has existed is of no interest to them and that art for them should be my definition of what will 'raise' them or 'free' them, is contemptuous. Honesty requires that I admit my tastes and that I respect theirs. To see people as totally media-brain-washed and culturally deprived is to ignore ethnic, racial and gender-based traditions; and the way we all become immune to propaganda after a while. The TV runs all day perhaps, but we make phone calls, fry an egg, make grocery lists, do homework or tax returns, play cards or chat with a neighbor over the clamor. Conversation is sprinkled with 'As long as you're up, get me a Grant's' and 'Please don't squeeze the Charmin', but the mockery is apparent. Sometimes I think we forget how smart our parents were, how sharp our kids are, how the guy who pumps gas on the corner and the woman who sells yard goods on Main Street are shrewd, shrewd, shrewd, never taken in in any graspable situation. Their 'conservatism' is more realistic than our 'radicalism' until social situations make change practicable, programs for action are organized in ways that actually relate to people's lives, and 'radicals' stop thinking they know so much more than the people they want to help and stop being overimpressed with media as seamless waterproofing against reality.

New ideas, new art, new situations do not displace history; they modify it. They create a new dialectic. It is our job as people who care to sort out the contradictions, to integrate new with old. We have to, as Adrienne Rich said, dive into the wreck to find what is salvageable. We have spent too much time killing our mothers and our fathers. Let's pick their brains instead, subject their knowledge (our heritage) to analysis based on what we need and want.

Theory. A proposed pattern to understand the world by. We look for patterns (meaning) in the world. When we think we see one that works (fits our experience), we apply it for as long as it holds up. But when it begins not to fit, we re-examine the pattern, correct it, refine it – if it is salvageable. Mystification of theory prevents its organic development; anti-individualism prevents users of mystified theory from matching it to their own experience. Theory is for *us*, not the other way round. Example: The Women's Liberation Movement causes socialists to re-think the words *liberation, class, family, sexuality.* Socialist theory must meet the feminist challenge or give way to a fuller theory, a fairer practice. Similarly, feminists must meet the challenge of class division and differentiation.

Individualism. The society we want to build will be composed of politically sophisticated women and men, conscious of history, of their own needs, of

177

social responsibility, and of sharing, learning and growing together. We can become that kind of human by practising and developing those skills along the way. The pluralism of the 'hundred flowers' impulse, the patience to go slow and not force compliance, the concern for process and feeling – these are the things women can bring to socialist practice, attitudes so badly needed, so shockingly absent. The relation of means to ends is still the sticky problem socialists have always understood it to be (at least they have sometimes understood it in theory). But the solutions given have too often been expedient. We must go slow if we do not want to go alone. To win is not enough – if it means jettisoning the things we need when we get there. We want to like who we become.

Feeling. The touchstone. Our theory must fit our feeling. Puritanism, 'should' and 'ought' won't work, won't – ultimately – help. We have to deal with the individual and with feeling, sensitively, not condescendingly. If we are not attuned to feeling, our own and others', the theory will not hold. It will not have taken into account powerful forces that will drag it down and eventually defeat it – as indeed it must be when it is one-sided (indifferent to women, indifferent to individual conscience, to personal feeling).

Relation between feeling and theory. Theory cuts off its roots, loses its connection to reality when it ignores feeling; feeling needs structuring, a means of evaluating betwee conflicting feelings. A *balancing act* where contempt has no place since it is not theoretical and is not a feeling that can exist between equals.

Saints with hatchets in their heads, or carrying their two eyes on a twig, or Christ's own face wiped onto a handkerchief, Noah drunk, Adam and Eve embarrassed, sinners smitten or knocked down by a great light, kings carrying pots of ointment to the baby king. Lessons all of them. From another time and place and way of thinking that exists for us only as history or fairy tale or fairy tales on history told by a man who (whatever his own perceptions may have been) was paid by a richer man to assuage conscience, impress friends, out-do rivals.

But seeing in contradiction one of the meanings of art, we examine Masaccio's *Expulsion from the Garden* for more than its Christian propaganda. On one hand it proposes institutional and cultural control of sexuality. It demonstrates pain and loss as punishment for breaking law. It marks intellectual curiosity and sexual gratification as cardinal sins, thus preserving the church's power over mind and body.

At the same time it speaks to and of human consciousness, in a profound way. The woman and the man, their clumsy bodies clearly not intended to be seen, stumble into nakedness, into knowledge of difference, of otherness from the orders of animal that surrounded them in the pre-conscious garden. They stumble, bent, under the weight of unbearable knowledge; they must justify themselves. They are sentenced to harshest labor (production and reproduction) to the end of their days and to the end of the days of their kind. Their painted bodies have the look of flesh without decency of pelt: they are upright, uncovered, aware, condemned. Masaccio has found a metaphor for the essential in the myth. He shows us humanness newly self-aware.

Workers with words and images create and propagate myths, re-form and re-interpret them (feeling using theory, theory using feeling). Myths live because they carry usable answers (or so it seems). They sustain; for a while they nourish. The Judeo-Christian myths, like the myths of all religions, embody concepts that function as armature for civilization, as method and goal for socialism (love and sharing, equality and dignity through works). We use myths (partial truths, temporary understandings) to criticize myths. We measure achievement against dream, the myth made up of both. We shuck off the non-nourishing parts of myth as we grow and change, as we see how myths are also *used* by those who would control us – used to delude us, to quiet us.

The myth of art itself confounds with notions of elitism, of mystification, of commodity fetishism. But equal is not same, mystery is not mystification, and its objecthood is not the aspect which makes a work of art a work of art. Questions of audience are instructive but not the sole criteria. Art in its propaganda aspect must speak to audiences through form accessible (culturally, geographically) to that audience. Art will speak effective working-class propaganda only when members of that class are 1) conscious of being working class and 2) not alienated or fragmented by the frictions within the working class.

Art as propaganda must help to bring about the conditions under which it can achieve its fullest propaganda function. This means propagation of respect for art, respect which can help bridge the gap between art of the highest order and working-class experience. When Mary Kelly makes art out of baby nappies and documents her child's development with Lacanian theory, she attempts to integrate the artifacts of a woman's daily reality, charged with complex emotional affect (Marxist/feminist/artist/mother raising a male child on the edge of the working class), with the keenest contemporary intellectual analysis she can bring to bear. This art swings between the nursery and the tower and shows again the way we are split – worker from knowledge, woman from science.

Political theory, like aesthetic theory, can produce an art which disdains aesthetics as trivial ('retinals' à la Duchamp) or redefines aesthetics as a scientific uncovering of art's essential nature (à la Greenberg). But this reduces sensory input which might have given pleasure and substitutes an intellectual austerity totally inaccessible and uninteresting to the working class, which thus becomes objectified.

Rosa Luxemburg said about her major theoretical work *The Accumulation of Capital* that not a half-dozen readers were able to appreciate it scientifically:

> My work is from this standpoint truly a luxury product and might just as well be printed on handmade paper.

And she was not even making art; she was writing theory. By utilitarian views of culture, the question of audience would disqualify her work.

What of art which does not have communication as its primary intention, or knows it will communicate with only a half-dozen? And this, as with Luxemburg's work, not a deliberate choice, but a simple concomitant of the level (area, discipline, issue) where one chooses, or is chosen, to work. Luxemburg addresses herself to working-class culture:

> The working class will not be in a position to create a science and an art of its own until it has been fully emancipated from its present class position.
>
> The utmost it can do today is to safeguard bourgeois culture from the vandalism of bourgeois reaction, to create the social conditions requisite for a free cultural development. Even along these lines, the workers, within the extant form of society, can only advance in so far as they can create for themselves the intellectual weapons needed in their struggle for liberation.

Now, sixty years after Luxemburg wrote, we would probably prefer to speak of all oppressed people, including the working class. Notice the value she assigns to bourgeois culture and the refusal to substitute a vulgarized view of working-class culture for it.

In our contemporary museums and galleries we can find 1 art which ignores social questions, 2 art which directly supports reaction, and 3 art which informs/agitates for justice. All three hang on museum walls although formalists (those who advocate the primacy of form over content) have seen to it that 3 is rare, and 2 often masquerades as 1. In 1934 Isamu Noguchi exhibited a bronze figure representing a lynched black man hanging from a piece of rope. Critic Henry McBride wrote in the *New York Herald Tribune* that this was 'just a little Japanese mistake'. Noguchi (now an internationally known abstract sculptor) did not exhibit again for fourteen years. A culture hostile to protest art makes its position known in both obvious and subtle ways. A tradition of strong protest work needs time and attention to develop; it needs the support in its adolescence that allows critical exchange among artists (who are always their own first audience) to bring about the deeper layers of expression.

The formalist rule in the U.S. has effectively prevented most contemporary critics (with the exception of Lucy Lippard and Max Kozloff, who were themselves committed activists) and historians from acknowledging, much less documenting, the body of anti-war art produced by a wide range of artists throughout the sixties. For them, somehow, the work never had enough intellectual rigor, formal purity, or piquancy to make its way up. Where are the art critics and historians interested in examining its failure – if such it was? Or, better, whose was the failure?

When Honore Sharrer's *Workers and Paintings* and Ben Shahn's *Sacco and Vanzetti* hang at the Museum of Modern Art, do they lose their meaning? Museums are still places where hundreds of schoolchildren, retired persons and working-class people spend an afternoon, people who do not go to galleries or read an art magazine. (In fact, I wonder if the imposition of admission fees cannot be related to, in addition to financial difficulties, the feeling expressed in the *New York Times* by Hilton Kramer that so many people attend museums nowadays that it makes it hard for the cognoscenti to enjoy the art; and related to, in the case of the Ben Shahn retrospective at the Jewish Museum, Kramer's remark that the kind of people who attend the exhibition respond to it uncritically.)

These enthusiastic – and outraged – museum-goers buy postcards of works they want to remember. The golden lion in Rousseau's *Sleeping Gypsy*, Meret Oppenheim's *Fur Lined Teacup*, Boccioni's city rising, the great water lily room, *Guernica*'s running woman and Maillol's falling woman play creative roles in their fantasies along with *Annie Hall* and the Rolling Stones. (Substitute your own choices.)

In a filmed version of Zola's *Nana*, a French family has trundled all its many members, from oldest to youngest, to skitter from side to side, moving as a rag-edged group, to thrill to the paintings in their heavy frames lining the long Louvre gallery. They burst from painting to painting, tittering, exclaiming, saying things like, 'Oooh! With a swan! Don't let the children see!'.

I do not think the meaning of the effort for social change implicit or explicit in the works of social realism, surrealism, futurism, neo-plasticism, conceptual art, black art and feminist art is negated by hanging these works in galleries and museums. Until the intent is realized, they hang like unopened letters, unanswered invitations. They will look different when those battles are won – more formalist, I suppose. They testify to capitalism's appetite for sensation. They testify that art is not a gun; a manifesto is not a military command. They also testify that *possibility* lives in art, like weeds in an untended lot.

Art from any of these three categories may challenge us to think and feel and analyze. And complexity allows that art may give us feasts for unprudish sensibilities while, at the same time, it lets in women and other groups on the edge of traditional white male western culture in dribblings calculated to pique bored tastes and whet market appetites. But these motivations *cannot taint the art so used*, any more than oil paint poisons the content of art expressed by its physical means (a possibility suggested by John Berger and emphasized by his cruder disciples), any more than the promotion of abstract expressionism by U.S. imperialism as flagbearer of American power and culture expresses the true and only meaning of the work of Pollock, de Kooning, Joan Mitchell, Rothko, and the rest.

Utilitarianism – defining things by use, or excluding things by measuring their purposefulness and effectiveness for certain specific aims – may be a great way to bake a cake. It is hardly adequate as an attitude for making or judging art, art being one of the more complicated, layered and resonant areas of human work. It is true that one makes art by asking *is that form (color, shape, word) useful in this context?* This is not the same as saying (by implication or omission) that art must move the revolution forward as directly, as forcefully as possible, now (because people are indeed suffering and dying now under oppression), or be classed as part of the oppression. We must take art with us to the revolution – all kinds of art, including that which is funny, beautiful, puzzling, provocative, problematic. Think of it like music, or writing. Will we leave out that which doesn't give us instruction on how to get to our destination, or provide us with a marching beat?

Art often deals with unclarities, looking for new understanding true to feeling – the basic measure – and to theory, which is to say fitted correctly to the artist's concept (a part of her/his larger world-view). Murkiness allows germination. Since it is not all knowable, plannable, and the nature of being is explored in the nature of art. The nature and praxis of art must be seen as reflexive, as well as reflective.

Bonnard's shimmering bathroom with Parisian housewife dappled in light refracted from water, tile and skin is a moment of health and cleanliness, sensuality incorporating woman into nature experienced as urban, indoor, gentled and domesticated. This experience of water, sun and skin partaking of each other, generating warmth, wetness and rainbows of vibrating light, is part of contemporary life, life in the bourgeois era – less dramatic perhaps than woman and nature visualized or hypothesized as cave and moor, dolmen and megalith, but more accessible and more significant to most of us. This does not negate the power and the wildness of the older, more primitive image. I don't have to choose between them. Fortunately, art provides us with both.

Art *is* political. But one also has to understand that the uses to which it is put are not its meaning. Its status as object and commodity is not its meaning: there are many objects and commodities. They are not all art.

What makes art different? Exactly the ways in which it is not an object, can never in its nature be a commodity. (Humans can be sold as slaves: to be human is essentially not to be a slave, in one's nature.)

A socialist and feminist analysis of culture must be as careful as it is angry - fierce *and* responsible.

This article is reprinted with a new introductory paragraph.

LUCY R. LIPPARD

SOME PROPAGANDA FOR PROPAGANDA

A picture is supposed to be worth a thousand words, but it turns out that a picture plus ten or a hundred words may be worthiest of all. With few exceptions, most effective social/political art (propaganda) being done today consists of a combination of words and images. I'm not just talking about 'conceptual art' or paintings with words on them, but also about writing that integrates photographs (and vice versa), about comic strips, photo-novels, slideshows, film, TV and posters – even about advertisements and fashion propaganda. In the last decade or so, visual artists have had to begin to think about problems of narrative, detachment, drama, rhetoric, involvement – *styles of communication* – which hitherto seemed to belong to other aesthetic domains. And in order to deal with these issues, they have had to overcome the modernist taboo against 'literary art', which encompasses virtually all art with political/social intentions.

'Literary art' either uses words or, through visual puns and other means, calls up content more specific and pointed than that promulgated by modernist doctrines. It is a short jump from *specific* to 'obvious', 'heavy-handed', 'crowd-pleasing', 'sloganeering', and other epithets most often aimed by the art-for-art's-sake establishment at Dada's and Surrealism's recent progeny – pop art, conceptual art, narrative art, performance and video art. Even the most conventional kinds of representational art come in for some sneers, as though *images* were by definition literary. God forbid, the taboo seems to be saying, that the content of art be accessible to its audience. And God forbid that content mean something in social terms. Because if it did, that audience might expand, and art itself might escape from the ivory tower, from the clutches of the ruling/corporate class that releases and interprets it to the rest of the world. Art might become 'mere propaganda' for *us*, instead of for *them*.

Because we have to keep in the back of our minds at all times that we wouldn't have to use the denigrated word 'propaganda' for what is, in fact, *education*, if it weren't consistently used against us. 'Quality' in art, like 'objectivity' and 'neutrality', belongs to *them*. The only way to combat the

184

'normal' taken-for-granted propaganda that surrounds us daily is to question *their* version of the truth as publicly and clearly as possible. Yet in the artworld today, clarity is a taboo: 'If you want to send a message, call Western Union'... but don't make art.' This notion has become an implicit element of American art education and an effective barrier against artists' conscious communication, the reintegration of art into life.

After at least two decades in which the medium has been used primarily to subvert the message, the very word 'message' has degenerated into a euphemism for commercial interruptions. So what's left of the avant-garde, rather naturally, rejects the notion of a didactic or 'utilitarian' or 'political' art, and socialist artists working in a context dominated by various empty fads and formalisms tend to agonize about the relationship between their art and their politics. 'Formalism' (in the Greenbergian, not the Russian sense) is denied them; it has been co-opted by those invested in the idea that if art communicates at all, what it communicates had better be so vague as to be virtually incommunicable, or it won't be 'good art'. This leaves the disenfranchised formalist (or 'socialist formalist', as one artist has called himself in an attempt to reclaim the term) on a tightrope between acceptance for her/his formal capacities alone and rejection for her/his need to 'use' these capacities to convey social content.

Feminists, on the other hand, should be better equipped to cope with this dilemma. Women artists' historical isolation has prepared them to resist taboos. Our lives have not been separate from our arts, as they are in the dominant culture. 'Utilitarian', after all, is what women's work has always been. For instance, many women artists today are rehabilitating the stitch-like mark, swaddling and wrapping, the techniques and materials of women's traditional art and work. Feminist art (and feminist propaganda) expands these sources to include what we learn from our own lived experience as women, from our sense of our bodies, from our subcultural lives as a 'vertical class'.

True, the feminist creed 'the personal is the political' has been interpreted far too widely and self-indulgently in the liberal vein of 'my art is my politics', 'all art is political', 'everything a woman artist does is feminist art', and so forth. The 'I' is not necessarily universal. The personal is only political when the individual is also seen as a member of the social whole. There is a plethora of a certain kind of 'feminist art' which, like other prevailing avant-garde styles, looks into the mirror without also focusing on the meaning of the mirror itself – on the perimeter, the periphery which forms the images (form as veil; form as barrier; form as diversionary tactic). Yet despite all this, feminism has potentially changed the terms of propaganda as art by being unashamed of its obsessions and political needs, and by confirming the bonds between individual and social experience.

Jacques Ellul (in *Propaganda*, Knopf, New York 1965) sees propaganda as totally dangerous, as a sop, a substitute for some loftier appetites, a false cure for loneliness and alienation. He reduces to propaganda all of our needs for shared belief, for a community of values. Feminists may be able to see it differently. The dictionary definition of the word is 'propagating, multi-plying, disseminating principles by organized effort'; it acquired its negative connotation in a colonializing male culture, e.g., the Roman Catholic Church. In its positive sense the word 'propaganda' can be connected to women's classic role as synthesizer. Our culture of consumption draws women to the market, which, as Batya Weinbaum and Amy Bridges have shown, 'provides the setting for the reconciliation of private production and socially determined need' ('The Other Side of the Paycheck', *Monthly Review*, July-August, 1976). Similarly, women artists, few of whom have escaped traditional women's roles, might understand and clarify a viewpoint rarely if ever expressed in the arts, and create new images to validate that viewpoint.

The goal of feminist propaganda is to spread the word and provide the organizational structures through which all women can resist the patriarchal propaganda that denigrates and controls us even when we *know* what we are doing. Since the role of the image has been instrumental in our exploitation (through advertising, pornography, etc.), feminist artists have a particular responsibility to create a new image vocabulary that conforms to our own interests. If, as Ellul says, 'non-propagandized' people are forced to live outside the community, then as feminists we must use our tools of consciousness-raising, self-criticism, and non-hierarchical leadership to create a 'good propaganda' that enables women of all races and classes to form a new, collective community. Such a 'good propaganda' would be what art should be – a provocation, a new way of seeing and thinking about what goes on around us.

So far, the audience for feminist art has been, with a few exceptions, limited to the converted. The greatest political contribution of feminism to the visual arts has been a necessary first step – the introduction and expansion of the notion of autobiography and narrative, ritual and performance, women's history and women's work as ways to retrieve content without giving up form. This has involved the interweaving of photography and words and sometimes music, journal entries and imitations thereof, and the instigation of a dialogue that is particularly appropriate to video, film or performance art. For instance, while so much 'narrative art' is simply a superficial and facetious juxtaposition of words and images, it can, when informed by a politically feminist consciousness, open a dialogue between the artist and the viewer: Look at my life. Now look at yours. What do you like/hate about me/my life? What do you hate/like about you/yours? Have you ever looked at your oppression or your accomplishments in quite this way? Is this what happened to you in a similar situation? And so forth, hopefully leading to: Why? What to do? How to organize to do it?

In a literate (but anti-literary) society, the words attached to art, even as mere titles, may have more effect on the way that art is perceived than some of the strongest images do. As a public we (but especially the docilely educated middle class) look to be told by the experts what we are seeing/thinking/feeling. We are told, taught or commanded mainly in words. Not just criticism, but written captions, titles, accompanying texts, soundtracks, taped dialogues, voiceovers all play major roles in clarifying the artist's intent – or in mystifying it. A title, for instance, can be the clue to the image, a hook pulling in a string of associations or providing a punch line. It can also be obfuscating, unrelated, contradictory or even a politically offensive publicity gimmick whereby the artist so vaguely identifies with some fashionable cause that the meaning is turned back on itself.

At what point, then, does the word overwhelm the image, the combination become 'just a political cartoon'? Still more important, at what point does visual or verbal rhetoric take over and either authoritarianism or an insidiously persuasive vacuity overwhelm dialogue? *This* is the point at which the image/word is no longer good propaganda (socially and aesthetically aware provocation) but bad propaganda (an exploitative and oppressive economic control mechanism). Authoritarian written art is basically unpopular with all except the most invested and/or specialized audiences. Feminists too are more likely to be swayed and moved to tears or rage by music, novels, films and theatre than by visual art, which is still popularly associated with imposed duty and elitist good taste, with gold frames and marble pedestals. Yet the feminist influence on the art of the seventies is evident in the prevalence of art open to dialogue – performance, video, film, music, poetry readings, panels and even *meetings*. It not only suggests a merger of art and entertainment (with Brechtian overtones) but also suggests that speaking is the best way we know to get the message across while offering at least the illusion of direct content and dialogue. It also implies that the combination of images and *spoken* words is often more effective than the combination of images and *written* words, especially in this day of planned obsolescence, instant recycling and anti-object art.

Although most of the propaganda that survives is written, it tends to get diluted by time, misunderstandings and objectification. The spoken word is more real to most people than the written word. Though more easily forgotten in its specifics, it is more easily absorbed psychologically. The spoken word is connected with the things most people focus on almost exclusively – the stuff of daily life and the kind of personal relationships everyone longs for in an alienated society. It takes place *between* people, with eye contact, human confusion and pictures (memory). It takes place in dialogues with friends, family, acquaintances, day after day. So one's intake of spoken propaganda is in fact the sum of daily communication.

This more intimate kind of propaganda seems to me to be inherently feminist. It might be seen as gossip, in the word's original sense: 'Godsib' meant godparent, then sponsor and advocate; then it became a relative, then a woman friend, then a woman 'who delights in idle talk', 'groundless rumor' and 'tattle'. Now it means malicious and unfounded tales told by women about other people. All this happened through the increased power of patriarchal propaganda, through men gossiping about women and about each other on a grand scale (history). Thus, in the old sense, spoken propaganda, or gossip, means *relating* – a feminized style of communication either way.

Over my desk hangs a postcard showing a little black girl holding an open book and grinning broadly. The caption reads: 'Forge simple words that even the children can understand.' This postcard nags at me daily. As a writer who makes her living mostly through talking (one-night stands, not full-time teaching), I am very much aware that writing and speaking are two entirely different mediums, and that they translate badly back and forth. For instance, you can imitate writing by speaking, as anyone knows who has dozed through the presentation of an academic 'paper' spoken from a podium. Or you can imitate speaking by writing, as anyone knows who has read the self-conscious chitchat favored by many newspaper columnists. The best way of dealing with speaking seems to be to skip, suggest, associate, charm and perform with passion, while referring your audience back to the

written word for more complex information and analysis.

Holding people's attention while they are reading is not so easy. Like 'modern art', the thoughtful essay has had a bad press. Popular magazines imitate speech by avoiding intimidating or didactic authoritarian associations with the text-filled page and by breaking the page with pictures, anecdotes or intimate 'asides'. Right and Left depend equally on colloquialism to reach and convince a broad audience. Popular dislike of overtly superior or educated authority is reflected, for instance, in an anti-feminist characterization of 'most women's lib books' as 'cumbersome university theses'. The visual/verbal counterparts of long-running TV soap operas are the comic book and the photo-novel, which, significantly, are the closest possible imitations of speaking in writing, as well as the cheapest way of combining 'spoken' words with images. As a middle-class college-educated propagandist, I rack my brain for ways to communicate with working-class women. I've had fantasies about peddling socialist feminist art comics on Lower East Side street corners, even of making it into the supermarkets (though it would be difficult to compete with the plastically slick and colorful prettiness of the propaganda already ensconced there). But this vision of 'forging simple words' also has a matronizing aspect. I was taken aback at a recent meeting when a young working-class woman who did not go to college stood up for a difficult language and complex Marxist terminology. Her point was that this terminology had been forged to communicate difficult conceptions and there was no need to throw the baby out with the bathwater because of some notion that the working class wasn't capable of developing its minds. 'We can look up the words we don't know,' she said, 'but people want to *grow*.'

So are my comic book fantasies simply classist? Should I stick to the subtleties of four syllable words? Both of us seemed to be leaning over backwards to counteract our own class backgrounds. A similar conflict was expressed by Cuban Nelson Herrera Ysla in a poem called *Colloquialism* (*Canto Libro*, vol. 3, no. 1, 1979):

> *Forgive me, defender of images and symbols:*
> *I forgive you, too.*
> *Forgive me, hermetic poets for whom I have boundless admiration.*
> *but we have so many things left to say*
> *in a way that everyone understands as clearly as possible,*
> *the immense majority about to discover the miracle of language.*
> *Forgive me, but I keep thinking that Fidel has taught us dialogue and*
> *   that this, my dear poets,*
> *has been a decisive literary influence.*
> *Thank you.*

Such conflicts between high art and communication have recently been raised in the visual arts by public feminist performance art, by Judy Chicago's cooperatively executed *The Dinner Party* and by the community mural movement – the visual counterparts of verbal colloquialism in their clear images and outreach goals. But how much conventional visual art in fact has been successful as propaganda? From the twentieth century we think of a few posters: 'Uncle Sam Wants *You*'; 'War Is Not Good for Children and Other Growing Things'; 'And Babies?' (this last one, protesting the My Lai massacre, was actually designed collectively by a group of 'fine artists' from the now defunct Art Workers Coalition). And we think of a few modern artists – the Mexican muralists and, ironically, several Germans: the Berlin Dadas, Heartfield, Kollwitz, Staeck, Beuys, Haacke. Compare this lackluster record with the less brutal consciousness raised by songs (those in which the musical foreground doesn't overwhelm or neutralize the lyrics). And compare it with the kind of historical consciousness-raising offered through oral history, accompanied by old photographs, letters, memories of one's own grandparents' stories. We keep coming back to words. And not just to words, but to words set in visual frameworks that are emotionally as well as intellectually stimulating.

realistic images are not seen as 'illustrations'. Yet I have to admit I'm constantly disheartened by the content of art using the 'new mediums' as vehicles not for communication or social awareness, but simply for

My own preference is for an art that uses words and images so integrally interwoven that even narrative elements are not seen as 'captions' and even realistic images are not seen as 'illustrations'. Yet I have to admit I'm constantly disheartened by the content of art using the 'new mediums' as vehicles not for communication or social awareness, but simply for unfocused form and fashion. Effective propaganda obviously has to be aimed at a specific audience, not just shot into the air to fall to earth we know not where. (This should hardly be anathema to an art already, if often unconsciously and involuntarily, aimed at a very limited audience of curators, critics, collectors and other artists.) Targeting one's audience is very different from finding one's audience – the former having to do with marketing and the latter with strategy. If we assume that *moving* a large and varied audience is at the heart of the matter, perhaps we should spend our energies making art for TV, where information can be communicated in a manner that is simultaneously intimate and detached, and where there might be some hope of turning that huge passive, consuming audience into a huge, active, critical, potentially revolutionary audience. And *if* (a monstrous if) we were ever to succeed in wresting TV time from 100% corporate control, would this lead to solid alliances, or to a wishy-washy pluralism? And where would artists come in?

Most 'art video' (as opposed to documentary, real-time political video) is still limited to art audiences and is, or would be, rejected by people accustomed to a kind of entertainment most avant-garde artists are not skilful enough to produce, even if they did decide to stop boring their audiences to death. Most artists prefer not to move out of the competitive, incestuous, but comprehensible art context into the unwelcoming Big Time of the real world. In the late sixties, a few conceptual artists did make newspaper pieces, but they were usually artworld 'in' jokes or rhetorical arguments plunked down with no attempt to adapt to the new medium, becoming in the process another kind of ineffectual cultural colonialism. (Ellul says that ineffective propaganda is simply *not* propaganda.) Despite its idealistic beginnings, most book art is now a pale imitation of gallery art, the page becoming a miniature wall instead of something to be *read* (i.e., understood). In turn, written art hung on gallery walls is difficult to read and arrogant in its enlargement from the book form it imitates. There have been some genuine and successful attempts to integrate art into street and community life, and others to analyze and compete with public advertising in the form of posters and rubber-stamp commentaries, but for all the theoretical acumen of some of this work, it tends to be visually indistinguishable from the mass media it parodies.

This opens a can of worms about satires and 'parodies' that aren't comprehensible if one isn't in the know. Ambiguity is chic *and* modernist, lending itself to esoteric theories that inflate the art and deflate any possible messages. A left-wing film, for instance, might be a 'parody' of macho fantasy films of violence, but in fact uses parody as an excuse to wallow in just that 'politically incorrect' imagery. This happens often in feminist art and performance too. When women artists use their own nude bodies, made-up faces, 'hooker costumes', etc., it is all too often difficult to tell which direction the art is coming from. Is this barebreasted woman mugging in black stockings and garter belt a swipe at feminist 'prudery' and in agreement with right-wing propaganda that feminism denies femininity? Is it a gesture of solidarity with prostitutes? Is it a parody of the ways in which fashion and media exploit and degrade women? Is it an angry satirical commentary on pornography? Or does it approve of pornography? Much so-called 'punk art' (politically aware at one point in Britain, although almost never in the U.S.) raises these questions in a framework of neutral passivity masquerading as deadpan passion. Similarly, a work might cleverly pretend to espouse the opposite of what it does in fact believe, as a means of emphasizing the contradictions involved. But how are we to know? Are we just to be embarrassed when the artist says, 'But I didn't mean it that way. How naive, how paranoid and moralistic of you to see it that way. You must be really out of it...'? Are we to back down because it is, after all, art which isn't supposed to be comprehensible and isn't just about appearances? Or can we demand to know why the artist hasn't asked her/himself what kind of context this work needs to be seen 'right' or 'not taken seriously' – to be

seen as the satire it really is?

Women are always assumed by the patriarchy to be suckers for propaganda – less educated, less worldly, more submissive, more emotional than men. Looking at it a different way, acknowledging the edge we have in empathy, feminist consciousness of communication, narrative, intimate scale and outreach networks, why aren't women artists taking the lead in inventing, say, a new kind of magazine art that transforms a legitimate avant-garde direction into propaganda with an aesthetic character of its own? Why aren't many women artists making imaginative public art focused on feminist issues? Why do the Right-to-Lifers have more compelling demonstration skits, poster and pamphlet images than the Pro-Choice movement? (One reason, of course, is that the right wing has money and CARASA doesn't. But surely there are enough economically comfortable women artists to lend some time and talents and aesthetic energy to causes they believe in?) Why does *Heresies* receive so few pertinent visual pieces? Why have the few artists committed to such work often found it easier to use words than images? And how can we get more visibility for those word and word/image pieces that do tackle this problem? Some crucial factor is lacking in our strategies for making memorable images or emblems that will move, affect and provoke a larger group of women. Some crucial breakdown in confidence or commitment, or caring energy, seems to occur when an artworld-trained artist is confronted with the possibility of making 'useful' art. I could make a lot of psychological guesses why (fear of the real world, fear of being used by the powers that be, of being misunderstood and misperceived, fear of humiliation and lack of support...) but I'm more interested in encouraging artists to move into such situations so we can see what happens then.

A lot of these questions and problems may be the result of our own misunderstanding of propaganda turning back on us. No one on the Left would deny the importance of propaganda. Yet it is a rare left-wing feminist who is interested in or even aware of the resources visual artists could bring to the struggle. The current lack of sparks between art and propaganda is due to a fundamental polarity that is in the best interests of those who decide these things for us. There are very effective pressures in the artworld to keep the two separate, to make artists see political concern and aesthetic quality as mutually exclusive and basically incompatible; to make us see our commitment to social change as a result of our own human weaknesses, our own lack of talent and success. This imposed polarity keeps people (artists) unsure and bewildered amid a chaos of 'information' and conflicting signals produced by the media, the marketplace, and those who manipulate them and us. It keeps us desperate to be sophisticated, cool, plugged in, and competitively ahead of the game (other women artists, that is). It makes us impatient with criticism and questions. It deprives us of tools with which to understand the way we exploit ourselves as artists. It makes us forget that words and images working together can create those sparks between daily life and the political world instead of hovering in a ghostly realm of their own, which is the predicament of the visual arts right now. It keeps us from forming the alliances we need to begin to make our own lives whole.

This article owes a great deal to dialogues with the Heresies No. 9 *collective and the New York Socialist Feminists, and especially to those with Joan Braderman in both groups.*

CHILA BURMAN

THERE HAVE ALWAYS BEEN GREAT BLACKWOMEN ARTISTS

We face many problems when trying to establish the very existence of Blackwomen's art, and a strong social and political base from which to develop our study of it. Firstly, we have to struggle to establish our existence, let alone our credibility as autonomous beings, in the art world. Secondly, we can only retain that credibility and survive as artists if we become fully conscious of ourselves, lest we are demoralised or weakened by the social, economic and political constraints which the white-male art establishment imposes and will continue to impose upon us.

This paper, then, is saying Blackwomen artists are here, we exist and we exist positively, despite the racial, sexual and class oppressions which we suffer, but first, however, we must point out the way in which these oppressions have operated in a wider context – not just in the art world, but also in the struggles for black and female liberation.

It is true to say that although Blackwomen have been the staunchest allies of black men and white women in the struggle against the oppression we all face at the hands of the capitalist and patriarchal system, we have hardly ever received either the support we need or recognition of our pivotal role in this struggle. Blackwomen now realise that because of the specific ways in which we are oppressed by white-male dominated society, we must present a new challenge to imperialism, racism and sexism from inside and outside the established black liberation movement and at a critical distance to the white-dominated feminist movement. It is this realisation which has a lot to do with many second generation British Blackwomen reclaiming art, firstly as a legitimate area of activity for Blackwomen as a distinct group of people, secondly as a way of developing an awareness (denied us by this racist, sexist, class society) of ourselves as complete human beings, and thirdly as a contribution to the black struggle in general.

Having said this, Blackwomen's ability to do any or all of these three things is restricted by the same pressures of racism, sexism and class exclusivity which we experience in society in general. The bourgeois art establishment only acknowledges white men as truly creative and innovative artists, whilst recognising art by white women only as a homogenous expression of femininity and art by black people (or, more accurately, within the terms of reference used, black men) as a static expression of the ritual experience of the daily lives of their communities, be they in the Third World or the imperialist hinterland. In this system of knowledge, Blackwomen artists, quite simply, do not exist.

Nevertheless, if we look at the way in which these assumptions have been challenged to date, particularly by white women, we can still see nothing that acknowledges that Blackwomen exist. Art history is an academic subject, studied in patriarchal art institutions, and white middle-class women have used their advantageous class position to gain access to these institutions by applying pressure to them in a way which actually furthers the exclusion of black artists in general. White women's failure to inform themselves of the obstacles faced by black artists and in particular Blackwomen artists has led to the production of an extremely Eurocentric theory and practice of 'women's art'. It seems that white feminists, as much as white women in general, either do not attempt to or find it difficult to conceive of Blackwomen's experience. Some of those who do not attempt to may claim that they cannot speak for Blackwomen, but this is merely a convenient way of sidestepping their own racism. The fact remains that in a patriarchal and sexist society, all black people suffer from racism, and it is quite possible for white women to turn racism, which stems from patriarchy, to their advantage. Black men are unable to do this and, theoretically, are unable to turn sexism to their advantage, although they can do this for short-term gains which in the long term will never benefit black people as a whole. This has happened to a certain extent in the art world, where black men have failed to recognise Blackwomen artists or have put pressure on us to produce certain kinds of work linked to a male-dominated notion of struggle. However, because of their race and class position, black men have been unable to use the resources of art institutions in the same way that white middle-class women have.

The struggles of Blackwomen artists

The first stage of most Blackwomen artists' encounter with the art establishment is their entry into art college. There are hardly any Blackwomen attending art college in Britain, and those who do, according to a survey of Blackwomen artists I carried out, seem to have experienced a mixture of hostility and indifference from their college. Because their white tutors work within an imperialist art tradition, using the aesthetic conventions of the dominant ideology, they are unwilling to come to terms with Blackwomen students and their work. This resistance manifests itself in many ways – some Blackwomen art students have found themselves asking why they as individuals found it easy to get into art college, only to realise that they are there purely as tokens, and in general it appears that Blackwomen's very presence in white-male art institutions is frequently called into question. Apart from denying us the support and encouragement that white art students receive, art colleges make us feel as though we don't belong inside their walls by the way in which our work is looked at. Those of us who have done more overtly political work have made white tutors very uncomfortable and, as a result, hostile, whilst students who have done less obviously challenging work have been questioned for not producing the kind of work which tutors expect black people to produce. Class differences amongst Blackwomen are significant here, for working-class Blackwomen have generally been quicker to reject the ideology of the art establishment and have therefore found it difficult to accept any kind of token status or to produce work of a more acceptable nature. Those who have not taken such an oppositional stance have still suffered from having their work analysed within a very narrow framework because their tutors have expected them to produce 'ethnic' work which reflects their 'cultural origin' using, for example, 'bright carnival colours', and white tutors and students alike have expressed confusion when such work has not been forthcoming. Another tendency of white tutors, irrespective of the type of work they are presented with, is to discuss art from the third world with Blackwomen in a patronising and racist manner.

Of course, the assumption that Blackwomen will produce work with 'ethnic' or 'primitive' associations is one that white tutors make about black men as well, but it is important to point out that male *and* female white tutors are more inclined to see black men as having a more prominent role in this misconceived tradition. One Blackwoman student at Bradford art college commented:

'Funny how they always refer to you as some sort of bridge or crosssing point between two things. Black meets woman. That's handy. As if you don't have an experience which is your own, but borrow from the brothers and sisters in struggle.'

It seems, then, that when art colleges and universities give places to Blackwomen, which in itself is a rare event, all the forces of the dominant aesthetic ideology are brought to bear on us. Blackwomen artists are ignored, isolated, described as 'difficult', slotted into this or that stereotype and generally discouraged in every conceivable way from expressing ourselves in the way that we want to. This system of oppression and exclusion extends well beyond our time as art students. There are no full-time lecturing posts at art colleges and universities filled by Blackwomen in the entire country – instead we are offered 'freelance' work as visiting lecturers, which will never be enough to initiate a critique of contemporary art practice which is so desperately needed in every single art department in the country.

In addition, Blackwomen artists are denied the opportunity to develop their work as individuals in the same way that white artists can through grants from sources such as the Arts Council, the Greater London Council, regional arts associations and the Calouste Gulbenkian Foundation. Even though some of these sources such as the GLC and the Greater London Arts Association have recently begun to realise how much they have neglected Black visual arts, on the only occasion that a Blackwoman has received funding from the GLC as an individual, this has still been on unsatisfactory terms which differ significantly from the terms on which the only black man in this position has been funded. The man in question has been funded without any preconditions except that he produces a certain amount of work, whilst the woman was funded by the Arts and Recreation Department of the GLC for a year on the condition that she was attached to a community arts centre as a 'community artist', and the stipulation was made that the work she produced should not reflect her desires as an individual but 'the interests of the black community'. The GLC had ignored the importance to the black community of the experience of individual Blackwomen and had funded her on the basis of an ahistorical notion of 'community' or 'ethnic minority' arts, but when it came to applying to the Arts Council, it appeared that the role she had been pushed into was not individual enough. The rejection of her application to this body read:

'We do not think that your proposed project fits the terms of reference for this training scheme which is specifically aimed at developing the individual's skills, and is not to assist with research projects.'

If even the GLC funded a Blackwoman artist only as a 'community artist', this illustrates our position in a kind of funding no-woman's-land, because the Arts Council, racist and sexist as it is already, will continue to see our work as unfundable research projects and, as was the case with the application mentioned, refer us to bodies such as the Association of Commonwealth Universities, further relegating us to the marginality of the 'ghetto artist', completely outside the mainstream British art world.

Blackwomen artists fight back

The resilience of Blackwomen in the face of oppression has manifested itself in the art world through our ability to produce and exhibit work despite all the social, economic and political constraints described above. The first all-Blackwomen's show at the Africa Centre in 1983 was not just a beginning; Blackwomen artists have been actively involved in exhibitions with white artists and Black men artists for several years, but this all-Blackwomen's show and the ones that have taken place since then – *Blackwoman Time Now, 1985 International Women's Day Show, Mirror Reflecting Darkly*, etc. – represent a significant new direction which has much to do with the development of what Barbara Smith describes as 'our own intellectual traditions'.

It is obvious that the majority of Black artists see their work in opposition to the establishment view of art as something that is 'above' politics, and Blackwomen artists see their work as integral to the struggles of Blackwomen and black people in general, but although Blackwomen's own culture plays a large part in determining the content and form of our work, we often concentrate on different issues to black men, who, as one Blackwoman artist points out, often believe that 'artists who are making through their works a collective, aggressive challenge to cultural domination are "real" black artists and making Black Art. But some male artists fail to understand or comprehend the struggles women artists go through to assert their identity and survive'.

Alice Walker illustrates the difference between these two ideas of Black Art in 'In Search of Our Mothers' Gardens' and goes on to put forward an alternative way for the black artist to operate:

'I am impressed by people who claim they can see every thing and event in strict terms of black and white but their work is not, in my long contemplated and earnestly considered opinion, either black or white, but a dull, uniform gray. It is boring because it is easy and requires only that the reader be a lazy reader and a prejudiced one. Each story or poem has a formula usually two-thirds 'hate whitey's guts' and one-third 'I am black, beautiful and almost always right'. Art is not flattery, and the work of every artist must be more difficult than that.

'My major advice to young black artists would be that they shut themselves up somewhere away from all the debates about who they are and what colour they are and just turn out paintings and poems and stories and novels. Of course the kind of artist we are required to be cannot do this (our people are waiting)'.

Alice Walker's advice is important here, for she is not suggesting that we cut ourselves off from the outside world, because we cannot forget the mark our oppressions as black women have made on us, or the fact that 'our people are waiting'. The point is that what we need as artists is the opportunity to create the situation she describes so that we are allowed to develop an understanding of ourselves and of the struggle we have to wage within British society for recognition and respect. If we are able to do this by having adequate resources put at our disposal, we hope to share our experiences with, awaken the consciousness of and impart our strength to the whole society.

This is a synopsis of a talk delivered at the Black Visual Artists Forum, ICA London, October 1986.

REVIEWED by LAWRENCE ALLOWAY

OLD MISTRESSES:
WOMEN, ART AND IDEOLOGY
BY ROZSIKA PARKER AND
GRISELDA POLLOCK

Women artists have access to as wide an array of styles and iconographical systems now as men, but they do not have an adequate place in the support system of commercial art galleries, museums, and magazines. Art critics, for instance, aside from Lucy Lippard, have not contributed much, but unexpectedly women art historians have. One reason for this is that they write outside the market. Traditional art history has numerous connections to the market of course (consider Bernard Berenson), but the historians here are innovative in relation to values, not occupied with the authentication of works in dealers' hands. Another reason is that historians' readers have higher expectations than art critics' readers. In the growing literature on women's art, there are half-a-dozen survey books, none of which existed before 1974. The ones not by art historians are certainly the worst: Petersen's and Wilson's *Women's Art: Recognition and Reappraisal*, the equivalent of a half-informed art appreciation lecture course; Germaine Greer's *The Obstacle Race*,[1] parasitic in its reliance on others' work; and Eleanor Munro's *Originals*,[2] ameliorating and conformist in the tone of its retelling of women's art as to a museum Junior Council.

The art historically-based studies by Eleanor Tufts, Elsa Honig Fine, and Charlotte Streifer Rubinstein[3] are informative texts, but the overall effect is that they lack intellectual rigor. Satisfaction at supporting a good cause can blunt the sense of critical inquiry. It is as if the chronicle form weakens the procedures of argument. The compilation of fact, accurate but not organised by vigorous ideas, has its limits. The lack of ideas about art or ideas derived from other fields, in which research is often more informed than in the visual arts, has restricted the scope of the surveys. The chroniclers have convincingly added to the expanding index of women artists, but possible patterns and clusters in the list of names have not been pursued with enough curiosity or zeal.

The positivistic accumulation of fact is a procedure to which I am sympathetic, but it becomes inertial if the data is not grouped by acts of interpretation. Of the surveys only *Women Artists 1550-1950* by Anne

Sutherland Harris and Linda Nochlin seems fully attuned to the tensions set up by women's art; the other books are comparatively bland and self-confirming compared to this decisive study. Given Harris's and Nochlin's authoritative performance in the area, it is natural that they should be called by two younger art historians, Rozsika Parker and Griselda Pollock, in *Old Mistresses*,[4] a book that echoes in fact their predecessors' bite and thoughtfulness.

Parker and Pollock complain that Harris and Nochlin are susceptible to the values of a male-serving art history. Here is their comment on Nochlin's sociological explanation of the slowing down of women artists: 'If these social or institutional restraints had indeed been effective, or, more importantly, were the central causes of women's "problems" in art practice, the only logical conclusion one could draw would be that there have been no women artists at all.' This would sound better in debate than it reads on the checkable page. Historically the problem of women artists has to do with retardation and re-routing, not obliteration, and Nochlin addresses those conditions specifically. It is not an either/or situation in which either there are women artists or there are not, because we know there are: a part of the value of Harris and Nochlin is that they accept the complexity of women in history as a part of the subject.

The locating of women artists in art history on terms compatible with the discipline's given form is flawed by acquiescence to male standards, according to Parker and Pollock. Both Harris/Nochlin and Eleanor Tufts are treated on this basis, as if Tufts's *Our Hidden Heritage* and *Women Artists 1550-1950* were symptoms of a single impulse to conform, but this is not so. Tufts thinks that women artists are great, whereas Harris/Nochlin stay within the scepticism of Nochlin's original question, 'Why have there been no great women artists?' Tufts may seem radical in her openness, but she is intellectually soft; it is Harris and Nochlin who are actually revisionists with their insistence on the causes of inequality. Their use of art history's received forms is more the retention of an evidential methodology than the sign of conformity. Sisterly appreciation across the centuries, in Tufts' auntly style, is by comparison a kind of consolatory art appreciation.

Parker and Pollock require a total dismantling of art history. This ultimatistic view rests on their ideological reading of art history which they regard as part of a nineteenth-century inheritance of prejudiced ideas. These include the 'collapse of history into nature and sociology into biology'. This is a deterioration of information as comparatively precise terms became progressively less differentiated. The destructive idea is the notion of 'different spheres for men and women' which leads to the trivialisation (by men) or the mystification (by women) of women's art. Women, owing to home-running and childbearing, were said to be closer to nature than to culture, the terms taken, as Parker and Pollock point out, from Lévi-Strauss.

Old Mistresses follows the normal chronological form, but the authors bring to it analytical judgment and up-to-date ideas. There are good sections on individuals as different as Sophonisba Anguissola and Rosalba Carriera, and on broad topics, such as craft. The book is free of sentimental excursions into the lives and motives of women. Although biography has a great deal to contribute to the study of art, the homiletic or exhortatory episodes that stylize the real course of women artists' lives are hard to tolerate. (Kathe Kollwitz, for instance, is at present frozen into a set of these tableaux.)

The subtitle of the book is 'Women, Art and Ideology', and ideology, however it gets defined, at a minimum assumes the present as viewpoint. It is the way in which we estimate how contemporaneity informs/distorts the past. Why then does the book, with its authors' strong ideological awareness, collapse at the end, in the present time? After four incisive chapters the fifth is inconclusive and prejudiced. It starts with conventional appreciations of Leonore Fini and Meret Oppenheim, according to the authors' arguable but interesting notion of Surrealism's implicit feminism. Then it proceeds to Helen Frankenthaler, Marisol, and Eva Hesse, and here the authors lose their art historical grip; Frankenthaler is discussed as if she were a first rather than a second generation abstract expressionist and Marisol is recruited to the ' "beat generation" in New York' (sic). Owing to Lippard's book on Hesse there are not gross errors like these about her, but the fact remains that these artists represent anti-feminist (Frankenthaler, Marisol) and pre-feminist (Hesse) attitudes. Why are they here when there are so many substantial feminist artists to choose from in the United States?

They are here because the authors, trained as art historians at the Courtauld Institute, have run into their profession's standard problem in coping with contemporary art. The art of the present exists in a state of unruly, pre-linear simultaneity, which does not provide clear guidelines or homing points. In addition there is a related difficulty concerning the United States, the main place for the production and study of women's art. Parker and Pollock are capable of a closely-argued book until their chronicle intersects with the present, and the present is American. Recognition of American culture is traditionally awkward in British thought. Hence the oddity of the American triad, after which the authors dwell on small-scale London matters: first a Hayward Annual exhibition of 1978 which was selected by but was not even wholly the work of women artists; then an over-intense account of an English Conceptual artist, Mary Kelly. This is precipitously less than what the 1970s have provided feminists in the way of subject matter. The parochial conclusion is especially unsatisfactory after the standard set by the authors' confident handling of earlier periods. For a book that begins with penetrating arguments about Anguissola and Artemesia Gentileschi, this is a steep descent, or as Humpty Dumpty might have said: 'There's a whimper, not a bang, for you.'

Despite their reservations about the ideology of conventional art history, Parker and Pollock, after all, share it. Their feminism does not protect them from nationalism or a belief that the present does not require the same evidential standards as the past. Their commitment to feminism is in conflict with these professional habits. The connection of art history and living artists which characterises the development of feminism in the United States escapes them.

NOTES

1 Reviewed *WAJ* (Fall 1980/Winter 1981), 64-9.
2 Reviewed *WAJ* (Spring/Summer 1980), 60-3.
3 Excerpted *WAJ* (Spring/Summer 1982), 6-9.
4 The title repeats, as the authors acknowledge, that of an exhibition at the Walters Art Gallery, Baltimore in 1972. It was a facetious title then, but the show was very early in the feminist movement and the title was tolerable for that reason. To come across it again, ten years later, is deplorable. The British authors are blithe about the words, but a *mistress* is an illegal sexual companion (not at all the equivalent of the honorific term master) and *old* suggests the loss of those qualities that mistresses rely on. The term hovers between jocularity and disparagement.

GRISELDA POLLOCK

WOMEN, ART AND IDEOLOGY: QUESTIONS FOR FEMINIST ART HISTORIANS

It ought to be clear by now that I'm not interested in the social history of art as part of a cheerful diversification of the subject, taking its place alongside other varieties – formalist, 'modernist', sub-Freudian, filmic, feminist, 'radical', all of them hot-foot in pursuit of the new. For diversification, read disintegration.
T.J. Clark, 'On the Condition of Artistic Creation',
    The Times Literary Supplement, May 24, 1974, 562.

Almost ten years ago, Clark warned of a crisis in art history which was the product of the loss of a cogent historical project for the discipline and the result of its severance from the other social and historical sciences. He was, however, fiercely dismissive of several alternative tendencies being offered, which he designated pseudo-solutions, themselves proliferating symptoms of intellectual desperation. These mere novelties, reflecting fashions in relevant but distinct disciplines, included literary formalism, psychoanalysis, film theory, and feminism. In this article I consider the question of how feminism, which has grown steadily in art history since 1974, positions itself in relation to both mainstream art history and its radical critiques.

Criticisms of mainstream art histories are being made through what Clark designated for his own and others' work, the social history of art. A superbly summary, but accurate, assessment written many decades ago can be found in the review which Meyer Schapiro published in 1937 of A.H. Barr, Jr.'s *Cubism and Abstract Art* (Museum of Modern Art, 1936). Schapiro wrote:

> ...Barr's conception of abstract art remains essentially unhistorical. He gives us, it is true, the dates of every stage in the various movements, as if to enable us to plot a curve, or to follow the emergence of the art year by year, but no connection is drawn between the art and conditions of its moment. He excludes as irrelevant to its history the nature of the society in which it arose, except as an incidental obstructing or accelerating atmospheric factor. The history of modern art is presented as an internal, immanent process among the artists; abstract art arises because, as the author says, representational art had been exhausted.[1]

The obvious paradigm for a genuinely historical, alternative art history lies within those schools of thought and historiography which insist upon the social character of all practices, including artistic practice which is shaped by concrete social relations, and works within and on socially produced ideologies. The most sustained example is, of course, within Marxist cultural theory and historical practice. As a feminist I find myself obliquely placed within this debate. Inasmuch as society is structured by inequal relations at the point of material production, so too is it deeply founded on inequal relations between the sexes. The nature of the societies in which art has been produced has not only been, for instance, feudal or capitalist, but in historically varied ways, patriarchal and sexist. Neither form of exploitation, moreover, is reducible to the other. As Jean Gardiner has pointed out, no social perspective can remain innocent of the importance of the sexual divisions of society and still claim to be an adequate account of social processes:

> It is impossible to understand women's class position without understanding the way in which sexual divisions shape women's consciousness of class... No socialist can ignore this question.[2]

The solution cannot lie in simply adding one approach to another with the concomitant danger of merely subordinating feminism to the more developed analyses of Marxism. Domination and exploitation in gender relations are not just a supplement to the more fundamental conflicts between the classes, even if it is difficult in practice to disarticulate them. Feminism in both practice and theory has exposed new areas of social conflict and has thus generated new kinds of analysis – of kinship structure and the family, of the construction of gender and our sexualities, of reproduction, of domestic labor and the employment of women and, of course, of the powerful place of cultural images in the cementing of the hierarchical relations between social groups and genders. Indeed, from the inception of the women's movement, one of the major targets of political activity has been the representation of women in advertising, cinema, photography, and the fine arts. Art history has a particular, if overlooked, role in all this. On the one hand, art history takes as its object of study a form of cultural production and ideology – art. On the other hand, the discipline itself is a component of cultural hegemony maintaining and reproducing dominative social relations through what it studies and teaches and what it omits or marginalises, and through how it defines what history is, what art is, and who and what the artist is. For instance, the major figure in art historical discourse is the artist, the singular, solitary genius whose creativity is recorded almost exclusively in a biographical or autobiographical mode in monographs and *catalogues raisonnés*. This figure functions, however, as a social ideal, a complement to and embodiment of the prime bourgeois myth of the universal, classless Man.

The myth of free, individual creativity is gender specific; it is exclusively masculine. We never talk of men artists or male art; if you wish to specify that the artist is female the term must be qualified with a feminine adjectival prefix. Recognition of this came early in feminist art history. Gabhart and Broun commented in their introductory essay to *Old Mistresses* the exhibition of art by women they organised in 1972:

> The title of this exhibition alludes to the unspoken assumption in our language that art is created by men. The reverential term 'Old Master' has no meaningful feminine equivalent. When cast in its feminine form, 'Old Mistress', the connotation is altogether different to say the least.[3]

Gabhart and Broun exposed the relationship between language and ideology, but did not ask why there is no place for women in the language of art history despite the fact that there has been a continuous tradition of women's practice in art. In *Old Mistresses: Women, Art & Ideology* (Pantheon, 1982), Rozsika Parker and I took up this question, feeling, moreover, that the neologism 'Old Mistress' was still pertinent as a reminder of what is at issue. It is not a question of merely overcoming the neglect of women artists by art historians. The consistency and variety of women's contribution to culture has been adequately demonstrated in feminist art histories of the last decade. Investigating the nature of the obstacles women faced, listing the diverse forms of discrimination, though necessary, is not a complete answer. As Parker pointed out in a review of Germaine Greer's *The Obstacle Race* (1969): 'It is not the obstacles that Germaine Greer cites that really count, but the rules of the game that demand scrutiny'.[4]

We started from the premise that women had always been involved in the production of art, but that the historians of our culture were reluctant to admit it. Our research revealed that it was in fact only in the twentieth century, with the establishment of art history as a widely-taught, institutionalised academic discipline, that women artists were systematically obliterated from the record. There is, however, considerable literature on women artists prior to this century and a certain amount of reference to women in modern art criticism. But this literature consistently employed a particular cluster of terms and evaluations which we labelled the 'feminine stereotype'. What was suggested unquestioningly was that all that women have produced bears witness to a single, sex-derived attribute – femininity. This attribution of a pervasive and irrepressible femininity then justified a complacent judgment on women's innate inferiority in the arts. We pondered the meaning and pervasiveness of the equation between art by women and femininity, and between femininity and bad art, and concluded that the feminine stereotype was an important, structuring category in the discourse of art history. It is set up as a necessary term of difference, the foil against which a never-acknowledged masculine privilege can be maintained. The hidden sexual prerogative of masculine appropriation of creativity as an innate attribute of that sex is secured by the repeated assertion of a negative, an 'other', the feminine, as the necessary point of differentiation and lack. We found, furthermore, that the foundations for this process lay in the social history of the artist and of the roles and positions of women.

Tracing the history of the evolving concept of the artist from the sixteenth to the nineteenth century and mapping at the same time the changing social definitions of woman, we discovered that men and women had followed historically different and finally contradictory paths so that by the nineteenth century what was understood by the term woman (a passive dependent to be fulfilled through domestic and maternal roles) and what the artist represented (an anti-social, independent creator) were set in an antagonistic relationship. This conflict is expressed aptly by one nineteenth century commentator: 'So long as a woman refrains from unsexing herself, let her dabble in anything. The woman of genius does not exist. When she does, she is a man'.[5] This polarisation occurred during the formation of bourgeois society in the critical period of the late eighteenth and early nineteenth centuries. Just as we recognise in the modern women's movement that changing women's position is a challenge to the structure of

the same – all these views served to make the status quo seem inevitable. The bourgeois image of the world combines, therefore, both a repression of the real social conditions of its present rule and the necessary repression of any recognisable difference between itself and past societies. This is accomplished first by 'modernising' history, i.e. assuming a complete identity between the present and the past, and secondly by projecting back into the past the features of the present order so that they come to appear as universal, unchanged, and natural. This has special significance for feminist analyses. The fiction of an eternal, natural order of things is employed monolithically to ratify the continuing power of men over women. The justification for making women exclusively responsible for domestic work and child care is assumed to be the 'nature' of women. Historically produced social roles are represented in bourgeois ideologies as timeless and biologically determined. Feminists have, therefore, a dual task: to challenge this substitution of Nature for History and to insist on understanding that history itself is changing, contradictory, differentiated.

Furthermore, art history belies historical scholarship in another way. It often has nothing to do with history at all for it amounts only to art appreciation. Recent critiques of what literary criticism does to the history of literary production are helpful in alerting us to similar ahistorical tendencies in art history. The way in which literature is studied, as Pierre Macherey has pointed out, does not explain how literature is produced: it teaches students how to consume the great fruits of the human spirit. In initiating students into the mysteries of aesthetic appreciation, submission to the inexplicable magic of creativity is instilled. But paradoxically, while literature is being presented as ineffable, the text is usually stripped naked, an apparently hidden nugget of meaning extracted through the exercise of sensitive, informed criticism, the whole 'translated' by the words of the critic who, while pretending merely to comment upon, in fact, refashions the meanings of the work of art in his or her own ideological image (i.e. modernises it). These dual procedures do not encourage students to ask the important questions – how and why an art object or text was made, for whom was it made, for what purpose was it made, within what constraints and possibilities was it produced and initially used? For, as Macherey states: 'In seeing how a book is made we also see what it is made *from*; this defect which gives it a history and a relation to the historical.'[9]

Literary appreciation and art history as appreciation are concerned with positive and negative evaluations of artifacts. Careful gradations and distinctions are established between the major and minor, the good and bad, the eternally valued and momentarily fashionable. This kind of evaluative judgment has particular implications for women. Art created by women is consistently assessed as poor art. Take, for instance, Charles Sterling's explanation for reattributing a portrait thought to be by Jacques-Louis

David to Constance Charpentier (1767-1849):

> Meanwhile the notion that our portrait may have been painted by a woman, is, let us confess, an attractive idea. Its poetry is literary rather than plastic, its very evident charms and its cleverly concealed weaknesses, its ensemble made up from a thousand subtle artifices, all seem to reveal the feminine spirit.[10]

And James Laver on the same painting: 'Although the painting is attractive as a period piece, there are certain weaknesses of which a painter of David's calibre would not have been guilty.'[11] Both Sterling and Laver have a norm of good art against which women are judged and found wanting. This establishes difference on a sexual axis and a different set of criteria for judging art made by women.

To counter this kind of criticism of women's art, some feminists assert that women's art is as good as men's, it just has to be judged by another set of criteria. But this only creates an alternative method of appreciation – another way of consuming art. They attribute to women's art other qualities, claiming that it expresses a feminine essence, or interpret it saying that it tends to a central 'core' type of imagery derived from the form of female genitals and from female bodily experience. All too familiar formal or psychologistic or stylistic criteria are marshalled to estimate art by women. The effect is to leave intact that very notion of evaluating art, and of course the normative standards by which it is done. Special pleading for women's art to be assessed by different values ensures that women's art is confined within a gender-defined category and, at the same time, that the general criteria for appreciating art remains that which is employed in discussing work by men. Men's art remains the supra-sexual norm precisely because women's art is assessed by what are easily dismissed as partisan or internally constructed values. These feminists thus end up reproducing Sterling's and Laver's hierarchy.

I am arguing that feminist art historians should reject evaluative criticism. They should concentrate instead on historical forms of explanation of women's artistic production and consider the usefulness of Marxist paradigms. There has been considerable development with Marxist cultural theory in the last decades, particularly with regard to notions of ideology and representation. But there are also elements of Marxist thinking about art and society to be avoided, among them: treating art as a reflection of the society that produced it or as an image of its class divisions; treating an artist as a representative of his/her class; economic reductionism, that is reducing all arguments about the forms and functions of cultural objects back to economic or material causes; and ideological generalisation, placing a picture because of its manifest content in a category of ideas, beliefs, or social theories of a given society or period.

All these approaches strive, however crudely, to acknowledge the complex and inescapable relations between one specific social activity – art – and the totality of other social activities which constitute the 'society' in, for, and even against which art is produced. The problem with reflection theory is that it is mechanistic, suggesting at once that art is an inanimate object which 'mirrors' a static and coherent thing called society. Treating art as a reflection of the society that produced it oversimplifies the processes whereby an art product, consciously and ideologically manufactured from specifiable and selected materials represents social processes which are themselves enormously complicated, mobile, and opaque. A slightly more sophisticated version of reflection theory is one in which art is studied 'in its historical context'. History is, however, too often merely wheeled on as background to artistic production, swiftly sketched in as a story which provides clues to the picture's content.

The attempt to place the artist as a representative of a class outlook registers the need to recognise point of view and position in class society as determinants in the production of art. Even so, it involves considerable generalisation. Hadjinicolaou, for instance, suggests that paintings carry a visual ideology. Artists such as David or Rembrandt produced works that can be read as embodiments of the visual ideologies of a particular class or fraction of a class – art of the rising bourgeoisie at the end of the *Ancien Régime*, for example. Whole *oeuvres* or groups of works become unitary examples of a social group's singular outlook via the service of the artist.[12] But the inadequacies of this approach become evident when applied to women. Some feminist art historians treat women artists as representatives of their gender – their work is seen to express the visual ideology of a whole sex. This condemns women effectively to a homogeneous, gender-defined category which is exactly what the feminine stereotype of mainstream art history does. The process effaces the specificity and heterogeneity of women's artistic production which is shaped variously and historically by factors such as class, race, nationality, period, and patronage.

Art is inevitably shaped by the society that produces it, but its particular features are not created by economic structures or organisation. In application to women the poverty of the economic reductionists becomes obvious because women's position in the workplace is shown to be a complement to, an extension of, or even a product of the complex forms of exploitation women experience in the home, in sexual relationships, in child care duties, or on the streets as a result of sexual domination.

The fourth element to avoid – ideological generalisation – is a response to the inadequacies of reductionism. Relations between areas of intellectual culture occur, but it is not enough to make great chains of ideas linking social philosophies and ideas to movements in art (e.g. Positivism and Realism). Ideology is not just a set of ideas but a process of masking contradictions thrown up in the life of society. Ideologies are often fractured and contradictory. Referring art to ideology as ideas merely displaces the necessary study of what ideological work specific pieces of art are doing. The parallel to this approach in feminist art history is to place what women artists produce in a singular category: women's art. While it has been necessary to reclaim that often pejorative category in order to insist that there is art made by women, it is also dangerous. It may lead us to believe that there are such unitary ideological categories as women's art, women's culture, or women's consciousness. To treat work by women simply as exemplars of some supposed essence of womanness is to reproduce a tautology which teaches us nothing about what being, doing, or thinking as a woman at different historical moments and in different social conditions might be.

Society is a historical process and history cannot be reduced to a manageable block of information; it has to be grasped as a complex of processes and relationships. We must, therefore, abandon all the formulations such as 'art and society', 'art and its social context', 'art and its historical background', 'art and class formations', 'art and sexual politics'. The real difficulties which are not being addressed reside in those 'ands'. We instead have to deal with the interplay of multiple histories, of the codes of art, the ideologies of the art world, the forms of production, the social classes, the family and sexual practices whose mutual determinations and interdependences have to be mapped together in precise but heterogeneous configurations.

Art is a part of social production; it is productive and actively produces meanings. Furthermore, art is constitutive of ideology, it does not merely illustrate it. It is one of the social practices through which particular views of the world, definitions and identities for us to live by, are constructed, reproduced, and even redefined. How this approach can be relevant for feminists was shown by Elizabeth Cowie in her study of women in film. For many feminists, woman is an unproblematic category defined by biological sex, by anatomy. For others, woman is not born, but made, conditioned by a series of socially prescribed roles. From these points of view, images of women in films are reflections or, at best, representations of those biological identities or social models. Films are to be judged, therefore, by the accuracy or distortion of that representation in relation to lived experience. It has, however, been argued that film has to be understood as a signifying practice, i.e. an organisation of elements which produce meanings, construct images of the world, and strive to fix certain meanings, to effect particular ideological representations of the world. So instead of seeing films as vehicles for preformed meanings or reflectors of given identities, the practice has to be seen as an active intervention:

> Film is a point of production of definitions but it is neither unique and independent of, nor simply reducible to other practices defining the position of women in society.[13]

As such, film is one of the practices which actively constructs and secures the patriarchal definitions for the category Woman.

Cowie then argues that the term Woman and its meanings are not given in biology or in society but produced across a range of interrelating practices; the term has been constructed by concrete historical, social practices – for instance, familial or kinship structures. Cowie draws on Lévi-Strauss's argument that the exchange of women between men is the foundation of sociality. The exchange of objects, which by their exchange are endowed with value and thus acquire meaning, institutes the reciprocal relationships and duties which are the basis of cultural (i.e. social) organisation as opposed to the natural state.[14] All culture is to be understood as exchange and therefore as communication. The most developed form of this is, of course, language. Language is composed of signifying elements ordered into meaning-producing relationships. Woman as a category is a product of a network of relationships created in the exchanges of females as mother, daughter, wife, sister in apposition to a concurrent production of man as father, son, husband, brother. If woman is a sign, then the meaning of the sign will always have to be determined within a system of relationships, i.e. within the specific organisation of kinship, reproduction, and sexuality. Because the meaning of the sign is a product of social relationships it can alter, and because it can alter, it must be reconstrued repeatedly. Furthermore, woman as sign implies that woman signifies something other than female sex. When women are exchanged in marriage, for instance, the empirical signifying thing is a woman, a female person. The meaning carried through the exchange by that signifying element is not femaleness but the establishment and re-establishment of culture itself, i.e. of a particular order of socio-sexual relationships and powers.

Woman as a sign signifies social order. The category Woman is of profound importance to the order of a society. It is therefore to be understood as having to be produced ceaselessly across a range of social practices and institutions and the meanings of it are constantly being negotiated in those signifying systems of culture, for instance, film or painting. To understand the precise disposition of meanings for the terms Man and Woman and the social order based upon them, we have always to attend to the specific work that is done within and by a particular text, film or painting. At the same time, this formulation allows us to recognise the centrality and critical importance of the representation of woman in patriarchal culture – and hence to grasp the radical potential of its analysis and subversion.

It thus becomes possible to redefine and refine the projects of feminist art historians. Women have not been absent from the history of culture but have spoken from a different place within it. The art they have made has been determined by the diverse ways in which they negotiated their specific situations as women and as artists at a given historical moment. In many cases they have struggled against the given definitions and ideologies of femininity and have resisted what has been expected of them. At other times they have worked within genres or forms which have been collusive with dominant ideologies. Moreover, artistic representations are not produced as passive reflections. In art, as elsewhere, we can discern the attempts to keep in place dominant ideologies about women and the order of the sexes. The relations between women, art and ideology have to be studied as a set of varying and unpredictable relationships.

In *Old Mistresses: Women Art and Ideology*, Rozsika Parker and I tried to construct a conceptual framework for the analysis of women, art and ideology. We attempted to provide ways of connecting the specific histories of women artists with the ideologies and structures which shaped their interventions in art practice. In place of the traditional survey, we studied women's history in its genuine discontinuities and specificities in order to understand how the paradox of the present developed. Three examples drawn from the book explore those ideas.

1 Anguissola: Artist and Social Class

And even if Sofonisba Anguissola's contribution to Renaissance portraiture does not earn her a place in a Renaissance chapter, her historical impact as the first woman artist to become a celebrity and therefore open the profession to women certainly does.

Ann Sutherland Harris, *Women Artists:1550-1950*, 44.

There are several points to remark in this quotation: Anguissola (1535/40-1625) is being given a gold star for initiative, for being the first woman in a profession, and for starting a linear sequence of women artists; she is an exception – unusual by virtue of her sex. As such she is being evaluated by special criteria reserved for women, for it is only her sex and novelty that can merit her an otherwise undeserved place in Renaissance art history. Anguissola was discussed by Vasari in Volume III of his book on his contemporaries, *The Lives of the Most Prominent Painters, Sculptors and Architects* (1568). Why did he include her? As a novelty perhaps. That would be typical of an emerging strategy among men writing about women artists in the Renaissance. In an earlier text by the Italian poet Boccaccio, *On Famous Women* (1370), there is the paradox of an author who mentions several women artists – in his case from antiquity – but only in order to represent them as atypical of their sex, to create the idea that women and art

214

are incompatible. Boccaccio states:

> I thought these achievements worthy of some praise, for art is much
> alien to the mind of women, and these things cannot be accomplished
> without a great deal of talent which in women is usually very scarce.

The effect of the above is the same as that in Harris's analysis. Celebrity,
novelty, exceptionalness are the myths made up by a masculine dominated
culture to 'frame' the facts of women's unbroken participation in artistic
production. But this does not entirely explain Vasari's discussion of
Anguissola.

Some evidence may be gleaned from Anguissola's 1561 *Self Portrait*
(Althorp, Northampton; Collection Earl Spencer). The artist presents
herself seated at a musical instrument accompanied by her chaperone. She
stresses not her artistic skills but the cultured accomplishments which
signify her class position. Anguissola was the daughter of an Italian noble
family of Cremona and was at the time of the portrait employed as lady-in-
waiting and painter to the Queen of Spain. Artists from the nobility were
uncommon, but the attributes of the aristocratic classes and their circles –
knowledge and accomplishment – were coveted by artists wishful of
severing themselves from the artisan class and becoming members of the
educated and learned communities. Such aspirations were supported by a
growing literature on the artist. For instance, Alberti fabricated the story
that artists of classical antiquity came from elevated social classes in order to
underwrite the ambition of contemporary artists.[15]

This shift away from the conditions and class base of medieval art
production had somewhat adverse effects on the practice of many women
who had been hitherto involved in art production through households,
convents, workshops, and family connections. Women's participation in
family businesses and craftwork was further undermined in the new
tradesmen's families where, in imitation of aristocratic fashions, women
were withdrawn from commerce and supposed instead to be occupied with
leisure activities, i.e. unpaid, in and for the home. But at the same time, in
some aristocratic circles, new and favorable attitudes towards women's
education were being encouraged within the literature of the courtier. These
included training daughters of the nobility in several accomplishments,
among them painting and drawing. It was in this context that Anguissola
was able to exploit a complex of circumstances and make of her painting an
occupation that gained her patrons and a place at the Spanish court. She
presents herself as a member of the cultured elite; the chaperone and dress,
the musical instrument and her playing signify the class whose attributes
coincided at that period with the evolving ideologies of the new artist. It was
therefore her class position that rendered her activity as an artist both
possible and indeed worthy of notice and comment. Furthermore, a careful

reading of what Vasari selects to mention about women artists shows his concentration on precisely those features which accorded with the elevated social concept of the artist he was attempting to secure.

This favorable coincidence for some women artists between class and artistic discourses was a historically determined conjuncture. It was compromised, however, by concurrent claims for an almost divine status for the artist, as second only to the Prime Creator – in Judeo-Christian mythology a definitively masculine persona. Moreover, at another historical moment, in the late 19th century, aristocratic and even *haut-bourgeois* connections were a disadvantage to women artists as both Marie Bashkirtseff (1859-1884) and Berthe Morisot (1841-1895) found. By then the relations between femininity and class were such as to bind women to the domestic performance of social duties in the drawing room in ways that were radically opposed to the public, professional sphere in which artistic activity was pursued. These two women's practice as artists was facilitated not by their class but by a quite different constellation of forces around the institutions of art training and exhibition – the impressionist and independent movements in art. However, the purpose of this discussion of Anguissola has been to stress the necessity for seeking out and understanding the conditions which favored women's art making as much as those which limited it, and seeing these conditions in real historical terms.

2 Academies of Art: Naked Power

Most feminist art historians misunderstand the nature and effects of the constraints placed upon women artists in the heyday of the academies in the eighteenth and nineteenth centuries. The restricted access to academic art education has been represented as a major obstacle, an effective form of discrimination which prevented women from being able to participate in all genres of art. Admittedly the fact that women were excluded from the life class did prevent them from officially being able to study human anatomy from the live human model. For almost 300 years, from the Renaissance to the late nineteenth century, the nude human figure was the basis for the most highly regarded form of art – history painting. Prevented from studying the nude, many women were constrained to practise exclusively in the genres of still life, portraiture, and landscape, genres considered less prestigious and thought to demand less skill or intellect. By association, artists specialising in these 'lesser' genres were regarded as artists of lesser talent. Yet in cases where men, Reynolds (1723-92) or Chardin (1699-1779), for instance, practised them, their abilities as artists were never questioned. However, from the point of view from which women artists have been assessed then and since, their concentration in these areas signified their inferiority. Take, for instance, this comment:

Flower painting demands no genius of a mental or spiritual kind, but only the genius of taking pains and supreme craftsmanship...In all three hundred years of the production the total practitioners of flowers down to 1880 is less than seven hundred...Whilst only a very small proportion are artists of the highest or even high merit. Actually more than 200 of these are of the late eighteenth and nineteenth centuries and at least half of them are women.[16]

The academies' refusal to allow women to study the nude had an even more far reaching significance. Women could hire a nude model unofficially or get a friend or husband to pose. But as it was not acknowledged officially that women were involved in the making of major history painting, they were prevented from contributing to what those history paintings pictured. It was the men of the academy who determined what images were produced in the most prestigious and ideologically significant arenas of high cultural production.[17] Control over access to the nude was instrumental in the exercise of power over what meanings were constructed by an art based upon an ideal of the human body. Official exclusion from life classes ensured that women had no means to determine the language of high art or to make their own representations of the world, and thus resist and contest the hegemony of the dominant class or gender.

Concurrently in the late eighteenth century, another development can be traced which was to create an even more rigid set of sexual divisions in art. Johann Zoffany's 1772 group portrait of the *Academicians of the Royal Academy* (Royal Collection) depicts the artists as gentlemen of learning assembled in the life room surrounded with examples of classical art and in the company of a nude model striking a heroic pose. The official portrait fulfills both the necessity of document – we can identify all the sitters through the skilful record of face and feature – and of the ideal. The picture is 'of' the Royal Academicians, but the painting is about the ideal of the academic artist, about eighteenth century notions of the persona of the artist and about how art should be pursued and practised – learnedly, with reason, and by men. There were two female academicians at the time, Angelica Kauffman (1741-1807) and Mary Moser (1744-1819), both of whom are included in Zoffany's picture, but only by small portraits on the wall. In the interests of historical accuracy they could not have been omitted, but in the interests of the men – masked by pleading decency and propriety – they could not be seen to have access to the nude model. They are therefore excluded also at another level – from the idea of the artist. As paintings on the wall, treated with somewhat less detail than the other Academicians, they can easily be mistaken for part of the studio furnishings. Woman is thus represented as object for art rather than art producer. Indeed, close scrutiny of other written texts in which women artists of the period are represented reveals a growing discourse on the woman artist who is not the embodiment of reason and learning, but the spectacle of beauty, sexually desirable, an artistic inspiration – a muse.[18] In considering the conditions of women's practice in the late eighteenth century, it is simplistic to argue that women were left out or discriminated against. Rather, the evidence suggests the active construction of differences, of separate spheres for men's and women's work, distinct identities for the artist who was a man – the artist, and the artist who was a woman – the woman artist. The category 'woman artist' was established and the sexual discourse in art constructed around the growing hegemony of men in institutional practices and in the language of art itself.

3 Revolutionary Defeat: The Bourgeois Order of Things

> Finally no biography will do her justice that does not take into account the historical context of her career, a gradually disintegrating aristocratic society of which she was an ardent supporter and for which her work, both written and painted provides an incomparable record.
>
> Ann Sutherland Harris,
> *Women Artists: 1550-1950*, 192.

The passage above, which refers to Elizabeth Vigée Lebrun (1775-1842), exemplifies the kind of pitfalls that occur when history is treated as mere background and art as social document. It is indeed necessary to treat Vigée Lebrun as an historically interesting figure rather than dismiss her work as sweet and sentimental, her usual treatment when cited in art history books. But her relationship to the events of the 1780s and 1790s is neither clear nor simple.

Vigée Lebrun was employed as Marie Antoinette's official portrait painter, and many of her patrons were members of the aristocratic circle around the court. In the violent struggles attendant on the Revolution of 1789, that class and the artists it employed were shaken momentarily. Vigée Lebrun's flight from France on the Revolution's eve announced not so much her political loyalties as her fear of what would come of her professional and financial connections with the court, and after the initial upheavals, a petition was signed requesting that her name be removed from the list of proscribed émigrés. Vigée Lebrun's career raises important questions about artists' relationships to social change, for artists do not reproduce dominant ideology passively; they participate in its construction and alteration. Artists work in and also on ideology. Vigée Lebrun's practice as an artist was shaped by the conflicting ideologies emerging in a period of radical social upheaval in which not only the structure of political power in society was dramatically shifted, but more relevantly, with the new class formation, women's roles were transformed.

Vigée Lebrun painted many self-portraits and portraits of other artists. Comparison of her *Self Portrait* (London, National Gallery) in a silk dress and a hat bedecked with flowers that match the array of colors on her unused and very decorative palette with her painting of *Hubert Robert* (1788; Paris, Musée du Louvre) is instructive. In the latter portrait Vigée Lebrun prefigures the Romantic ideal image of the artist casually dressed in workmanlike clothes, unmoved by the creases in his jacket or the lumpiness of his cravat. Robert looks not towards the viewer, but at some unseen point of real or imaginary inspiration. He holds his palette and used brushes with easy confidence. At work and in private, the artist, self-generated, self-absorbed, dressed only to suit his convenience and work, is represented here as someone apart whose behaviour is directed by the exigencies of artistic creation. Vigée Lebrun's image of herself as artist constructs a totally different set of concerns. Her dress is social and fashionable, her hairstyle and decorations set down faithfully. They add up to a picture of a beautiful woman, an overlapping notion of beauty and femininity entangled in dress, hair, skin texture, fabric, and the carefully organised interplay of artifice and nature. Moreover, she gazes at us, not asserting her look over ours, but rather inviting us to look at her. Everything from the shadow of the hat to the sweep of her welcoming hand combines to signify her existence for us, her presentation of herself as a spectacle for the viewer. In the gulf that separates the two paintings of artists lies what was to become in bourgeois society an insuperable distance between the notion of the artist and the notion of woman.

In a study of late eighteenth-century genre painting, Carol Duncan charted the emergence of a new moralistic, emotionally charged representation of family life in which domesticity and the relationships between parents and children were not only presented as pleasant but as blissful. Responsible for this new treatment of mothers, children, and the family, she argues, was the development of the new, bourgeois institutions of the family and childhood, which replaced the *ancien régime's* idea of family as dynasty.[19] The clearly differentiated roles for father and mother, the insistence on gratifying emotional feelings between members of this social unit were all constituent elements of what was, at that date, progressive bourgeois ideology. One of its most salient novelties was the cult of the happy mother, the woman fulfilled by childbearing and childrearing. However symptomatic of emerging bourgeois ideas this insistence on family and motherhood, it was not restricted to that class nor celebrated only in the domestic genre often associated with its patronage. Note for instance the portrait of *Marie Antoinette and Her Children* by Vigée Lebrun (1787; Versailles) in which the Queen is portrayed dandling a lively baby on her knee while a daughter leans affectionately against her and the heir to the throne plays with the baby's cradle.

In a 1789 *Self Portrait* (Paris, Musée du Louvre) Vigée Lebrun showed herself with her daughter. The portrait is articulated across this ideological shift. The novelty of the painting lies in its secular displacement of the image of the Madonna with male child for a double female portrait – mother and daughter. In her presentation of self, the artist doubly stresses the contemporary conception of woman. Partly revealed, smooth-limbed and beautiful, 'naturally' coiffed, she is viewed also as an affectionate mother. The painting links the two females in a circular embrace, the child a smaller version of the adult. The mother is to be fulfilled through her child; the child will grow to be identical to her mother.

By the nineteenth century, with the consolidation of a patriarchal bourgeoisie as the dominant social class, women were increasingly locked into place in the family; the category Woman was limited to those familial positions, and where women lived and worked beyond them they were penalized for it and treated as unnatural, unwomanly, unsexed. Femininity was exclusively domestic and maternal. At the same time a new notion of the artist evolved that associated the creator with everything that was antidomestic – the Romantic ideal of outsiderness and alliance with sublime Nature, or the Bohemian model of free living, sexually energetic, and socially alienated outcasts. The categorical difference of identity between terms such as artist and woman thus were historically produced within the social formation of the bourgeois order. The French Revolution, which established the hegemony of the bourgeoisie, was in many ways a historic defeat for women as it created the special configuration of power and domination with which women still contend. It is the history of its consolidation, i.e. of bourgeois social relations and of their dominant ideological forms that we need to analyse and subvert. Hence, the relationship of Marxism and feminism in art history cannot be a cobbling together. It must be the fruitful raiding of Marxism for its explanatory instruments, for its analysis of the operations of bourgeois society and its ideologies in order to identify the specific configurations of bourgeois femininity and forms of mystification which mask the reality of social and sexual antagonisms. Denying women vision and voice deprives them also of power.

NOTES

The above is a shortened version of 'Vision, Voice and Power: Feminist Art History and Marxism,' *Block*, 6 (1982). I thank Deborah Cherry, Shirley Moreno, and Janet Wolff for reading and commenting on this article. I have freely used their advice.

1 Meyer Schapiro, 'On the Nature of Abstract Art', *Marxist Quarterly* (January-March 1937), 77-8.
2 Jean Gardiner, 'Women in the Labour Process and Class Structure', in *Class and*

Class Structure, A. Hunt, ed. (London: Lawrence and Wishart, 1977), 163. See also L. Comer, 'Women and Class: The Question of Women and Class', *Women's Studies International Quarterly*, 1 (1978), 165-73.

3 'Old Mistresses: Women Artists of the Past' (Walters Art Gallery, Baltimore, April 17-June 18, 1972). Catalogue essays by Ann Gabhart and Elizabeth Broun.

4 Rozsika Parker, 'Breaking the Mould', *New Statesman*, November 2, 1979, 682. Reviewed also in *WAJ* (F '80/W '81), 58-64.

5 Cited in Octave Uzanne, *The Modern Parisienne* (London: Heineman, 1912).

6 Frederich Antal, 'Remarks on the Method of Art History', reprinted in his *Essays in Classicism and Romanticism* (London: Routledge & Kegan Paul, 1966), 175-89.

7 *Ibid.*, 187.

8 Nicos Hadjinicolaou, *L'Histoire de L'Art et la Lutte des Classes*, (1973). Louise Asmal, trans. (London: Pluto, 1978), Chapters 2-4.

9 Pierre Macherey, *A Theory of Literary Production* (1966), G. Wall, trans, (London: Routledge & Kegan Paul, 1978), 80.

10 Charles Sterling, 'A Fine David Reattributed', *Metropolitan Museum of Art Bulletin*, IX (January 1951), 132.

11 James Laver, 'Woman Painters', *The Saturday Book* (London, 1964), 19. For a critical study of those stereotypes see Cindy Nemser, 'Stereotypes and Women Artists', *Feminist Art Journal* (April 1972), 1, 22-3.

12 Hadjinicolaou, *L'Histoire*, Chapters 8-10.

13 Elizabeth Cowie, 'Woman as Sign', *M/F*, 1 (1978), 49-64, 50.

14 Claude Lévi-Strauss, *The Elementary Structure of Kinship* (1949) (London: Eyre and Spottiswood, 1969).

15 See Margot and Rudolf Wittkower, *Born Under Saturn* (Oxford: Oxford University, 1963), for this history of the change in status and identity of the artist in the Renaissance period.

16 Martin H. Grant, *Flower Painting Through Four Centuries* (Lee-on-See, Eng.: F. Lewis, 1952), 21.

17 I found Cora Kaplan's work on women and their 'intervention into the high patriarchal discourse of bourgeois culture' – epic poetry – very helpful on this point. In poetry women were likewise permitted to write in the lesser modes of lyric poetry or ballads and sonnets but the prestigious forms, like epic poetry were preserved for men; a woman daring to use the form was threatening to abrogate the power of public speech, the authority of her own voice for her own causes. See 'Introduction' to the Women's Press edition of Elizabeth Barrett Browning's great epic poem on women and art, *Aurora Leigh* (London: Women's Press, 1978).

18 See for instance, Denis Diderot, *Diderot Salons*, Jean Adhémar and Jean Seznec, eds. (Oxford: Oxford University, 1957-67), especially Vol. III, or Elizabeth Vigée Lebrun, *The Memoirs of Madame Elisabeth Louise Vigée Lebrun, 1755-1789*, Gerard Shelley, trans. (London: John Hamilton, 1927).

19 Carol Duncan, 'Happy Mothers and Other New Ideas in French Art', *Art Bulletin* (December 1973), 570-83.

ANN SUTHERLAND HARRIS

LETTER TO THE EDITOR

Griselda Pollock's essay, 'Women, Art and Ideology: Questions for Feminist Art Historians' (*WAJ*, Spring/Summer, 1983), was submitted as a response to Lawrence Alloway's critical review (*WAJ*, Fall 1982/Winter 1983) of the book, *Old Mistresses: Women, Art and Ideology* (Pantheon, 1981), that she wrote with Rozsika Parker. It is a puzzling reaction for she addresses none of his points but merely reiterates some of her favorite arguments from the book in a more polemical tone. While there are many points that should be challenged in this essay, I will limit myself to those sections prefaced by quotations from my section of the exhibition catalogue, *Women Artists, 1550-1950* (New York: Knopf, 1976). Pollock misrepresents my methods and my positions and I would like to set the record straight.

The first quotation chosen by Pollock in her essay as exemplifying the kind of attitudes of which she disapproves comes from the concluding paragraph of my share of the catalogue introduction where I outlined the most essential points about the contribution of women artists before 1800 to the history of art to be included in future survey course texts. I was addressing authors such as H.W. Janson, who believed that no woman had changed the history of art in any fundamental way and therefore none deserved a place in his book, *History of Art*. In that context, my statement ('...even if Sofonisba Anguissola's contribution to Renaissance portraiture does not earn her a place in a Renaissance chapter, her historical impact as the first woman artist to become a celebrity and thereby to open up these professions to women certainly does') is, I think, perfectly valid. 'Celebrity, novelty, exceptionalness' (*sic*) are not 'myths made up by a masculine dominated culture to "frame" the facts of women's unbroken participation in artistic production', as Pollock asserts, but factors of historical significance that affect both sexes. (Far more people can name the first man to walk on the moon than any of his successors and now Sally Ride is, for the time being, as famous as Neil Armstrong.) The fact that the next generation of Italian women artists emerged in cities near Cremona substantiates my position that Anguissola influenced historical developments more by being a famous woman artist than by what she painted. We may regret the combination of social conditions that determined this but we would be foolish to deny it. Further, as Pollock knows very well, that statement was far from being the only positive one that I made about Sofonisba and her work. Indeed, Parker and Pollock liked one sentence so much that they borrowed it without acknowledgment in their book ('Sofonisba painted

222

more portraits of herself than any artist between Dürer and Rembrandt', p. 107 of our catalogue; p. 86 of their book, although they refer to her as Anguissola here). Most of the other points that Pollock makes in her essay on medieval craft guilds, on the desire of Renaissance artists for higher social (and intellectual) status, and on the social context of Sofonisba's portrait at Althorp can be found either in my share of the catalogue introduction or in the section on Sofonisba in the catalogue. While I am now quite used to finding my words and ideas in this publication plundered without acknowledgment, I have not previously encountered a scholar who then uses my own arguments against me.

In the book, Parker and Pollock acknowledge the point I made about Baldassare Castiglione's *Book of the Courtier* opening up educational opportunities for women of the upper classes by arguing that the ideal female courtier should receive the same training as the male courtier, only horseback riding, fencing, and playing the trumpet being regarded as unsuitable. She agrees that it was this cultural innovation that enabled some daughters of some noblemen to be taught to read and write, and even to paint and play musical instruments. Thus class was certainly an important factor in the discovery of Sofonisba's gifts, but it does not explain everything, for otherwise we should have seen many more women of her social standing emulating her example, which was not the case. It must be remembered that Cremona was then a small town and her father only a minor member of the Italian nobility. Had he not promoted his daughter as energetically as he did, largely, as I suggested, because he had no male heir to guarantee the preservation of the family name until he was fifty-seven and Sofonisba about twenty, and had her talents not been considerable, she would not have enjoyed the success she did. Class alone is also a crude explanation of her *Self Portrait at the Virginals* (1561, cat. no. 3). When Sofonisba painted herself as a noblewoman, she did not do so, as Pollock believes, for the same reasons as a male artist aspiring to a higher status than his birth or membership in a manual profession then gave him, for she was born with more rank than any male Italian Renaissance artist I can think of. Further, her decision to present herself playing a musical instrument puts this *Self Portrait* in an altogether different category than that of the standard noblewoman, who rarely does anything but fill out her expensive clothes, glance at a prayer book, or fondle a lap dog (e.g. Lavinia Fontana's *Portrait of a Noblewoman*, cat. no. 6). Portraits of either men or women playing musical instruments in the sixteenth century are extremely rare, more so than I realised when preparing the catalogue entry for this work or for Caterina van Hemessen's *Portrait of a Young Woman at the Virginals* (cat. no. 2).[1] Male sitters evidently preferred to stress more serious, masculine accomplishments (they have swords, large hunting dogs, account books, globes, ancient statues, and libraries at hand). Sofonisba thus portrays herself in an exceptional, not a standard, manner by telling us that she was a gifted musician as well as a fine painter. In none of her other self-portraits does she present herself as a passive object of contemplation. Even the steady, direct gaze of her first dated self-portrait (1554; cat. fig. 2) is disconcerting in the context of normal female portraiture of the sixteenth century, when women are nearly always shown with their gaze averted.

Pollock then passes on to the issue of women and the Academies, which she asserts 'most feminist art historians misunderstand' (I do not think she adds anything substantial to the subject either), before tackling 'Revolutionary Defeat: The Bourgeois Order of Things', which is prefaced by the last sentence from my biography of Vigée Lebrun in the catalogue: 'Finally, no biography will do her justice if it does not take into account the historical context of her career, a gradually disintegrating aristocratic society of which she was an ardent supporter and for which her work, written as well as painted, provides an incomparable record'. This statement, declares Pollock, 'exemplifies the kind of pitfalls that occur when history is treated as mere background and art as social document'. Readers of *Old Mistresses* may be puzzled because the same quote is used there approvingly (p.97). Even in the *WAJ* essay, Pollock admits that 'it is indeed necessary to treat Vigée Lebrun as an historically interesting figure rather than dismiss her work as sweet and sentimental'. It then emerges that she disagrees with my (and everyone else's, including her own expressed in the book) explanation of why Vigée Lebrun left Paris on the eve of the Revolution. The artist's decision 'announced not so much her political loyalties as her fear of what would become of her professional and financial connections with the court'. Is this a roundabout way of saying that she doubted patrons whose heads had been removed would pay their bills? If her loyalties were not with the royalists, why did she not stay around to paint their opponents, as did Adelaide Labille-Guiard? Did she not have legitimate reasons to fear for her own life, fears that she would have found justified after Anne Rosalie Bocquet Filleul, who painted the royal children, was guillotined? Further, Vigée Lebrun's flight to Rome was certainly interpreted as a declaration of royalist sympathies by the Revolutionary Councils, hence her classification as an 'émigrée', which was not so easily revoked as Pollock thinks. Despite the efforts of her husband and many friends, her name was not removed from the lists until 1800. Until then, her life was in danger and her property could be confiscated if she returned to France. In brief, Pollock's comments illustrate not so much the value of feminist-Marxist historical analysis as the pitfalls of drawing historical conclusions without doing your homework.

Whether Vigée Lebrun's career as a portraitist 'raises important questions about artists' relationships to social change' more acutely than that of many of her contemporaries can be questioned, as can Pollock's statement that 'her practice as an artist was shaped by the conflicting ideologies emerging in a period of radical social upheaval', for Vigée's style and class of patron remained remarkably consistent whether she was working in Paris, Rome, Vienna, or Leningrad. Labille-Guiard's shift from aristocratic patrons to those of the middle class and her far more varied portrayals of women surely offer the Marxist or socially aware feminist art historian more scope.

Pollock's comparison of Vigée Lebrun's superb portrait of Hubert Robert, which I described in the catalogue as a 'masterpiece of truly romantic fervor, an idealisation of artistic genius conveyed with striking realism', with Vigée's *Self Portrait* in London (only a copy of the original, which is in a private collection) is 'instructive', but conveys more of Pollock's methodology than of the 'significant gulf that separate(d)...in bourgeois society...the notion of the artist and the notion of woman'. At no point in the Renaissance or later has society's 'notion' of an artist ever matched its 'notion' of a woman, yet the number of women who became serious artists grew exponentially from the mid sixteenth century onwards.[2] Pollock's theory, explicated at great length in the book she co-authored, fails to explain why successful women artists emerged in Europe only late in the Renaissance, most of them from the same social strata as male artists, or why their numbers rapidly increased, despite the professional, practical, and psychological barriers they always faced. She also overlooks the fact that while stereotypical characterisations of the male artist changed in the nineteenth century, the male 'gentleman' artist still flourished along with social misfits and rebels and all shades of social class and aspiration in between, from Wintherhalter to Courbet, Bouguereau to Van Gogh. Parker and Pollock noted Vigée's source for this *Self Portrait* in *Old Mistresses*, namely Rubens's so-called *Chapeau de Paille* (now also in London), but while recognising the feminine stereotype that the artist successfully exploited for her own professional purposes in this and other self-portraits, other readings of its image are possible. It can be argued that Vigée cleverly transformed her source by posing herself with erect frontality and gazing directly at us, an image of self-confidence to go with the picture's message, namely that she paints as well as Rubens. Rubens's subject lowers her head and looks askance, rather like Princess Diana before her marriage, an image that conforms with the ideal of feminine modesty, then and now.

Pollock ends with some references to Carol Duncan's excellent article, 'Happy Mothers and Other New Ideas In French Art' (*Art Bulletin*, December 1973), which she believes bolsters her case. But she misreads Duncan if she believes that Vigée Lebrun's huge *Portrait of Marie Antoinette with her Children* (Versailles) belongs to this 'happy family' category rather than to the older category of 'the *ancien régime's* idea of family as dynasty'. The formality of this enormous picture excludes it, even if the Queen is shown as a mother with a faint smile. The Dauphin points solemnly to the empty crib whose most recent occupant had just died, as did the Dauphin shortly after the picture was finished. What could be more dynastic and less happy than that?

Old Mistresses has its faults, but it is also a stimulating attempt to understand the situation of women artists, past and present, by using approaches that would not have been appropriate to the catalogue of the exhibition curated by Linda Nochlin and myself. Pollock's essay, however, is flawed by its angry tone, by an ungenerous attitude towards the work of other scholars, male and female, on whom she has depended more extensively than she is willing to acknowledge, by a reluctance to name most of the male scholars whose work she finds wanting, and by some misinterpretations of the historical evidence that invalidate her conclusions. Feminist scholars have been reluctant to criticise each others' work, but we cannot advance our positions unless we will engage in critical debate. Serious Marxist analysis can certainly offer feminist art historians some useful methodological tools and insights, but so can more traditional methods. As Mao said, 'Let a thousand flowers bloom'.

Ann Sutherland Harris, New York City

NOTES

1 The only sixteenth century male *Self Portrait as a Musician* that I know of is a picture in Vienna of about 1512 by the Master of the Self Portraits (L. Goldscheider, *500 Self Portraits*, Vienna, 1937, no. 79); he is tuning a small stringed instrument. Titian's *Concert* (Palazzo Pitti, Florence) and Cariani's *Man with a Lute* of about 1525 (Strasbourg) hover on the edge of genre but are both probably portraits. Caterina van Hemessen's picture was inspired by the Master of the Female Half Lengths, who produced many genre pictures of female musicians but no portraits of women making music. Lavinia Fontana used the formula for herself (Rome, Accademia di S. Luca). The next example seems to be Jan Steen's *Self Portrait* (c. 1661-63; Thyssen Collection, Lugano), whose mood is very different.

2 That there are striking parallels nevertheless between the positions of the woman and of the artist is the point of June Wayne's wonderful lecture. 'The Male Artist as a Stereotypical Female', reprinted in Judy Loeb, ed., *Feminist Collage* (New York: Teacher's College, 1979), 128-37.

GRISELDA POLLOCK

REPLY TO ANN SUTHERLAND HARRIS

May I point out in response to Ann Sutherland Harris's letter that my 'Women, Art and Ideology: Questions for Feminist Art Historians' was *not* submitted in response to Lawrence Alloway's review of the book I co-authored with Rozsika Parker, *Old Mistresses: Women, Art and Ideology*. It was solicited by the editor of *WAJ*, and was published as a shortened version of an article first published in *Block*, 6 (1982). It did, however, provide the opportunity to explain some of the methodological and theoretical concerns which had informed our book and which Alloway's review had completely ignored. My purpose was never to counter or cut short responses – critical or otherwise – to our contribution to feminist debate. Ann Sutherland Harris's letter is welcome in the same spirit, but even more so because it genuinely comes from within the feminist art historical community. In our book Rozsika Parker and I did undertake a critique of the work of our sisters (and in the article, too, but not in anger as Harris suggests) for we felt that feminism was strong enough now to sustain the necessary and open discussion of conflicting interpretations and emphases. Some of the points Harris makes are welcome corrections or modifications; other points I would still dispute, but that seems to me a healthy sign in feminist art history. Harris agrees with the desirability of 'critical debate'. For this to flourish, however, a cheerful plurality of viewpoints must be complemented by vigorous explication of premise and method. The article I wrote extended the principles Parker and I had developed in our collaboration on *Old Mistresses* precisely in order to indicate the need for a feminist art history which offers a substantive critique of the norms and canons of art history's mainstream practice. Disagreement over the interpretation of particular paintings or correction of particular historical materials as Harris provides does not really address the central issue of the structural sexism of art historical practice and the way its apparently gender-blind discourse nonetheless limits and constrains what can be said about artists who are women, and about gender relations in history. It was the way in which the discourses of art history perpetuate and reproduce through their specialised treatment of art and artist the hierarchical gender divisions of our society which constituted the project of *Old Mistresses: Women, Art and Ideology* and my subsequent article. The issues are not fact or error, judgment or homework, but the politics of knowledge. It is the truth-knowledge-power nexus of our society which feminist art historians in Great Britain are currently addressing.

Griselda Pollock
Leeds, England

ANGELA PARTINGTON

FEMINIST ART AND AVANT-GARDISM

This essay is a contribution to long-running debates about strategies in feminist art, in particular the conflict over whether visual work should 're-colonize' or re-claim the imagery of patriarchal culture and invest it with feminist values, or whether it has to formulate a 'new language' with which to articulate feminist meanings.[1] My arguments are in support of work which re-cycles or appropriates traditional and/or current/popular imagery, using its symbols, metaphors, formulas and reference-systems; and which re-utilizes a variety of traditional, established, even 'bourgeois' media and forms as well as exploiting the conventions and styles of mass-produced imagery. I want to argue against any notion of a 'correct' textual strategy in feminist art. Ultimately this essay suggests that there is no feminist art, that there is only art which can be read as feminist.

One of my main concerns is that feminist artistic practices involve strategies around the institutional and economic circumstances under which (women's) art is produced, distributed, and consumed, as well as the more familiar textual strategies which concern the visual organization and formal structure of the work itself. In order to argue that this is a priority, rather than an optional extra, the objectives of feminist art practice have to be clarified. Feminist art practice is an intervention in the reproduction of *gender relations* (power and subordination) through the use and manipulation of the *means and processes* of artistic production. This definition differs significantly from those which allow femininity (rather than gender relations) to become the object of attack, and which assume art objects in and by themselves (rather than the manipulation of artistic means and processes) to be more or less of an intervention.

It is because extra-textual strategies are a priority that I consider eclectic, imitative, formulaic, or reference-making work to offer more possibilities, in terms of acknowledging the gendered viewer and addressing a female audience, by allowing specific (feminine) knowledges and interests to determine the meaning of the work. On these grounds I want to argue against claims made for 'innovative' work which has been produced by feminists over the last decade or so, and place it within an avant-garde tradition. Artists who claim to pursue a 'new language' with which to

228

express feminist values have enthusiastically deployed 'deconstructive' textual strategies which ultimately deny the possibility of gendered (or interested) viewing, because they belong to the very tradition (avant-gardism) by which high culture defends its claim to disinterestedness (is enabled to appear value-free, supposedly beyond the demands of a market economy or a patriarchal system). Not only does such work inevitably revive the techniques and motifs of formalism and modernism (grids, fields, bands) and therefore fail to invent a new language, but it also exploits the technologies and conventions of mass-produced and reproducible imagery (photography, typography, montage) in order to make unique examples of gallery art which are easily as elitist and inaccessible as any painting, thereby demonstrating its indifference to extra-textual problems.

What follows is by way of substantiation for these arguments, and an attempt to offer some encouragement to women working in modes and media for which there has not been much support from feminist critics recently. First I will suggest that although extra-textual problems have been addressed in the areas of production and distribution, they have been significantly neglected with regard to the consumption of (women's) visual work. Then I will outline some of the differences between audience-orientated and deconstructive work, argue that the former has been systematically devalued and marginalized by critics while the latter has been publicised and promoted, and suggest that this development is a result of the failure to take consumption seriously. Finally I will try to point out some of the ways in which audience-orientation, and the notion of the gendered consumer, is crucial to the development of a feminist art practice.

Feminism and the relations of artistic production

The function and status of artistic and critical practices have been rendered problematic by feminist artists and critics themselves.

Projects such as *Feministo, Mother's Pride Mother's Ruin*, and even *The Dinner Party*,[2] whatever their problems, do at least signify an intention to renegotiate the relations of artistic production, and an awareness of the necessity and urgency of such a renegotiation. Similarly, what has now become a tradition of collective exhibition for feminist artists represents a challenge to the complex of meanings and values surrounding the 'one man show'.[3]

The difficulties of attempting to 'break away from individual creative production (when)...the habit of individual activity has been the norm'[4] derive from a series of crucial issues surrounding the concept of 'creativity' and its political use. On the one hand it has been recognised that there are significant dangers in pursuing 'greatness' or 'a piece of the poisonous pie'.[5] On the other hand, it is acknowledged that having women in positions of power (both as activists and as feminine role models) can be invaluable.

On the understanding that 'we have inherited a conception of art as something removed from other forms of social activity...the antithesis of work...mythologized as an oasis of creativity in the desert of alienated and mass-production capitalism...idealized as the product of a few gifted and privileged people,'[6] feminist art represents an attempt to 'break with the dominant notions of art as personal expression, instead connecting it in with the social and the political and placing the artist as producer in a new situation of responsibility for her images'.[7]

In feminist criticism there has been considerable concern about the nature and function of critical practice, and acknowledgement that its place within the tradition of high culture must be questioned. Since the nineteenth century, criticism has tended 'to assume that what is at issue is a correct reading of a pre-given text, for which the critic's subjectivity is required to evaluate various texts as in some way representing "quality" ...'[8] Deriving from an understanding of the ways in which this 'critical publicity' contributes to the reproduction of the power relations of the art-world, feminist critical practice represents an attempt to adopt a consistently questioning attitude, to provide 'provisional instruments constantly subject to correction in the interaction with new material, new insights and collective political work', in sharp contrast to the 'universal' values offered by traditional criticism.[9] Feminist criticism does not look for artistic 'quality', it looks for feminist meanings, that is, it *constructs feminist readings*, and in doing so radically re-locates the source of aesthetic pleasure. This is an unforgivably tendentious approach from the perspective of 'value-free' traditional approaches, but one towards which those who see themselves as both critics and feminists have increasingly moved.

But culture cannot be reduced to the social relations of production and distribution alone. Meaning-production is made possible by conditions existing simultaneously at various levels of social formation. Feminist meanings then, are not created exclusively by feminist artists and critics. Relations of consumption, – the conditions under which the works are read/viewed – are a crucial instance in the generation of cultural meanings and values, providing one of the material circumstances for the context without which cultural objects cannot signify.

Reading practices are productive. They constitute a labour which transforms a material resource (the text) into a meaningful object, i.e. one which has a social function, a use in an exchange ritual, a symbolic or sign-value. This requires both energy and skill; competences which are always acquired in the context of socially and culturally specific experience; cultural capital the value of which depends on the fields within which it can be invested in the form of knowledges and tastes. (As described by Pierre Bourdieu, see note 43). Reading practices are the *means* by which texts can or cannot represent the interests of (be meaningful to) specific social groups, for example, women. Representation always implies a specific position within social relations rather than a relation to a pre-signified reality, the means of representation therefore involve a whole economy of competences as well as the languages which bear the traces of their circulation.

Some examples of feminist theory have acknowledged the need to define consumption as something other than the passive absorption of a message which is somehow 'transmitted' to the consumer by the producer via the text, or 'mediated' by the critic. It has been conceded that 'meaning is socially created in the consumption of the work...(it is) impossible to separate the production of the work from its consumption',[10] but often such acknowledgements are qualified by the assumption that *some* texts nevertheless manage to provide their own conditions of intelligibility.[11] My own view is that the importance of this aspect of meaning-production (the text's *insertion* within a series of discourses) has been seriously neglected, to the detriment of feminist attempts to intervene in the power relations inscribed within artistic discourses.

These arguments (about reading) will be returned to in a later section. At this point, I want to try to show how this neglect has created a situation in which the interchange between feminist artists and critics has brought forth a dominant textual strategy in feminist art. For the first time, much of the work produced by feminist artists recently has had a similar 'look'. For the first time, it seems to belong within the artistic avant-garde because, in formal terms, it is 'innovative' in relation to contemporary stylistic orthodoxies. This is a result of the adoption of 'deconstructive' strategies, which have their history in the succession of avant-garde art movements witnessed throughout the twentieth century. Avant-gardism is defined by the constant imperative to break with the conventions of 'readability', in favour of strategies which are intended to demonstrate the 'facticity', 'opacity' or 'productivity' of the text. It is this tradition which has made possible the mythologies of modernism (art about art) and of an art history which reduces the meaning of all art to its place within the history of form/style – despite the often overtly political *intentions* of many avant-garde movements.

The project of feminist art, to re-negotiate the relations of artistic production, is in danger of being reduced, as a result of this development, to the search for a rule of textual organization which is somehow intrinsically feminist or radical. Such a strategy assumes that texts can carry with them their own conditions of intelligibility, obscuring the fact that representation and meaning-production are processes involving multiple levels of practice.

One of the ways in which artistic discourses defend their claim to disinterest, is by describing artistic production in idealist terms, i.e., as the 'phenomena' of what is assumed to be an 'essence' (truth, knowledge, beauty, purity, etc.). By focusing on consumption as a productive practice, ideologies (knowledges, pleasures, meanings, values) can be properly located as instances of the social formation. Any practice aspiring, then, to challenge the relations of artistic production is committed necessarily to a materialist approach to meaning-production. (This is taken up again in a later section).

Deconstruction, prioritizing the producer-text relationship as it does, retains idealist categories and concepts (or at least their theoretical effects). Defenders of deconstruction would argue to the contrary, that it represents a challenge to idealist epistemology. I will therefore substantiate this claim by first, showing how the ways in which deconstructive strategies have been critically prioritized above other strategies in feminist art depend on a series of idealist assumptions; second, by looking at deconstruction in its context of avant-gardism and emphasizing its hegemonic function (achieved by appearing 'independent' of the economic forces operating on popular culture); third, by arguing that it derives (as do all avant-garde strategies) from a theoretical reduction of the 'material' to the 'formal'. These three characteristics are related and interdependent.

Deconstruction vs celebration and negation

Deconstruction has emerged as dominant partly because other strategies have been critically discredited.

There is, or has been, a strand in feminist art of 'celebratory' strategies which are not reducible to a series of textual innovations. They share a particular approach to the concept of 'women's experience' and its value within the women's movement, rather than a particular mode of textual organization. Aspects of it include heroinization, vaginal iconography and body-art, and references to domestic skills and preoccupations. Classic examples of heroinization are Monica Sjoo's *God Giving Birth* and Ann Grifalconi's *And God Created Woman in Her Own Image*, others can be found amongst the work of Margaret Harrison, Ann Newmarch, Nancy Spero, May Stevens, Susan Hiller, and Judy Chicago, to mention a few. Well-known examples of vaginal iconography include the *Dinner Party* plates, Betty Dodson's *Vaginal Drawings*, Suzanne Santoro's *Towards New Expression*, and Shelley Lowell's *Rediscovery*. In different ways, work as diverse, in formal terms, as Margaret Harrison's *Craftwork*, projects like *Feministo* and *Mother's Pride* and Miriam Schapiro's fabric collages, all rely heavily on connotations of the 'domestic'.

What this work has in common is an aspiration to celebrate the feminine, *not* as an essence, but as it is experienced by women, in their different circumstances, so that a sense of sisterhood, or solidarity, might be generated at an emotional level.

Heroinization exposes the contradictions of a society which produces a dominant notion of 'women' as physically and mentally inferior, unable or unwilling to act, while simultaneously *depending* (for its own reproduction) on women's abilities to act, to take initiatives, to be independent, and indeed to be depended on by men. At the same time it traces the production of contemporary symbols for women's strength and ability. (It is *not* about selecting 'special' women for the rest of us to 'look up to' – arguments about which women 'deserve' to be heroinized and which women 'deserve' to do the selecting are irrelevant).

Vaginal iconography is a similar attempt to construct symbols of shared femaleness, involving the transformation of the 'unspeakable' into a cause for celebration. Uses of the discourses of domesticity attempt to mobilize the 'feminine' as a challenge to the hierarchies of aesthetic pleasure which, by opposing art to craft, public to private, work to leisure, cultural to natural, etc., devalue or render 'invisible' women's work as non-work or 'non-productive' labour. It is *not* about rehabilitating domestic skills within the realms of fine art, rather it is about 'femininity' as a terrain for the production of dominated knowledges, pleasures and values.

Above all, celebratory strategies aspire to provide a means of identification between women, in a society where isolation and fear divide and control women, whose knowledges are systematically represented as neuroses, aberrations, fantasies, etc., within the discourses of patriarchal culture. It is important to demonstrate that there is such a thing as feminine knowledge, a specifically feminine experience of the world, and that therefore culture is not 'un-gendered'. In this, celebratory strategies strike at one of the central concepts of idealist thought, and at the foundation of art's hegemonic function.

In general however, feminist criticism of celebratory strategies has been surprisingly thorough and virulent in its condemnation. The most common, if not only, justification for this criticism has been that this kind of work is 'essentialist' because it relies on a concept of essential femininity. For example, it has been argued that heroinization is essentialist because 'the very notion of positive (lesbian) images of women relies on the already constituted meaning of "woman"...(because it) considers the notion of femininity as unproblematic and positions women's culture as separate and different from mainstream culture',[12] and because it involves 'terms of evaluation which we (feminists) have developed a critical stance towards'.[13]

Vaginal iconography has been referred to as 'anti-phallic self-valida-tion...feminist essentialism in art...(which) simply reverses the terms of domination and subordination. Instead of the male supremacy of patriarchal culture, the female (the essential feminine) is elevated to primary status'.[14] Apparently it 'assumes' that an emphasis on women's experience or a concern with the female body, and the production of feminist meanings are the same thing.

Work which refers to the domestic is, it is argued, similarly essentialist because it is a 'glorification' of feminine skills which assumes that women have an 'inherent creativity'[15] or because it represents an attempt 'to retrieve embroidery and china-painting from the inglorious role of women's drudgery (or at best "craft") and re-allocate them to the realm of "high art"...'[16]

One might summarize the general response by quoting thus – 'It is just not possible to say that "women-centred" writings have any necessary relation to feminism'.[17] These criticisms share a tendency to distinguish firmly between the femi*nine* and the femi*nist*, and a conviction that a pre-occupation with the former is a sure indication of essentialism.

Undoubtedly there are difficulties with celebratory strategies, not least problems deriving from the aspiration to address the commonality of women's experience, which *can* obscure important differences. For example, it might be said that 'the idea of "the community of all women"...is an idea more popular among middle-class than among working-class women'.[18] But there is no reason to assume that these difficulties are insurmountable. Surely a feminist politics *must* depend in some way on the possibilities of generalizing, at a symbolic level, about women's lives, indeed the impact of the women's movement on our society to date derives, I would suggest, from exactly this. Having acknowledged that feminist criticism is not about recovering the meaning of a pre-given text, or about intrinsic (even feminist) 'quality', but about making feminist readings, I find it puzzling that feminist critics have generally blocked off such possibilities in the case of celebratory work.

Why has the criticism been conducted at such an 'in general' and abstract level? If it had been pitched at the level of concrete specificities it might have been possible to argue that, in certain contexts, and, under certain circumstances, the celebration of femininity is a highly appropriate and useful strategy for artists who wish to put their work at the service of the women's movement. It has a distinct advantage above avant-garde strategies in that it dismisses all claims to 'independence' and tries to produce work specifically for an audience (women) instead of adopting the traditional fine art attitude of indifference to audiences.

If heroinization is unacceptable because it introduces the concept of a hierarchy of women, how then could a feminist be 'horrified' to see literary giants such as Woolf and Dickinson reduced to vaginal sculptures?[19] They can't have it both ways. It simply is not necessary to equate heroinization with hierarchization, nor to see vaginal imagery as a contradiction of the richness and variety of women's experiences and achievements.

The tendency for challenges to cultural hegemony to be 'rehabilitated' is a product of critical judgements and readings, so why do feminist critics collude in this process by referring to work which uses domestic skills as 'elevating' or 'glorifying' instead of emphasizing their potential for the construction of symbols for women's knowledge of their own oppression?

Why have celebratory strategies been rejected on the grounds that they are not a 'new phenomena'? [20] This is a naive and simplistic equation of 'the new' with 'the radical'. And, worst of all, why have these criticisms introduced distinctions (usually associated with anti-feminism) between women's experience and feminism? [21] There is a suggestion here that political values, ideological interests, do not derive from specific, concrete, lived relations but from the professional practices of an elite group. The experience of white, middle-class educated women is being accorded the status of 'analysis' while other women's experience is seen simply as evidence of their subordination.

Rather than concluding that 'women centred' or celebratory work is of no particular value to feminism it would be considerably more helpful to develop a critical practice in which the gender of an artist (or indeed a consumer) *increases its significance*. The failure to do so is evidence of the retention of idealist theories of meaning-production, because it does not construct readings on the basis of historically specific ideological identifications but claims to recover the meaning of the work which is assumed to reside at the level of 'production'.

Another strand in feminist art which has been the object of much unfavourable criticism consists in strategies of 'negation'. These include role-reversal, parody and graffiti, all of which represent attempts to negate masculine representations and patriarchal values.

The classic example of role-reversal is Sylvia Sleigh's *Philip Golub Reclining*; its function is the reversal of the gender relations of 'normal' viewing situations, in this case by taking the famous *Venus of Rokeby* by Velasquez and replacing the woman in the original image with a passive, inert, objectified, to-be-looked-at male who is 'on display' in relation to the viewer who is presumed to be female (Sleigh's own reflection is visible in the mirror). As a result, the 'male gaze' is robbed of its hegemonic value, since it cannot claim disinterest or appear 'ungendered'. [22] This reversal of viewing relations was the theme of the ICA exhibition *Women's Images of Men*. Whatever the differences, at a formal level, amongst the works exhibited, its feminist meaning was constituted in its shared approach to an aspect of women's experience, in its insertion in a series of discourses which structure gender relations. To turn men into the object of the female gaze is 'to return the scrutiny...to appraise the male...as bearer, rather than maker of significance'. [23]

Parody is a common element in the work of many feminist artists, including Hannah Wilke, Lynda Benglis, Alexis Hunter, Judith Bernstein, Aimee Rankin and Barbara Kruger. This kind of work may 'exploit the fetishistic style and content of glamour advertising, reproducing its timescale for viewing and reading, echoing its themes of auto-eroticism and violence. However, this is subverted by an edge, an ambiguity and an excess which is too incisive to sit within the parameters of the genre'.[24] The purpose is often to 'reclaim the sign – woman's body – from masculine fantasy, de-colonise it and reintegrate it to express aspects of female experience...',[25] so a necessary element is provided by work which ridicules masculinity, subjecting its 'weltanschaung' to derision and caricature, as in May Stevens' *Big Daddy* series.

Ad-graffiti is a way of directly confronting and commenting on patriarchal representations in an attempt to negate their meanings.[26] On one level, by 'disfiguring' advertisements, graffiti represents a vandalism of male property, expressing contempt for it and trivialising it at the same time. And on another level, it 'invests' advertisements with meanings which their producers could not have anticipated. Sometimes it involves changing the image and/or adding to, or changing, the written text, and sometimes it consists simply in adding a word or a phrase so that the same image, its formal organization remaining completely unaltered, acquires a completely new significance by being 're-anchored'.

Negation strategies assert a culture of femininity as a culture of negation. They tend to use humour as a political weapon, and since the source of amusement is invariably men, their ideas and values, women are united in their pleasure through the symbolic come-uppance of the self-righteous, dominating male. Again the over-riding concern is to provide means of ideological identification for women, and to demonstrate that culture is not value free, but that knowledge of the world is gender-specific. It depends absolutely on a concept of a female audience, and tries to make images function in the interests of that audience as a social group with its own ideological and economic interests.

But strategies of negation have also been criticized on the grounds that they are essentialist. Usually it is argued that this kind of work depends on a 'realist' approach to representation, which results in a simple countering of 'true' female experience against the 'false' masculine version of it. Again these criticisms tend to devalue the 'feminine' by trying to locate the meaning of the text at the level of 'production' (in the relationship between producer and text) rather than accounting for the broader relations of consumption which also provide its conditions of intelligibility. Thus, these criticisms are themselves 'essentialist' since they depend on a notion of a privileged subject position from which the meaning of the text can be determined.

For instance, role-reversal has been criticized on the grounds that it cannot produce the same meanings for women as the 'original' did for men.[27] I would agree that to expect that it should derives from an inadequate understanding of the processes of signification, because representations are related differently (asymmetrically or unevenly) both to specific objects of representation and to specific viewing subjects. Representation is not a process of reflection but of the insertion of images within a series of discursive contexts. The criticism is that, while role-reversal can demonstrate this 'asymmetry' of discursive oppositions (so that difference always implies power), it is ultimately ineffective because it remains 'trapped' within them. The implication is that a genuinely radical strategy would somehow have to undercut these oppositions altogether.

Similarly, parody has been criticized on the grounds that it reinforces what it should subvert. It 'fails to challenge conventional notions of female sexuality...has no theory of the representation of women...what is assumed to be progressive is actually retrograde. Being-a-woman is the essential presupposition underlying this art-work'.[28]

Criticisms of ad-graffiti also tend to rely on the notion that strategies of negation are somehow inevitably 'caught up' in the values of patriarchal culture. It has been argued that 'male iconology which carries women's subordination into visual images and subsequently legitimizes women's secondary social status, is not a mere surface gloss on an advert which can easily be peeled back to reveal "true woman"...graffiti is caught up in, and negated by, the advert's own meaning'.[29]

As with the criticisms of celebratory strategies, I find this response to negation perplexing. If the function of the feminist critic is to make readings which might encourage a proliferation of feminist meanings, (necessitating a view of the text in which it has no intrinsic 'qualities' of its own but must have values invested in it in productive practices, including consumption), why have these attempts to negate the values of patriarchal culture been attributed such intrinsic expressions of authorial intent?

Why is it assumed that the purpose of role-reversal is to 'produce' the same 'effect' on women as the original had on men? This prioritizes the role of the producer to an unnecessary degree. If one emphasises the reader/viewer contribution, and its function in 'viewing relations', as I have tried to do, it can be argued that role-reversals engender a proliferation of meanings beyond (but including) the discursive oppositions structuring the original.

Why is the meaning of the original (masculine) representation attributed with such a degree of fixity? Once an image has a specific set of meanings invested in it by a specific social group, it is not prevented from becoming the site of struggle over new meanings for an ideologically opposed group. The relationship between an image and the concept to which it refers is arbitrary; to become fixed it has to be motivated by a series of investments, insertions within the discourses of social relations. Any disruption in this process (which must be continual to produce its effects) results in changes in the conditions of intelligibility and therefore in the meaning of the text.

Criticisms of negation strategies, by implying that images already 'made' and their meanings secured within the institutions of patriarchal culture are somehow beyond this kind of intervention, are retaining the theoretical effects of an idealist theory of meaning-production, in which the relationship between a concept and its 'image' is deemed 'natural' or inevitable.

Why is it assumed that, by countering patriarchal representations with women's knowledges of the world, negation is naively realist? It is not a question of challenging the 'false' with the 'true', but of demonstrating the gender-specific nature of experience and knowledge. The imposition of these motives makes it more difficult, rather than less, to construct feminist readings of this work.

My reasons for choosing celebration and negation as examples of strategies which are being 'squeezed out' by deconstruction, and for arguing that this is wrong, are that they seem to me to have unexploited potential for addressing women as an audience (a potential lacking in deconstruction). Both represent some attempt to encourage ideological identifications between women as the consumers in certain processes of representation, by privileging the feminine reader through an emphasis on women's experience. I appreciate that the concept of 'women's experience' is vague and contradictory but this is an imperative to carry out further work rather than to abandon the whole notion as too difficult to approach. Celebration and negation are audience-orientated because they subordinate the text, *as text*, to its function (representing the ideological interests of women as a dominated social group). The text is not given the status of 'a representation', but of a symbol of the processes of representation, so that its formal existence is only *one* of the conditions of its meaningfulness. This seems to me to be a necessary aspiration for a practice which claims to adopt a materialist approach to culture, since it defines production as a practice rather than an effect of textuality.

A common assumption of the critics of celebration and negation is that feminist art must construct a 'new' language with which to articulate radical meanings. Here the text, the relationship between its formal elements, is afforded a position as *the* determinant of meaning which, in any given instance of meaning-production, it never attains. From this perspective, the audience figures only as a group of initiates familiar with the range of textual moves which have been undertaken, rather than as providing the conditions under which those textual moves can carry significance.

Deconstruction in feminist art

Deconstructive strategies are based on a theory of meanings as the productions of texts. Emphasis is laid on the means of representation, but these means are reduced to the language of texts, so that texts are deemed to provide their own determining conditions of reading and meaningfulness.

Mary Kelly's work, for example, 'stresses the fact that the production of the subject is primarily a question of positionality in language'.[30] The aim is to encourage a 'critical distance' between viewer and text, so that this 'positionality' is displaced, and meaning is 'deconstructed'. Examples can also be found in the work of Marie Yates, Yve Lomax, Sarah McCarthy, Martha Rosler, Judith Barry and others.

Deconstruction as a textual strategy is not confined to feminist art. (Indeed it is the means by which artistic 'revolutions' have taken place throughout the history of modernism). But it has become widespread in feminist art because of certain theories of femininity now associated with it. These derive from theories of language and the subject originating in post-Freudian psychoanalysis. The work of Julia Kristeva and Luce Irigaray has been instrumental in the dissemination of these theories.

Briefly, the argument is that a 'feminine' relation to language is characterized by 'process' and 'heterogeneity', whereas a masculine relation is fixed and homogenous. It therefore threatens to subvert the meanings of patriarchal discourses by placing subjectivity 'in process' and transforming the moment of reading into one where meanings are set 'in play' rather than fixed. However, this 'feminine relation' has nothing to do with being a woman, because a woman's relation to a text usually involves identifying with a masculine viewing subject.[31]

So-called classic-realist texts (Hollywood films are notoriously exemplary) set up this masculine relation, constructing 'ideological' (patriarchal) subjects as a result. By contrast, deconstructive texts encourage a heterogeneous, or 'feminine' relation, thereby 'unfixing' this ideological subject. The difference between the two is provided by their *formal existence*, their modes of textual organization.

Claims that deconstruction represents a break from idealist epistemology are based on a critique of 'logocentrism' (metaphysical relations whereby concepts appear to be 'present' in representations. These relations function through series of oppositions in which one term – the logos – is deemed superior to the other e.g. spiritual vs. material, natural vs. cultural, masculine vs. feminine, etc. In this way the world is 'ordered', made sense of, meanings and values are generated). Logocentric thought can, thus, conceive of a 'reality' which is opposed to an 'imaginary', an 'objective' to a 'subjective', a 'literal' to a 'metaphysical', and so on. As a consequence, some representations are described as scientific, objective, naturalistic, etc., and others as artistic, subjective and metaphorical.

Deconstruction seeks to demonstrate that these oppositions are constructions, and that supposedly 'objective' representations only appear so because their *textuality* is effaced through a process by which its formal conventions appear 'transparent' and its texts achieve a 'realist' status. All representations (including verbal, and even thought itself) are textual, it is claimed, therefore the ways in which some are elevated above others as reflecting or expressing truth must be constructual rather than inevitable.

There are several problems here, which I will go into further in the next section, involving a series of reductive moves. A process (representation) is reduced to an object (the text), a network of material circumstances (discourse) is reduced to an abstract, formal system (language), consequently the opposition between the 'real' and the 'imaginary', for example, is seen as not only contractual, but somehow meaningless or without effects.

In order to explain how logocentric thought is reproduced in the individual subject, a theory of the entry into language (into the 'symbolic order') has been developed using Lacanian psychoanalysis. A 'signifying practice' is the setting in place of a system of signs requiring the identity of a speaking subject. Very briefly, this subject is the product of a series of events tracing the development of the psyche, involving the 'mis-recognition' of the self (making future identification with others possible), and the entry into the symbolic which accompanies this first articulation of the 'I' of subjectivity.[32] The symbolic order of Western patriarchy gives primacy of signification to the phallus, hence the masculine subjectivity is the 'ideal ego'. So if women are to make sense of patriarchal representations, identification with the masculine subjectivity is required. Therefore, the desires which women bring to each viewing/reading experience derive from their lack of the phallus.[33]

Thus logocentrism is inevitably *phall*ogocentrism, a concept combining patriarchal authority, unity of meaning, and certainty of origin. This is why the term 'feminine', in the discourses of deconstruction, refers to any force which disrupts or subverts the meanings of the symbolic order. Any language which prioritizes 'process' above homogeneity, the semiotic[34] above the symbolic, becomes a 'dynamic' signifying practice as opposed to a 'stabilizing' one. The 'feminine' and 'women's experience' are distinguished in this way.

Deconstruction aspires to be a dynamic signifying practice, 'a form of anarchism which will express in behaviour and in action the discourses of the historical avant-garde: the destruction of the traditional western subject'.[35] It is the need for such a practice which, according to Kristeva, is the main problem of feminism.

Deconstruction involves making 'plural' or 'writable'[36] texts which demand active reading (as a result of 'critical distance'), in contrast to the realist or 'readable' texts of dominant (stabilising) signifying practices which, it is argued, demand 'passive consumption'. This is achieved by various strategies, usually involving bringing textuality to the surface, making texts refer to themselves, to reveal the 'productivity' of language. The formal properties and relations of the text become its own subject-matter, and in this way the distinctions between writing and reading, between artistic and critical practices, are 'displaced'. The purpose is not, however, to produce a 'feminist' text, because political tendentiousness involves a degree of textual closure which is anathema to the deconstructive project, rather it is to produce an alternative 'thrill', a *jouissance* [37] which replaces the old pleasures of passive consumption. The alternative pleasure results from 'transcending outworn or oppressive forms, or daring to break with normal pleasurable expectations in order to conceive a new language of desire'. [38]

This aesthetics of transgression is common to all avant-gardes, ensuring that strategies are always determined, through relations of symmetrical opposition, by the very (dominant) forms they claim to challenge. Modernism* is the other side of the coin to Realism* (where both are conceived in terms of modes of textual organisation), they define each other by being what the other is not: they are complementary aspects of the same formalist approach. The apparent contradiction is embedded in the very means by which cultural hegemony is secured and maintained.

This explains why Western capitalism has succeeded in putting modernist art to various uses (in cultural imperialism or cold war politics, for example). This is also why male artists have consistently managed to produce meanings which depend on a 'feminine' relation to the text, and why the avant-garde continue to occupy an 'alternative space'[39] in relation to the mainstream, even finding this a cause for self-congratulation rather than self criticism. [40]

This blindness to the ways in which artistic 'independence' naturalises 'good taste' within a hierarchy of aesthetic pleasures, is what makes avant-gardism so inappropriate for feminist art. The transgressional (or subcultural) position is occupied by the romantic 'outsider', a modern ideology of masculinity. [41] The ambiguous and uneasy relationship which women artists have tended to have with avant-garde movements is evidence of this. [42] Avant-gardism is an intellectual field defined by the 'creative project' which outlives any individual manifestation of it. Homage is paid to the intrinsic value of this every time a new 'heresy' emerges and succeeds in dethroning the current orthodoxy. There is an underlying complicity between the contenders then, their relationship is one of competitive complementarity between 'champions' and 'challengers'. The stakes, it is agreed, are worth fighting for, they are the social resources specific to the field, i.e. the power to legitimate and consecrate aesthetic experiences.

In order to engage in this competition, however, certain knowledges (cultural capital) have to be invested in the field. Knowledges, as feminists

---

* Though the former is often based on a critique of the latter, both assume that there is a representable 'reality' beyond the 'illusions' of a mediated world.

must insist, are gender-specific, but those demanded by this field are specifically artistic competences claiming to be un-gendered, and therefore must be masculine. These competences provide the basis for the 'critical distance' required for deconstructive reading/writing. This critical distance is an 'aesthetic disposition' in which (it is claimed) formal relations, in and by themselves, become the generator of meanings and values. This aesthetic disposition makes possible the claim to economic disinterest – the 'disavowal of economic necessity'[43] which is at the heart of the field and provides the foundation for bourgeois hegemony (because middle-class taste can appear as 'naturally' superior). This contrasts sharply with strategies in which the text's subordination to its ideological function is acknowledged, as with celebration and negation.

Formalism and materialism

Deconstruction's claim to challenge realism, like all avant-gardes' claims to be 'materialist', are based on a theoretical reduction of discourses (which are concrete, motivated, worldly, institutionalized social relations) to languages (abstract, unmotivated systems of difference), and therefore of the material (productive practices) to the formal (level of technology).

This explains why deconstruction has to maintain a distinction between those texts which enable productive reading, and those (realist) ones which defy deconstruction and supposedly maintain the reader in a passive position. (So texts *are* pre-given after all. How does this account differ from idealist theories of meaning-production?) It also explains why deconstruction has to maintain some notion of a privileged subject position where artistic practices are concerned. Not just anyone can be deconstructive, it all depends on the extent to which the semiotic can filter through the symbolic. Artists may not be born but they nevertheless emerge through the oedipal phase which occurs at a very early age. The accumulation of class and gender specific educational and cultural capital, after this climax in the psychoanalytic narrative, pales into insignificance.

Formalism is an idealist tradition. From Bell (1913)* and Fry (1920)* to Greenberg (1947)* and Fried (1966)* it is defined above all in opposition to the material, the social, the experiential, the worldly. It has always been committed to the maintenance of art as an autonomous realm of knowledge-production. It is not as a result of the influence of materialism that art resists capitalization and the demands of a market economy.[44] On the contrary, this is absolutely compatible with a modern (romantic) idealism where only art can transcend the restrictions of the material world. For modernist/deconstructive artists to claim that their work is materialist on the grounds

---

* Prime examples of modernist theory, which continue to heavily influence both the teaching and criticism of art.

that it is about the means of the production is to mistake one of those means (language) for the totality. It is an over-simplification of the marxist de-mystification of idealist thought.

Althusserian concepts of ideology, the subject, and reproduction, are often referred to in support of deconstruction. Yet the two are incompatible in my view. The development from structuralism to post-structuralism (which advocates deconstructionist strategies) via semiology, depends, I would argue, on a particular reading of Althusser which is controversial.

Structuralism is about social relations and practices, not formal relations and texts. It is a theory of the conditions of intelligibility which positions the reader at the centre of the production of meaning, as the point at which the text achieves some unity, can signify. It is an investigation of a text's relations to structures and processes. Structures are present in the text only to the extent that formal conventions are collectively recognized. They are the (shared) competences which make readings possible. Competences are always specific to the reader and his/her position within various sets of social relations. Therefore, the meaningfulness of the text is dependent on the degree to which it is invested with ideological functions, made to refer to a specific but not pre-signified experience of the world ('reality') and becomes *vraisemblable* (becomes a relation of the intertextuality which makes it intelligible). The production of meaning does not occur at the abstract level of textual difference, but at the concrete level of practice (reading) at which signifiers become 'motivated'. This is what defines structuralism as a materialist approach, not attention to the formal existence of codes and conventions in the text, but attention to reading as a material practice which transforms the text into an intelligible object by giving it an ideological function.

Althusser's concept of 'relative autonomy' refers to the ways in which the economic 'base' (mode of production) confers a dominant role on another (ideological) level of the social formation. But:

> the mode of production is... conceptualized as consisting, neither as economic relations *per se*, nor of anything so vulgarly material as 'level of technology' but as a combination of relations... social relations themselves progressively become 'a productive force'... (for) theoretical fields and discourses.[45]

Determination (of ideology by practice) involves a structural, rather than sequential, causality. Materialism is defined not as a crude reversal of idealist thought, but a de-mystification in which both the terms of the dialectic and the relationship between them are revised. So:

> on the one hand, *determination in the last instance by the (economic) mode of production*; on the other, the relative autonomy of the

superstructures and their *specific effectivity*. This clearly breaks with the Hegelian theme of *phenomena-essence-truth-of*. We are really dealing with a new relationship between new terms.[46]

An idealist dialectic is the product of a 'simple truth' whereas a materialist dialectic is 'overdetermined'.

But post-structuralist semiology[47] and advocates of deconstruction have re-established a sequential causality, a 'simple truth', by addressing the problem of ideology in terms of the reduction of the subject, rather than of social relations. It is claimed that 'Ideology produces the individual in relation to representation within the social processes in which he or she is situated, as an identity'.[48] This is the result of the reduction of productive practices (and their institutional contexts) to languages (of representation). Althusser's materialism depends on an understanding of ideology as an instance of the social formation, and an understanding that there is no ideology except for concrete subjects, whereas in the post-structuralist reading the theoretical effects of idealist concepts remain active because this determination (of ideology by practice) is not in evidence. The outcome is a 'dominance orientated' theory of meaning-production, where reproduction can only be interrupted by deconstructive (avant-garde) practices.

The specific effectivity of the superstructures, and the relative autonomy of the processes of representation, are reduced in deconstruction to the 'productivity of language'. The effects of this can be seen in attempts to separate 'realist' modes of representation from deconstructive representation which, by acknowledging its own textuality, supposedly breaks with idealist epistemology. This position tries to argue that 'realism' is an effect of textuality, that the source-of-representation (institutions, practices) does not exist independently of the text, or that the relationship between them is arbitrary. While realism may be defined at the level of signification (see above reference to the *vraisemblable*), signification is a function not only of language but of all the means of representation, including the productive force which is social relations. Thus, while

> there is no simple correspondence between classes at the economic level and classes as social forces constituted at the political and ideological planes... neither is the connection accidental and arbitrary. What relates them is a process of representation, properly understood, in which a representation of the one is produced at the other distinct and 'relatively autonomous' levels.[49]

The connection is always motivated, as I have already argued, in specific competences located beyond linguistic systems of representation in social relations themselves.

What has become known as the *Screen* critique of realism (which proposes that a) realism interpellates individuals as coherent subjects 'in thrall to the text' and b) this is achieved via textual operations of the signifying practice which exceeds any reading) 'makes the analysis of specific texts produced and consumed in concrete, historical circumstances difficult, if not impossible'.[50] Realism is not a mode of textual organization, it describes the particular place which a text occupies (within discourse) by virtue of the circumstances it is given in specific readings. The 'represented' is *not* equated with a pre-signified 'reality', *nor* is it equated with the 'representation'. The text has a specific situation in relation to the apparatuses of reading (the site of competences) which determine how, when, why and *to whom* it appears 'realist' (or anything else). The text is implicated in actuality by historical and ideological (as well as formal) circumstances. This means that *as a text* (with internal relations distinct from external forces) it is a unity which is contingent, circumstantial. 'The multiplicity of codes which make up the work is focused in the very historical conjuncture in which it is delivered'.[51] The production of feminist meanings therefore requires more than the elaboration of a particular (deconstructive) mode of textual organization, but a negotiation of the text's insertion within the discursive limits of a specific conjuncture (at the points of production, distribution, and consumption).

This is why I consider the strategies of celebration and negation to be of importance. By acknowledging this subordination of the text to these functions, they emphasise imagery as 'a relational term... the multiple intersection of a range of discourses',[52] and in so doing, inhibit the processes of reproduction.

Women as an audience - conclusion

This article is in part a plea for a feminist art which is accessible to, and pleasurable for, women. But what does this mean? It suggests the need to prioritize feminine knowledges and competences, feminine desire, since these are the means by which objects can signify and be meaningful for women and represent their relation to, or interests in, the world. Feminism *is* the representation of these interests.

This raises certain difficulties about what feminine experience (from which knowledges and competences derive) is, or indeed what femininity is. There have been attempts made by feminists to separate femaleness from femininity in order to try to explain how, for instance, a cultural object both addresses a gender-specific audience (already formed as it were) and at the same time contributes to the 'gendering' of the viewer.[53] I see no need to draw such a distinction. Gendering processes never end; a feminine subject is never completely 'formed'. For an individual to be maintained in a feminine subject-position, she has to experience continually the reality of being feminine. Every encounter with a cultural object must be able to confirm and re-affirm the gender of the subject. It may seem obvious that patriarchal society has an interest in ensuring that this process continues, but the reproduction of *gender relations*, on which patriarchy depends, requires a great deal more than this. Gendering processes, *per se*, are not intrinsically oppressive or exploitative; the domination of women depends not on ideologies of femininity but on the reproduction of gender relations, which cannot take place outside the institutional contexts which give those relations meaning and consequences. Feminine taste represents women's desire to be addressed as feminine subjects, and this is evidence of their shared cultural identity not their oppression. It is not as if there were a residual 'femaleness' to turn to instead.

For artists to mobilize a concept of feminine knowledge strikes a blow at the very justification for art's claim to disinterest (to transcend the social), which is its production of 'universal' values. Moreover, that art should continue to occupy such a de-socialized sphere is necessary for the reproduction of social relations in a climate of constant technological and mass-cultural change. How else might a concept of dominance continue to make sense in the face of the possibilities offered by modern technology?

Concepts of feminine desire have suffered most from the idealist notion of desire-as-acquisition (the making good of a lack), where acquisition is defined in opposition to loss. Psychoanalytic theory has placed the surveillance and control of feminine desire at the centre of social reproduction; through its preservation of the family in the wake of industrialization, it has enabled the survival of dominance through gender. This moralized discourse of mental pathology has, more than anything else, provided the conditions under which feminine knowledge has been made visible/readable as fantasy. Consequently attempts to use the concepts of gendering offered in psychoanalysis, by feminists, results in circular arguments in which women's desires are seen simply as a passive response to the empty promise of 'completion' offered by ideologies of femininity.[54] Femininity is reduced to passivity, feminine desire is reduced to a predictable response to patriarchal power. According to this, feminism itself might also be seen as a huge male conspiracy.

These issues have serious implications for our understanding of women as an audience. It has been deemed necessary to maintain a spurious distinction between 'the social act of consuming', and the moment when consumers 'engage in the processes and pleasures of meaning-making attendant on watching a film or a T.V. programme', so that a concept of 'interpellation' (deriving from psychoanalytic theories of subjectivity) can be preserved. This distinction between 'audience' and 'spectator' involves a further separation of the context of watching T.V. (which has to insert itself into the discourses of domesticity/familial relations) and the context of cinema-going (which, it is argued, involves looking 'in a more pristine way' at the image). To suggest that women watching films are subject to cinematic 'regimes' of pleasure whereby they are 'constructed' as gendered spectators rather than that the film inserts itself into the discourses of feminine experience (at home, 'work', leisure, etc.) is unacceptable. It is simply a way of maintaining the object of film within the domain of literary criticism. Moreover, it colludes with the representation of women's desires as contradictory fantasies of masculinization and masochism.

If concerns with women-as-an-audience are to get beyond token acknowledgements of the need to see both context and reading practices as productive, followed by a series of qualifications which allows everything to continue as before, these (psychoanalysis-informed) concepts of feminine desire/knowledge must be replaced. For an object to become a repository for meaning and pleasure (or un-pleasure) for women, it must undergo a process in which a series of investments (of women's competences) are made, so that women's desire becomes a condition of its meaningfulness, and knowledge (of the place of the feminine within the social) is produced, (contributing to the accumulation of feminine competences in the viewer).

There is no need to look for a 'new language' with which to articulate feminine meanings. These investments are continually being made and remade at the point at which cultural objects are inserted within the discursive relations of women's lives. That women's pleasures are not redeemable (as cultural capital) in the context of legitimate (patriarchal) institutions, such as education, the media, the family, the art-world, is a function of hegemony not a product of language. Hegemony is the rationalization of dominance, in relation to which feminine desire often asserts itself as a de-rationalizing impulse. Women's 'obsessions', with their bodies for example, inhibit their subordination as often as they facilitate it. Women take pleasure, they are not given it. Women can turn anything into an object of desire in order to experience pleasure, and it is the latter which is at stake not the former. Women's use of 'fashion', for example, to structure their tastes, runs counter to the individual/universal dualism of patriarchal discourses, creating identifications and difference at the same time. The tension between the conditions of existence and these dominated pleasures is a constant threat to hegemony.

Intervention in the reproduction of gender relations then, must increase this tension by addressing the knowledge/values produced by women's commodity-consumption as specifically feminine. For art this involves its dissociation from the pursuit of intrinsic value (feminist or otherwise) and an engagement with the contingencies, however transitory, of women's social position now.

As well as being an argument for a feminist art for a feminine audience, this article is also intended as one against avant-gardism. Popular distaste for 'form-over-function' (or looking 'in a more pristine way') is no accident or whim. Avant-gardism is always necessarily recruited to defend art's claim to disinterest, without which relations of domination and subordination could not continue to make sense in a contemporary society.

NOTES

This paper carries an amended introduction.

1 Although this paper was originally written three years ago, this conflict still thrives in areas of feminist debate. A recent example, in which the innovative or avant-garde was prioritized above the derivative or populist, was included in Gina Newson's film *Imaginary Women* in 1986.

2 *Feministo* (1975) was a 'mail art' project involving women all over the country, *Mother's Pride Mother's Ruin* (1978) was an exhibition of photographs, films and installations by Tricia Davis and Phil Goodall, *The Dinner Party* (1979) was an installation attributed to Judy Chicago but worked on by dozens of women in California and exhibited recently (1985) in London.

3 Examples include *Issue* and *Women's Images of Men* (at the ICA, 1980, the latter toured), *Sense and Sensibility* (at the Midland Group, Nottingham, 1982) and more recently *Pandora's Box* at the Arnolfini, Bristol (and touring) in June, 1984.

4 T. Davis, and P. Goddall, 'Personally and Politically' in *Feminist Review* no. 1 (1979) pp. 21-35.

5 See for example G. Pollock, 'Vision, Voice and Power' in *Block* No. 6 (1982) pp. 2-21 and Lippard, 'The Women's Art Movement – What Next?' in *From the Center* (1976) pp. 139-148.

6 M. Barrett, 'Feminism and the Definition of Cultural Politics' in *Feminism, Culture and Politics* (1982) pp. 37-58.

7 J. Barry and S. Flitterman-Lewis, 'Textual Strategies' in *Screen* vol. 21, no. 2, 1980, pp. 35-48.

8 R. Coward, 'This Novel Changes Lives' in *Feminist Review* no. 5, 1980, pp. 53-63. See also Duncan, C., 'When Greatness is a Box of Wheaties' in *Art Forum*, October 1975, pp. 60-64.

9 G. Pollock, Introduction to *Sense and Sensibility* catalogue (1982).

10 Barrett, *op. cit.*

11 See, for example, E. Cowie, 'The Popular Film as a Progressive Text – a discussion of *Coma* in *m/f* no. 3, pp. 59-81 and 4, pp. 57-69, (1979 and 1980), where a spurious distinction is made between texts which have their meaning constituted in their insertion within a series of discourses, and those which provide their own determining conditions of reading and meaningfulness.

12 Barry and Flitterman-Lewis, *op. cit.*

13 Barrett, *op. cit.*

14 Barry and Flitterman-Lewis, *op. cit.*

15 *Ibid.*

16 Barrett, *op. cit.*

17 Coward, *op. cit.*

18 Rosler, 'The Private and the Public' in *Art Forum*, September 1977.

19 Barrett, *op. cit.*

20 Coward, *op. cit.*

21 See G. Pollock, 'Feminism, Femininity and the Hayward Annual' in *Feminist Review*, no. 2 (1979) pp. 33-54.

22 J. Berger, *Ways of Seeing* (1972) p. 47.

23 L. Tickner, Introduction to catalogue for *Women's Images of Men* (1980).
24 G. Pollock, (1982) *op. cit.*
25 L. Tickner, *op. cit.*
26 For some examples, see J. Posener, *Spray it Loud* (1982).
27 G. Pollock, 'What's Wrong With Images of Women?', *Screen Education* no. 24 (1977) pp. 25-34.
28 Barry and Flitterman-Lewis, *op. cit.*
29 J. Ryland, 'Feminist Graffiti of Adverts', *Feminist Art News* no. 6 (1982) p. 5.
30 Mary Kelly, quoted in the catalogue for *Sense and Sensibility* (1982).
31 See A. Kuhn, *Women's Pictures* (1982) pp. 11-13 for a more detailed account.
32 See J. Kristeva, 'Signifying Practice and Mode of Production' *Edinburgh Magazine* no. 1 (1976) pp. 64-75.
33 See L. Mulvey, 'Visual Pleasure and Narrative Cinema' *Screen* vol. 16 no. 3 (1975) pp. 6-18.
34 Kristeva's term for the pre-lingual realm of sounds, rhythms, gestures etc., which are anterior to meaning.
35 J. Kristeva, from interview in *L'Espresso* April 1977.
36 Jacques Derrida's term, see J. Culler, *On Deconstruction* (1983) Routledge pp. 88-110.
37 R. Barthes, *The Pleasure of the Text*, (1975).
38 L. Mulvey, *op. cit.*
39 S. Harvey, 'Independent Cinema?' *Independent Video* no. 1 (1981).
40 As Peter Wollen does in *Readings and Writings* (1982) p. 214.
41 See A. McRobbie, 'Settling accounts with Subcultures, a feminist critique' *Screen Education* no. 34 (1980), pp. 37-49.
42 As referred to in R. Parker and G. Pollock, *Old Mistresses*, (1981) pp. 134-157. See also Joyce Johnson's *Minor Characters* (1983) for a personal account.
43 P. Bourdieu 'Aristocracy of Culture' *Media, Culture and Society* vol. 2 no. 3 (1980) pp. 225-254.
44 See B. Miege, 'The Cultural Commodity' *Media, Culture and Society* vol. 1 no. 3 (1979) pp. 297-311.
45 S. Hall, 'Re-thinking the "Base and Superstructure" Metaphor', *Class, Hegemony, Party* (1977), ed. J. Bloomfield, (1977) pp. 43-72.
46 L. Althusser, 'Contradiction and Overdetermination' in *For Marx* (1969) pp. 87-128.
47 Eg V. Burgin, 'Looking at Photographs' in *Screen Edcucation* no. 24 (1977) pp. 17-24.
48 R. Coward, and J. Ellis, *Language and Materialism* (1977).
49 J. Tagg, 'The Currency of the Photograph' *Screen Education* no. 28 (1978) pp. 45-67.
50 D. Hebdige, and G. Hurd, 'Reading and Realism' *Screen Education* no. 28 (1978) pp. 68-78.
51 J. Tagg, *op. cit.*
52 N. Green and F. Mort 'Visual Representations and Cultural Politics' *Block* no. 7 (1982) pp. 59-68.
53 A. Kuhn, 'Women's Genres' *Screen* vol. 25 (1984) pp. 18-28.
54 For example, R. Coward, *Female Desire* (1984).

ROSEMARY BETTERTON

HOW DO WOMEN LOOK?
THE FEMALE NUDE
IN THE WORK OF SUZANNE VALADON

The representation of women in the visual media has become a crucial area
of concern for the Women's Movement over the last few years. Most
energies have been put, quite rightly, into countering the stereotyping and
sexism of media images. Evidence of how wide such concerns have become is
shown by the very useful booklet published by the Trade Union Congress
this year, *Images of Inequality: The Portrayal of Women in the Media and
Advertising* (TUC, 1984).

At a more theoretical level, a body of feminist work has been developed
which analyses the position of the male spectator in relation to the female
image as being one of power and control. This work has developed a
powerful feminist critique of the ways in which women are represented in
the visual media. It has constituted an important challenge to the notion that
there can be a common experience of images across gender (and also race
and class) divisions. However, an analysis of images which focuses
exclusively on their relationship to a male spectator leaves certain problems
unexplained and difficult to resolve. Centrally, it offers no explanation of
how *women* look at images of women. It is this question which I want to
develop here in two main ways. Firstly, what does it mean to look from a
woman's point of view? And, secondly, how do women appear in images
made by women?

The focus of the first part of the article will be on the question of
spectatorship, both male and female, in relationship to representation of
women's bodies. I want to argue that women can and do respond to images
of themselves in ways which are different from and cannot be reduced to,
masculine 'ways of seeing'. The work of Suzanne Valadon (1865-1938)
shows how a woman artist working within a male tradition of
representation *could* produce images which disrupt the conventions of a
genre. My starting point for looking at Valadon was a general interest in
women artists working at the beginning of the century many of whom are
perhaps known by name, but whose work is difficult to see either in

reproduction or in exhibition.

It was the discovery that she worked extensively on the female nude, a subject linked almost exclusively to male artists, which seemed to connect up with wider questions about the relationship of women to images of themselves. In particular it raised the issue of what kinds of pleasures are offered to women as spectators within forms of representation which, like the nude, have been made mainly by men, for men. If 'pleasure in looking is split between active/male and passive/female' (Mulvey, 1975) then how do I, as a woman, explain my enjoyment of certain images, especially within a category such as the nude? On what basis would it be possible to make critical distinctions between images which work for women and those which work against them?

In a culture where images of female sexuality are multiplied endlessly as a spectacle for male pleasure, there is a crucial political point in feminist arguments that *all* representations of the female body draw upon the same visual codes, and reinstate the same relationships of sexual power and subordination. No images can ever entirely escape the circle of voyeurism and exploitation which constitutes male power in representation. Even Valadon's nudes, whether flicked through in a book or hung on a gallery wall, are defined within a regime of looking which is oppressive to women. Such a view, however, although powerful and persuasive, seems unnecessarily pessimistic politically and for reasons I indicate below, theoretically dubious. It is necessary to argue that some forms of representation *are* better than others, on the basis that they offer women images of themselves which are not humiliating or oppressive.

It also seems important from the point of view of feminist cultural production and criticism to begin to map out the shifts and changes within representations of the female body which might offer a basis for developing new kinds of imagery. It is a political project to search for and construct more positive images for women, as well as to denounce and deconstruct those which are limiting and oppressive. Feminists working in different areas of cultural production are developing strategies of intervention which have a critical function towards dominant stereotypes and also try to find and to develop new kinds of representation for women. Rose Garrard's recent work shown at the Ikon Gallery in Birmingham earlier this year has precisely this critical relationship to an existing tradition of representation.

Female sexuality is clearly a problematic area of representation for women artists to work on, given the bias of western culture towards fetishizing the female body. The nude in art has been enshrined as an icon of culture since the Renaissance, and epitomizes the objectification of female sexuality. For both these reasons it is peculiarly resistant to change by women artists. Suzanne Valadon is unusual as a woman artist in taking the nude as a central theme of her work. Her work therefore poses some interesting questions about the relationship of women to a 'masculine' genre. Does a woman artist necessarily produce a different kind of imagery from her male counterparts? Can a woman who is not a feminist produce work which is feminist? If the nude is embedded in a structure of gendered looking, based on male power and female passivity, is it possible for a woman artist to 'see' it differently?

I want to try to answer these questions by looking at those aspects of Valadon's experience as a woman and as an artist which made her relationship to the nude distinctly different from that of her male contemporaries. In her work, I will argue, we can see a consciousness of women's experience which challenges the conventions of the nude. But first I want to look in more detail at some of the arguments which have been developed around the question of male spectatorship and to suggest some ways in which we might usefully think about women's pleasure in looking.

Through men's eyes...

> Representation of the world, like the world itself, is the work of men; they describe it from their own point of view, which they confuse with the absolute truth.
>
> de Beauvoir, 1972:175

De Beauvoir's perceptive comment points to two important strands within feminist analyses of representation. The first emphasises that representation is a particular construction, rather than being a reflection, of reality. The second shows that the world which is represented to us can be seen in other ways. A body of writing has emerged in the last few years which has provided a framework for the critical re-examination of the representation of the female body in images.[1] It has exposed the nude as a particular construction of female sexuality which signifies male desire. At the same time the privileged position assigned to the fine-art nude in European culture has come under attack, by situating the nude in relation to a whole range of representations which exploit female sexuality in pinups, pornography and advertising. Male artists and critics have consistently justified their enjoyment of the nude by appealing to abstract conceptions of ideal form, beauty and aesthetic value. Such a view renders invisible the relationships of power and subordination involved when a male artist depicts the female body. It ignores or denies the difference between looking at the body of a woman and looking at a pile of fruit.[3] Therefore a feminist critique of the nude has focused upon analysis of the ways in which the act of viewing itself reinstates male power.

In a painting by Ingres from the early nineteenth century, which is representative of the 'classic' tradition of the nude, the address to the spectator is made explicit in a number of ways (Figure 29). The naked

29 J. A. D. Ingres, *The Great Odalisque*, 1841. Musée du Louvre, Paris.

woman is shown reclining, and although her body is turned away from the
viewer, the glimpse of her breast and the expanse of her buttocks and thighs
emphasise her sexual availability. Her glance too invites the gaze, so that the
fiction of her complicity with the viewer's look can be maintained. The act of
viewing is accentuated by the device of the drawn curtain which suggests
that a sight which is normally hidden has been revealed to us. Finally, the
treatment of the body itself as smooth, fleshy and boneless reinforces the
passivity and languor of the pose. What is specific to the nineteenth century
is the theme of the odalisque, a harem setting which has connotations of
extreme sensuality, represented by the rich materials and jewellery, and of
slavery. It suggests that the woman in the image is literally possessed by the
man who looks at her. Women's sexuality is represented as exotic and at the
same time firmly in male possession. Under the guise of disinterested
aesthetic contemplation, the spectator/owner was given a privileged access
to the spectacle of the naked female body, a sight normally tabooed in
western culture.

What this analysis shows is that the gender of the viewer and the nature
of his response was not a postscript to the production of the image, but
crucial in the construction of the nude as a genre. The representation of the
nude in art could not be seen as being produced outside or apart from the
social and sexual relations of a given society in any period.

The idea of gendered audiences with differing responses, needs and
desires emerges from this critique. Women and men look differently
because their social experience is different. John Berger put this succinctly in
his essay on the nude:

...men act and *women appear*. Men look at women. Women watch themselves being looked at. This determines not only most relations between men and women but also the relation of women to themselves. The surveyor of woman in herself is male: the surveyed female. Thus she turns herself into an object – and most particularly an object of vision: a sight.

Berger, 1972:47

Characteristic of women's looking, then, is that it is split between surveyor and surveyed. Women see themselves through men's eyes. Yet Berger offers no account of the process by which women become objects of their own vision. It has largely been assumed, without argument, that women have a passive or negative relationship to their own image in visual art.

A more theoretical analysis of spectatorship, drawing mainly on a psychoanalytic perspective, has come from the study of cinema. Laura Mulvey's influential piece 'Visual Pleasure and Narrative Cinema' (1975) provides a starting point for analysis of sexual difference and spectatorship in relation to the narrative structures of film. She argues that, structurally, the narrative film presumes a male gaze and a female object:

In a world ordered by sexual imbalance pleasure in looking has been split between active/male and passive/female. The determining male gaze projects its phantasy onto the female figure which is styled accordingly. In their traditional exhibitionist role women are simultaneously looked at and displayed, with their appearance coded for strong erotic and visual impact so that they can be said to connote *to-be-looked-at-ness*.

Mulvey, 1975:11

While offering a complex analysis of the voyeuristic and fetishistic drives of the male spectator, Mulvey's argument, though this was not her intention, rendered the female spectator doubly unseen. Through her attention to male spectatorship Mulvey appeared to give theoretical weight to the evacuation of a woman's point of view. The position of the female spectator became not only invisible but impossible since, in the cinema at least, what she was seeing was already determined and encompassed by the male gaze.

I have used these two instances to suggest that during the 1970s the woman under discussion was placed firmly within the image, an object if not a mere fiction of male fantasy. Where did this leave women as viewers then? Such analysis offered no space to examine the question of what active female pleasure in looking could be. Does it exist, and what might its components be? How are we to explain such pleasure?

Looking as a woman...

I want first to review briefly some arguments which have been put forward to explain the position of women as spectators and to account for women's pleasure in images of women. In most analyses, the position offered is a profoundly contradictory one for women. On the one hand, woman as spectator is offered the dubious satisfaction of identification with the heterosexual masculine gaze, voyeuristic, penetrating and powerful. This may offer the pleasure of power and control, but at the expense of negating women's own experience and identity. The problem with this is that it cannot offer any positive explanation of women's pleasure as *different* from male pleasure. On the other hand, it is argued, women's pleasure is bound up with a narcissistic identification with the image of the female body, usually shown to be desirable but passive. This second explanation seeks to account for the frequency with which the female image appears, often semi-nude, in women's magazines and in advertising which is addressed specifically to a female audience.

The first explanation suggests that images of women are attractive because, as women, we are subject to socialisation. We inhabit a patriarchal culture in which we, no less than men, are socialised into the acceptance of women's bodies as desirable and accessible. We are bombarded with images of style, glamour and seduction through magazines, adverts, cinema and television. No wonder these images become objects of fantasy and desire for us, too. No wonder they seep into our consciousness as models of what we really want to be. Recourse to the concept of socialisation alone, however, can only provide a partial explanation. It cannot fully explain the different ways in which certain images affect us (Page Three Girl, no; Marilyn Monroe, perhaps...), nor on what basis we might make critical distinctions between different images. It also does not explain why women might respond to the same image in different ways. For example, while I am quite clear that my pleasure in a female nude by Valadon is greater than in one by Renoir, I certainly cannot assume this to be true for all women. What makes the difference? Not socialization, but certain kinds of knowledge and experience, of which for me the most important is an awareness of feminist ideas.

Socialization can also suggest a particular notion of 'false consciousness' in which women, and men, are duped into a passive absorption of current ideologies of femininity, an acceptance of the status quo as given. This does not seem to accord with the reality of most women's experience of being confronted, at some moment in their lives, with a gap between the ideal image of femininity presented to them and their own less than ideal selves. Such awareness may lead to depression or to consciousness raising, but either way it suggests that the 'fit' between experience and ideology is never complete.

The other kind of explanation of women's pleasure draws upon the concept of narcissism. If the male look is characterised by voyeurism, observing and taking pleasure at a distance, the female look, it is claimed, is narcissistic, finding pleasure in closeness, in reflection and in identification with an image. Narcissism as concept has a dangerous ambivalence for women, however. In popular usage, the myth of Narcissus who fell for his own reflection and pined away for love of it stands for unhealthy obsession with self-image. When transferred to women, it has traditionally been cited as a confirmation of innate frivolity and self-indulgence. (In medieval and Renaissance iconography the woman holding a mirror signified Vanity.) It therefore points to a kind of essentialism which has reactionary implications for women. But as Rosalind Coward has recently argued, women are in love with their own desirability for very real reasons:

> because desirability has been elevated to being the crucial reason for sexual relations, it sometimes appears to women that the whole possibility of being loved and comforted hangs on how their appearance will be received.

> Coward, 1984:78

It follows then that women will anxiously scrutinise images held up as ideals of femininity for signs that they can appropriate to themselves. But since there is usually a mismatch between ourselves and the images held up to us, the response cannot be one simply of pleasurable narcissism. The relation of women to their images is profoundly uncomfortable, a relation which, describing the negative sense women have of their own self image matched against the ideal, Coward terms 'narcissistic damage'.

The concept of narcissism has been deployed by some feminists, however, in an argument for a specifically feminine erotic experience. Luce Irigaray in 'This Sex Which is Not One' (1977) claims that the kind of look which separates the subject from the object of the gaze and projects desire on to that object is essentially masculine. Female eroticism is bound up with touch much more than with sight, women's pleasure being autoerotic. This, she argues, means that women have a problematic relationship with the whole process of looking in western culture. Women are bound within visual discourse to become objects and never subjects of their own desire. Since distance is an absolute condition of viewing and women's pleasure is autoerotic, any pleasure women have in the visual image is vicarious and even masochistic.

Irigaray, then, takes the idea of narcissism a stage further in suggesting women's pleasure in self cannot be mediated through the experience of other images. Her argument is problematic in that it posits an essential feminine erotic experience apparently outside cultural and social definitions. But what she does do is offer an account of women's pleasure which is not bound within the parameters of male experience, and which is seen as distinctly different. This is important for any positive analysis of women's pleasure, though it needs to be explained as a *social* process rather than assumed as an essentially feminine characteristic.

So far I have written about a 'masculine' and a 'feminine' viewpoint as if these were unproblematically assumed by 'real' men and women whenever they look at an image. Both 'masculine' and 'feminine' are not essences, but social categories formed through changing social experiences. They are not only imposed from outside us, they are also experienced subjectively as part of our understanding of who we are. But in a patriarchal culture it is clearly the case that women are forced to adopt a masculine viewpoint in the production and consumption of images far more often than men are required to adopt a feminine one. Since gender relations are not equal women, in looking at paintings or watching films, may indeed be placed in the position of adopting a voyeuristic gaze: but that position involves discomfort, a constant process of readjustment. For example, a woman looking at the nude illustrated in Figure 29 could quite easily adopt a position of aesthetic detachment, since that is the way we are all taught to look at art in this culture. However, if she began to refer the image to her own experience of being treated as a sexual object (for example, of walking down a street past a group of staring men), the way she looked at the image could change her point of view.

In Mulvey's re-examination of the structures of spectatorship in cinema she develops the idea of the 'mobile' position of the female spectator. The woman watching the film is caught up in the pleasures offered by 'masculinization' but is unable completely to adopt a masculine viewpoint. Mulvey explains this mobility in Freudian terms. The woman is torn between the memory of her 'phallic phase' before the development of femininity, and her assumption of 'correct femininity' which demands that the active phallic phase be repressed: 'the female spectator's phantasy of masculinization is always to some extent at cross purposes with itself, restless in its transvestite clothes' (Mulvey, 1981:15).[3] But I want to argue that this ability to switch points of view may be seen in a more positive way as opening up a critical space between a masculine or a feminine position and the actual experience of a woman watching a film or looking at a painting. We need to make a distinction between looking 'as a woman' and the fact of being one, between a feminine position and female experience.

In looking at a glamour photo or a nude it is possible to be both fascinated and attracted by the image, and *at the same time*, well aware of the difference between the image and our own experience: just as in reading a romance or in watching a melodrama one can be swept up by, and yet recognise, the seductive pull of fantasy. This suggests a certain ability to move between and to acknowledge different viewpoints at once, to look critically 'against the grain' while still enjoying the process itself. I am not arguing that this ability is innate to women by virtue of biological sex, but that it *is* a condition of women's viewing under patriarchy. Men too can look critically, but within forms of culture made for and by men they are less likely to be forced constantly to negotiate a viewpoint. Nor do I want to suggest that women automatically look in a detached and critical way. Looking (or producing) as a woman is dependent on a certain consciousness that such looking is, or could be, different from a masculine viewpoint. Such consciousness in turn depends on a recognition that women's social and cultural experience is itself differently arrived at. It also requires a consciousness that women's experience could be positive and productive, capable of giving voice and vision.

This enables us to ask what kind of imagery might be produced which *would* address women's experience. In the case of the nude, what kind of struggle over discourses of representation would signal an attempt to break with male iconography? In Suzanne Valadon's work precisely this critical space is opened up between the iconographic tradition of the nude and the representation of female experience. Her work is characterised by a certain tension between expectations set up by the genre and the way she actually represents the female body. This tension within the generic codes of the nude marks a point of resistance to dominant representations of female sexuality in early twentieth-century art. It may also account for some of the confusion of critics, who have described her work as both 'masculine' and 'feminine'. (Figure 30.)

A woman artist cannot be assumed to have 'seen' differently from her male contemporaries, but it can be argued that the particular force of her experience produced work which was differently placed within the dominant forms of representation of her period. It is necessary therefore to look at how Valadon's background and position as a woman artist affected her representation of the nude.

Artist as model

Suzanne Valadon worked for about ten years as a professional artist's model. This is significant for her own work as an artist and for the ways in which her subsequent identity has been established. Modelling in the late nineteenth and early twentieth century signified a particular relationship of artistic practice to sexuality. The period of Valadon's working life from the 1880s to 1938 saw the popularity of Bohemia as a central myth of artistic life. At its core was the relationship between the male creator and his female model. Alfred Murger's *Vie de Bohème*, published first as short stories and then in book form in 1851, set a pattern for fictional accounts of young artists and doomed models. Clearly part of the success of Bohemia lay in its mobilisation of existing ideologies of masculinity and femininity. In the

30   Suzanne Valadon, *The Blue Chamber*, 1913. Musée Nationale d'Art Moderne, Paris.

artist-model relationship there seemed to be a 'natural' elision of the sexual with the artistic: the male artist was both lover and creator, the female model both his mistress and his muse. Some male painters explicitly connected their artistic powers with sexual potency. August Renoir, for whom Valadon modelled in the 1880s, was alleged to have said: 'I paint with my prick.'

The connexions between phallic and creative power became a well-worn theme in the discourses of artists and critics of the period. This ideology is clearly restated in a book published in 1930 by C. J. Bulliet called *The Courtezan Olympia, An Intimate Survey of Artists and their Mistress Models*. The title neatly conveys the book's qualities of titillation and sexism:

> Genius is creative, and our guardians of morals, professional and amateur, rightly (even if ignorantly) sense a connection between the lusts of the body and this creative energy of the mind and emotions.
>
> Bulliet, 1930:2

The essential complement of the lusty artist was the female model, who was never seen as a contributor in the production of an image, but only as a passive material to be posed and manipulated, subject to the transforming power of the artist. In popular myth, and sometimes in fact, the model's exploitation as the object of the artist's gaze led directly to her exploitation as his sexual object. In paintings of the nude by some modernist artists of the 1900s this connexion is represented explicitly, as for example in the various versions of 'Artist and Model' by the German painter, Kirchner.

The fusion of the sexual and the artistic in ideologies of art production clearly created problems for a woman artist. Painting from the female model formed part of the definition of what it meant to be an artist, but at the same time it had come to signify a sexualised relationship. For a woman to become a 'serious' artist then, a transgression of contemporary ideals of femininity was implied: yet if she kept to the 'safer' subjects of domestic scenes, flower paintings or landscapes, she risked relegation to the secondary status of 'woman artist'. In Frances Borzello's (1982) study of the artist's model it is suggested that the normative value of the male artist/female model relationship was such that it rendered all other relations between artist and model deviant.

But what of the ultimate 'deviation' – when both artist and model were female? The social relations of artistic production in the late nineteenth century still made such a relationship unlikely, however, despite the growing numbers of women entering the artistic profession in the 1880s and 1890s. In France the 'Union des Femmes Peintres et Sculpteurs' was founded in 1881 to promote the interests of women artists and support their demands for access to education and exhibition. Over a twenty-year period the Union fought for, and gradually won, rights to academic training at the Ecole des Beaux Arts and finally in 1903, the right for women to enter the competition for the Prix de Rome, the height of an academic artist's aspirations (Diane-Radycki, 1982). Such an entry into the art establishment and the right to be treated on an equal basis with male art students was important for the professional recognition of women as artists, even though academic honours were by then scorned by the avant-garde. Sources such as the painter Marie Bashkirtseff's diaries, first published in 1887, emphasise the conflict between middle-class femininity and the paradigm of artistic life. The respectability afforded by academic training did enable women to study the nude without loss of social position.

Although the classes for women were available in Paris, for instance at the Academie Julien where nude male models were used, painting from the nude must still have been a relatively rare experience for women before 1900. It has been taken for granted by most writers on women in art that institutional exclusion from study of the nude was damaging to women artists. But it is not clear what drawing from the naked body would have meant to a middle-class woman. What relationship could she have to the male iconography of the nude? Even viewed through the distancing veil of aesthetic values, the nude in painting was uncomfortably close to the sexually explicit discourses of pornography. The fact that both shared the same regime of representations meant that at any moment the image could become dangerously ambivalent, as did Manet's painting of *Olympia* in 1865. For a woman brought up within definitions of bourgeois femininity which tabooed the sight of her own body, let alone anyone else's, painting the nude must have been fraught with difficulty. Intervention in a genre bound up with the fundamental premises of male creativity involved problems far beyond institutional exclusion. It questioned the definition of femininity itself. It is therefore not surprising that few women artists working at the end of the nineteenth century made the nude a central theme in their work, despite increased access to life classes.

Yet Suzanne Valadon did just that. From her first drawings in the 1880s throughout her working life she produced images of the nude. What made this possible? The answer seems to lie in her background as a model which made her experience of art markedly different from the majority of both male and female artists. Her sexual identity was constructed outside bourgeois femininity and, by selling her body as a model, she entered the art world by an 'underground' route. Furthermore, her class background barred her from access to professional or academic training. As the illegitimate daughter of a part-time seamstress and cleaning woman, she occupied an extremely marginal position even within the working-class milieu of Montmartre in the 1880s.[4] She was apprenticed at the age of nine to an *atelier de couture* in the Place de Clichy, where she worked under sweatshop conditions for three years. A succession of jobs followed as waitress and dishwasher, street vendor, groom in a livery stables and acrobat in a circus troupe. After an accident at the circus she was forced to give up acrobatics for the insecure and badly paid work of artist's model.

In the 1880s, the suburb of Montmartre was becoming a favoured area for artists in search of cheap studio space and picturesque views. Women in search of work stood in the Place Pigalle waiting to be viewed and picked out by artists in search of models. The parallels with prostitution are clear; a model also offered her body for sale, she was usually of lower-class origin and dependent upon her middle-class 'client', her rates of pay were low and established by individual negotiation. Even if a model led a blameless life, she was clearly defined outside the codes of respectable femininity.

Valadon had both sexual and non-sexual relationships with the various artists for whom she modelled: Puvis de Chavannes, Renoir, Toulouse Lautrec and less known now, Henner, de Nittis, Inais and Zandomeneghi. By her own account Valadon was a very good model and extremely successful at it, and there is nothing to suggest that she felt exploited. But modelling placed her both outside the respectability which was still accepted by most women artists and at the opposite pole from their aspirations. She was situated between the harsh world of the exploitation of women's work in low-paid jobs, with prostitution as an alternative, and the Bohemian world of the artist. What made Valadon almost unique was her successful transition from one to the other. This transition of Valadon's from model to artist was a hard process, both in terms of acquisition of technical ability and in the struggle to form a new identity as a professional artist.

In becoming an artist Valadon took on, and lived out, the characteristics of the male Bohemian stereotype: a succession of lovers, a scorn for money and a wild lifestyle. Yet it was not a role which, as a woman, she could inhabit without contradictions. This is evident in the complicated and difficult relationships she had with her mother and with her son, Maurice Utrillo, which created enormous tensions throughout her life. It is also evident in her work. While her early drawings used nude subjects, these were often based on her own body or that of her child. Her relationship to the nude therefore could not be the same as that of a male artist using female models, although she learnt to draw using conventions of representation common to artists of her period.

Her work was based on direct experience of the way her own body was used as a model, and it is clear from the self-portraits that she saw herself in an uncompromising and independent way. She is both subject and object, viewer and viewed, in her nude studies, in a way which begins to redefine and reconstruct the relationship of artist and model and, in turn, of spectator and image. Valadon's interest lies partly, then, in the way she combined roles of model and artist and by doing so disrupted the normative relationships of masculine creativity and feminine passivity. But she is interesting also because as a model she did not conform to the respectable image of the 'woman artist' and thus was able to work within the male-defined iconography of the nude. Valadon's disruption of those codes comes neither from a conscious feminist perspective nor from mere circumstance, but from the consciousness which she developed as a woman who experienced different but overlapping definitions of femininity and masculinity, creativity and class.

Model as artist

When Valadon began to produce her first drawings during the 1880s the academic tradition of the nude was already fragmenting. During her working life as an artist the formal conventions of art were radically transformed by the modernist aesthetics of the Parisian avant-garde.[5] But as Carol Duncan has pointed out (1973), the modernist 'break' did not challenge the ideological assumptions embedded in the representation of the nude. The social and aesthetic radicalism of avant-garde artists did not necessarily imply a critique of existing gender relations. In the work of Picasso or Kirchner the theme of male sexual dominance and female passivity is reproduced in an even more explicit and violent way. Valadon's work has to be situated in a complex set of discourses of modernist aesthetics and more traditional ideologies of gender relations.

I want to draw out one strand which is relevant to Valadon's choice of a particular mode of representing the nude. This was the desire in the second half of the nineteenth century to represent the 'modern' nude, no longer veiled in history or mythology, but the woman 'as she is', seen on the modelling couch, in the studio and in a landscape. The notion of woman 'as she is' in itself signifies an ideological construction at work. In the bathers of Renoir, Degas and Cézanne and in Gauguin's women of Tahiti, for instance, can be seen the reworking of the powerful myth of woman as nature. The nude in landscape in particular came to signify an identification of women's bodies with the forces of nature. Women could be seen as 'naturally' representing fertility and unthreatening eroticism.

How do Valadon's drawings of the nude relate to this theme of the natural woman? Clearly she too was concerned to represent the modern nude, stripped of historical and mythologising trappings. But her work departs significantly from the repressive connotations of the work of her male precursors and contemporaries. Her choice of theme – women seen naked in the studio, in domestic interiors and in landscape – suggests that she should be placed with painters who sought to demystify the nude and develop new forms of realism. Yet in her treatment of the theme women are not shown to be instinctual and natural beings, but individuals engaged in social relationships and activities.

What Valadon tried to capture in her drawings was the intensity of a particular moment of action rather than a static and timeless vision. This suggests a conscious and deliberate attempt to change existing codes of representation which, in the case of the female nude, emphasised beauty of form, harmony and timelessness. She chose in her portraits and nudes to show women caught in moments of action and engaged in relationships with each other. This choice was not governed by an uncontrollable emotional urge, as some of her biographers have suggested, but by a thorough familiarity with the work of contemporary artists, in particular Degas and Toulouse Lautrec. It was these two artists who recognised her drawing ability while she was still a model, and who encouraged her to exhibit her work in the Salon de la Nationale for the first time in 1894. Her work was shown alongside that of Degas and Lautrec in private galleries in the 1890s and 1900s, and after 1909 she exhibited regularly at the most important venues for modern art in Paris, the Salon d'Automne and the Salon des Indépendents. The social milieu she frequented included most of the leading members of the Parisian avant-garde. Such a position suggests that Valadon was quite familiar with current discourses on art and was capable of consciously transforming them.

A comparison between her early drawings and the work of Degas shows

31   Edgar Degas, *Women In A Tub*, c.1885, pastel on paper. Collection Mrs. Anne Kessler.

32   Suzanne Valadon, *Young Girl Sitting At Her Toilette*, 1894. Collection Robert Lehman, New York.

very clearly how she drew on his conception of the nude but fundamentally changed its character. Degas produced a set of ten pastels for the Eighth Impressionist Exhibition in 1886 on the theme of nudes at their toilet (Figure 31). According to Degas his intention was to show:

> a human creature preoccupied with herself – a cat who licks herself; hitherto the nude has always been represented in poses which presuppose an audience, but these women of mine are honest and simple folk, unconcerned by any other interests than those involved in their physical condition... It is as if you looked through a keyhole.
>
> Royal Academy, 1979-80:64

His statement is interesting in two ways. Firstly in the contradiction between his stated desire to represent the nude in a way which denies its traditional voyeurism and yet which reinstates voyeuristic looking in an even more intense way as if 'through a keyhole'. The body on display is to be replaced by peeping into the intimate and hidden world of women. Secondly, he reproduces precisely the ideology of women as nature, absorbed in their physical beings – like cats they perform purely instinctual and reflexive rites of cleanliness. In these images, then, the viewer is given a privileged access to a private, narcissistic moment: seeing a woman alone and caught unawares, intimately framed. Compared with the sensuous and intimate voyeurism of Degas, Valadon's drawings and pastels on the same theme look curiously awkward (Figures 32 and 33). Her women are seen usually in middle distance, isolated in space and uncomfortably posed. Rather than

33 Suzanne Valadon, *Nude Getting Into Bath Beside Seated Grandmother*, c.1908. Collection Paul Pétridès, Paris.

attributing this to lack of facility, it may point to a rather different treatment of the theme.

In Valadon's drawings of women getting in and out of baths, drying themselves and getting dressed, the viewpoint is more distant and placed artificially high in the picture plane. The effect is to flatten and to distort space so that the spectator is offered no ideal viewing position from which to look at the nude figure of the woman. This distortion of form and flattening of space was part of modernist aesthetics, but as used by Valadon here, it disrupts the continuity between the viewer and the viewed, the illusion of a continuous space. But more than this, Valadon's use of the drawing medium alters the seductive quality of Degas' nudes. Where his pastel is soft and sensuous, suggestive of the softness of flesh or the blurring half-tones of shadow, Valadon's lines are abrupt, edgy and harsh, denying any erotic sensation. Valadon's drawing (Figure 32) transforms the narcissistic and private gesture of Degas' woman, who gazes at and touches her arm, into a movement which is both more awkward and more immediate. She reaches towards the edge of the space for a towel while clutching her foot. The beautiful, undulating line of Degas' figure has become lumpy and discontinuous, the lines are sharper and no longer voluptuous. Degas himself acknowledged the difference in letters to his 'terrible Maria', written around 1900, when he refers to her 'wicked and supple drawings' which are 'drawn like a saw'. (Rey, 1922:9-10.)

These differences in composition and technique are crucial to the very different experience which the viewer has in relation to Valadon's drawings as opposed to Degas' nudes. But the employment of modernist distortions and stress on the constructed nature of the image do not in themselves imply a radical change in the representation of the nude. (Picasso, Matisse and others pushed those formal distortions much further in their versions of the nude, but could not be said to challenge its voyeuristic premises.) It is the combination of the visual style with the innovations Valadon makes in the iconography of the nude which makes her work specifically different. The naked woman is very frequently shown in a social relationship with another woman, often clothed and older, a servant or mother figure. Valadon used her own mother, as well as her son, friends and servants, as models for her drawings in the 1900s. Both figures are shown engaged in some activity which implies a moment in a series of relationships and activities, and also a kind of communication between the women (see Figure 33). The experiences represented are familiar and banal ones, not mystified through representation into a timeless moment.

By doing this Valadon is not simply offering us another version of the nude, she is challenging a central truth which it embodies. This myth is of Woman who, changeless and unchangeable, is identified with her biological essence, identified with her naked body. One of the peculiar features of the nude in art from 1500 to 1900 is that it offers us a woman who remains essentially unchanged through a kaleidoscopic variety of sets and costumes, landscape or harem, Venus or prostitute:

> Thus against the dispersed contingent and multiple existences of actual women, mythical thought opposes the Eternal Feminine, unique and changeless.
>
> de Beauvoir, 1972:283

Valadon's nudes, in showing women's nakedness as an effect of particular circumstances and as differentiated by age and work, therefore challenge the idea that nakedness is essence, an irreducible quality of the 'Eternal Feminine'.

Taken as a sequence, Valadon's drawings from the 1890s and 1900s show a series of interactions between women and children. This theme of

34 Suzanne Valadon, *The Abandoned Doll*, 1921. Collection Paul Pétridès, Paris.

35 Suzanne Valadon, Self-Portrait, 1932. Collection Paul Pétridès, Paris.

women's relationships is continued in her paintings, though more frequently here the naked woman is seen in isolation. Many show two women of different ages – as in the works on the theme of mother and daughter, *Little Girl at the Mirror,* 1909 and *The Cast Off Doll,* 1921 (Figure 34). In both paintings a naked adolescent girl looks at herself in a hand mirror, while in the second her mother gently dries her back with a towel, the abandoned doll lying at her feet. The two pictures together suggest a narrative of the onset of puberty and the girl's awareness of her own sexual being. In the earlier work the older woman shows the girl her reflection in an almost violent gesture. In the later picture the girl herself twists away from the mother, and while their poses echo each other, the physical contact between them is broken by their separate glances. In such works Valadon is questioning the dominant tradition of the nude as a spectacle for the male viewer by focusing upon women's sense of the relationship between their state of mind and their experience of their bodies in processes of changing and ageing.

In a series of paintings from the 1920s and 1930s she draws, in common with her contemporaries, on existing iconographic codes of the reclining nude, but her versions differ from theirs in the attention given to the individuality of the sitter. In some, women look discomforted by their

36 Suzanne Valadon, *Reclining Nude*, 1928. Metropolitan Museum of Art, New York, Robert Lehman collection.

nakedness, while in others they seem unaware of their bodies; but in either case, the viewer is made aware of the woman's face which is as strongly and individually delineated as her body (see Figure 36). Some critics have noted that Valadon brings together the two separate genres of the nude and portraiture:

> Everything is portraiture as far as she is concerned, and a breast, thigh, wrinkle are interrogated with no less attention than a facial expression. The models, often chosen for their ugliness, their commonplace nature, – heavy breasts, sagging stomachs, wide hips, prominent buttocks, thick wrists and ankles – are depicted with a gift for individual characterisation which we find in both individual and collective portraits.
>
> Dorival, 1958:34-5

Dorival's comments are descriptively accurate while at the same time revealing his well-bred disgust for women who do not conform to the idealised, classless stereotype of the nude. Other male critics have found the stress on individual identities marked by class and age similarly difficult to take. One critic even accused Valadon of misogyny, of taking her revenge on women through a refusal to idealise their bodies.[6] Embedded within such critical confusions is the clear assumption that the aesthetic value of the nude is bound up with the sexual desirability of the model. Valadon's insistence on the individuality of her models, their differences in body size and shape, in age and in class, suggests relative indifference to conventional ideals of sexual attractiveness. Two of her own Self Portraits painted when she was fifty-nine and sixty-seven respectively, show herself naked from the waist up, confronting the viewer with made-up face, jewellery and cropped hair (Figure 35). This painting is disconcerting in its combination of self-image and nude form, and in Valadon's refusal to compromise with old age. Even more now than when it was painted, the image asserts the recognition of women's own view of their bodies against the tyranny of images of youth, beauty and attractiveness endlessly reflected in contemporary culture.

I am not arguing that more 'realistic' representations of women's bodies are necessarily better *per se*, but that Valadon ruptures the particular discourse of the fine art nude in which nudity = sexual availability = male pleasure. In doing so, she offers us a way of looking at the female body which is not entirely bound in the implicit assumption that all such images are addressed only to a male spectator.

Conclusion

Valadon's representation of the nude can be differentiated in a number of ways from the dominant imagery of female sexuality current in fine art in the early twentieth century. Although she worked within the category of the 'modern nude', and at times reproduced elements of its essentialist ideology of woman as nature, her work taken as a whole significantly departs from the norm. In showing naked women as diverse individuals engaged in daily social activities, the nude's primary signification as a sexual object for men is reworked as a site of different kinds of experience: of pleasure and embarrassment; of intimacy and sociability; of change and of ageing. In another way the formal characteristics of her drawing and painting deny the sensuous illusionism of the painted pin-up and render the woman's body less available to a voyeuristic gaze. If a male spectator's presence is always clearly signified in the traditional discourse of the nude, Valadon's work at least makes it more difficult for a male viewer to assume such a position unconsciously, as the comments of the male critics quoted above would indicate.

I do not want to suggest that Valadon's work should be retrieved uncritically, to be dusted off for feminist consumption. Her acceptance of male definitions of art is undeniable, and so too is her success as an artist within those definitions during her own lifetime. But what she did do was to open up different possibilities within the painting of the nude to allow for the expression of women's experience of their own bodies. Although she worked within the given forms of her own period, she redrew their boundaries in order to represent and engage with a woman's viewpoint. Her work shows that it is possible for women to intervene even within a genre which has such a powerful tradition of male voyeurism as the nude in painting.

Such attempts to re-present and re-imagine dominant iconographic codes are important for feminists now engaged in visual culture as producers and as critics. The transformation of existing codes and symbols is necessary because there is no alternative visual language readily available to express women's experience. But it is also important to recognise that such a transformation at the level of representation cannot be achieved without taking on problems of institutional change. So long as the practices of history, criticism, reproduction and publishing continue to marginalise, negate and isolate women's role in the production of culture, then we will continue to see their work in terms defined by a male critical tradition. In 'recovering' the work of a woman artist we can begin to challenge and oppose the sexist assumptions of dominant cultural discourses from a feminist critical perspective. In that sense, 'looking as women' not only means bringing different kinds of experience to the making and reading of images, it demands a conscious attempt to transform the conditions under which such images are produced, seen and understood.

NOTES

1 I am referring here to a range of work produced in the early and middle 1970s which shared broad assumptions about the relationship between the female nude and the male spectator, although differing in theoretical levels of analysis. For example see Berger (1972), Brooks (1977) and Pollock (1977).
2 A modern variant of this claim to have their minds 'on higher things' is made by contemporary artists and critics who argue that all experience of art is subjective and individual, so that any feminist who attacks sexist imagery is failing to understand the basic premises of 'Art'. This comment is still heard frequently in art schools. It also surfaced in the debate over Allen Jones's painting and sculpture in the mid-1970s.
3 The psychoanalytic implications of Mulvey's ideas of transvestism and the female spectator in cinema have been taken up by Mary Ann Doane (1982). Since I do not pursue these ideas here, I would refer the reader to her work. Dyer (1982) and Myers (1982) both raise questions about the relationship of the female spectator in relation respectively to the male pin-up and to advertising.
4 In references to Valadon's life her mother, Madeleine, is frequently described as a laundress. A reason for this mistake possibly lies in the popularity of the laundress as a stereotype of female working-class sexuality in late nineteenth-century French culture. For further details see Lipton (1980). Valadon herself becomes a stereotype of sexual promiscuity in many versions of her biography.
5 Modernist art movements in the 1900s were characterised by a rejection of the spatial illusionism, narrative and figuration of the European art tradition in

favour of forms of art which used distortion of space and form and a greater degree of abstraction, and stressed the expression of subjective experience. This has been seen by most art historians as a radical turning point in the history of art, though this view is itself under attack from 'post-modernist' critics.

6 Jean Vertex cited in Warnod (1981:73, no source given). An analysis of critical responses to Valadon's work requires a separate study in itself. Such comments reveal very clearly the patriarchal discourses of art history, which are incapable of dealing with women artists in other than stereotypical ways. For a general analysis of critical stereotypes see Nemser (1973).

REFERENCES

Berger, J. (1972) *Ways of Seeing* London: BBC and Penguin.

Borzello, F. (1982) *The Artist's Model* London: Junction Books.

Brooks, R. (1977) 'Woman Visible, Women Invisible' *Studio International* vol. 193, no. 987.

Bulliet, C.J. (1930) *The Courtezan Olympia, an Intimate Study of Artists and their Mistress Models* New York: Covici, Friede.

Coward, R. (1984) *Female Desire: Women's Sexuality Today* London: Paladin.

de Beauvoir, S. (1972) *The Second Sex* London: Penguin.

Diane-Radycki, J. (1982) 'The Life of Lady Art Students: Changing Art Education at the Turn of the Century' *Art Journal*, Spring.

Doane, M.A. (1982) 'Film and Masquerade – Theorising the Female Spectator' *Screen* vol. 23, nos. 3-4.

Dorival, B. (1958) *Twentieth Century Painters* New York: Universe Books.

Duncan, C. (1973) 'Virility and Domination in early 20th Century Vanguard Painting' *Art Forum*, December.

Dyer, R (1982) 'Don't Look Now – the Male Pin-up' *Screen* vol. 23, nos. 3-4.

Irigary, L. (1977) 'This Sex Which is Not One', in Marks and de Courtivron (1981).

Lipton, E. (1980) 'The Laundress in Late Nineteenth Century French Culture: Imagery, Ideology and Edgar Degas' *Art History* vol. 3, no. 3.

Marks, E. and de Courtivron, I. (1981) *New French Feminisms* Brighton: Harvester Press.

Myers, K. (1982) 'Towards a Feminist Erotica' *Camerawork* no. 24.

Mulvey, L. (1975) 'Visual Pleasure and Narrative Cinema' *Screen* vol. 16, no. 3.

Mulvey, L. (1981) 'Afterthoughts ...Inspired by Duel in the Sun' *Framework* vol. 6, nos. 15/16/17.

Nemser, C. (1972) 'Stereotypes and Women Artists' *Feminist Art Journal* vol. 1, no. 1.

Pollock, G. (1977) 'What's Wrong With Images Of Women?' *Screen Education* no. 24.

Rey, R. (1922) *Suzanne Valadon* Paris: Editions de la Nouvelle Revue Francaise.

Royal Academy (1979) *Post Impressionism* London: Royal Academy.

TUC (1984) *Images of Inequality – The Portrayal of Women in the Media and Advertising* London: TUC Publications.

Warnod, J. (1981) *Suzanne Valadon* Switzerland: Bonfini Press.

I would like to thank Ahmed Gurnah and Sylvia Harvey for their very helpful comments and criticisms.

CAROLEE SCHNEEMANN

LETTER TO THE EDITOR

To the Editor:

Thomas McEvilley's recent analysis of the shamanistic origins of performance art, 'Art in the Dark,' leads me to some considerations of essential differences between the works of male and female performance artists. For all of us the violence and offensiveness of our shamanistic explorations have been in proportion to the metaphysical fractures which fuel patriarchal oppositions. But an iconographic identification of the contradictory implications and uses of related materials and actions for female versus male performers mentioned in the article would be highly instructive.

From a feminist perspective, a great deal of shamanistic male performance art has been centered on unravelling a repository of collectively unconscious guilt, and on desire for power or for contact with generally despised aspects of nature and body – the femaleness suppressed in our culture. McEvilley focuses on the critical neglect of these unconscious processes and on the sexual prohibitions which activated shamanistic performance art, but he fails to identify the denied 'femaleness' of 'areas that were previously as unmapped and mysterious as the other side of the moon'. What he notes as 'behavior deliberately contrived as the most inappropriate and offensive' (suggesting personal exorcism of social taboos and prohibitions) remains bound to the patriarchal psychosocial structures that it attempts to illuminate. In early male performance art the panoply of physical taboos, mutilations, and violations – which had its apotheosis in 'fucking female corpses' – is understood by feminine analysis as the crazed expulsion of female complementarity (which was socially annexed and denied primacy).

The erotic female archetype, creative imagination, and performance art itself are all subversive in the eyes of patriarchal culture because they themselves represent forms and forces which cannot be turned into functional commodities or entertainment (to be exchanged as property and value), remaining unpossessable while radicalizing social consciousness. The shamanistic performances of women usually relate to a historic tradition that is pre-Greek, pre-Christian in its inspiration. My mythic associations are *not* Dionysian but properly Aphroditean – Goddess of human passion and of unity of desire and will. Dionysus is the son of Aphrodite – his attributes were derived from her and eventually absorbed into the succeeding patriarchal infrastructures. Dionysus represents the ancient Indo-European bull god in transition from deifying the Goddess to annexing her powers. His potency evolves from a hermaphroditic form, to consort, to dominator. Shamanistic mythology in women's performance art must be acknowledged as what lies behind and is obscured by Greek mythology. Our performance of taboo acts is linked with an identification of our bodies with nature, with the celebration of the cosmic and the sacredness of the ordinary and the lived experience. Ordeals of endurance, physical violation – binding, shooting, puncturing, tying up – are not characteristic of the work of those women artists mentioned in the article (Mary Beth Edelson, Barbara Smith, Rachel Rosenthal, myself – Linda Montano's Christian references the exception). Our use of the body in ritual inculcates not male mysteries but female or communal ones, aligned with intuitions of ancient Goddess presence and investigating those integrations of body and spirit which masculist culture and mythos have torn asunder. The differences in male and female approaches are epitomized by a pair of performances in Holland in 1979. Hermann Nitsch's drenching of tied, shivering performers with gallons of cow's blood was assimilated by the audience, while the fabric coil of menstrual blood that I extracted in my work was considered 'obscene'.

Finally, McEvilley describes *Meat Joy* as a 'fertility rite', diverting its motivation back toward a male birth fetishization. *Meat Joy* was what I described as 'an erotic celebration to sensitize my guilty culture'. As Henry Sayre wrote recently in *The Minnesota Review* (Spring 83), 'the real distinction between most male body art and that of most women lies in the fact that, as a rule, the male's relation to his body is one of self-violation while the female's relation is one of self-exploration and definition.'

Carolee Scheemann
New York

SANDRA LAHIRE

LESBIANS IN MEDIA EDUCATION

This is written in a building called the Darwin building at the Royal College of Art, London[1]. Darwin, whose revolution in science legitimated the socially created differences between men and women and gave them an apparent biological justification. Lesbians were excluded as 'unnatural' or an impossibility (see the monument of Queen Victoria over the road).

This is what many women artists in education have said to me:

> Women sit on the TV production line. Men take the fruits of this labour to use them against us. The tools of government, the means of evaluation in media education, the core disciplines to be learned, are dictated by the latest technological acquisition, by an establishment of design and media education that does not share its power. Let us take it.

> I kept it silent, even in a group of women working with performance and media, because I feared it was disruptive of some more important struggle, which was predesigned for me to carry out. Now I know that it is my body, my room, our daughters' employment that is at stake, and my film-making with other dykes – that could be all other women. Our tongues and eyes meet in our words, in the tastes, smells, sinking and biting that we enjoy together. In its growth, our media work does not coerce people, it is how we make ourselves self-responsible.

> Wherever I am and come from, my tongue is Lesbian. I do not feel I should have to support the debate of middle-class intellectuals with it. I and others I have worked with have accepted my Lesbian identity. My Jewish identity is my work now in terms of 'where is my homeland?'.

> If you have enough money and privilege you can separate yourselves from heterosexist oppression. Let us not forget, though white middle-class feminism would like us to, that Lesbians are constantly threatened. 'Passing' – staying invisible and presumed to be heterosexual – is a central issue in Lesbian culture. Often, the less privileged you are, the more necessary is passing for survival in a harsh urban environment.

> In the frightened mood of the eighties, there is a kneejerk reaction to the economic recession that warns Blacks not to be too Black, Jews not to be Jewish, and the unemployed and Lesbians not to be too visible. The

274

more we let ourselves be pushed out now, the less room we will have for manoeuvre and formulating our own imaginative tactics of resistance. The time to manoeuvre is now, with our work, whilst we still have a foothold.

Unless we are affirmed, the feeling that we often get is that Lesbians must stop being selfish and giving joy to each other when the birth of a nation is at stake. But precisely by eschewing the family and marriage structures of white society, free Black women negotiated their own forms of autonomy. This contrasts with the framework of the USA and its satellites in which the family has been defined as a closed nuclear unit, the foundation of capitalism.

Instead of being bound up behind veils and distortion, let us establish the forms that we need and begin to manipulate them for ourselves. As a teacher I see this works best in an atmosphere of warmth amongst women.

You read flashes of body-language, some of self-dismissal and at the same time stubborn affirmation. And it is not necessarily that women would find out that they were Lesbian, but even to take that route and look at things from that angle is turning the world inside out. Turning negation back on itself. Adrienne Rich argues[2] that when we stop lying about our love (sexual or not) for other women, when we stop mutilating ourselves simply to survive our subjection, we can begin to resist our mutilation by values and laws based primarily on male needs. She posits our resistance[3] as a Lesbian continuum or network for action, which women might move in and out of all the time. This must not be cut. As there have not been many Lesbian film-makers, we study our lives to show the following generations. 'When a woman tells the truth she is creating the possibility for more truth around her.'[3] There is no aspect of the dominant culture that does not contribute to the enforcement of heterosexuality in some way, whether it is the witholding of technical knowledge, the burning of documents and archives, the burning of witches ('witches' meaning quite literally those who have wits, who know).

Who was that haggard twin of hers staring through the screen? The night was chilly. She summoned her in, and helped her unfreeze. They resembled each other.

Being a Lesbian is not in itself political. However, the conditions in which we live as women are available to political change because they can be seen to be socially caused and not naturally destined. This is about actively politicising areas of our lives that are assumed to be unchangeable.

Sex between women opens more channels of communication and

strengthens the network through which every issue is being fought. One may ask, are our identities really so bound up with sexual choice? The human essence is the assembly of social relations, and sexuality *is* social relations.

If our work were ambiguous, it would pull us back to a false, not Lesbian, continuum. When our work is forthright we illumine for each other territories that we can no longer allow to be obscured.

Lesbians should strive to minimise the chances that radical content will be perceived in terms of style alone, '*Lesbianism*'.

Operating on the premise that the culture of resistance uses all the media at its disposal, Lesbian culture – if not censored, stifled, or invisible – is 'tolerated' or imitated in a colonising way for commercial or high art purposes. As a former anorexic, I am sensitive to all forms of subtle manipulation of women.

Our fight grows out of our women's circle of discourse. This must spread wide to make interference in the millenia of talking men. We are not abstractions in male psychoanalytical debate. Laughing, working, touching, we are putting our own psychic health first. I am hoping that our voices may derange those who support the leadership of this police-state.

What a relief to feel solid against that alienating stare of ownership to which women may be subjected at any time of day or night.

Far from being a riddle to ourselves (as we seem to be held out to men) we are restrained by double bindings in a male language that is as cramping as Grace Poole's attic. Catatonia would be the end result, the gesture of a lunatic having to separate herself from her language and eventually killing herself off: 'Words dry and riderless/The indefatigable hooftaps'.[4]

What was the price of subjection to the Law of the Father? A violent denial of my mother's body and bonds of feeling by which we clarified each other's images. A mother is a woman, not the easy target for our repressed anger; and, childless, I am a woman.

Is 'mother' or 'language' primary? Or 'phallus as signifier'? The female body is complete, not a negative to the phallus. Ultimately the Lacanian debate is redundant to the Lesbian, both because it is class-based and because the influence of the mother is as primary as a hieroglyph. Now we are thinking of two women imaging together, lips speaking together, maybe in conflict but so making a discourse in and of and for itself, not embedded in one certain psychoanalytic schema of construction of femininity, e.g. mother/daughter roles.

Because it forced itself upon me I told the absence-of-signifier theory of women to get knotted. It was.

Even now there is little material support for Lesbian couples apart from within the Lesbian community. Any public display of a relationship problem

276

is seen as having to do with its being Lesbian. No one ever thinks that the ownership politics of heterosexual culture may have eaten holes in the Lesbian relationship. Or maybe the trouble is one-to-one relationships. Or that women ever have relationships together whilst at art school. Women students consolidating each others' meaning are an asset that had better be liquidated, in the interests of the management and a culture that would rather fragment the body, and make lucrative fetishes out of those fragments.

One aspect of our practice has tried to operate on the very terrain of stereotype itself, trying to undermine and change the readings of certain stereotypes, by showing up the contradictions between them and the double-think that is necessary to believe in them. Those who control stereotypes are never exposing *themselves*. This is also true for straight 'experimental' practice.

For women filming women, what we need now is to restore the integrity of the whole body, which is what Chantal Ackerman and Helke Sander have chosen to do.[5] 'Narcissism' was adopted by Freud in his libido theory to describe a condition in which the ego turns its energy back on itself. And without the shared experience of being female, some spectators are unable to see the revelations of Lesbian work as anything but narcissistic, in a sense of being trapped in herself, or indulging her ego. How can women committed to producing socially engaged work confront this narrow view of narcissism encouraged by the art world and promoted by the video apparatus? Turning the camera to the world, yes, and if it is oppressive, turning the monitor to the wall, or manipulating the Barbie-doll imagery sold to us. In the case of the woman dealing with autobiographical material and self-perception, turning the camera on herself is necessary, not because she is reinforcing the male fetishising of parts of her body. She opposes externally imposed images of her sexuality by building up a dialogue with aspects of herself, with doubles or twins or alter-egos, as Sylvia Plath does by her writing of *The Bell Jar*. The mirror is a common-sense method of crystallising a twin through inward dialogue. Far from mimicking the isolated self-obsession of the male narcissist, a woman working with herself and devoting her love to herself in another woman, instead of gaining access to power via men, is working with the self-reflection essential for self-determination and political change. Men who feel 'left out' of this woman's work blame the Lesbian element, this completely autonomous self through which women address social issues such as work and nukes and pit closures.

Returning yet again to the Lesbian Body, I remember *Focii* by Jeanette Iljon[6] centering on a relationship of self to self and self to other. And some work by Chantal Ackerman in which she uses a fixed camera that disrupts the Hitchcockian pleasure in looking associated with traditional or 'experimental' techniques such as close-ups, quick cuts, zooming, panning, tracking (see ads, promos and male 'experimental' film discourse). For every reason hinted at so far, I find Steven Dwoskin's, and much of Godard's work, offensive when it plays around with pictures of women ostensibly alone, yet who are penetrated by the male camera with as much inherent violence as the *Psycho* shower scene.

Women filming women and our own sexuality

Through this very negation I feel this work pressing on me to make a positive imprint. Such work could relate the emotional freedom of women to the freedom of society itself. This is a great pleasure to any woman viewer, and it makes a change and revolution in the material world irresistable.

I thought that it was a lethargy that dulled me, a repressive force; but I've begun to understand it as an energy that strikes icy-bright. I'm paralysed, caught for a while in its bright focus. My response seems so ingrained, its line marked out over so many political scenarios. Paralysed, I become flustered. It must be obvious to all who look. Tattooed at mouth and eyes. I'm not sure what happens next. No matter. Too long I've gone back over those old tracks. Where? The thing is to get off, pushing into that light. This feeling, all such feelings, are not transgressions.

No more time for that limited 'romance' which feeds off being forbidden. My positive Lesbian feelings have come out simultaneously with my work. You learn about yourself as you make the work with the materials around you in installations and film and performance, and that learning process becomes part of the meaning of the work.

> The erotic has often been misnamed by men and used against women. It has been made into the confused, the trivial, the psychotic, the plasticised sensation. For this reason we have often turned away from the exploration and consideration of the erotic as a source of power and information, confusing it with its opposite, the pornographic.[7]

We are making images for our sexuality, and there are more responses like touch and hands holding.

> Not as public spectacles like hanging, violence, murder,
> Not making a public spectacle of ourself,
> But the visibility and touch of our works to each other,
> So that we crystallize each other's thoughts.

She needs warm compresses for her eyes if nowhere else, due to the dearth of Lesbian films and the need to do a salvage job on Supergirl. Shut-away Lesbians, without the particulars of wider social encounters, become abstractions in any current debate on sexuality in media work.

Our media work is not just about positive images of Lesbians, but an impact suggesting a positive guide to action. Being that obtuse and cussed we are already not such a welcome choice for design-orientated education, and perhaps being thrown out on the streets from our brief intervention at the Royal College of Art is the beginning of becoming visible and fighters. We are already listening to each other and weaving a picture-poem patchwork of protest.

Within Environmental Media which moves out from the walls, I am taking space for a Lesbian voice. Where to for all the undergraduate women I chatted to for this issue? Lesbians are not an exclusive club or ghetto but all women's desire for each other's full expression of our bodies and language. We oppose the predefined category of woman in male theory and its derivatives, in which woman is a lack, of power, of penis, and who bears a very heavy negative relation to the jolly pageant of male art and design history. Through my very negation in a system of feudal chivalry, that does not use our discourse of body and loving/being in love, I use strong – sometimes angry – images to tell the stories of our lives. It is essential that we be a mirror to each other. Hearing, feeling. Many images of feeling boxed in, and bound. Together exploring each other's solitary confines, and together weaving a very large space.

Rooms within rooms, with doors opening in different directions. Men have always wanted to identify a hierarchy and an 'ism', and women at the peace camps and in *Women Challenge Film and TV Education* have none. Drawing breath from each other, we say the same thing in different ways. At any one point along the timescale, there is always a woman who is guiding herself past her male assessors as if by a thread.

I was alone and I wanted to express my Lesbian feelings in the Darwin Building so intensely that I even resented the ingrained and casual male-female habits of chivalry...and the 'blondes' and 'redheads' lights. It was a chasm inside of me. Now that chasm is space out of which I spin my images. The darkness of this well inside contains all colours. I never want to hear you say that blackness is the colour of despair and negativity.

The position of Black Lesbians, when working with/for white people is fundamentally different from that of white Lesbians. I am a white woman, I think that any feminist work at the Royal College of Art is bound to be limited when there are not many Black women and women of colour.

I remember very clearly when I was nine and she was twelve, and we kissed and caressed each other and played tricks on the boys and grownups.

Lesbians aren't oppressed by the Law...?

Anti-Lesbian practice ranges from a verbal omission to actual physical violence. In media education Lesbian images represent the ultimate threat to the patriarchal order: independence from their whole art-historical debate based on ownership of the female body and exploitation of her work.

At work particularly, teachers are permanently forced to conceal our

Lesbian identity. This means living in constant strain, whilst still being subject to anti-Lesbian attitudes and behaviour from colleagues, employers, male technicians (which is most technicians), and critics parasitical to the art establishment.

Here is one Staff Group's proposals for inclusion in a school statement on sexism, adapted to higher and art education:

> Lesbian students must see their sexuality positively reflected in the society of the school, and all students must be actively encouraged to see that their sexuality can be a matter of positive choice. This can best be achieved by Lesbian and gay teachers being visible within the school. This means that teachers who are Lesbian or gay should not be pressurised into hiding this fact from students or into allowing students to make a wrong assumption about their sexuality. Their decision to come out must be actively supported by all members of staff right to the rector.

In no way should being Lesbian be made to feel like a sinister activity ('sinister' in the McCarthy sense, not in the sense of subversive and transforming). The homophobia that faces young Lesbians in colleges does not exist in a vacuum. It is all part of a learned response and attitude that everyone in our society assimilates through subtle means in the dominant media.

> Lesbian teachers, whether they are out or closeted, are helpful as role models, implicit support etc.[8]

The Gay Teachers Group put forward the following motion at the 1984 NUT National Conference:

> This conference rejects all discrimination on the grounds of sexual orientation and instructs the Executive to support vigorously all teachers discriminated against on these grounds...Conference also instructs the Executive to promote constructive and positive attitudes to homosexuality in school curricula. Furthermore...to press the TUC to include sexual orientation in its model Equal Opportunities Clause.

So far, none of the teaching unions has a policy on the rights of Lesbian teachers and students. Some teachers and some LEA's – notably the ILEA (if it remains intact) – are tackling this issue. Get a clear statement of support from a local branch.[9]

Nothing contributes to anti-Lesbian attitudes and Lesbian self-loathing and neglect of her sexuality so much as a feeling of insecurity with regard to the world of work, the law, and union activity. Yes, a Lesbian working to encourage women's strength in an art college has, even now, been nicknamed 'he' (strange that this appears unusual, as the generic term 'he' usually embraces 'she'). Often we feel like staying at home, or are frightened when returning late from our shows and meetings, because we are not accompanied by the chivalry of a man. At the same time, men seem afraid of the strong woman and her autonomous sexuality.

Lesbian mothers must tailor work around bringing up children, who are not an abstraction during 'working hours'. Men have been conducting a debate in colleges into which we may step when we are not at home. This is the social condition which work made by women must oppose, or this work will tend to be seen either as 'evidence' of some essential (essentially inferior) femininity, or else as some special kind of 'achievement' like that of circus animals.

Being Lesbian is not a soft option. Surprisingly, we also have housework to do, bills to pay, children to get to school, ill people to care for. Anti-Lesbianism occurs every time our childrearing is scrutinised in an unsupportive way and every time it is assumed that what we ought to want is to raise 'normal' children...the argument for denying Lesbians custody of our children. Mothers do not have to be mothers only. Our access to jobs ought not to be limited by access to child care and by male-engendered expectations of what a 'good' mother is.

My hope is that every woman teacher and student choosing to remain with a man will require of him that he treat her as a person who has the very needs Lesbians have been asserting. This is the only way we can gain our full heretical strength.

Pulling out the magical cliché of male thought – 'it's not men who oppress women, it's the capitalist system' – is a long-standing cop-out and denial of men's responsibility. Of course it is the system of capitalism which oppresses us. But this 'system' *is* a collection of people's actions and attitudes.

There is a subversive perception of the order of things developing. Men always want to identify and recuperate a hierarchy and 'ism', but we are all spokeswomen. Conversely, we are free to see men as people who can change rather than as fixed tormentors, providers, lovers and, worst of all, judges of our validity. To fear a knowledge of our own Lesbian love is to fear a knowledge of our work in performance art and media.

Sexuality between women opens more channels of communication and strengthens the network through which we will bring about material changes. Our Lesbian continuum:

Paradigms,
folding mirrors,
multiple and serial loves,
coming and going through out rooms
within rooms

...an ongoing collation, not a preset line of argument. The only line is a Lesbian Line.

NOTES

This is an unedited version of the article which first appeared in *Undercut*, Summer 1985.

1 Sandra Lahire was a student in the Environmental Media department of the Royal College of Art. She makes reference to this at other points in the article. This was the only department in the college with a strong feminist presence and a tradition of students engaging with oppositional politics in their work. It was closed down by the new, Thatcherite Rector, Jocelyn Stevens. The last students left in 1986. (Ed.)
2 *Women and Honour: Some Notes on Lying.*
3 *Compulsory Heterosexuality and Lesbian Existence.*
4 Sylvia Plath.
5 See *Jump Cut* no. 22 for Helke Sander.
6 Distributed by *Circles*.
7 Audre Lourde, 'The Erotic as Power', Chrysalis, 1979.
8 Woman, 17.
9 NUT: National Union of Teachers; TUC: Trade Union Congress; LEA: Local Education Authority; ILEA: Inner London Education Authority.

K A T H Y M Y E R S

TOWARDS A FEMINIST EROTICA

This paper is a response to the ideas which came out of the *Camerawork* one-day discussion for women on the subject of pornography. This discussion aimed to set the problematic area of pornography within the wider issue of the politics of sexual representation. It was also hoped that discussion would deal with the controversial subject of a 'feminist erotica': this did not take place, a resistance which speaks of a fundamental dilemma in sexual politics. Many feminist critiques of the representation of women hinge on the assumption that it is the act of representation or objectification itself which degrades women, reducing them to the status of objects to be 'visually' or 'literally' consumed.

I want to argue that this assumption can lead feminism into deep water. On the one hand, it works to deny women the right to represent their own sexuality, and on the other it side-steps the whole issue of female sexual pleasure. I want to suggest that questions of representation and of pleasure cannot be separated, and that a feminist erotica could examine the nature of this relationship. This in turn demands examination of the forces which produce dominant ideas of sexuality and pleasure. Rather than seeing power as a force which 'represses' or 'holds down' our sense of pleasure and sexuality, I want to suggest the opposite: that power actually produces forms of pleasure and sexuality. The forms of sexuality and pleasure produced through pornographic representations are not acceptable for a variety of reasons. However, I want to argue that through a relocation, a respecification of the nature of power, new, potentially progressive images may be produced: the perception of power as a positive force provides the groundwork for a feminist erotica.

Finally, this article holds that images themselves cannot be characterised as either pornographic or erotic. The pornographic/erotic distinction can only be applied by looking at how the image is contextualised through its mode of address and the conditions of its production and consumption.

The workshop

Feminists working on the politics of female sexuality have all but ignored the issue of female sexual pleasure: caught on the defensive, most have devoted their energies to a counter offensive against the dead weight of patriarchy, fighting images which are deemed sexist or exploitative. One of the most organised and coherent groups in this sexual defence lobby is WAVAW (Women Against Violence Against Women). As this group was dominant both in force and number at the *Camerawork* day event, it would be useful to outline their analysis.

WAVAW's objection to pornography, unlike that of groups on the right, is not premised on moral or health grounds, but is rooted in their understanding of the role which pornography plays in the antagonism between the sexes. Pornography is objectionable because it 'humiliates' 'denigrates' and 'exploits' women.

Exploitation operates on several levels. Firstly, through the process of representation, women are 'objectified'. Women's gender and social status is reduced to the level of a commodity which may be possessed and exchanged by men. Secondly, pornography restricts female sexuality by reducing it to specific anatomical characteristics: eg, the repetitive fetishisation of breasts, legs, vagina, etc. Through this fetishisation, sexuality is fragmented, the part is left to stand for the whole. Thirdly, WAVAW suggest that the proliferation of pornography has actually led to an increase in sex crimes against women. These three processes of objectification, fetishisation and violation are central to the WAVAW critique of pornography.

What is missing from the WAVAW analysis is an understanding of how and why these processes occur: all their analyses are simply traced back to a monolithic notion of patriarchy. All imagery, all practices within the 'dominant ideology' are interpreted as further evidence of 'patriarchal oppression'. This defensive tactic continually reduces women to victim status and leaves very little space within which an alternative female sexual practice may be negotiated. The only alternative which is presented as viable is a total withdrawal from heterosexual relations not as a matter of sexual preference but of political necessity.

WAVAW's concept of power is premised on a fundamental contradiction. On the one hand, power as synonymous with patriarchal oppression works to victimise women. Its force is monolithic and cohesive, and from the point of view of women, politically negative. On the other hand, WAVAW's intentional withdrawal from men, and endorsement of separatism, suggests that women can establish new ways of organising their sexuality, relationships and experiences: that women have the power to positively establish a separate identity. Whilst women may positively organise their 'real' experiences, this sense of positive organisation is not extended to the construction of 'positive' representations of women. The domain of representation is perceived as essentially colonised by patriarchy and leaving little room for manoeuvre.

As an alternative, I want to draw on some of the ideas of Foucault as a way of exploring the power-pleasure-representation nexus, and look at how these relations are produced by, as opposed to held down by, power.

Foucault, in his book *The History of Sexuality* aims to investigate 'The regime of power-knowledge-pleasure that sustains the discourse on human sexuality'. For Foucault, sexuality has become a means of controlling and administering social relations. The idea that control over sexuality provides a way of controlling a society is not new. What makes Foucault's approach novel is his rejection of the idea that control is exercised through systems of repression. On the contrary, Foucault suggests that the history of sexuality has been characterised by an 'explosion' of 'polymorphous discourses on sexuality'.

One of the characteristics of this 'explosion' is the making verbal, the putting into words, of sexuality. Foucault traces this back to the model of the church confessional. The model of the production of truth through the process of confessing can for example be found in modern practices of psychoanalysis. Our society's obsession with sexuality also permeates many 'unspoken' practices. For example, Foucault argues that the architecture of the eighteenth and nineteenth century poorhouses, schools, factories, homes, etc were all 'saturated' with sexual knowledge. This knowledge informed the layout of bedrooms, toilets, school doors, cloakrooms, etc. In addition, discourses on sexuality spread through the institutions of welfare, jurisprudence, psychiatry, medicine, exercising complex and often contradictory influences on the development of personal and sexual relationships within society.

Foucault refrains from combining these constituent elements into a monolithic theory of the relations between power and sexuality. Power, like sexuality, is perceived as multifaceted, emanating from many institutional 'power-bases'. It is this polymorphous quality of power which gives it its strength and flexibility, but which also denies the possibility of any simple causal or deterministic analysis of power relations.

For Foucault, power works to produce a multiplicity of female sexualities which work to insidiously maintain the social order: eg, the production of the ideology of 'romance', of 'hysteria', the 'nervous woman', 'frigid wife' or insatiable 'nymphomaniac'. Certain forms of female sexuality support the family structure, others are outlawed from it: eg, pornography, prostitution and lesbianism. For Foucault, this public/private dichotomy far from challenging the social order, works to secure and legitimate the parameters of acceptable and unacceptable behaviour.

This analysis also challenges the idea of an 'essential sexual instinct' waiting to be uncovered, or freed from repression. The concept of power as positive and productive both gives us the tools to analyse the patriarchal order (not as a monolithic system of oppression, but as a specific socio-historic articulation of power relations) and also provides the ammunition for change (a re-organisation of power relations). It shifts feminism from the site of oppositional practice (a defence against the bastions of patriarchal power) to that of a positive practice working to deploy power.

But to say that power produces sexuality and pleasure is itself inadequate: we have to understand how this process specifically occurs. The experience of pleasure is both a social and emotional activity. The two are inextricably linked: we need to ask how the powers of the imagination and fantasy can actually produce and sustain dominant notions of sexual practice. One of the biggest problems with WAVAW's empiricist analysis of pornography, is their inability to explain this connection.

The real and the representational

One of the central characteristics of WAVAW's argument is the distinction they make between the material world of 'real' relationships and the imaginary world of representation and fantasy. This separation of the imaginary and the material seems too simplistic an account of the way we live our lives, ignoring the crucial position of systems of representation, whether images or language, in our 'real' relationships.

This separation points to a central contradiction in their argument. On the one hand, they see 'real' relationships and representations as totally separate; on the other hand, they point to the ways in which pornographic imagery not only reinforces but actively instigates the sexual abuse of women. They continually invoke imagination and fantasy as agents of sexual oppression with no possible positive role.

For WAVAW, the sin of pornography is its ability to structure and organise fantasy in ways which are thought to be oppressive. Fantasy, the guilty party, becomes the breeding ground for violent actions. But there is a difference between criticising the social discourses which structure the form and content of the imagination and blaming fantasy and imagination themselves. This is a distinction which WAVAW seem unprepared to make. Yet fantasy, and all the associated mechanisms of daydreaming, the imagination, inspiration and creativity are a fundamental part of experience.

Rather than dismissing the power of the imagination and fantasy as politically undesirable, what is required is a greater understanding of their determination and structure under a phallocentric order. Such an analysis may bring women closer to understanding the nature of their oppression. Of course it also presents the ultimate challenge: how to restructure the systems of language, association and meaning which organise our consciousness.

Pornography and sex

As I've already suggested, the sexual isn't already given, but is produced through a variety of social practices which extend across the fabric of daily life. Some of these practices are socially condoned (eg, heterosexual relations within marriage) and others condemned (eg, hard core pornography). Even heterosexual relations within the family are not simply legitimated but governed by social mores about the kind of sex act allowed, the age of participants, etc: there is a complex web of regulation, channelling and development which is not fixed or innate but directly related to the social and historical attitudes of the social formation.

Whilst WAVAW interpret pornography as evidence of the continuing conflict between the sexes, the libertarian tradition, equally starting from the premise of an essential sexuality which is socially repressed, has tended to defend pornography on the grounds that its outlaw status directly challenges the status quo.

The 'sexual radicals' such as Reich and Marcuse played a central role in the development of the libertarian tradition. Following Freud's analysis, they proposed that sexuality was subject to social censorship when it threatened to disrupt the social order. This invested sexual practices with a potentially revolutionary power. However, their idea of a rebel sexuality is continually undermined by the notions of sexuality with which they worked: that is that an 'essential' sex could be uncovered if layers of repression and social oppression were stripped away. Obviously this idea of an essential sex is not a particularly fruitful avenue of enquiry for feminists who wish to challenge dominant notions of the essentially feminine which in the end are found to rest on biologistic or universal criteria.

The heritage of the libertarian tradition has continued to inform many popular notions of sexuality, for example the so-called 'permissiveness' of the sixties as well as many aspects of the male gay liberation front. Libertarianism also informs Angela Carter's influential book, *The Sadean Women*. She suggests that the Marquis de Sade's documentation of nightmarish sexual exploits are fundamentally concerned with the nexus of power, sex and class under bourgeois relations. By caricaturing these relations in their most oppressive and violent forms, pornographic literature, Carter argues, is capable of offering a critique of 'accepted' social relations, where oppressive power relations are continually disguised and denied by reference to the natural order, romance, desire, etc.

However, while pornography is apparently invested with the power to subvert accepted gender relations, it may have the opposite effect. Because it lies outside the accepted, it implicitly acknowledges and accepts social privileging of the family, reproduction and heterosexual union. It basks in its role as deviant. Caught in this binary model of acceptability/unacceptability, pornography works to restrict the expression of sexuality.

For example, soft core pornography reduces female sexuality to genital sexuality: a woman's sexuality is defined in terms of her orifices. The sexual no longer refers to the potential of the erotic body as a whole, but to fragmented, fetishised aspects of a woman's anatomy. The sexual is reduced to a series of well-worn scenarios which have their ultimate resolution in the promise of penetration (by the imagined reader, or more explicitly by a male actor). The images are dulled by sameness, a constant repetition of the imagined fuck. The pornographic colludes with what the libertarians purport it to disrupt. The sexual is located in the organs of reproduction. Pornography works to celebrate the union of sexuality and alliance, of pleasure and reproduction; sex is genital sex, and nothing more.

Libertarianism also falsely assumes that everything which is socially unacceptable (and hence subject to censorship) is inherently subversive and liberating. This is because they focus only on pornography's claim to be erotic. It is the eroticism in pornography which is thought to be liberating, symbolising the life giving forces of love, pleasure, desire, etc.

Thus, libertarianism leaves unexplored the implicit power relations with which pornography is invested. Power is exercised through pornography on many levels which speak of an implicit gender fascism: eg, that the magazines are produced for the consumption of men, the recurrent portrayal of women as victims, the fact that their sexual pleasure is produced for an imagined male audience, etc.

These power relations within pornography challenge the libertarian claim to its liberating potential. It is this continual overdetermination of the sexual by power relations which renders the pornographic image unacceptable.

Libertarianism also positions freedom as the antithesis of power relations. It is power which keeps freedom down. But to accept this is to see power as repressive, as hindering the development of sexual expression. Foucault's analysis of power, in contradistinction to this, sees power as actually producing sexual discourses. It seems to me that if we are to understand the role of pornography in our society and understand the ways in which our conception of female sexuality is produced, we have to see power as a productive as opposed to a simply oppressive force. Our conception of freedom, of sexual pleasure, needs on the one hand to negotiate the existing power forces, and on the other move towards the construction of new sexual experiences. What is required is a shift in the location of power, not a denial of its existence. It is through this reworking of power relations that a sense of freedom may be established.

This idea of power producing pornography cannot be confined to an examination of the image. An analysis of pornography which focuses purely on its content is in danger of falling into a kind of 'reductive essentialism', ie, the notion that exploitation resides in the representation of female sexuality per se, rather than in its contextualisation: the conditions of its production and consumption; the ways in which meanings are created, etc. Unless we can shift the debate on representation away from the image, there is very little 'positive' work which can be done.

Whilst it is true that we designate certain images as pornographic, pornography also refers to a particular mode of productive relations which market and sell sexuality: eg, the choice of model/subject matter, the photographer-model relationship and the conditions under which they work, the choice of medium and distribution, all affect our reception and interpretation of what constitutes pornography. This economy of pornography works to structure the audience to whom the material is made available, and also the kinds of pleasures and responses which are elicited.

The false claim of libertarianism is to suggest that eroticism lies outside the nexus of existing power relations. But this is not the same as saying that the erotic is powerless, and that work cannot be done to explore its full potential. This is the ultimate meaning of a feminist erotica; to reappraise the ways in which versions of female sexuality have been produced, and to use this as a springboard to develop new dimensions and meanings for female sexuality. We have to understand the ways in which images work to construct our own experience of our sexuality. Rather than running away from the powers of the imagination and fantasy, we have to reappraise the role of representations in structuring our needs and desires as a step towards constructing new meanings for the experience and representation of our sexuality.

I want to illustrate this point with one image taken from a soft core porn magazine and one from a woman's journal. By comparing them, I want to suggest that woman's sexuality is deployed in a variety of ways. This deployment is dependent upon the context in which the image appears, its mode of production as well as consumption (Figs. 37, 38).

On first impression, the two images seem remarkably similar: the model's pose and attitude, the seaside setting, etc. The main difference appears to be that the Slix model sports a bikini whilst the porn model is naked. It could be argued that women's exploitation is only a matter of degree along a scantily clad continuum. However, the surface similarities belie fundamental differences in the representation of female sexuality and in the kinds of pleasures offered to audiences.

Many of these differences are hidden from the viewer. For example, the production of pornography differs in most respects from the production of a fashion advert. This affects their economic foundation, the choice of studio, photographer, model, etc. They are specialist discourses which retain their autonomy. For example, the 'photographic life' of models is extremely limited. Few nude models ever make the transition to become fashion models, partly because of the stigma which certain forms of nude modelling

37   Image from a girlie magazine.

carry, and partly due to the fact that different selection criteria operate. Fashion models have become increasingly slender, younger and taller. Most nude models are considered too 'curvy' for fashion work: different 'aesthetics' operate. In turn this visual aesthetic cannot be divorced from the respective audiences for fashion and pornographic imagery. To put it simply, there is an overall tendency to market 'fleshier' women to men and thinner, sometimes sexually androgynous, images of women to female audiences. This micro-politics of body style speaks of the aesthetic and pleasurable segregation of sexuality across a range of visual discourses, which cannot be simply explained away in terms of 'taste' nor patriarchal oppression but require further examination.

Selling female sexuality to a woman is not the same as selling it to a man. The anticipated gender of the audience is crucial in structuring the image. For example, look at the angle of the women's heads in the two images. The pornographic model's face is angled towards the viewer. Her mouth is open, a classic signifier of sexual receptiveness and anticipation. In the small inset photo the same model faces and acknowledges the camera. Behind the camera, we, the audience are located.

By comparison the Slix model, sweeping back her hair, looks across the scope of the camera. She does not face us, her mouth is closed. Not so much a sulky pout as an expression of relaxed langour. Like the pornographic image, she is aware of being on display. But the tenor of her demeanour is

38 Swimsuit advertisement from a women's magazine.

proud and inaccessible. She sweeps back her hair from the heat of the sun, not from passion.

By comparison, her legs are together. The Slix model's mouth and legs offer no point of entrance. The body of the Slix model is a matt sandy tone, she is relaxed. The skin of the nude model is oiled to give the effect of a sheen of perspiration which can signify sexual activity and tension.

The girls in the background of the Slix image look at each other not at the camera. Self-absorbed, they reiterate the confident, self-engrossed narcissism of the foregrounded model. She takes pleasure in her sunbathing, not in the presence of her audience. Only the small inset model in the beach jacket to the right of the image pays the camera a cursory glance.

What differentiates the pornographic image from the fashion shot is the mode of address. The Slix mode of address is characterised by the tension which it establishes between the model's desirability in conventional terms, and her inaccessibility. The advert works to secure a distancing effect between image and audience.

By comparison, the nude model's sexuality is posed as invitational. The pleasure of looking at her merges with the pleasure of being with her. Her sexuality stretches out to embrace the viewer. The nude model 'asks' the audience to possess her. It is a form of sexual consumption which implicitly genders the audience as male. The model's apparent expression of pleasure is not for herself. She is not autonomous, her pleasure is always for the consumption of another, and herein lies one of the fundamental alienations of pornographic imagery.

By comparison, the Slix advert positions the audience as spectator, to keep a safe distance and to observe, not to touch. Sexual inaccessibility is conveyed through the structure of the image. For example, the self-absorbed pose of the model, the cropping, editing and retouching of the photograph work together to reinforce the displayedness of the model, and in doing so, distance the audience.

The impact of the Slix advert is based on the strength of the photograph. Its scale and use of full colour work to dominate the page. The seaside location, the pattern on the bikini, the sense of displayed style are all anchored in the copy line 'New Waves'. These associations are cemented by reference to the brand name of Slix which is in bold type. Image and copy line work together. 'New Waves' links the image to the body of the text.

Whilst the image celebrates the tension between desirability and inaccessibility, the body of the text suggests sexual provocation. Unlike the provocative pose of the pornographic image, the Slix advert suggests sexual power as opposed to sexual availability and perhaps vulnerability. The wearer of the Slix bikini is promised power over others, the power of sexual display: 'Slip into Slix and make a few ripples'.

The target audience for this advert is women. The advert is designed to appeal to women. One of the pleasures which the advertising system offers women is the promise of a kind of power and self-determination. Images of women marketed to women rarely present female sexuality purely in terms of vulnerability, accessibility or availability. But the power which the advertising of beauty and personal products offers women is always of a limited kind, located in terms of sexual display, appearance and attractiveness. What the advert may offer for consumption is an ideal version of self. It also plays on women's pleasure in looking at attractive women. This kind of visual pleasure is inscribed in the image.

We may find many images of women unacceptable, glamorised, exploitative or whatever; but we cannot simply interpret women's pleasure in reading them as evidence for the extent to which the female consciousness has been colonised by patriarchy. We have to account for women's pleasure in looking at images of women.

The advertising image and the pornographic image offer different kinds of pleasure to their respective audiences. If audiences did not find them in some way pleasurable they wouldn't work; magazines and products wouldn't sell. It is their pleasurable associations which perpetuate them. But pleasure as a concept cannot be tackled in isolation, we need to understand how pleasure is produced through the structuring of power and sexuality.

Towards a Feminist Erotica

One of the central objections put forward by feminists in their critique of pornography and other modes of representation is that it 'objectifies' women. Objectification has become a much abused term. There is a sense in which the process of sight and perception necessarily entails objectification in order to conceptualise and give meaning to the object of our gaze. Within feminism, objectification has quite a specific meaning: through the process of representation, women are reduced to the status of objects. This is partly derived from a commonsense use of the marxist idea of commodity fetishism: images of women have become commodities from which women are alienated. Their status as commodity works to deny their individuality and humanity. The second sense of objectification which has informed its current usage is derived from Freud's concept of sexual fetishism: the idea that objects or parts of the anatomy are used as symbols for and replacements of the socially valued phallus. Hence, the argument goes, men have difficulty in coping with women's sexuality because of its castrating potential, and because of its lack of a phallus. In order to cope with this anxiety, men fetishise aspects of female sexuality – for example, the legs or breasts – as symbols of acceptable sexual power.

The use of the term 'objectification' is coupled with a tendency to interpret all forms of sexual symbolisation as evidence of sexual fetishisation. In the analysis of female imagery two processes of symbolisation are brought under closer scrutiny: that of sexual fragmentation and sexual substitution. Frequently these processes of metonym (where the part stands for the whole) and metaphor (where one object or aspect of the anatomy stands for another) operate together. For example, the depiction of female sexuality through the representation of a stiletto-shod foot isolates and fragments the sexual by focusing on a part of the anatomy and fetishises the foot by over-valuing it as a phallic symbol. Psychoanalytic interpretations of this kind of imagery have suggested that the stiletto as phallic symbol serves to 'give' the woman her missing phallus, thus circumnavigating the castration threat which she poses for male sexuality and rendering her safe.

Whilst this kind of analysis may provide an adequate interpretation of the dominant associations of stilettos in our culture, can we say that all forms of sexualised imagery can be interpreted in terms of phallic substitution? There exists a repertoire of conventionalised symbols which have become imbued with fetishistic associations of which the stiletto is only one example; but symbolisation is not a closed system of limited or fixed meaning. Symbolism is polysemic (has no one, fixed meaning), there always exists the possibility of powerful symbolism which works to activate forms of sexual expression which are not recognised by phallocentric interpretation.

Because fetishisation usually employs a fragmented image there is a danger of assuming that all fragmentary images are necessarily fetishistic. The process of sexual fetishisation (specific phallic associations) is always complicated by that of commodity fetishisation, whereby the image of a woman's legs for example becomes isolated and estranged. They become a commodity, an object of display to be visually consumed by an audience.

What is at issue is not so much the perceptual processes of objectification and fragmentation which are a necessary part of rendering a complex world meaningful but rather the specific forms of objectification entailed in commodity and sexual fetishism. It therefore seems important to create a working distinction between the process of fragmentation, which implies a breaking up or disabling of the physical form, and what could be termed 'a pleasure in the part' – the pleasure derived from looking at a picture which depicts the curve of an arm or the sweep of the neckline. Such images could be interpreted not as a butchering of the female form but as a celebration of its constituent elements, giving a sense of the scope and complexity of sensual pleasure which breaks with specific genital sexual associations and with the necessity of overdetermining phallic substitution in the representation of the female form.

It seems that we have to clarify whether it is the process of necessary objectification entailed in perception which we object to (used for example whenever we look at the world, at art, at a book, etc) or the meanings which it carries for women under specific patriarchal formations. These are two separate issues which tend to be collapsed into each other when feminists talk about the representation of women in art, photography, etc. To refuse to differentiate between the two modes of objectification is to endorse a kind of perceptual essentialism – that objectification is inherently exploitative and demeaning.

To see objectification in essentialist terms is to deny the possibility of any alternative practice within the representation of women. Feminists would be denied the possibility of visual communication and new forms of perception.

What is crucial is that existing theories of male power based on phallocentrism cannot provide a basis for the development of a progressive female sexual politics. One of the oppressions of patriarchy is to constrain female sexuality through a system of binary oppositions: eg, masculine as opposed to feminine, passive versus active, emotional versus physical, sexual receptiveness as opposed to sexual drive, etc. This binary system works to perpetuate unacceptable ideologies about the nature of sexual relations. This means that feminist sexual practice cannot simply position itself in opposition to the dominant ideology. The kind of questions which it must ask have implications not only for what is meant by a representational system (and the part which it plays in structuring fantasy and the imagination) but also what is meant by power, sexuality and pleasure.

It is in terms of the pleasure derived from representational systems that we need to reintroduce a notion of the erotic. Within sexual politics we have to find a way of accounting for women's sexual attraction to each other; the visual pleasure of leafing through a glossy women's magazine; the appeal of the heroine star systems, etc. Such pleasure cannot be simply dismissed as more evidence of patriarchal oppression, that women are continually gulled into a search for the ideal type simply to appeal to 'their man'. We cannot dismiss sexual attraction as further evidence of patriarchal mystification.

What we need to do is explore the ways in which female sexuality is marketed and represented. As I've tried to show with the help of two images, this representation is far from homogenous. Nor can we assume a fixed meaning for an image with which we are familiar. Meaning is produced through the process of representation, the context in which an image appears, its mode of production and consumption.

I haven't attempted to problematise definitions of the pornographic and erotic which are historically and socially defined. At any one moment there will exist competing definitions: for example, those which exist within the feminist movement, as opposed to the liberal Williams lobby or the Whitehouse brigade. Rather than looking for any simple causal analysis we need to further our understanding of how the exercising of power produces forms of sexuality which work to structure the process of pleasure, fantasy and the imagination. Ultimately the distinction between pornography and other modes of sexual representation cannot rest on the characteristics of the image. The differences between pornographic vaginal imagery and medical vaginal imagery are learned through contextualisation: they are not innate.

In the reappraisal of our sexuality, there may appear to be an overlap between the kind of images designated as pornographic as opposed to erotic. This means that the exploration of female sexual pleasure through imagery will remain politically controversial.

Some suggestions for the kind of questions which need to be asked when producing or appraising potentially progressive images of women:

How is the image produced?
Whose fantasy is being recorded?
What power relationship exists in the photographer-model relationship?
How are models selected, what is their relationship to the overall production process?

How will the image be distributed and where will it be circulated?
The politics of distribution cannot be separated from those of production, nor of consumption. Where an image is distributed will affect who will see it, in what context, etc. It is obviously important to sort out whether an image is for private or public consumption, whether it will be seen in a gallery or a magazine, etc. It needs to be asked whether an image's validity or 'usefulness' depends on how an audience will use or interpret an image. For example, does the risk of appropriation by men invalidate producing erotic imagery for women? This risk could be countered by showing these images in, for example, *Camerawork*.

Visual conventions of the image
How do we classify an image as erotic? What conventions and genres of representation does an image trade on?
To what extent does an oppositional system need to reuse and question familiar styles in order to go forward and create new meaning?
What are the signifiers of sexuality?
How do we recognise the gender of the subject?
In fact how important is the thwarting of easy gender assignment for erotic pleasure?

The audience and pleasure
What kind of pleasures does an image offer its audience?
How is the sexuality and subject position of the audience constructed – are they sexed as male or female?
What kind of emotional responses does the image demand?
Does it demand any kind of audience interaction to interpret the meaning of the image? To what extent does the image challenge assumptions already held?

ROS COWARD, YVE LOMAX, KATHY MYERS

BEHIND THE FRAGMENTS

This conversation picks up on a number of debates currently in circulation around the notion of 'positive images' of women. Some of the ideas presented here have been rehearsed elsewhere. For example, Ros Coward's article on 'Sexual Violence and Sexuality' in *Feminist Review* no. 11; artist Yve Lomax's exhibitions, and Kathy Myers' article on a 'Feminist Erotica' in *Camerawork* 24. This conversation draws upon this work and tries to take the debate a stage further. Of central concern is whether or not the concept of a 'positive image' might not be based upon some impossible utopian ideal of a 'whole' or 'unified' woman. The problem of 'wholeness' inevitably touches upon its counterpart, the fragmentation of the female form.

Kathy Myers: One thing that I would like to talk about is fragmentation and particularly to ask: what is happening when images fragment? One way of reading fragmentation is solely in terms of sexual fetishism, something which is specifically bound up with patriarchy. Within the article I wrote for *Camerawork* 24, 'Towards a Feminist Erotica', I was very much concerned with fragmentation in terms of metonymy, where the part or fragment stands for (the lack of) the whole. Within that article, however, I began to wonder whether or not fragments work in their own right, without any recourse to a whole. When I was talking about the pleasure of the part, I wondered if the idea of there being a whole woman is not in fact a myth, because you can never know a whole woman. The idea of there being a whole unified woman, who can be totally possessed, is a religious one. Are those arguments which are concerned with fragmentation or the break up of images misconstrued because they are always searching for a holy grail, which in fact no longer exists and never really has existed? Has feminist analysis got itself caught up in this search?

Yve Lomax: I think that those questions very much rest upon the issue of representation. In particular, the idea that beyond every representation there exists a 'whole woman' which the act of representation either positively or negatively represents – the idea that the referent of a representation remains external to and independent of the representation itself. In many senses this idea beholds us to conceiving of all representations as fragments. What else but a fragment allows us to

297

presuppose a whole? As far as I am concerned the whole has trailing behind it a theological cortège. Only from a vantage point such as God's can one ever pronounce The Whole. Within my work I have been attempting to take up with the whole, or referent, as a part which is produced alongside other parts and which does not totalise those parts. I feel that questioning fragmentation and representation opens up a new load of questions as regards not only images of the body, but also politics, power and style. I am not saying that I am opposed to whole, as if it were a matter of making a choice between wholes and fragments – that would be absurd! Rather, I am concerned with the extent to which the desire for the whole can work against women's multiplicity and becomes a reductionist enterprise which attempts to bundle up all the parts which women are and produce, and make them into a neat rounded off whole.

Ros Coward: I absolutely agree that the idea of a personality which somehow can be utopically or ideally represented is a red herring. Nevertheless, I wouldn't dismiss the argument about fragmentation.

Yve Lomax: I wasn't dismissing the argument: on the contrary, I am very much concerned with opening it up. For instance, opening up rather than closing down our conception of the whole, which I feel is important for the way that we regard the body, the image and moreover, what is crucial to this argument, namely, power.

Ros Coward: There is a regime of fragmentation which I feel is quite pernicious. What I think is most problematic about it is the way that an awful lot of advertising images imply that the rest of the body is either dead or drowned. I am thinking in particular of the Veuve du Vernay ad: all you see are legs sticking out of a bath and a hand holding a glass which implies that the rest of the body is under water, dead or drowning. There is also the Pretty Polly ad – 'No means of visible support' – where the body is floating off the ground, which could be somebody hanging. So, I do think that there is definitely a regime of death fragmentation images where what is being evoked are parts of a dead body.

Kathy Myers: One of the problems is that a lot of the arguments about fragmentation imply that fragmentation means the same thing under very different circumstances. I am wondering if there are not different vocabularies arising from what fragmentation can mean. For example: you have a Marxist version of commodity fetishism, you have a Freudian version which is expanding notions of fetishism and sexuality; and you have a sort of Barthes version which is concerned with the poetics of the part.

Ros Coward: Barthes is very interesting on the part; he talks about what it is that really engages you with a photograph. In his most recent book,

Camera Lucida, he develops and tries to analyse the idea that the fragment is more erotic than the whole. He talks about the way that some photographs move you intellectually but, he says, what is really powerful for you is that some element of the photograph pierces, moves or captures you. Personally I agree with that. A lot of photographs that I find erotic are ones in which some element captures or moves me, in the sense that he speaks of it.

Kathy Myers: But where do we have to look for the reasons for that capture?

Ros Coward: Unfortunately, Barthes doesn't really analyse that; it is one of the problems with the book. He does, however, give three reasons why a photograph can move you. One is that you are moved socially and intellectually – he shows examples of photographs of Russia and says, 'look, this shows what they really looked like in that period'. In many senses it is a rather uncritical use of the photograph as real. Secondly, that a photograph captures personal memory; he shows pictures of a young boy in an Eastern European village and says that for him it brings back strong memories of his travels. Thirdly, that which is much more intensely personal, where some aspect of the photograph really bites you. But he is not very analytic about that, presumably it is to do with his own personal and sexual construction. One of the photographs of which he talks the most, and which is not reproduced in the book, is a picture of his mother when she was a young girl. I don't think that Barthes is into fragmentation in and of itself, it's more that he thinks what actually stirs you is often a part rather than a whole. This is one of the things that is most interesting, for it provides a means of unifying, cutting across the distinctions between snapshots, high art and magazine photos because, as he says, he is not particularly interested in one person's work but rather what it is that moves you about a whole number of different photos.

Yve Lomax: Parts moving or affecting other parts is very much what interests me too. Rather than posing the question of images in terms of representation, of asking 'what does it represent?' and then proceeding to assess the success of a representation in terms of some binary schema of good or bad, negative or positive, I am interested in how and what an image moves or affects and also, how and what moves or affects an image.

Kathy Myers: That brings up the issue of what kind of images women are allowed to find appealing. I feel that within feminism there are many implicit assumptions as to what images you should or shouldn't find appealing. What do you do when you discover that something quite abhorrent, like an image from Italian *Vogue*, which is heavily into S/M, leather and sexual androgyny, moves or affects you in some way? Such an image may have quite a strong affect upon you, which is not about, 'Oh my God, look how men are representing women!', nor necessarily about an overt erotic sexual desire towards the image, but rather about some aspect of the image being pleasurable in its own right.

Ros Coward: But what is your sexual desire towards the image?

Kathy Myers: I don't think that it can be completely specified; any response to an image is never just one thing.

Ros Coward: But that is the whole problem with the debate concerning pornography. What I think is being objected to, and one should capture the positive side of this objection, is that what pornography is meant to be doing is producing sexual arousal and the possibility of masturbation. It is about providing women as things for men to masturbate over. This objection, however, poses two questions. One, is that a problem in itself – do we really object to men having any sexuality and do we object to them having a sexuality towards women? Two, what is going on when women themselves begin to find such images attractive? Should this be stamped upon because men's masturbatory arousal around such images has been a source of problems, because it also means that men go out and harass women on the street and assume that they are available in the same way that images are; or, is it that we are repressing our own responses? I think there are many complicated issues around all this which we have got to sort out. A lot of the problems regarding porn, which Kathy brought up in her article, 'Towards a Feminist Erotica', are about the context of consumption – that porn is sold almost exclusively to men.

Kathy Myers: In that article I argued that not only are there different contexts, but that these produce different modes of address in relation to fashion and pornographic images, which is to imply that they are somehow different. In practice they are not, there is a cross-over in the way that images are produced; for instance, the technological innovations of fashion lighting and sets are now being used in pornography.

Ros Coward: I think that way of approaching pornographic images can go completely off beam because one is never analytic as to what images are actually doing. By saying that porn is in and of itself degrading and that when it spills over into advertising you can also designate that pornographic, completely neglects that what one is dealing with are codes of how the sexual is constituted. Although you can't say that pornography and advertising are the same, you can say that the codes of what designates the sexual and sexual availability are identical. The codes are exactly the same in pornography as they are in fashion and art photography and even snapshots. The issue is that of a sexualised body which is organised according to codes which are dominant, general and available.

Kathy Myers: I agree that there is a regime, or commonness, of sexual codes but I have been working with the idea that this is not static, that there is a multiplicity of codes with which we are engaged. Often this multiplicity is reduced to just a game of spot the code where it is believed that once you have located the code you can solve all else. If you get an expansion of sexuality, of female sexuality, the codes expand as well. The issue for me is no longer that women are exploited but rather how they are exploited. Women are exploited in a number of ways which are shifting and which are not finite. What you have to do is search for the difference rather than for a common denominator.

Yve Lomax: I think the idea that our sexuality is coded can lead to the somewhat spurious conclusion that if we decode we will reveal or liberate the truth of our sexuality. There is a danger of conceiving a code as some sort of framing device, something which has an inside and outside, something which is negative and incarcerates. This can lead to the precarious and rather arrogant assumption that images can be produced which are free from, an alternative to, the negative enframing of the codes. This is one of the things which I find problematic regarding the notion of positive images of women.

Ros Coward: It also brings up the question as to whether you can at present show sexualised images of women.

Kathy Myers: The only feminist erotica that I have seen first hand, except for some shots of gay women in American magazines, are by two Dutch women. The images were sexually androgynous. They either used blur or some optic effect which meant that you got a lack of definition and specificity about the sexual gender assignment of the image and also what exactly the image was of. Often it was two women, you thought, and the emphasis was on movement, muscle, texture, light and dark.

Yve Lomax: The images which I find really tedious are those making endless analogies between cabbages, flowers and women's vaginas. Although I may find cabbages erotic in their own right, I don't find those images erotic in the least.

Ros Coward: I find a lot of straight porn erotic. I think that one of the big problems is that we don't quite know where exactly our past reservations have come from when we are looking at sexualised images. Quite rightly we rejected all that sixties stuff which said that we have got to own up to images, look at them and become as sexual as everybody else, ie men. We realised the problems of that, but at the same time I am not prepared to go along with the idea that we shouldn't look at existing erotic or porn images just because they are men's. I think that idea doesn't confront the fact that in our society the showing or detailing of explicit sex is still considered to be not on. And that is precisely what porn gets off on, for it shows all that. As it exists at the moment, porn is catering for men and I agree that it is massively selling images of women and that some of it is horrific. I object to the violent side of it: I don't object to the sex side of it.

Kathy Myers: In terms of violence, conventional erotica can be worse. I was looking through John Hedgecoe's *Possessions* and Helmut Newton's *Sleepless Nights* and in one Hedgecoe image a woman is leaning back suffocating with a stocking over her head beside which is a pair of men's shoes; she is gasping for air and you have the feeling that she has been done unto by the presence which belongs to the shoes. You have got sadism, necrophilia, all aestheticised.

Ros Coward: I wouldn't use the terms erotica and pornography in distinction.

Kathy Myers: I am using them in the conventional sense – where you see the word 'erotica' inside a book jacket and the book is sold under the letter 'E' on the bookshelf.

Yve Lomax: Isn't the distinction between porn and erotica a red herring?

Kathy Myers: It is and isn't. It can be said that it is a class difference. With a named photographer any image which is produced is not called pornographic but erotic. There is a market distinction.

Yve Lomax: I think that the distinction very much relies on notions of good and bad – if it's classy then it's good.

Ros Coward: I think that we must be clear as to what we are objecting to; that is, that we are objecting to certain codes or constructions of sexuality rather than to anything to do with explicitness or sexuality, or genitalia, or to the fact that we might have sexual responses. I realised that when I said 'I object to violence' that was too simplistic.

Yet I do think that there are certain things which are out, given that we live in a context where men do attack and kill women on the street. Sex and death are, in a way, what we should be thinking of very closely. That women can be enjoyed erotically, although they are dead or dying, is such a dominant image in pornography. What the hell is it about a culture where men get turned on by the sight of a dead woman? And I really do think that it is men; I think you would be hard put to find a woman who is turned on by the sight of a dead man.

Kathy Myers: Isn't it something to do with vulnerability being sexually arousing? What that means in terms of the male is a simultaneous bringing out of the protector and the exploiter. I think that is an integral part of patriarchal relations. If you have a hierarchical structure of domination and submission then you are going to get that play of power. The definition of the strong is always dialectically moving between the power to protect and the power to exploit. And what that means is that the blame is always attached to the vulnerable side because, so it is said, the vulnerable woman has the power to produce such emotions in the other (man). The notion of the vulnerable is very dominant in rape, and rape is the only crime in England where the victim is guilty until proven innocent; you are guilty by virtue of being as opposed to doing.

Ros Coward: Changing the subject slightly, I think that we are in a situation where our sexuality is very much about the visual. We look at images of brown bodies, say in *Cosmopolitan*, and say, 'that is so lovely, I'd like to be like that'. What is so pernicious about this is that it always constructs us as objects even if we are making an active response to such images. Those images always have a shadow behind them which is about being beautiful; even though we know that people don't just exist like that without a lot of hard work, the fantasy, nevertheless, has a pernicious relationship with reality and our psyche. Locked into a regime of the visual, of seeing the beautiful, we never explore what other sorts of sexual responses we have, like touch. But I don't mean that we should give up photographs and get into feeling things. Yet how is it that there are very few images around of feeling things, of hands holding or touching things?

Yve Lomax: I get the utmost pleasure out of producing images, touching photographs, moving them around. I think that it is important to stress that desire is not merely about what we see in an image. Desire is very much bound up with the production, circulation, flow and usage of images; it is operative in all sorts of images which are not necessarily overcoded by or saturated with 'the sexual'. I feel that it is important to expand our conception of desire, particularly the notion that desire only takes place in accordance with absence, that it is primarily about lack.

Kathy Myers: I think that in attempting to find a rationale of why women find images of other women pleasurable, one can be too reductive. There is often this desperate desire to look for one answer: it is narcissism, it is identification; it is the desire to look like or be that ideal. But I think that the pleasure of the image is like an over-determined moment; it is not a fixed thing which is happening. That is one of the problems I find with rigid image analysis: it is always looking for one causal explanation as to why we get turned on by an image. I think that it is to do with a multiplicity of psycho-sexual codes and that the pleasure of the image is to do with an intensity of those codes.

Yve Lomax: Perhaps that is what the pleasure is all about: one thing erupting into an intensity of many things.

Kathy Myers: One of the problems with the notion of positive images of women is that it can impose new forms of inflexibility upon what is allowed as female sexuality. The notion often operates as a binary opposition – either you stay within patriarchy and become masculinised, in order not to be dominated, or you leave, divorce yourself completely and become more woman than woman. In the end, however, you just go round in circles. For me the notion of positive images of women is quite different; it plays the role of deviant, confusing boundaries, playing with codes of sexuality, style, acceptable roles etc. However, you are still left with the problem that the definition of deviance is always produced by the supposed norm from which it deviates.

Yve Lomax: That is the problem I find of setting oneself up as an opposition believing that somehow you are different from, opposite to and outside of that which you oppose – it is believed that there is a frontier which you oppose – it is believed that there is a frontier which can be transgressed. But it doesn't turn out like that, for you find that you are always affirming that which is opposed. There is no outside, no other side of a frontier which is free; both sides belong to one and the same instance. If you like, the outside of patriarchy is already produced from within. Believing that you can oppose this thing called patriarchy from the outside is to actually collude with it, because such opposition presupposes that patriarchy has a fully-fledged identity, an essential centre. Such opposition affirms patriarchy and its power. *In the end it allows what is protested against to be nourished.* I really do think that we have got to go against the idea that you can be outside of what you oppose and also the idea that if you stay within patriarchy you will be contaminated. I don't want to affirm patriarchy's existence. Transformation yes, but certainly not affirmation. I think that we have to challenge our conceptions of power regarding patriarchy and that means changing what we mean by resistance.

Kathy Myers: Another thing which is problematic as regards positive images of women is representation – the idea that the photographic image can represent women for what they really are.

Yve Lomax: So often it is believed that you have two things: women and representations of women. It is taken for granted that no matter what representational means are employed, you can return to women, the referent, find them still the same and then judge a representation as a failure or success, good or bad, a mis-representation or a re-presentation. But how can we guarantee that something has been 'represented' (or come to that, mis-represented) without resorting to dogmatism? The referent or represented, if we are still going to use the terms of representation, which I have my doubts about, is something which is produced by or alongside representation; it is not something which in the last instance remains outside. I think that we need to question the apparent correspondence and distinction between the referent and the representation.

Ros Coward: What you are saying means that we can produce or construct our own definitions of women. I agree that the argument about positive images of women tends to imply that photographs can show women as they really are.

Yve Lomax: There is another thing which I feel it is important to say, we perpetually talk of representing or representations of desire, but it doesn't work like that, desire is invested within the production of an image; it concerns, also, what an image produces and affects. It is not a question of images representing desire, for images, as much as words or politics, *are* desire, if you get my point.

Ros Coward: I really do think we can and must create positive images of women, although one of the things that I am hesitant about is the assumption that this can be done just upon the sexual level. That is one of the problems with the debate; it is about can you or can't you and tends to occlude everything else, whereas, like you say, there are all kinds of images and different photographic means. We need to construct all sorts of images; it shouldn't solely revolve around the question of our desire towards 'sexual' images. At the moment we have a regime which affects us all as to what is desirable and beautiful. This regime conditions our eroticism and belongs to an incredible fantasy or work of construction: people don't actually exist like that. I think that we have got to find ways of developing a much more contradictory sense of what is sexual.

Yve Lomax: ...scrambling the codes.

Kathy Myers: Although you say that those beautiful images of women are constructions or fantasy, ie not real, I think that it is crucial to say that fantasy or desire deconstruct our idea of the real. That which makes not-real in images is not necessarily an evil device.

Ros Coward: It is not necessarily an evil device but the problem at the moment is that it does claim to represent the real.

Kathy Myers: Then it is that claim which we should be challenging and not the one about fantasy. But then I think that a lot of erotica doesn't claim to represent the real.

Yve Lomax: But isn't that just the other side of the coin?

Ros Coward: The surreal as opposed to the real, which leaves untouched the photograph's claim to represent the real, such that all those photographs of women in pornography are received as recordings of what those women really looked like.

Kathy Myers: The readers' pages of pornographic magazines are very interesting as regards that. What you get are people who send in pictures of themselves or their girlfriends; they pick up on the idea that images are really for real, for what they do is to imitate the poses. But it always looks wrong or tacky because it has been taken with an instamatic camera. When you see such pictures you realise on what level people pick up on the conventions of photography, which they think is only the pose and not the technology. There is that innocence of how the final effect is created.

Ros Coward: That idea of representations of real can be found in Andrea Dworkin's work, which says, look this really is going on, this is dreadful for it is really happening and claims it was better when it was written for then it infers it didn't really happen. Photography does have this curious, privileged claim of representing the real.

Yve Lomax: And perhaps that is what we have got to debunk if we want to open the sexual body of the photographic image.

ABOUT THE CONTRIBUTORS

Parveen Adams was founder of *m/f* and a member of the editorial group from 1978-1986. She is a psychology lecturer at Brunel University.

Karen Alexander is a London-based independent film and video producer.

Lawrence Alloway is a New York based art critic born in England.

Sutapa Biswas is an artist who was born in Bolpur, India, in 1962 and moved to Britain in 1966. Exhibitions include *The Thin Black Line*, ICA, London; *The Third World Within*, Brixton Art Gallery, 1986; *The Issue of Painting*, Rochdale Art Gallery and Air Gallery, London, 1986. She was artist in residence at the City Museum and Art Gallery, Stoke on Trent, in 1986.

Judith Barry is an American-based artist who works in video and a variety of other media. She was an editor of *Discourse* from 1981 to 1985, and has written for *Screen, Wedge*, and *Museum Journal*. She exhibited in *Echo*, Museum of Modern Art, NY, 1986 and *First and Third*, Witney Museum NYC, 1987.

Rosemary Betterton teaches art history and women's studies at Sheffield City Polytechnic, England. She has written on women and representation in a variety of journals and is the editor of *Looking On: Images of Femininity in the Visual Arts and Media*.

Anna Bonshek is an English painter, writer and lecturer currently teaching art history in Washington D.C.

Chila Kumari Burman was born in Liverpool, England, and is a visual 'artist' and activist.

Fiona Byrne-Sutton grew up in Switzerland, studied Fine-Art at Goldsmiths School of Art and Social Anthropology at Cambridge University. Work has included sculpture; teaching; a 1984 art auction which raised £30,500 for the African famine and War on Want; the Artangel Trust; and currently, organizing the first East Midlands trade unions arts festival for the Regional TUC in 1988.

Beatrix Campbell is a journalist with the London listings magazine *City Limits*, whose work also appears in *Marxism Today, The Guardian*, and on TV. She is co-author with Anna Coote of *Sweet Freedom* (1981) and author of *Wigan Pier Revisited* (1984) and *The Iron Ladies* (1987).

Gloria Chalmers was born in Glasgow in 1948. After studying photography at the Polytechnic of Central London from 1980-83, she worked as Exhibitions Organiser at the Cockpit Gallery, London. In 1985 she was photographer in residence at Leigh College and is currently Gallery Coordinator at Stills Gallery, Edinburgh.

Michelle Cliff is a Jamaican writer based in California. She is the author of *Claiming an Identity They Taught Me to Despise, Abeng*, and the novel *No Telephone to Heaven*, published in the USA by Dutton.

Rosalind Coward lectures in visual communications at Goldsmiths College, London. Her books include *Language and Materialism*, 1977, with John Ellis; *Patriarchal Precedents*, 1984; and *Female Desire*, 1984.

Rosalind Delmar is a London-based writer and lecturer.

Dinah Dossor has taught art history and theoretical studies at Liverpool Polytechnic, England, since 1970, and is currently teaching in the Fine Art Department where she specialises in women's studies and community art.

Sandy Flitterman-Lewis teaches film in the English Department at Rutgers University, New Jersey. She was one of the four founding editors of *Camera Obscura* and has written on feminism, film theory and television for numerous publications including *Women and Film, Screen, Wide Angle* and *Enclitic*. Her work is anthologised in three collections: *Theories of Authorship, Regarding Television*, and *Channels of Discourse*. She is currently writing a book on French women directors.

Rose Garrard trained as a sculptor in London and Paris. The title 'sculptor' no longer seems appropriate; it is too confined and traditional for an artist whose investigations have been enriched by her work in television, theatre and magazines and who now challenges the conventions of categorisation.

Ann Sutherland Harris is a professor of art history at the University of Pittsburgh specialising in Italian and French seventeenth century art and the work of women artists of the sixteenth to eighteenth centuries and the present. In 1972 she was a founder and president of the Women's Caucus for Art in the U.S. Publications include monographs and catalogues on G.L. Bernini, Alice Neel, Roman seventeenth century landscape painting and *Women Artists, 1550-1950*.

Zena Herbert, aged 42, was a mature student on the fine art course at Leeds Polytechnic, England. In her last year she produced a controversial series of photographs of male nudes which contrasted the men's projected macho image with their fear of being exposed.

Alexis Hunter has exhibited in many solo and major touring shows internationally and has taught at art schools and universities in Great Britain and overseas. At present she teaches at St. Martin's School of Art and the Byam Shaw school in London.

Julia James worked as a nurse and health visitor before studying art. She left the Slade School, London, in 1985 and now works as an artist, photographer and mother. She has been involved with feminism and art for several years, co-founding Cinestra Pictures, a women's video co-op, and working as a member of the *Feminist Art News* collective.

Mary Kelly is an artist who lives and works in London. She is best known for *Post Partum Document* which has been exhibited extensively since 1976 and was published in book form by Routledge & Kegan Paul in 1983. Her current project, *Interim*, featured recently in *The State of the Art* on Channel Four.

Yasmin Kureishi was born in London in 1958 and read philosophy at the Polytechnic of North London. She has written for *Dawn* in Pakistan, for *The Daily Jang* in Britain, and for *Inside Asia* magazine. She is currently a contributor and collective member of *Spare Rib*.

Sandra Lahire is a film maker whose work is distributed by Circles, Women's Film and Video, London, and shown with the Art's Council's *Film Makers on Tour*. 'With our images we can haunt those in power to expose their collusions. Women join in conversations and film-poems to make a cancer-free bodyscape and landscape, where there is food for all lives.'

Lucy Lippard is a New York based writer and activist and the author of thirteen books on contemporary art, the most recent of which are *Overlay: Contemporary Art and the Art of Prehistory*, 1983 and *Get the Message? A Decade of Art for Social Change*, 1984. She is a co-founder of *Heresies* collective, PADD (Political Art Documentation/Distribution) and Artists Call Against US Intervention in Central America.

Susan Lipshitz Phillips is a psychotherapist who lives and works in London.

Yve Lomax is an artist and writer and teaches at the London College of Printing.

Laura Mulvey, writer and film maker, lectures at the London College of Printing. Her collected essays are to be published in 1987.

Kathy Myers is a London-based journalist who has edited *Camerawork* magazine and *City Limits'* TV and media section. She has published *Understains: The Sense and Seductions of Advertising* and co-produced Channel 4's *The Media Show*. She freelances for *The Guardian* and *The Independent*.

Mica Nava is a lecturer in the Department of Cultural Studies at North East London Polytechnic and an editor of *Feminist Review*.

Gloria Feman Orenstein is an associate professor of comparative literature. She teaches in the programme for the study of women and men in society and comparative literature at the University of Southern California. She is the author of *The Theatre of the Marvellous: Surrealism and the Contemporary Stage*, and co-founder of The Woman's Salon for Literature in NY. She has written widely on women in literature and the arts.

Caroline Osborne teaches art history in London and works for *Feminist Review*.

Angela Partington studied painting and is currently researching for a Ph.D at the Centre for Contemporary Cultural Studies in Birmingham, England. She lectures at Bath College of Higher Education, St. Martin's School of Art, and Dartington College of Arts.

Griselda Pollock teaches the history of art and film and is Deputy Director of the Centre For Cultural Studies at the University of Leeds, England. She has written books on Van Gogh, Millet and Cassatt. She is co-author with Rozsika Parker of *Old Mistresses: Women, Art and Ideology* and *Framing Feminism: Art and the Women's Movement 1970-85*.

Carrie Rickey writes on art and film and contributes to *Artforum, Art in America, The Village Voice* and *The New York Times*. She is film critic of *The Philadelphia Inquirer*.

Anne Robinson was born in 1959 in Scotland. She studied painting at the Glasgow School of Art and film at St. Martin's School of Art. She is currently working with experimental video and film.

Hilary Robinson writes: 'I trained as a painter and am now a drawer, a writer, a teacher, a student (again), a cat-keeper, and a (bad) Irish fiddle player. I am finishing an MA by thesis at the Royal College of Art, London, researching how contemporary feminist artists are dealing with body-image and sexuality in their work. Having lived in Oxford, London, Newcastle and Glasgow I am now in Hull. When in Glasgow I helped organise the Women Artists Conference held there in March 1984.

Carolee Schneemann is a US painter known for her explorations in combinations of media. She has been involved in performance art, choreography and film and video. The Max Hutchinson Gallery presented a twenty-year retrospective of her work in 1982. Her complete performance works and selected writings are published by Documentext/McPherson.

Monica Sjoo is a self-taught artist who was born in Sweden and now lives in England. *Women's Lives* with Anna Sjodahl toured Scandinavia in 1974-6. A four-women show, *WomenMagic, Celebrating the Goddess Within Us*, has toured Europe since 1979. She is involved in the matriarchy network, radical paganism, the women's peace movement and spiritualism and healing, and is the author with Barbara Mor of *The Ancient Religion of the Great Cosmic Mother of All* (1981 and 1987).

May Stevens calls herself a socialist feminist artist. A founding member of the *Heresies* collective in New York, her work has been widely shown in the US and Britain. She received a Guggenheim grant in painting in 1986.

Moira Vincentelli is a lecturer in art history in the Visual Art Department at the University College of Wales, Aberystwyth. She has a special interest in feminist art history and women's art traditions outside Western fine art. She has published articles and organised exhibitions on women's banners, Algerian women's ceramics and women artists working in Wales.

Margot Waddell is a principal child psychotherapist at the Tavistock Clinic, London.

Michelene Wandor is a poet, playwright, critic and short story writer.

Karin Woodley was born in Britain in 1961 of African descent and studied music, which she has taught for the past decade. She is administrator of the Minorities' Arts Advisory Service, a member of *Artrage* editorial advisory board, and is involved in consultancy and campaign work related to the development of Black arts and culture in Britain.

Penny Woolcock works 'long hours for Trade Films in Newcastle, England. Sometimes I decide to stop painting but although I don't believe paintings make the world miss a heartbeat, when I stop it makes me feel like a cardboard cutout of the real person I used to be. So I save tiny bits of time like a miser. I paint most often on Sundays so I must be a Sunday painter and that feels fine.'

Marie Yates is a London-based artist and lecturer working in photography and fine art. Her work was shown in *Difference: Representation and Sexuality* 1985.

BIBLIOGRAPHY

This bibliography is far from comprehensive. It is intended to supplement, rather than replace, the one compiled by Rozsika Parker and Griselda Pollock in *Old Mistresses*, and therefore contains few of the texts that they mention. In addition, it reflects the books, catalogues and magazine articles that I've come across, which in turn reflect the women who have gained access to print, to critics, and to distribution of such information. Thus, although many women work collectively on a local level to publish, the lack of resources for publicity and distribution can mean that few outside the area know of it. The Women Artists Slide Library in London has a growing collection of published and unpublished information, catalogues and dissertations; I recommend them to people searching for information and also to those with information to pass on to others. For a more general bibliography of feminist literature I recommend Cheris Kramarae and Paula A. Treichler's *A Feminist Dictionary* – though be warned: where books are published in the UK and the USA, they only list the USA publisher.

Books and catalogues

Ainsley, Sam, *Why I Choose Red*, Glasgow: The Third Eye Centre, 1987.

Arbour, Rose Marie, *Art et Feminisme*, Quebec: Minestière des Affaires Culturelles, 1982. (Catalogue of exhibition at Musée d'art contemporain, Montreal. Text in French).

Barrett, Michele, 'Feminism and the Definition of Cultural Politics' in: Brunt & Rowan, eds, *Feminism, Culture and Politics*, London: Lawrence and Wishart, 1982.

Borzello, Frances, *The Artist's Model*, London: Junction Books, 1982.

Boyce, Sonia, Exhibition Catalogue, London: Air Gallery, 1986.

Broude, Norma & Garrard, Mary D, eds, *Feminism and Art History: Questioning the Litany*, New York: Harper and Row, 1982.

Cahn, Miriam, *Das Klassische Lieben*, Basel: Kunsthalle, 1983. (Catalogue of exhibition Arbeiten 1979-1983. Text by Theodora Vischer & Miriam Cahn in German).

Calvert, Gill; Morgan, Jill & Katz, Mouse, eds, *Pandora's Box*, Rochdale: Rochdale Art Gallery & Womens Images, 1984.

Chadwick, Helen, *Of Mutability*, London: ICA, 1986. (Exhibition catalogue. Text by Marina Warner & Richard Cork).

Chicago, Judy, *Through the Flower: My Struggle as a Woman Artist*, London: The Women's Press, 1982.

Coward, Rosalind, *Female Desire: Women's Sexuality Today*, London: Paladin Books, 1984.

Ecker, Gisela, ed, *Feminist Aesthetics*, London: The Women's Press, 1985.

Edge, Sara & Morgan, Jill, *The Issue of Painting*: Sutapa Biswas, Margaret Harrison, Glenys Johnson, Rochdale: Rochdale Art Gallery, 1986.

Eiblmayer, Silvia; Export, Valie and Prischl-Maier, Monika, *Kunst mit Eigen-Sinn: Aktuelle Kunst von Frauen*, Wien/Munchen: Locker Verlag, 1985. (Catalogue of exhibition held at Museum Moderner Kunst/Museum des 20 Jahrhunderts, Vienna. Text in German).

Garrard, Rose, *Between Ourselves*, Birmingham: Ikon Gallery, 1983. Exhibition catalogue. Text by John Roberts & interview by Sue Arrowsmith).

Harris, Ann Sutherland & Nochlin, Linda, *Women Artists 1550-1950*, L.A. & NY: Los Angeles County Museum of Art & Alfred A Knopf Inc., 1978.

Hiller, Susan, *The Muse My Sister*, Glasgow: The Third Eye Centre, 1984.

Himid, Lubaina, exhibition selector, *The Thin Black Line*, London: ICA, 1985. (Exhibition catalogue. Includes: Brenda Agard, Sutapa Biswas, Sonja Boyce, Chila Burman, Jennifer Comrie, Lubaina Himid, Claudette Johnson, Ingrid Pollard, Veronica Ryan, Marlene Smith, Maud Sulter).

Hunter, Alexis, *Photographic Narrative Sequences*, London: Edward Totah Gallery, 1981. (Exhibition Catalogue. Text by Lucy Lippard & Margaret Richards).

Kappeler, Suzanne, *The Pornography of Representation*, Cambridge: Polity Press, 1986.

Kelly, Mary, *The Post-Partum Document*, London: Routledge and Kegan Paul, 1985.

Kent, Sarah and Morreau, Jaqueline, eds, *Women's Images of Men*, London: Writers and Readers, 1985.

Kramarae, Cheris & Treichler, Paula A, *A Feminist Dictionary*, Boston, London & Henley: Pandora Press, 1985.

Kruger, Barbara, *We Won't Play Nature to your Culture*, London: ICA, 1983. (Exhibition catalogue. Text by Craig Owens & Jane Weinstock).

Kuhn, Annette, *The Power of the Image: Essays on Representation and Sexuality*, London: Routledge & Kegan Paul, 1985.

Kuhn, Annette, *Women's Pictures: Feminism and Cinema*, London: Routledge & Kegan Paul, 1982.

Lippard, Lucy, *From the Center: Feminist Essays on Women's Art*, New York: EP Dutton, 1976.

Ni Chuilleanain, Eilean, ed, *Irish Women: Image and Achievement*, Dublin: Arlen House, 1985.

Nunn, Pamela Gerrish, ed, *Canvassing*, London: Camden Press, 1986.

Parker, Rozsika & Pollock, Griselda, *Old Mistresses: Women, Art and Ideology*, London: Routledge and Kegan Paul, 1981.

Roth, Moira, ed, *The Amazing Decade: Women and Performance Art in America 1970-1980*, Los Angeles: Astro Artz, 1983.

Santoro, Suzanne, *Per una Espressione Nuove/Towards a New Expression*, Rome: Rivolta feminile, 1974. (Artists book. Text in Italian & English).

Schneemann, Carolee, *More than Meat. Joy*, New Paltz, New York: Documentext 1979.

Sense and Sensibility in Feminist Art Practice, Nottingham: The Midland Group, 1982. (Exhibition catalogue. Text by Griselda Pollock).

Sjoo, Monica & Mor, Barbara, *The Ancient Religion of the Great Cosmic Mother of All*, Trondheim: Rainbow Press, 1981.

Spence, Jo, *Putting Myself in the Picture*, London: Camden Press, 1986.

Sprüth, Monika, ed, *Eau de Cologne*, Cologne: Monika Sprüth Galerie, 1985.

Stevens, May, *Ordinary/Extraordinary: A Summation 1977-1984*, Boston: University Art Gallery, 1984. (Exhibition catalogue).

Suleiman, Susan Rubin, ed, *The Female Body in Western Culture: Contemporary Perspectives*, Cambridge, Mass. & London: Harvard University Press, 1986.

Wagner, Judy K Collischan van, *Women Shaping Art*, NY, Praeger, 1984.

Warner, Marina, *Monuments and Maidens: The Allegory of the Female Form*, London: Wiedenfeld and Nicholson, 1985.

Williamson, Judith, *Consuming Passions: The Dynamics of Popular Culture*, London: Marion Boyars, 1986.

Women Artists Slide Library, *Eye to Eye: Irish Women Artists*, London: Women Artists Slide Library, 1986.

Women's Work, *Two Years in the Life of a Women Artist's Group*, London: Brixton Art Gallery, 1986.

Magazine Articles

Applebroog, Ida, et al, 'The Women's Movement in Art, 1986', *Arts Magazine* vol. 61 no. 1, Sept. 1986. (Ida Applebroog, Josely Carvalho, Susan Gill, Chris Heindl, Fran Hodes, Bea Kreloff, Ura Lerman, Sabra Moore, Joan Semmel, Joan Snyder, Nancy Spero: Ten leaders discuss the women's art movement today in a panel generated by the Women's Caucus for Art annual conference in New York in April 1986).

Asphodel, 'Womanmagic', *Spare Rib* no. 110, 1981.

Berman, Avis, 'A decade of progress, but could a female Chardin make a living?' *Artnews*, Oct. 1980.

Bonney, Claire, 'The Nude Photograph: Some Female Perspectives', *Women's Art Journal* vol. 6 no. 2, Fall 1985/Winter 1986.

Bosch, Annette van den, 'Susan Hiller: Resisting Representation', *Artscribe* no. 46, May/June 1984.

Burman, Chila Kumari, Interviewed by Errol Lloyd, *Artrage* no. 11, 1986.

Coward, Rosalind, 'Sexual Violence and Sexuality', *Feminist Review* no. 11, June 1982.

Elinor, Gillian & Matlow, Erica, 'Art Education', *Feminist Review* no. 18, Nov. 1984.

Glueck, Grace, 'Women Artists '80: A matter of redefining the whole relationship between art and society', *Art News*, Oct. 1980.

Goodall, Phil, (interviewed by Lynn Alderson & Sophie Laws), 'Feministo: Art and Parcel of the W.L.M.', *Trouble and Strife* no. 5, Spring 1985.

Harper, Paula, 'The first feminist art program: A view from the 80's', *Signs*, Summer 1985.

Harrison, Margaret, 'Notes on Feminist Art in Britain 1970-77', see under *Studio International*.

Hunter, Alexis, 'Feminist Perceptions', *Artscribe* no. 25, Oct. 1980.

Kelly, Mary, 'Beyond The Purloined Image', *Block* no. 9, 1983.

Kelly, Mary, Interviewed by Terence Maloon, *Artscribe* no. 13, Aug. 1978.

Kelly, Mary, 'No Essential Femininity: A Conversation between Mary Kelly and Paul Smith', *Parachute* no. 26, 1982.

Kelly, Mary, 'Re-Viewing Modernist Criticism', *Screen* vol. 22 no. 3, 1981.

Kent, Sarah, 'Feminism and Decadence', *Artscribe* no. 47, July/Aug. 1984.

Kraft, Selma, 'Cognitive Function and Women's Art', *Woman's Art Journal*, Fall 1983/Winter 1984.

Kruger, Barbara, Interviewed by Kate Linker, *Flash Art* no. 121, Mar. 1985.

Kuspit, Donald B, 'From Existence to Essence: Nancy Spero', *Art in America*, Jan. 1984.

Lacy, Suzanne, 'The Forest and the Trees', *Heresies* vol. 4 no. 3 (Issue 15), 1982.

Larson, Kay, 'For the first time women are leading not following', *Artnews*, Oct. 1980.

Linker, Kate, 'Forum', *Artforum*, April 1983.

Lippard, Lucy, 'Sweeping Exchanges: The contribution of feminism to the art of the 70's', *Art Journal*, Fall/Winter 1980.

Millett, Kate, 'Interactions between sculpture and writing', Interviewed and with comment by Holly O'Grady, *Feminist Art Journal* vol. 6 no. 1, Spring 1977.

Millett, Kate, Interviewed by Arlene Raven and Susan Rennie, *Chrysalis* no. 3, 1977.

Mulvey, Laura, 'You don't know what's happening do you, Mr Jones?', *Spare*

Rib no. 8, Feb. 1973.

Nemser, Cindy, 'Four Artists of Sensuality', *Arts Magazine*, March 1975.

Parker, Rozsika, 'About Time', *Spare Rib* no. 102, 1981.

Parker, Rozsika, 'Censored', *Spare Rib* no. 54, 1977 (re: Suzanne Santoro).

Parmar, Pratibha, 'Hateful Contraries: Media Images of Asian Women', *Ten.8* no. 16, 1984.

Patel, Amina, 'Images of Asian Women in the (White) Media', *Artrage* no. 3/4, Summer 1983.

Pointon, Marcia, 'Interior Portraits: Women, Physiology and the Male Artist', *Feminist Review* no. 22, Spring 1986.

Pollock, Griselda, 'Art, Artschool, Culture: Individualism After the Death of the Artist', *Block* no. 11, 1985/6.

Pollock, Griselda, 'History and Position of the Contemporary Woman Artist', *Aspects* no. 28, Autumn 1984.

Pollock, Griselda, 'Issue', *Spare Rib* no. 103, 1981.

Pollock, Griselda, 'Vision, Voice and Power: Feminist Art History and Marxism', *Block* no. 6, 1982.

Pollock, Griselda, 'What's the difference? Feminism, representation and sexuality', *Aspects*, Spring 1986.

Robinson, Hilary, 'Women's Images of Men, Edited by S. Kent & J. Morreau, Reviewed', *Creative Camera* no. 252, Dec. 1985.

Rosler, Martha, 'The Private and the Public: Feminist Art in California', *Artforum*, Sept. 1977.

Screen, Sex and Spectatorship Issue, vol. 23 no. 3/4, Sept/Oct. 1982.

Spence, Jo, 'Beyond the Family Album', *Ten.8* no. 4, Spring 1980.

Spence, Jo, 'The Picture of Health?', *Spare Rib* no. 163, Feb. 1986.

Steyn, Juliet, 'The Women's Peace Mural (The Sankofa Bird)', *Aspects*, Spring 1986.

Studio International, Womens Issue, vol. 193 no. 987, 1977. (Includes articles by Rosetta Brooks, Margaret Harrison, Ellen H. Johnson, Sarah Kent, Lucy Lippard, Linda Nochlin).

Tickner, Lisa, 'Allen Jones in Retrospect: A Serpentine View', *Block* no. 1, 1979.

Tickner, Lisa, 'The Body Politic: Female Sexuality and Women Artists since 1970', *Art History* vol. 1 no. 2, June 1978.

Tickner, Lisa, 'May Stevens', *Block* no. 5, 1981.

Turner, Kay, 'Contemporary Feminist Rituals', *Heresies* vol. 2 no. 1 (Issue 5), 1982.

Undercut, Special double issue on women's work, no. 14/15, Summer 1985.

Wolverton, Terry, 'Lesbian Art Project', *Heresies* vol. 2 no. 3 (Issue 7), 1979.

Yates, Marie, 'Photography and Fine Art', *Ten.8* no. 23, 1986.

Magazines regularly reviewing art by feminists:
FAN (Feminist Art News) (UK), *Heresies* (USA), *Spare Rib* (UK), *Woman's Art Journal* (USA), *Women Artists Slide Library Journal* (UK), *Women's Review* (UK).